SOVEREIGN DEBT CRISES

There is an obvious need to learn more about why some countries succeed and others fail when dealing with debt crises. Why do some sovereign debtors overcome economic problems very quickly and at minor human rights costs for their people, while others remain trapped by debts for years struggling with overwhelming debt burdens and exacerbating economic problems and human suffering? This book analyzes fourteen unique or singular country cases of sovereign debt problems that differ characteristically from the "ordinary" debtor countries, and have not yet received enough or proper attention – some regarded as successful, some as unsuccessful in dealing with debt crises. The aim is to contribute to a better understanding of the policy options available to countries struggling with debt problems, or how to resolve a debt overhang while protecting human rights, the Rule of Law and the debtor's economic recovery.

Juan Pablo Bohoslavsky is the United Nations Independent Expert on Foreign Debt and Human Rights. He previously worked at the United Nations Conference on Trade and Development (UNCTAD) and as a consultant for the United Nations Economic Commission for Latin America and the Caribbean (ECLAC). A doctor of law with wide experience in international relations and litigation, he is the author of numerous books and articles on sovereign financing, economic complicity, and human rights.

Kunibert Raffer was an associate professor (retired September 2016) at the Department of Economics, University of Vienna; Honorary Professor of the Universidad Nacional de Río Negro, Argentina; member of the Sovereign Bankruptcy Group of the International Law Association; 1989 Visiting Fellow at the Institute of Development Studies (Sussex) invited by Sir Hans (HW) Singer with whom he co-authored two books; and 1990–93 Honorary Research Fellow, Department of Commerce, University of Birmingham (UK). In 1998 he participated in the UNDP's research project "International Development Cooperation and Global Public Goods." He is a former lecturer at UNITAR (on debt and MDGs), and he proposed a model of sovereign insolvency (Raffer Proposal).

Sovereign Debt Crises

WHAT HAVE WE LEARNED?

Edited by

JUAN PABLO BOHOSLAVSKY

United Nations Independent Expert on Foreign Debt and Human Rights

KUNIBERT RAFFER

Associate Professor (Retired September 2016), Department of Economics, University of Vienna

CAMBRIDGE
UNIVERSITY PRESS

CAMBRIDGE
UNIVERSITY PRESS

University Printing House, Cambridge CB2 8BS, United Kingdom

One Liberty Plaza, 20th Floor, New York, NY 10006, USA

477 Williamstown Road, Port Melbourne, VIC 3207, Australia

314–321, 3rd Floor, Plot 3, Splendor Forum, Jasola District Centre, New Delhi – 110025, India

79 Anson Road, #06–04/06, Singapore 079906

Cambridge University Press is part of the University of Cambridge.

It furthers the University's mission by disseminating knowledge in the pursuit of education, learning, and research at the highest international levels of excellence.

www.cambridge.org
Information on this title: www.cambridge.org/9781316510445
DOI: 10.1017/9781108227001

First published 2017

Printed in the United Kingdom by Clays, St Ives plc

A catalogue record for this publication is available from the British Library.

ISBN 978-1-316-51044-5 Hardback

To friendship as the basis of academic work

Contents

Contributors

José Antonio Alonso is Professor of Applied Economics at the Universidad Complutense de Madrid. He was General Director of Economic Cooperation at the Instituto de Cooperación Iberoamericana, Vice-Chancellor at Universidad Internacional Menendez Pelayo and Director of the Instituto Complutense de Estudios Internacionales (ICEI). He is a member of the *Committee for Development Policy* (ECOSOC, UN), the *Consejo de Cooperación para el Desarrollo* (Spain) and the *European Advisory Group of the Bill and Melinda Gates Foundation*. He is specialized in Growth and Development and International Economics and has written numerous articles in academic journals. His most recent books are: *Global Governance and Rules for the Post-2015 Era* (with J.A. Ocampo, 2015); *Lengua, Empresa y Mercado* (with J.L. García Delgado and J.C. Jiménez, 2015); *Alternative Development Strategy for the Post-2015 Era* (co-edited with G.A. Cornia and R. Vos, 2013); and *Development Cooperation in Times of Crisis* (co-edited with J.A. Ocampo, 2012).

Juan Pablo Bohoslavsky, Dr. iur. (Salamanca), LL.M. (Austral University) and LL.B. (Comahue), is Independent Expert on Foreign Debt and Human Rights of the United Nations. He previously worked at the United Nations Conference on Trade and Development (UNCTAD) and as a consultant for the United Nations Economic Commission for Latin America and the Caribbean (ECLAC). His published works include books and articles on public debt, direct foreign investment and human rights.

Daniel D. Bradlow is SARCHI Professor of International Development Law and African Economic Relations at the University of Pretoria and Professor Emeritus, American University Washington College of Law. He was previously the first Head of the International Economic Relations and Policy

Department, South African Reserve Bank. He has also served as Chair of the Roster of Experts for the Independent Review Mechanism at the African Development Bank; a member of the Board of Directors of New Rules for Global Finance, the Advisory Board of the Financial Regulation and Human Rights Project and the High Level Panel on the Governance of the Financial Stability Board; and Senior Special Fellow in the Legal Aspects of Debt and Financial Management Programme of the United National Institute on Training and Research (UNITAR).

Luiz Carlos Bresser-Pereira is Emeritus Professor at the Getulio Vargas Foundation where he has been teaching and conducting research since 1959. His Ph.D. and Livre Docencia in economics are from the University of São Paulo. He was awarded doctor honoris causa by the University of Buenos Aires, and received the James Street Scholar 2012 from the Association for Evolutionary Economics – AFEE. He was Finance Minister (1987) and Minister of Federal Administration (1995–98) of Brazil. Among his books in English are: *The Theory of Inertial Inflation* (1987); *Democracy and Public Management Reform* (2004); and *Globalization and Competition* (2010). Among his papers are: "Economic reforms and cycles of state intervention" (1993); "The Dutch disease and its neutralization: a Ricardian Approach" (2008); "The two methods and the hard core of economics" (2009); and "The global financial crisis, neoclassical economics, and the neoliberal years of capitalism" (2010). His current research is on new developmentalism and developmental macroeconomics and on the interpretation of Brazil.

Alfredo Fernando Calcagno is an economist with a Ph.D. from University Paris 1. He is the head of the Macroeconomics and Development Policies Branch at UNCTAD in Geneva. From 1984 to 1989, he held positions at the Secretariat of Planning, the National Economy Ministry, the Central Bank of the Republic of Argentina and the International Economy Center. From 1989 to 2003, he worked as an economist at ECLAC. He co-authored the book *El universo neoliberal* (2006) with Alfredo Eric Calcagno.

José Castro Caldas is currently a researcher at the Centre for Social Studies of Coimbra University, Portugal (CES). He holds a Ph.D. in economics. Previously he was an assistant professor in the Economics Department of ISCTE, Lisbon, Portugal. His teaching and research has been mostly devoted to the history and philosophy of economics. He has authored or co-authored articles published in *Revue de la Regulation, Journal of Economic Issues, The Journal of Artificial Societies and Social Simulation, Economics of Innovation and New Technology, Revista Crítica de Ciência Sociais, Cambridge*

Journal of Economics and *Environmental Values*. As an activist he has been a founder of the Portuguese Initiative for the Audit of the Public Debt.

Rodrigo Delgado holds a Master in Latin American studies from Universidad Nacional Autónoma de México. He holds a first degree in Public Administration and Political Science from the Universidad Autónoma de Baja California. He worked for the Economic Research Institute of the UNAM and currently works at the International Affairs Department of the National Banking and Securities Commission of México.

Adam Feibelman's teaching and research focus on bankruptcy law, regulation of financial institutions, legal issues related to sovereign debt and international monetary law. He joined the Tulane University faculty in 2009. Prior to that, he was a faculty member at the University of North Carolina School of Law and the University of Cincinnati School of Law and taught as a Bigelow Fellow at the University of Chicago. He clerked for Judge Gilbert S. Merritt of the U.S. Court of Appeals for the Sixth Circuit. His current scholarship explores the IMF's role in international financial regulation. Recent work includes "The IMF and Regulation of Cross-Border Capital Flows" (*Chicago Journal of International Law*), "Involuntary Bankruptcy for States" (*Duke Journal of Constitutional Law & Public Policy*), "Europe and the Future of International Monetary Law" (*Transnational Law & Contemporary Problems*) and "American States and Sovereign Debt Restructuring" (in D. Skeel and P. Conti-Brown, eds., *When States Go Broke*)

Jürgen Kaiser studied geography and regional planning in Berlin and Karlsruhe. He is the co-founder and coordinator since 1995 of the German Debt Crisis Network and Jubilee-Germany (erlassjahr.de). From February 2005 until January 2006, he was the Financial Flows and Debt Relief Adviser at UNDPs Bureau for Development Policy (Poverty Group). He has authored publications on debt workout mechanisms and debt conversion.

Manuel F. Montes is Senior Advisor on Finance and Development at the South Centre in Geneva. He was previously Chief of Development Strategies, United Nations Department of Economic and Social Affairs (UNDESA). Before that, he was Chief of Policy Analysis and Development in the UN's Financing for Development Office; UNDP Regional Programme Coordinator of the Asia Pacific Trade and Investment Initiative based at the Regional Centre in Colombo, Sri Lanka; Programme Officer for International Economic Policy at the Ford Foundation in New York, 1999–2005; Senior Fellow and Coordinator for Economics Studies at the East-West Centre in Honolulu, 1989–99; and Associate Professor of Economics at the University of

The Philippines, 1981–89. He has held visiting positions at the United Nations World Institute for Development Economics Research (UNU/WIDER) in Helsinki, the Institute for Southeast Asian Studies (ISEAS) in Singapore and the Institute of Developing Economies (IDE) in Tokyo. His most recent publications are "Obstacles to Development in the Global Economic System" (Research paper published by South Centre, Geneva, July 2014) and *Retooling Development and Global Economic Governance* (2014). He holds a Ph.D. in economics from Stanford University.

Thiago de Moraes Moreira received his Master in economics from the Federal University of Rio de Janeiro. His dissertation focused on the analysis of the micro-macroeconomic integration and its effects on the economic cycles and trend growth. Currently, he is a consultant of the Strategic Planning of Petrobras, in Brazil, working on elaborating and monitoring prospective scenarios for Brazilian and world economies. He has concentrated his studies on the analysis of the structural changes in the Brazilian economy, also analyzing relations involving these changes and the trajectories of important macroeconomics variables such as GDP and its composition, investment rate, interest rate and exchange rate. He is also Professor of Macroeconomics in the Regional Economic Council of Rio de Janeiro (CORECON-RJ).

Philip Pilkington is a macroeconomist working in the asset management firm Grantham, Mayo and Van Otterloo (GMO). He holds an MA in economics from Kingston University. He is a member of the Political Economy Research Group (PERG). Prior to working at GMO he maintained the popular blog *Fixing the Economists*. He also contributed many articles on economic matters to publications such as *The Guardian, Naked Capitalism* and *Al Jazeera*. He is the author of the forthcoming book *The Reformation in Economics*.

Marion Pircher holds a doctoral degree in economics from the University of Vienna, Austria. Her dissertation compared the policies that Indonesia and Malaysia used during the East-Asian Crisis. She is currently working at Oesterreichische Nationalbank.

Kunibert Raffer retired in October 2016 as associate professor in the Department of Economics at the University of Vienna. He is Honorary Professor at the Universidad Nacional de Rio Negro (Argentina), and a member of the Study Group on Sovereign Insolvency of the International Law Association. He was a consultant to UNIDO, the UNDP, the G24 and the OPEC Fund, and visiting professor at the Universities of Innsbruck, Klagenfurt, Complutense de Madrid, Buenos Aires and Universidad Nacional del Sur (Argentina).

He has lectured at the United Nations Institute for Training and Research. From 1990 to 1993 he was Honorary Research Fellow at the Department of Commerce, University of Birmingham (UK). In 1989 he was a visiting fellow at the Institute of Development Studies, Sussex, invited by Sir Hans (H.W.) Singer, with whom he co-authored two books. The Raffer Proposal to resolve sovereign debt crises by applying US Chapter 9, Title 11 (insolvency of municipalities) to countries was propagated globally by NGOs, especially the Jubilee movement, as Fair, Transparent Arbitration Process (FTAP)

Elizabeth Thurbon, Senior Lecturer at the School of Social Sciences, UNSW Australia. Thurbon's research specialization is the (international) political economy of techno-industrial development and change, with a particular focus on East Asia and Australia. Her most significant contributions to the field examine the rise and transformation of Northeast Asia's developmental states, and the relationship between international trade and financial integration and the pursuit of transformative economic and social goals in different national contexts. Her most recent book, *Developmental Mindset: The Revival of Financial Activism in South Korea* (2016), examines the ways in which developmental ways of thinking have informed a strategic approach to financial policy in South Korea from the 1960s to the present. She holds a Ph.D. in government from the University of Sydney. She also completed her economics (social sciences) degree at Sydney University, where she was awarded first class Honours and the University Medal for Academic Excellence.

Oscar Ugarteche holds a Ph.D. in history and philosophy from the University of Bergen in Norway, an M.Sc. from the London Business School of the University of London and a BS in finance from the College of Business Administration, Fordham University, New York. He has a Doctorate Honoris Causa from the Universidad Nacional de San Augustin (2015) in Arequipa, Peru, and is a senior researcher at the Institute of Economic Research, UNAM, since 2005, with tenure since 2008. Ugarteche was previously at the Catholic University of Peru, as well as an international consultant on foreign debt issues. He has worked and written on foreign debt issues since 1976, and published twenty-three books to date, with the most recent one being *Ideas towards a New International Financial Architecture?* (co-edited with Alicia Puyana and Alejandra Madi, 2015).

1

Introduction

We Need to Learn from Experience

JUAN PABLO BOHOSLAVSKY AND KUNIBERT RAFFER*

This book tries to find out what could be learned from debt crises that have occurred regularly since the early 1980s. This whole period can be seen as an age of sovereign debt crises, occasionally interrupted by a few years in which neither a crisis occurred nor countries had to suffer from the orthodox recipe against debt crises, i.e. harsh and undue austerity measures and 'structural reform' programmes. The number and recurrence of crises and their disastrous social and economic consequences distinctly reveal the inadequate response of states and the international community to this global challenge.

One reason for this inadequacy is fierce political resistance by stakeholders that actually benefit from this *status quo*; fear of trying alternative responses seems to be another. Unfortunately both were strong enough to block change for the better. This is nowadays crystal clear in the case of Greece, which experienced huge pressure from lenders (especially when decisions whether to accept or refuse bailouts and 'adjustment programmes' were to be taken by referenda or by democratically elected parliaments), combined with a government that does not dare reject the implementation of further austerity, which the electorate explicitly opposes, against its own promise.[1]

Under the current system, debt has become a form of political government through a relation of subjection,[2] a tool to bypass democratic institutions and

* The authors wish to extend their gratitude for the comments to the drafts of this chapter received from Alfredo Fernando Calcagno, José Caldas, Matthias Goldmann, Martín Guzman, Manuel Montes and Oliver Pahnecke.

[1] See on this Juan Pablo Bohoslavsky, report to the UN Human Rights Council on his visit to institutions of the EU, discussing the response of the EU institutions to the sovereign debt crisis from a human rights perspective, 14 December 2016 (A/HRC/34/57/Add.1).

[2] *See* on this Matthias Goldmann and Silvia Steininger, 'A Discourse Theoretical Approach to Sovereign Debt Restructuring: Towards a Democratic Financial Order', *German Law Journal*, 2016, Vol. 17, No. 5, pp. 709–46.

to govern debtor countries by creditors' whim – the replacement of democratic citizenship by market citizenship. This is why, in our view, the need to improve the way debt crises are tackled is not only about designing and implementing efficient economic policies and realizing economic and social rights but also about enhancing democratic governance.[3]

There is another important reason for why debt crises are not adequately prevented or tackled. Poor systematization of experiences with and reasons for debt crises certainly help to explain why crucial lessons have not been learned (Machiavelli *dixit*) and corresponding policy options and their consequences have not been fully explored. Valuable knowledge is not readily available and, hence, not used when confronting another crisis. Actually, there is no global data registry for debt restructurings.[4]

Lenders getting multibillion-dollar profits or political benefits under the current state of affairs are hardly keen on searching for more efficient and human rights–oriented options. This situation helps to understand why most creditors do not engage in any policy or institutional initiative that goes beyond Collective Action Clauses: it is not about preventing crises, nor about ensuring human rights, but only about minimizing losses and dealing with inter-creditor equity.

On the other hand, there is a certain unwillingness to learn on the part of politicians and decision-makers, as they appear to fear that new options may force them to acknowledge the seriousness of the situation (a news that nobody likes giving) and offer less room for manoeuvre in their negotiation with creditors, making this process even tougher and less popular in the eyes of the creditors. In addition, once politicians consider a crisis to be over, i.e. once they have absorbed the shock and defused the most threatening problems to creditors, they lose interest in designing, building consensus and implementing alternative responses. Yet, governments may perceive an incentive to learn and make an effort to implement alternative proposals: by giving priority to their population's rights, they would become politically stronger in domestic politics. We saw this happen in Argentina while the state was pushing for a meaningful haircut to its creditors. However, on the one hand – and this is obvious – creditors' pressure does not make this option easy at all. On the

[3] *See* on this Goldmann and Steininger, 'A Discourse Theoretical Approach to Sovereign Debt Restructuring'.

[4] There are in economic literature only a few academic attempts to systematize data on debt restructurings, such as Tamon Asonuma, 'Serial Sovereign Defaults and Debt Restructurings', IMF Working Paper Research Department, March 2016; Christoph Trebesch and Juan J. Cruces, 'Sovereign Defaults: The Price of Haircuts', *American Economic Journal: Macroeconomics*, 2013, Vol. 5, No. 3, pp. 85–117.

other hand, we need to keep in mind that crises and austerity do not hit all people in debtor countries the same way. A number of powerful domestic stakeholders stand ready to support austerity programmes instead of progressive tax reforms to overcome the crisis.

The first shock wave after Mexico's 1994–95 crash triggered a call by the Organisation for Economic Co-Operation and Development (OECD) for a larger 'officially provided safety net' for speculators, but also a short-lived revival of the idea of sovereign insolvency. Then Chairman of the US Federal Reserve System Alan Greenspan suggested thinking about international insolvency procedures as an appropriate mechanism to settle debt problems. The *Financial Times* reported that Treasury Secretary Robert Rubin said he carefully avoided the term 'international bankruptcy court', but that some procedures to work out the debt obligations of debtors were needed. In the *Wall Street Journal* (10 April 1995), Representative Jim Leach, Chairman of the House Banking and Financial Services Committee, recommended international insolvency proceedings: 'What is needed today is a Chapter 11 process for the global financial system, a technique to keep nation-states and their people from the impoverishing implications of insolvency.' Mentioning the little-known Chapter 9 proceedings briefly, he specifically pointed out its implicit understanding that local government must continue to function. It was even considered informally to bring the issue to the table of the Halifax G7 summit, but this was not done. New euphoria on capital flows to East Asia soon eclipsed the Mexican shock. The problem faded away from public interest again.[5] While the Highly Indebted Poor Countries (HIPC) Initiative, the increasing use of Collective Action Clauses and the promotion of code of conducts elaborated by private lenders[6] might tackle some of the collective action problems that every debt crisis entails, they do not seem to provide a robust legal or institutional framework to deal with the problems at stake.

And this even applies to rather global initiatives such as those promoted in the United Nations. In September 2015, the UN General Assembly approved a

[5] *Cf.* Kunibert Raffer, *Debt Management for Development – Protection of the Poor and the Millennium Development Goals*, Cheltenham and Northampton: Edward Elgar, 2010, p. 79; on internationalizing Chapter 9, Title 11 US Code v. Kunibert Raffer, 'Applying Chapter 9 Insolvency to International Debts: An Economically Efficient Solution with a Human Face', *World Development*, 1990, Vol. 18, No. 2, pp. 301ff; or Kunibert Raffer 'Debts, Human Rights, and the Rule of Law: Advocating a Fair and Efficient Sovereign Insolvency Model', in: Martin Guzman, José Antonio Ocampo, Joseph E. Stiglitz (eds) *Too Little, Too Late. the Quest to Resolve Sovereign Debt Crises*, New York: Columbia University Press, 2016, pp. 253ff.

[6] Such as the *Principles* for Stable Capital Flows and Fair Debt *Restructuring* of the Institute of International Finance.

resolution on 'Basic Principles for Sovereign Debt Restructuring'.[7] These principles adopted an incremental approach, offering a progressive guide so that debt-restructuring practices become gradually in line with a set of well-rooted international legal principles such as sovereign debt sustainability, good faith, legitimacy, impartiality and human rights. In light of the lessons drawn from the country cases described in this volume, these UN principles have learned a great deal from past experience and understood some of the fundamental problems underlying debt crises while crystallizing an effective guidance to prevent and/or minimize them in a sustainable and human rights–sensitive way.

However, there is a huge gap between theory and practice. One the one hand, most developed countries voted against or abstained from this resolution. On the other, Argentina was the main sponsor and promoter of this UN resolution. Actually, after this resolution was passed by the General Assembly, the national Argentine Congress explicitly incorporated it into the country's domestic law. Yet, after resisting for a decade the judicial battering of vulture funds, Argentina capitulated in 2016 and decided to reimburse the full amount defaulted in 2001, plus (in some cases exorbitant) interest and other costs, thereby violating the very essence of the principles.

We obviously need to learn more about why some countries succeed and others fail when dealing with debt crises. Why do a few sovereign debtors overcome economic problems very quickly and at minor human rights costs to their people (like Iceland), while others remain trapped by debts for years (Greece, for instance), struggling with overwhelming debt burdens and exacerbating economic problems and human suffering? What happens to the countries that try something different, and to those that follow options that have repeatedly failed? To what extent do debtors and creditors consider the real implications of each option to tackle debt crises before making a decision?

To explore these and other questions, our book seeks to highlight fundamental lessons that should be drawn from the past. A more informed decision-making process about available options to deal with debt and financial crises could help lenders, but more importantly governments, to perform more sophisticated cost-benefit analyses in order to decide strategies. It would also help *bona fide* creditors, by far the largest group of creditors.

[7] Which were built on the 'UNCTAD Principles on Responsible Sovereign Lending and Borrowing'; *see* Juan Pablo Bohoslavsky and Matthias Goldmann, 'An Incremental Approach to Sovereign Debt Restructuring: Sovereign Debt Sustainability as a Principle of Public International Law', *Yale Journal of International Law*, 2016, Vol. 41, pp. 13ff.

This challenge concerns most countries, even though some of them seem to ignore it. One the one hand, the continuously rising burden of sovereign and private debt in both developing and developed countries tells us that debt problems (and the political, social and economic problems they bring about) will be among us for the foreseeable future. On the other hand, as the April 2016 G20 Ministerial Meeting demonstrated, debt restructuring is not yet considered a policy option, remaining an elephant in the room that needs to be addressed. It would be of advantage to discuss this problem before another shock wave produced by the next debt crisis hits.

Drawing useful conclusions is all the more necessary, as UNCTAD has just warned of 'a new round of debt crises'[8] in developing countries that would send shockwaves through the global financial system, with disastrous human rights consequences.[9] UNCTAD's Report stressed the vulnerability of poor states to falling commodity prices and higher interest rates, the same scenario as during the pre-1982 years. Now that the Fed has stopped its policy of 'free' money, the danger of debt crises also looms over many OECD countries, especially euro-member countries. Their huge debt burdens are presently sustainable due to low interest rates or even negative interest rates for borrowing by countries like Germany. A change to normal interest rate levels – understandably not presently on the agenda of the European Central Bank (ECB) – let alone a period of high interest rates as in the early 1980s, would definitely raise gravest problems for quite a few countries worldwide. UNCTAD concludes:

> While the current situation seems less ominous than in 2008, it is proving more difficult to manage. With the financial system on a firmer footing, politicians and policymakers have recovered their sense of impotence in the face of supposedly insurmountable global forces, and have made 'business as usual' their default policy option. Financial markets are chastened but unreformed, debt levels are higher than ever and inequality continues to rise. Most of the upside gains have resulted from asset price rises and increased corporate profits. Meanwhile, most of the downside adjustment has fallen on debtor countries and working families, with wages, employment and welfare provision under constant pressure from a return to austerity measures.[10]

UNCTAD warns that Southern external debt stocks more than tripled between 2000 and 2015. In the North, Italy is already in an emergency situation now, at presently prevailing low interest rates and while the ECB is unreasonably

8 UNCTAD, 2016, *Trade and Development Report 2016*, p. I.

9 See Juan Pablo Bohoslavsky, report to the UN General Assembly on integrating human rights into debt policies to counter new debt vulnerabilities, 5 August 2016 (A/71/305).

10 UNCTAD, cit., II.

flooding markets with money. Greece is still stumbling under its debt burden, and so-called successes such as Spain, Portugal or Ireland are not really doing well either if one cares to lift the newspeak-veil that unaccountable and irresponsible eurocrats have pulled over these crises.

To make a long story short, drawing lessons from the past is probably more necessary right now than it has ever been.

The countries analysed in this book were chosen by the criterion of being different from the average or representative debtor country in distress. All have singularities that should help us to understand debt problems and ways to overcome them in ways that are economically indicated, consistent with the rule of law, and that take the human rights of debtors' population properly into account.

By analysing fourteen unique or singular country cases of sovereign debt problems that have not yet received enough or proper attention – some regarded as successful, some as unsuccessful, in dealing with debt or financial crises – this book aims at contributing to a better understanding of the policy and legal options available to countries struggling with debt problems. It tries to work out common trends and challenges and to find insights that could be useful to other cases.

Argentina is a fairly obvious choice for a number of reasons. Its history as a debtor, various unsuccessful attempts to overcome the debt crisis, its default only three months after the final futile IMF attempt to rescue Argentina in September 2001, among other interesting developments, predestine it as one case to be analysed in this book. It should be recalled that one reason for the scale of the crisis was the peso-dollar parity, introduced by Argentina in line with the IMF's fad at that time, namely currency boards and fixed pegs. The Ministry of Finance's attempts to put together a programme covering financial needs for 2001–02 while country spreads were about to reach 1,000 basis points was supported by nearly $20 billion of multilateral credits, $13.7 billion from the IMF alone. But as the unavoidable cannot be avoided, Argentina took the audacious step of unilaterally offering its creditors a cut of 75 per cent of nominal values, a proposal somewhat modified in 2004. In its desperate situation Argentina had no other choice but to get relief. As no formal framework existed, it chose this conflict-ridden strategy. It must be noted that Argentina openly opposed the IMF, even threatening not to pay the Fund as due (but later paying off what was owed to it). On several occasions Argentina prevailed against the IMF. Eventually, more than 90 per cent of creditors agreed to the reduction of Argentina's debts; only a small group of holdouts refused to do so.

Argentina's holding out against the holdouts was remarkable. So was the seismic decision by the New York judge Griesa to take consenting creditors as hostages, de facto expropriating them, which changed the rules in financial markets, and the final settlement with them by the new Argentine government, which in 2015 decided to pay them 100 per cent.

Brazil is an important debtor country, having a long history of currency or balance-of-payment financial crises, playing a major role both in the Latin American crisis of the 1980s and in the 'second-generation' crisis of the 1990s. But Brazil already faced debt problems much earlier: after negotiations in 1943, Brazil's debts were reduced by more than 75 per cent. Brazil and Argentina also spearheaded the new drive by Southern debtors to repay the IMF early, which created notable financial problems with the Fund. The IMF was on the brink of bankruptcy because of early repayments and a consequent shrinking of its outstanding claims from SDR 70 billion (2002) to some SDR 15.5 billion (end 2006), as well as income shortfalls that had been projected to surpass 40 per cent during 2008–10.[11] Another big international debt crisis once again saved the Fund. As in the early 1980s, it was an international debt crisis the IMF had helped to come about by propagating neoliberal agenda.

The interesting conclusion the chapter's authors draw from Brazil's experience is at odds with prevailing, orthodox theory. Developing countries should not get indebted in foreign money – in money that they can neither issue nor depreciate. In other words, they should not try to grow with 'foreign savings' (current account deficits). Growth should not be externally financed. In the last 70 years the highest growth period (1947–72) of the Brazilian economy occurred with low levels of current account deficits.

Ecuador was chosen because it was the first 'Brady country' that officially defaulted, putting an end to the illusion that the Brady Initiative – a scheme first proposed by the then – Brazilian Minister of Finance, Luiz Carlos Bresser Perreira, and called Debt and Debt Service Reduction schemes after Brady's term at the US Treasury – had helped to overcome the debt crisis of the 1980s. Later on, in 2007, Ecuador established a Public Debt Audit Commission to evaluate the country's debt incurred over the previous three decades. Without going into the merits of this Commission's findings, one has to say that it proved a successful instrument in convincing (or simply scaring) more than 90 per cent of creditors to eventually accept selling their bonds at a 65 per cent discount to Ecuador after the country had defaulted on two of its bond issues in 2008. After a number of years without access to capital markets, Ecuador

[11] Hector R. Torres, 'Reforming the International Monetary Fund – Why Its Legitimacy Is at Stake', *The Journal of International Economic Law*, 2007, Vol. 10, No. 3, pp. 1ff, available at www.networkideas.org/featart/aug2007/fa10_Hector_Torres.htm, p. 9.

agreed to repurchase most of its remaining defaulted debt and could issue bonds again in 2014. This sovereign restructuring of external debt is a rare case. Relief was obtained in the absence of acute financial stress. Furthermore, the sovereign obtained debt relief, at least in part, on the express assertion of illegitimacy of financial obligations.

Greece is the prime example of how incompetent and biased unelected bureaucrats that seem to have a different agenda than solving this crisis can easily turn a small problem into an outright catastrophe, snatching defeat from the jaws of victory. Any team of independent economists could have solved Greece's problem quickly and easily by obeying Art. 125 of the Maastricht Treaty. It shows how politicians can mess up a simple and easy-to-solve problem while purporting to 'rescue' a country. Greece's debt burden has increased substantially since 'rescue' efforts had started, its GDP has shrunk sizeably and avoidable (and sometimes irremediable) damages have been inflicted on Greece's people and economy, taxpayers in other euro-member states and the private sector. Future capital market access for euro countries may have been damaged. It is impossible to imagine how more damage could have been inflicted.

Greece is also an outlier in the EU-caused crisis. Whereas all other euro-countries are examples of what is called the second generation of debt crises (i.e. due to undue liberalization, a runaway private sector is allowed to destroy a sound economy and governments, whose fiscal indicators are wonderful), Greece recalls the Latin debt crisis of the 1980s (not Chile's, though). The government itself and the EU were the cause of problems, strongly aided and abetted by wrong regulatory decisions. Regulatory measures anointing euro-members with risklessness induced banks to hold too high amounts of euro-member-country debts that later turned out to have been very risky. As the euro-member could amass too high debts, these regulatory failures at least exacerbated the crisis if they did not create it. It is *the* showcase of incompetence of irresponsible functionaries.

Grenada might seem less obvious than the cases of Argentina and South Africa. It was chosen as an example representative of small island states. The small size of the island's economy and its limited diversification are customary features of such countries. A very special feature was the broad and forceful participation of civil society in the process of debt negotiations. Interventions of the influential Conference of Churches in Grenada resulted in a far more balanced economic reform programme than usual in highly indebted countries under pressure from the IMF and other creditors. Based on Grenada's example, the author of this chapter proposes a Heavily Indebted Small Island Developing States (HISIDS) initiative for all small island countries, which should build on the strengths of the HIPC Initiative while avoiding its weaknesses.

Iceland stands out as one of the few cases (arguably the only case) where the debt crisis did not result in abject poverty and austerity ruining the economy for years to come. Even with room for improvement, one may see Iceland as *the* blueprint for how to manage debt crises. Most significant, Iceland refused to bail out foreign investors (many of them speculators). Nevertheless, overcoming the crisis was not painless, but it was much less painful than in virtually all other debtor countries. International organizations and other countries can and should learn from the particular path chosen in Iceland, which included protecting its core social welfare system, progressive tax reforms, efforts to ensure citizens' participation in the decision-making process and endeavours to establish political, administrative and judicial accountability.

Indonesia was the country worst hit during the Asian Crisis in 1997–98. It was also the country that followed IMF instructions most obediently and faithfully. Once presented as a miracle by the Bretton Woods Institutions (BWIs) eagerly taking credit for another success due to their advice, Indonesia became a Severely Indebted Low Income Country (SILIC) as a result of BWI advice that produced the Asian crisis. From the paradise of an emerging – or newly industrializing – economy it fell into the category of the poorest countries. Indonesia was denied HIPC status, although simple divisions of total debts in present value terms and debt service by export revenues showed a debt/exports ratio of 252 per cent and a debt service/export ratio of 33 per cent in 1998. Economically and judged by HIPC-relevant debt indicators, it was a HIPC. As in Nigeria's case, the amount of debt was substantial ($150.8 billion). Seeing HIPC reductions as too costly, creditors denied HIPC treatment on economically unconvincing, bureaucratic grounds.[12] To put things into a nutshell: thanks to BWI advice and quick liberalization, Indonesia is another and a prime example of how a country can fall down the ladder from virtually developed to poorest. We need to pay attention to how all this happened.

Ireland, another recent case in euroland and a country also having better Maastricht criteria than Germany in jerry-built euroland before the country was forced to bail out foreign speculators, was chosen because it was abused by the EU to claim that its policies of bailing out speculators and foreign banks (often, though not always, necessarily identical actors) were successful. It also shows that the difference with Iceland is more than just one letter in spelling.

[12] Cf. Kunibert Raffer & H.W. Singer *The Economic North-South Divide: Six Decades of Unequal Development*, Cheltenham (UK)/Northampton (US): Elgar 2001 [paperback eds: 2002; 2004], pp. 191ff.

Malaysia's prudent and well-considered reaction to the Asian Crisis of 1997–98 makes it an obvious candidate for our list. Courageously defying IMF pressure, Malaysia followed its own policy strategy and imposed capital controls on short-term outflows. It opted for monetary policy autonomy and stable exchange rates, which are considered 'unorthodox' policies. This helped contain increases in non-performing loans. Legally, Malaysia simply used its membership right: any IMF member may exercise capital controls in a manner which will not restrict payments for current transactions, defined as 'not for the purpose of transferring capital' by the Fund's Articles of Agreement, right at the time when the IMF tried to change its statutes to anoint its illegal policy of forcing member states to liberalize capital accounts with legality. All countries had not only the right to control capital outflows – as the IMF had to admit when Malaysia exercised it; by forcing members to finance large and sustained outflows by speculators the IMF openly violated its own constitution, protecting speculators from those countries that control the Fund by their votes. Initially heavily criticized by the IMF and neoliberal economists, Malaysia's policies are meanwhile considered successful in shielding the country from the worst effects of this crisis, as especially the comparison with its neighbour Indonesia proves.

Mexico was again chosen for very obvious reasons. The historic fact apart that the Great Latin crisis 'officially' started in August 1982 when Jesús Silva Herzog, the then–minister of finance, informed creditors that Mexico would no longer be able to service its debt, Mexico shows a lot of peculiarities. Yet, officially dating Mexico as the start of the debt crisis of the 1980s is – like many official statements – at odds with the truth. Following BWI (especially IMF) advice, Chile suffered an enormous debt crisis in 1982, before Mexico. This was conveniently veiled by anointing Mexico as the first case. Poland also defaulted before Mexico. Progress overcoming yearly (and, for banks, highly profitable) rescheduling, so-called MYRAs (Multi-Year Rescheduling Arrangement) were first concluded with Mexico, even before the 'Brady Plan', a similar but limited debt exchange programme, was put into effect there under Baker, who officially demanded repayment of every cent. In a way, Mexico may be seen as some kind of test laboratory for sovereign debt management. Thus, the question of what can be learned from its experience is doubtlessly important.

Portugal, yet another euro-country cited as proof that the crisis could be overcome thanks to EU authorities, is equally worth a closer look. In May 2014, three years after the crisis broke, Portuguese authorities performed what was called a clean exit from the 'adjustment programme'. Analysing this case more closely and neutrally shows a very different picture. After the 'clean exit'

Portugal was left a much poorer country having to service a much larger debt. Other structural problems, such as the fragility of the financial system, remained unaddressed. After the 'clean exit' two banks had collapsed and were resolved with public resources. In Portugal, as in other euro-countries, one point becomes most clearly visible: austerity destroying human lives and denying human rights is no longer confined to the South. Unelected EU bureaucrats can be even worse and more inhuman than (also unelected) IMF functionaries.

South Africa (SA) is an equally clear choice. Lending to the apartheid regime – sometimes even in violation of UN sanctions – was considered by many experts as the clearest case of odiousness. If any country after Costa Rica in the 1920s had any chance of repudiating the past regime's financial commitments on legal, ethical and moral grounds, it was post-apartheid SA. Due to international sanctions, total foreign debt inherited from the racist regime was naturally relatively small. Nevertheless, or maybe because of that, the new government decided not to raise this issue.

South Korea was one of the countries gravely affected by the Asian Crisis. Egged on by the BWIs to liberalize and deregulate as quickly as possible, Korea – whose sovereign debt was a mere 8.3 per cent of GDP in 1996 – suffered its worst financial crisis in history in 1997, driving it into the arms of the IMF. Unlike Indonesia, Korea returned to its own policy as soon as that could be done. The result was a quick recovery and resiliency to the global 2008 crisis. Self-insuring against future crises by building up foreign exchange reserves – without any doubt a costly strategy – Korea defended its own policy space.

Spain, before 2007 a perfect example of responsible fiscal policy, became one of the euro-countries severely affected by the financial and economic crisis after 2008. Its Maastricht indicators were better than Germany's, but enormous current account deficits and external private debt accumulated at a scale only possible by its membership in the euro-area and the concomitant inflow of credit from surplus countries (in fact, especially one country) in the euro-area. This mechanism foreseeably triggered the crisis. To save Spanish speculators and even more so speculating banks from other euro-countries, Spain financed a massive public bailout programme, transforming private debts into public debts. The bailout of foreign speculators is one main characteristic of the present generation of debt crises, especially pronounced in the EU. Like other euro-countries, Spain is an example of how inappropriate policies can destroy countries and trigger crises at a huge human rights cost.

2

Managing Public Debt Crisis in Argentina

Between Sovereignty and Subordination

ALFREDO FERNANDO CALCAGNO*

ABSTRACT

Argentina has endured sovereign debt crises practically since its existence as an independent country in the early nineteenth century. This chapter concentrates on the sovereign debt problems related to the period of financial globalization that started in the mid-1970s. The country experienced two debt cycles (1977–80 and 1990–2000) in which a rapid rise of external debt was followed by severe crises (1980–82 and 2001–02). The chapter traces the factors that led to public over-indebtedness, including domestic financial liberalization, macroeconomic policies and the bailing out of private indebted agents. It also describes the economic consequences resulting from debt crises and the very different ways in which these crises were managed, first between 1983 and 1989, and then after 2003. The different approaches in handling sovereign debt crises and their consequences strongly influenced the economic performances and the social and political processes. In one case the government accepted the 'strategy for the debt' set by the main creditors, which was consistent with the Washington Consensus policy agenda. In the second case, the management of the sovereign debt problem was consistent with the national priorities and development options. The chapter examines how Argentina managed to restructure its sovereign debt in the latter period, in a way that restored its sustainability, but also the obstacles posed by vulture funds and the ruling of foreign justice courts. It finally extracts some lessons from the Argentinean experience and shows how it has contributed to the international process aimed at establishing a mechanism for restructuring sovereign debts.

* This chapter presents the views of its author and not of the institution where he is employed. The author wishes to thank Arturo O'Connell and Edgardo Torija-Zane for their valuable comments.

I. INTRODUCTION

Sovereign debt crises in Argentina have a history almost as long as the country's independent life. Starting with the first loans extended by Barings Bank of London in 1824, sovereign debt has strongly influenced economic and political life. Despite very different situations over the course of almost 200 years, issues relating to sovereign debt presented a number of similarities.

First, periods of high sovereign indebtedness were mostly linked to external debt, although sometimes the line between external and domestic debt was blurred. Second, large capital inflows responded more to 'push' factors (i.e. economic conditions in world financial centres) than to 'pull' factors stemming from Argentina's need for external financing. Third, a significant proportion of those inflows financed non-productive activities (e.g. defence procurement, imports of consumption goods and services, speculation on financial assets, private capital flight). Fourth, when a sovereign debt crisis eventually erupted, the way in which its burden was distributed depended on the capacity of different social groups to influence distributional policy decisions.

This chapter presents the Argentinean experience starting in the mid-1970s, when the country enthusiastically embraced the growing process of financial globalization.

II. DEBT BUILD-UP AND MANAGEMENT IN THE NEW ERA OF FINANCIAL GLOBALIZATION

II.A. *The Build-up of a Large External Debt*

The mid-1970s was a time of radical changes in the international economy, characterized by increasing financial globalization. It also witnessed dramatic changes in Argentina. During almost 40 years, Argentinean governments of different social constituencies and political orientations pursued the common goal of industrialization. As a result, by the early 1970s manufacturing accounted for one-third of total value added, 25 per cent of total employment and an increasing share of merchandise exports.

However, the economy tended to suffer from recurrent trade deficits due to the slow growth of primary exports and the high income elasticity of imports, which consisted essentially of intermediate and capital goods. This resulted in an external debt that amounted to $7.9 billion in 1975, equivalent to 22 per cent of gross domestic product (GDP) (Table 2.1).

A coup d'état in March 1976 changed the country's economic orientation. Industrialization strategies based on domestic markets and a developmental state were replaced by ultra-liberal policies that included trade and capital-account liberalization, income concentration and financial deregulation. These measures were complemented by an anti-inflationary policy that used the exchange rate as an 'anchor' (i.e. devaluing the peso at rates well below those of domestic inflation).

However, inflationary inertia was stronger than expected: between the end of 1976 and the end of 1980, consumer prices increased at an average annual rate of 140 per cent, compared to 68 per cent for the dollar rate (pesos per US dollar ($)). This provided excellent opportunities for carry-trade operations, since nominal interest rates in line with domestic inflation rate provided very high returns in dollar terms.

Real appreciation of the peso undermined the competitiveness of domestic production, prompting an upsurge of imports that negatively affected local manufacturing. Instead of financing industrialization as in earlier times, foreign debt was financing deindustrialization.

With the steep rise of interest rates in the United States in late 1979, debt servicing became a major burden on Argentina's balance of payments: the current-account deficit jumped from $500 million in 1979 to $4.8 billion in 1980. When in March and April 1980 several large domestic banks went bankrupt, private agents started to dollarize their financial assets. Banks increased their interest rates in a bid to retain deposits. This further dampened economic activity, but maintained the attractiveness of carry-trade operations as long as the exchange rate risk could be covered. This was done through 'back-to-back' operations, whereby a resident owning bank deposits abroad used those deposits as a guarantee for taking new credit which was used for short-term financial investments in pesos. The increased amount was then transferred abroad through the unregulated capital market, generating a new guarantee for a new carry-trade round. The rapidly increasing private external debt was registered in the Central Bank of Argentina (BCRA), while the accumulation of foreign assets and the reduction of foreign liabilities resulting from capital outflows remained unreported.[1]

Instead of recognizing that it was impossible to maintain an overvalued exchange rate, the government increased its own external debt and those of its state-owned enterprises in order to meet the private sector's demand for dollars. More than 80 per cent of the external debt contracted by both the

[1] BCRA, *Memoria Anual 1980*, Buenos Aires, 1981, 13.

public and private sectors between 1976 and 1983 (when the military government ended) was used to increase private assets abroad.[2]

II.B. *Managing the Debt Crisis*

This dynamic explains the rapid increase in Argentina's gross external debt, from $8.3 billion in 1976 to $27.2 billion in 1980 and $35.7 billion in 1981. However, as long as devaluation could be avoided, the debt-to-GDP ratio seemed bearable. When the peso was eventually devalued in 1981 and 1982, the external debt ratio jumped from less than 20 per cent of GDP in 1980 to almost 80 per cent in 1982 (Table 2.1). Interest payments on public debt (both domestic and external) accounted for 10.2 per cent of GDP and 32 per cent of current fiscal revenues in 1982. With international reserves held by the Central Bank falling to $3 billion, the country was heading towards default.

To avoid this, the government encouraged private firms to postpone their net external payments. Those that managed to refinance their foreign debt for at least 540 days, or obtained new credits, were eligible for exchange rate insurance, paying a fee much lower than the actual devaluation. In addition, the government paid private firms 23 cents per dollar of debt to compensate them for the devaluations in the first half of 1981, despite the fact that most of those firms held foreign assets at least as large as their foreign liabilities. In October 1982, the government nationalized private debts covered by exchange rate insurance against payment in pesos well below market price. It is estimated that the exchange rate insurance scheme provided to the private sector (public enterprises were excluded from such coverage) amounted to a bailout equivalent to 65 per cent of their insured debt.[3]

The democratic government of Raúl Alfonsín, who took office in December 1983, adopted some measures that could have led to a different form of debt management. In particular, it created a Central Bank committee to establish the legitimacy of public debt and to examine cases of possible fraud related to the exchange rate insurance scheme. The committee found many irregularities, such as transnational firms and local business groups benefiting from exchange rate insurance on self-lending operations, on foreign liabilities that had already been cancelled or on capital investment

[2] Word Bank, *Economic Memorandum on Argentina*, Report no. 4979-AR, Washington, DC, June 22, 1984.

[3] Eduardo Basualdo, *Deuda externa y poder económico en la Argentina*, (Buenos Aires: Nueva América, 1987).

disguised as external debt.[4] However, with only one exception (the *Cogasco* case), the government took no action to recover the money.

Regarding public debt, the objective was to renegotiate the debt that was reaching maturity, and to seek fresh financing from the International Monetary Fund (IMF). Argentina undertook successive rounds of negotiations with international bank lenders (in 1983, 1985 and 1987), the Paris Club (in 1985 and 1987) and the IMF (with which it signed standby agreements (SBAs) in 1983, 1984 and 1987). In this process, official and multilateral creditors provided financing that was used not for recovering growth but rather for servicing the debt owed to private creditors. At the same time, austerity measures were strictly monitored by the IMF. Through these negotiations, creditors also benefited from implementation of the on-lending and capitalization mechanisms, which allowed them to make extra profits and reduce the weight of the Argentinean debt in their portfolios without absorbing all the cost of selling it in a secondary market at 25 to 30 per cent of its face value.[5]

A similar approach to debt crisis management was pursued by other Latin American countries. It gave time and revenues to creditor banks to reduce their exposure to the region's debt and averted a banking crisis in developed countries. However, it was less favourable to the debtor countries. Argentina could not meet its macroeconomic commitments made under the SBA, which resulted in the interruption of the IMF programme in 1988. Argentina partially suspended its servicing of the external debt in April 1988, but this was 'too little, too late' to fix macroeconomic imbalances and avoid the uncontrolled currency depreciations and episodes of hyperinflation that followed in 1989–90.

With almost all Latin American countries running into arrears on their external debts, it was eventually recognized that there was a solvency problem and that some debt relief was needed. The US Secretary of Treasury, Nicholas Brady, proposed that indebted countries should be allowed to issue debt bonds that could be exchanged for bank credits, generally with a reduction in face

[4] *See* Eduardo Halliburton, José Mauro Bianco and Carlos Villalba, 'Deuda Externa Privada. El Destino de Una Investigación', *Realidad Económica* 87 (1989): 72–113.

[5] A detailed analysis of debt renegotiations was conducted for the Primer Informe de la Comisión Bicameral Permanente de Seguimiento y de la Gestión y del Pago de la Deuda Externa de la Nación, Ley 26984. Its report (still unpublished), coordinated by Eric Calcagno, President of the Commission, was presented to Parliament on December 2015. It draws on inputs prepared by the Central Bank of Argentina under the direction of Arturo O'Connell, the Latin American Faculty of Social Sciences team led by Eduardo Basualdo and the Centre of Economy and Finance for the Development of Argentina (CEFID-AR) team led by Guillermo Wierzba. Soon after, CEFID-AR was disbanded by the new Argentinean government.

value.[6] Argentina concluded such an agreement in April 1993, when loans for $28 billion were exchanged against $25.5 billion in 30-year public bonds.

III. A SECOND WAVE OF FOREIGN INDEBTEDNESS: FROM THE BRADY PLAN TO THE LARGEST SOVEREIGN DEFAULT IN RECENT TIMES

III.A. *Argentina's Convertibility Plan*

The debt strategy designed and conducted by a conglomerate of creditors failed to help Argentina recover its growth and its debt sustainability. It was the revival of 'push' factors in the early 1990s that led to a new wave of capital inflows. In fact, the Brady Plan was accompanied by a deep reduction in US interest rates that prompted a surge of financial flows no longer based on bank credits but on the purchase of sovereign bonds by (mostly) institutional investors.

To reduce high inflation, Menem's government resorted, yet again, to the exchange rate anchor. In March 1991 it established a convertibility regime, introducing a law that pegged the exchange rate to the US dollar and determined that the monetary base had to be backed by a similar amount of international reserves. The economic authorities argued that with such a backing there would be enough dollars to always maintain the exchange rate.

Disinflation was successful, as the inflation rate fell from 1,344 per cent in 1990 to 84 per cent in 1991 and to 17.5 per cent in 1992. However, it did not prevent a significant real appreciation of the peso. This created yet another opportunity to exploit carry-trade operations, which, along with the privatization process, prompted large capital inflows and a rapid increase in international reserves. Given the pro-cyclical monetary rule, rising reserves translated into a rapid expansion of domestic credit (mostly for consumption). This boosted economic recovery, but it also contributed to generating a large current-account deficit. Economic growth and privatizations initially improved fiscal revenues, but the resulting fiscal surplus turned into a growing deficit after 1995. The deterioration of the fiscal balance was partly due to social security reforms, which replaced a public pay-as-you-go system with a capitalization regime in which most of the contributions were diverted to private pension funds.

This exposed the vulnerability of the convertibility regime. With an overvalued currency, the only way to control current-account deficit was

[6] On the Brady Plan, *see* Arturo O'Connell, *Report on developing countries' finance and debt with commercial banks* (Buenos Aires: Centro de Economía Internacional, 1993).

by restricting imports through an economic recession; but this would increase the fiscal deficit and weaken the financial system, while the Central Bank could only marginally finance the government or serve as a lender of last resort.

A serious warning came in late 1994 with the Mexican crisis. Domestic agents withdrew time deposits from the banks and purchased dollars, resulting in huge capital outflows. The run on deposits and haemorrhaging of reserves only stopped when the government obtained sizeable foreign loans, starting with an IMF disbursement in April 1995.

The system could continue as long as Argentina was able to obtain enough foreign funds and constantly increase its external debt, which doubled between 1993 and 1998 (Table 2.1). But the sequence of financial crises that started in Thailand in 1997 reduced capital inflows into Argentina, pushing the country into economic depression.

III.B. *Into the Abyss*

Under De la Rua, who became president in December 1999, the government pursued the same economic policy, seeking to avert the risks to convertibility by securing large foreign financing and adopting a restrictive fiscal stance. Since market financing was virtually inaccessible, the government sought official financing (mostly from the IMF, but also from the World Bank, the Inter-American Development Bank and the government of Spain) of up to $19.7 billion. At the same time, 12 domestic 'leading banks' and pension funds announced that they would allow loans and credit restructuring of another $20 billion.

The confidence inspired by these measures was short-lived, as evidenced by a new wave of withdrawals of deposits and a reduction of international reserves in the first months of 2001. The government then undertook a massive restructuring of the public debt in April, aimed at postponing $7.8 billion of debt repayments of the principal, which were due in 2001–02. With the so-called mega-debt exchange (*Megacanje*), up to $30.4 billion worth of new bonds were issued in exchange for $28.2 billion of old bonds, at an exorbitant implicit yield of 15.3 per cent. However, both bank deposits and reserves continued to fall. Between the end of January and the end of July 2001, international reserves declined from $33.2 billion to $18.5 billion.

In July 2001, Argentina's National Congress passed the 'Zero Deficit' Law, which was expected to eliminate the fiscal deficit once and for all and generate a confidence shock that would trigger economic recovery. This law established that, if programmed public spending exceeded the anticipated fiscal revenues for the subsequent quarter, all public expenditure categories (except interests on public debt) would be uniformly reduced in order to balance the fiscal account. Accordingly, the government reduced nominal pensions and public wages, as well as other non-financial public expenditures by 13 per cent – the percentage that, according to official calculations, was required to eliminate the deficit. The IMF praised this measure and extended an emergency loan of another $8 billion, bringing the total amount of its rescue package for Argentina to $21.6 billion.

This generated a supplementary recessionary shock to an economy that was in its fourth year of recession. After a short respite, there was another run on deposits. The economy went into a free fall: in the third quarter, seasonally adjusted GDP plummeted by 4.6 per cent, and by a further 5.6 per cent in the last quarter (i.e. an annual rate of –24.4 per cent). In such a situation, fiscal revenues fell even more sharply than fiscal spending. A law voted by Congress could not repeal a macroeconomic law.

In October 2001, the ruling party lost the mid-term elections, and it was a politically weakened government that made two last-ditch efforts to rescue the economy. It first announced a new debt exchange aimed at reducing the high interest rates of the *Megacanje*, and postponing part of its debt servicing until 2005. The exchange was divided into two steps. The first related to $58 billion owed to domestic creditors. This replaced public bonds with 'guaranteed loans' issued under domestic law and backed by a tax on financial transactions. The second step of the debt exchange, which involved sovereign debt held by non-residents, never took place. Finally, the government tried to stop the run on bank deposits and reserves by introducing an almost total freeze on bank deposits. This exacerbated the economic and political crisis.

Since the government did not fulfil its fiscal commitments, the IMF withheld the disbursement of the $1.3 billion loan due in December and the World Bank also suspended a $650 million loan. Without any source of foreign financing – which had mostly financed private capital outflows throughout the year – the convertibility regime collapsed. After a few weeks of social turmoil and a bloody repression, the president of the Republic resigned.

In late December 2001, the provisional president, Adolfo Rodríguez Saá, declared a partial default on external debt, which affected the external bondholders and the Paris Club creditors but spared the 'guaranteed loans', the debt with multilateral creditors and the new debt to be issued. The defaulted debt of $79.7 billion more than doubled the previous default 'record' of $31.6 billion set by the Russian Federation in 1998.

Shortly after, Rodríguez Saá was replaced by Eduardo Duhalde, who declared the end of convertibility on 6 January 2002. In the following months, a steep devaluation resulted in a public-debt-to-GDP ratio of 150 per cent (Table 2.1). Restoring growth and debt sustainability seemed an insurmountable challenge, and the way forward was highly uncertain.

IV. A NEW APPROACH TO DEBT RESTRUCTURING

IV.A. *Reducing Indebtedness as Part of a Development Strategy*

The peso was devalued gradually. At first, a dual system was established, with an official segment, where 1 dollar equalled 1.4 pesos, and a floating segment. As most of the banking operations were denominated in dollars, the devaluation and dual currency market created considerable confusion. In February 2002 it was decided to convert all the banking loans into pesos at the rate of 1 dollar equals 1 peso, and all the deposits at the rate of 1.4 pesos per dollar. The government compensated the banks for the difference, issuing domestic public debt equivalent to $31 billion. Including the accumulation of interest in arrears, public debt reached $191.3 billion by the end of 2004 (Table 2.1). Under IMF pressure, foreign exchange markets were liberalized and the dollar jumped to 3.6 pesos in early June 2002.

It seemed that debt management would replicate previous experiences where private losses were socialized, keeping profits in the hands of private capital exporters and accepting the IMF's diktat on macroeconomic policy and structural reforms. However, there were some differences. First, the government did not nationalize private external debt. In fact, many private debtors defaulted on most of their debt up to an amount of $35.2 billion. Private external debt was concentrated in a small number of large firms and transnational companies; many were supported by their parent companies or benefited from debt restructuring and haircuts. In addition, several export-oriented firms achieved profitability that enabled them to repay their debts. As a result, private external debt fell between the end of 2001 and 2005, from $78.4 billion to $48.4 billion.[7]

Second, the government rapidly understood that sticking to IMF conditionality (e.g. a free floating currency regime, fiscal austerity and a flexible labour market) would be disastrous. Consequently, it turned to a 'managed float' regime, stabilizing the exchange rate at around 3 pesos per dollar, which was still a strongly undervalued level. Furthermore, it introduced a tax on exports which helped to recover public spending, particularly social transfers.

[7] Bicameral Commission, 120.

Under Nestor Kirchner's presidency starting in 2003, debt management was to be integrated into a general political and economic project. A major aim was to achieve debt sustainability by restoring economic growth and restructuring debt in default. It was believed that economic recovery would result from stronger domestic demand, while the new exchange rate would support import-substituting reindustrialization. Creditors were invited to negotiate without the intervention of the IMF.

Instead of a club of banks led by the main creditor institutions, Argentina now had to deal with many institutional investors and innumerable individual investors. There were 152 kinds of bonds, denominated in 14 different currencies involving eight different jurisdictions. Although a number of creditors started litigation against Argentina, most of them organized themselves into committees to conduct negotiations.

In March 2005, the result of the first debt restructuring was announced. Of an eligible debt of $81.8 billion (the previously mentioned $79.7 billion plus $2.1 billion in unpaid interest), $62.3 billion (or 76.2 per cent) worth of debt was replaced by new securities equivalent to $35.3 billion. These consisted of $15 billion in par bonds, without any discount but with very low (though rising) interest rates; $11.9 billion in discount bonds, with a haircut as high as 66.3 per cent and an interest rate of 8.28 per cent; and $8.3 billion in quasi-par bonds with a discount of 30.1 per cent and an interest rate of 3.31 per cent.[8] In addition, investors received GDP-linked warrants proportional to their participation, which would provide supplementary payments in the years when GDP growth exceeded 3.5 per cent. Thanks to very rapid GDP growth, warrants' holders received unexpectedly high payments: as much as $10 billion between 2006 and 2012.[9]

In 2006, the government paid its entire debt ($9.53 billion) with the IMF ahead of time. This early repayment did not alter economic policy, as no IMF-supported programme was being applied, but it was intended to reaffirm the government's independent policy orientation. The 2005 debt exchange, added to the cancellation of the IMF debt, and the rapid growth of GDP in current dollars reduced total public debt from 127.5 per cent of GDP at the end of 2004 to 64.0 per cent two years later, while the external public debt fell from 77.1 to 28.6 per cent of GDP.[10]

8 Ministry of Economy press release, 18 March 2005.

9 Martín Guzman, "An Analysis of Argentina's 2001 Default Resolution," Centre for International Governance Innovation Paper No. 110, October 2016.

10 These amounts do not include the debt of private holders that remained in default. If included, the debt-to-GDP ratio was higher by 12.2 per cent in 2006.

With a booming economy and fiscal surpluses, it was possible to limit new debt issuances, which mostly took place in the domestic market. Several measures further changed the public debt structure. In 2008, the social security system was renationalized, with pension funds' assets transferred to the public sector. As most of those assets consisted of public bonds, net public debt shrank significantly. By the end of 2009, public institutions held 48 per cent of gross public debt.

The new international framework adversely affected the trade balance. In addition, repayments of loans that were reaching maturity required considerable external financing. Therefore, the government used part of the Central Bank's reserves to service its external debt.[11] However, as international reserves were essential for coping with the challenging external environment, it appeared necessary to regain normal access to international financial markets.

In 2010, a second debt exchange was opened. Of an eligible amount of $18.3 billion, $12.2 billion (67 per cent) were exchanged against $7.2 billion of new debt: $1.9 billion in par bonds, $4.3 billion in discount bonds and $0.9 billion in global bonds. Investors also received a GDP-linked bond, as in the 2005 exchange.[12]

Efforts to normalize the relationship with foreign creditors also involved resolving several legal disputes. In 2013, Argentina paid $500 million to plaintiff firms that had won cases against Argentina in the World Bank's International Centre for Settlement of Investment Disputes (ICSID). In 2014, it transferred bonds worth $5.1 billion to Repsol as compensation for the partial renationalization of the oil company, YPF. Also in 2014, Argentina restructured its debt in default with Paris Club members for a total amount of $9.7 billion, including $3.6 billion in punitive interest payments.

At that point, many of the goals related to public debt pursued since 2003 were attained. The ratio of public debt to GDP had declined from 150 per cent in 2002 to 50 per cent in 2014–15. Moreover, 60 per cent of that debt was held by public agencies, meaning the net public debt was only 20 per cent of GDP. The recovery of debt sustainability resulted from successful debt restructuring and, even more important, from the economic recovery that increased real GDP by 77 per cent between 2002 and 2015; such an expansion would not have been possible without the breathing space

[11] The Fund for Reducing the Debt, created for that purpose in March 2010, cancelled $33.4 billion of debt between 2010 and 2015.

[12] Ministerio de Economía, Oficina Nacional de Crédito Público, Deuda Pública del Estado Argentino, data up to 30 June 2010.

provided by the partial debt default. As a result, the burden of the debt crisis was better distributed, employment recovered, income distribution improved and poverty levels fell significantly.

One major problem remained: the 7.6 per cent of non-restructured external debt (the 'holdouts'), part of which was held by vulture funds.

IV.B. *The Conflict with Vulture Funds*

Argentina was an attractive target for vulture funds, because much of its debt had been issued under foreign jurisdictions, which implied renouncing sovereign immunity, and the absence of collective action clauses (CACs) enabled minority bondholders to reject restructuring agreements accepted by a qualified majority. This explains why vulture funds started acquiring Argentinean debt in 2001–02.[13]

The funds easily secured judgements in foreign courts ordering Argentina to pay the totality of its debt in default. The country refused to comply, because its restructured bonds contained the 'Right Upon Future Offers' (RUFO) clause, which obliged Argentina to extend to all the restructured debt any condition that could be offered to the holdouts that would be more beneficial than the terms agreed to in the previous debt exchanges.

There followed several years of judicial and political harassment of Argentina. The vulture funds demanded the seizure of various Argentine assets, including those of its Central Bank and the public social security system, bonds backing Argentinean Brady securities, embassies, an Argentinean navy training vessel, the national airline and the energy company, YPF. They tried to block joint ventures with YPF by attempting to seize assets of its associated firms in the United States. They also called for an embargo on China's loans to Argentina to finance infrastructure projects. Most of these demands failed, but they created a climate of uncertainty for any investment project in Argentina. Furthermore, the vulture funds lobbied energetically, particularly through the American Task Force Argentina, financing hostile media campaigns and pushing to block the country's access to multilateral credit and capital markets.[14]

The most damaging measure against Argentina were the judicial cases that hinged on the *pari passu* (equal treatment) clause included in debt contracts, according to which a given debt could not be subordinated to that of any other creditor, restructured or not. The Argentine government understood that

[13] Carlos Burgueño, *Los buitres* (Buenos Aires: Edhasa, 2013), 15.

[14] Juan Hernández Vigueras, *Los fondos buitre, capitalismo depredador* (Buenos Aires: Capital Intelectual, 2015), 124–39.

clause to mean that all holdouts could ask for similar payments to those who accepted restructuring. To that end, in September 2013 the Argentine Congress authorized the government to organize a third debt exchange (which eventually did not take place). However, a New York District Court judge (Thomas Griesa) interpreted that clause to mean that Argentina should not be allowed to pay its restructured debt unless the plaintiff vulture funds received, concurrently or in advance, full payment on their claim. The ruling was upheld by the Appeals Court of New York, and the Supreme Court declined Argentina's request to review the case. Additionally, Judge Griesa issued an injunction under which any institution – banks or clearing houses – somehow supporting the Argentine government to pay service on the restructured debt without having fulfilled its obligations towards the holdouts would be under contempt of court. On 30 June 2014, Argentina deposited $539 million in the bank of New York Mellon (BoNY), which was in charge of payments to bondholders of the restructured debt. However, the bank did not transfer the money to the exchange holders.

Although the court ruling only concerned bonds issued under US legislation, the institutions that channelled payments on bonds issued under Argentinean, English and Japanese legislation[15] required clarification from Judge Griesa to ensure they were allowed to proceed with such payments. The judge first authorized them on a case-by-case basis, but on March 2015 he forbade further payments on bonds restructured under Argentinean law.

Affected bondholders sought recourse in European courts against payment suspension, and in February 2015 an English judge ruled that the euros retained by the BoNY were under British jurisdiction and belonged to bondholders, but did not order the bank to make payments. In October, a Belgian court ordered the bank to make the transfers to holders of bonds in euros, but to no effect.

The Argentinean government tried unsuccessfully to break the deadlock. Through the Sovereign Payment Law (10 September 2014), Nación Fideicomisos (a subsidiary of state-owned Banco Nación) replaced BoNY as payment agent, and bondholders were invited to exchange their bonds against others covered by Argentinean or French jurisdiction. It also took the case to the international arena by promoting an initiative of the Group of 77 and China, as a result of which the General Assembly of the United Nations called for 'the establishment of a multilateral legal framework for sovereign debt

[15] Citibank, Euroclear, JP Morgan Chase and Clearstream.

restructuring processes' (Resolution 68/604 of 9 September 2014), and adopted nine 'basic principles on sovereign debt restructuring processes' in the Resolution 69/316 of 10 September 2015. In particular, it recognized that deciding sovereign debt restructuring was a right of sovereign states, and reaffirmed the principle of sovereign immunity. In August 2015, Argentina sought to institute proceedings against the United States in the International Court of The Hague, alleging that its judicial power was violating Argentinean sovereignty and immunity. These initiatives contributed to the global debate on sovereign debt and vulture funds, but did not alleviate Argentina's problems. Meanwhile, Judge Griesa accepted 37 collective demands from 'me too' holdouts (those that had not undertaken litigation against the Argentine government) to receive the same benefits as the vulture funds. Therefore, the total debt to be paid under his ruling jumped from $1.4 billion to almost $8 billion.

Even though the RUFO clause expired on 31 December 2014, there was virtually no scope for negotiations during 2015, an electoral year. Indeed, the holdouts saw the possibility of obtaining the entire amount claimed if one of the front-runner candidates, Mauricio Macri, who had committed to abide by Griesa's ruling, won the election. Thus his victory on 22 November 2015 was also a victory for the vulture funds.

The new government sought to achieve an agreement with the holdouts as soon as possible. It offered all the holdouts 100 per cent of the capital plus 50 per cent of that amount as interest payments for the whole period in default ('basic offer'). In addition, those recognized as having been affected by Argentina's lack of observance of the *pari passu* clause could also opt to receive the entire amount they claimed less 30 per cent ('*pari passu* offer').[16] The first offer suited plaintiffs who had obtained an early ruling, because the interest rate applicable was that of the 1-year US Treasury bond (less than 1 per cent at the time). The second offer was in the interests of those whose claims had not received judgement yet, because they were entitled to the punitive rate of 9 per cent for a longer period of time.

In March 2016, Argentina's Congress voted on a law approving these offers, provided the US court cancelled the *pari passu* clause. The same law allowed issuance of $12.5 billion worth of bonds (covered by a foreign jurisdiction) for

[16] For no apparent reason, the vulture funds owned by Paul Singer obtained a lower reduction (25 per cent) on their claims of $5.9 billion. They also received $235 million to cover the cost of their litigation against Argentina. On the agreements with the vulture funds, see Sebastián. Soler, "Los Buitres Ganan la Partida," in *Macri lo Hizo*, ed. Ari Lijalad (Buenos Aires: Ediciones Continente, 2016).

repaying the remaining debt in default of $6.2 billion.[17] The government justified these terms on the grounds that it had an urgent need for new external debt issues to cover the fiscal deficit plus new investments for infrastructure development; in fact, new government debt was also needed to match private capital outflows. In the first seven months of 2016, the public sector issued dollar-denominated (mostly external) debt up to $34.6 billion (of which $6.6 billion was issued by eight provinces, $6 billion by the Central Bank and $22 billion by the Central Government), more than 35 per cent of the public external debt by the end of 2015. Thus, once again, a large amount of external debt is to be incurred, not for importing needed capital goods, but mostly for financing expenditure in pesos and covering capital flight.

V. MAIN LESSONS FROM THE ARGENTINEAN EXPERIENCE

Several lessons can be learned from the Argentinean experience, both to prevent future sovereign debt crises and to better handle them when they occur.

First, it is necessary to control the amount of capital inflows and be selective about their composition and use. Indeed, the seeds of debt crises are sown during the periods of easy access to foreign financing, when much of that capital is not used for productive projects and instead generates macroeconomic vulnerability (e.g. currency appreciation and financial bubbles). Domestic sources of investment finance need to be reinforced. Governments need to prevent excessive public as well as private indebtedness, as the latter also poses a risk to macroeconomic stability and government's solvency.

Second, when a solvency debt problem arises, postponing its actual resolution is counterproductive. Restrictive policies, including automatic adjustment mechanisms, such as Argentina's Convertibility Plan and the Zero Deficit Law, fail to generate confidence to restore credit and growth; instead, they aggravate the crisis. Rescue packages usually only help private creditors – in some cases private debtors are also bailed out – without restoring debt sustainability. When the solvency problem is eventually acknowledged, structural reforms are imposed by multilateral lending institutions, which generally end up only serving the interests of the creditors.

Third, private domestic and foreign agents with access to foreign finance have strong links with international financial markets and normally own large (often undeclared) foreign assets. Therefore, bailing out their foreign

[17] In the project of law, the government estimated that total debt in default, including punitive interests, amounted to around $20 billion.

debts in case of a debt crisis is unjustified, as they usually have the means to pay or restructure their debts.

Fourth, a necessary step in tackling a solvency debt crisis should be to suspend, at least partially, debt repayments. It allows breathing space to avoid further economic and social damage, and it brings creditors to the negotiating table.

Fifth, the negotiation process tends to be long and complex because of the large number and heterogeneity of creditors, including non-cooperative bondholders. Most of them, however, incline to accept long-term restructuring and large haircuts, which are more profitable than selling the bonds in the secondary market. The renegotiation process can be facilitated by clearly specifying the meaning of the *pari passu* clause and establishing CACs, but they would still have to face long and costly negotiations, including possible litigation, without the guarantee of a satisfactory resolution. An international framework that would allow a suspension of payments, a temporary halt to litigation and emergency financing for sustaining economic activity during the negotiating period would still be needed.

Sixth, vulture funds pose a formidable obstacle to resolving sovereign debt crises. They can litigate in jurisdictions (such as in the US courts) that only seek to safeguard creditors' interests. This adversely affects not only the sued country, but also other bondholders and the normal functioning of the international financial system. It may also compromise future debt restructuring or haircuts if the creditors can expect full payment, or even windfalls, through litigation; or, on the contrary, see payment blocked by the courts. Argentina's experience shows that US courts, by imposing a ruling on globalized financial institutions, exerted de facto universal jurisdiction, thereby impinging on other countries' (not only Argentina's) sovereignty and the rule of law. International law should effectively ban the predatory activities of vulture funds and curb the extra-territorial reach of the US judicial system.

Seventh, governments should never renounce to their sovereign immunity. They should avoid issuing debt in foreign jurisdictions, and if they deem this necessary, they should only resort to jurisdictions where the law protects issuers from vulture funds' activities, as in Belgium.

Eighth, a country can successfully pursue debt management policies as long as its government defends its national interests, resisting pressures to socialize costs and privatize profits and to follow pro-cyclical macroeconomic policies. In the case of Argentina, even after the new government accepted a costly defeat by the vulture funds, the overall result of the policy followed by the preceding Kirchner administrations was positive in terms of recovering sovereign debt sustainability through debt reduction and economic growth.

Annex

TABLE 2.1 *Public domestic and external debt, and private external debt and financial assets, 1975–2015*

	Public debt			External debt		Private	Total public	Total external
	Total	Domestic	External	Total	Private	External assets	Debt	Debt
	In current billion $						*In per cent of GDP*	
	(1) = (2) + (3)	(2)	(3)	(4) = (3) + (5)	(5)	(6)	(7)	(8)
1975	..	..	4.0	7.9	3.9	..	..	18.8
1976	10.4	5.2	5.2	8.3	3.1	..	28.7	22.8
1977	11.5	5.5	6.0	9.7	3.6	..	25.1	21.0
1978	10.3	2.0	8.4	12.5	4.1	..	17.5	21.2
1979	11.2	1.2	10.0	19.0	9.1	..	12.4	21.1
1980	17.1	2.6	14.5	27.2	12.7	..	11.4	18.1
1981	29.3	9.2	20.0	35.7	15.6	..	26.5	32.3
1982	30.4	4.0	26.3	43.6	14.4	..	55.2	79.3
1983	41.1	9.4	31.7	45.1	13.4	..	64.2	70.4
1984	43.7	8.2	35.5	46.2	10.6	..	54.6	57.7
1985	42.8	1.9	40.9	49.3	8.5	..	67.9	78.3
1986	46.1	1.4	44.7	51.4	6.7	..	55.9	62.4
1987	57.2	5.4	51.8	58.3	6.5	..	74.1	75.5

1988	59.3	5.8	53.5	58.5	5.0	..	76.0	74.9
1989	64.4	6.0	58.4	63.3	4.9	..	118.2	116.2
1990	60.6	..	..	62.2	5.9	..	48.5	49.8
1991	60.6	..	..	61.3	8.9	44.9	35.7	36.1
1992	63.3	12.6	50.7	64.0	13.3	44.4	30.1	30.4
1993	69.6	16.0	53.6	73.6	20.0	49.0	29.4	31.1
1994	80.7	19.4	61.3	87.6	26.3	49.8	31.3	34.0
1995	87.1	19.9	67.2	101.5	34.3	59.9	33.8	39.4
1996	97.1	23.0	74.1	114.4	40.3	65.7	35.7	42.1
1997	101.1	26.2	74.9	130.0	55.1	69.3	34.5	44.4
1998	112.4	29.3	83.1	147.6	64.5	72.7	37.6	49.4
1999	121.9	37.1	84.8	152.6	67.8	78.5	43.0	53.8
2000	128.0	43.1	84.9	155.0	70.1	79.4	45.0	54.5
2001	144.5	56.6	87.9	166.3	78.4	81.9	53.8	61.9
2002	137.3	46.1	91.2	156.7	65.5	90.1	149.4	170.5
2003	178.8	72.9	105.9	164.7	58.8	98.2	138.8	127.9
2004	191.3	75.4	115.9	171.2	55.3	102.0	127.3	113.9
2005	152.2	63.2	89.0	137.4	48.4	100.1	87.0	78.5
2006	162.8	75.6	87.2	135.0	47.8	109.1	76.2	63.2
2007	173.6	73.9	99.7	153.4	53.7	119.9	67.3	59.5
2008	175.0	81.6	93.4	153.9	60.5	121.0	58.5	51.4

(continued)

TABLE 2.1 (*continued*)

	Public debt			External debt		Private	Total public	Total external
	Total	Domestic	External	Total	Private	External assets	Debt	Debt
	In current billion $						In per cent of GDP	
	(1) = (2) + (3)	(2)	(3)	(4) = (3) + (5)	(5)	(6)	(7)	(8)
2009	176.9	85.3	91.6	145.3	53.7	133.5	58.7	48.2
2010	175.5	94.9	80.6	140.1	59.5	144.1	48.4	38.6
2011	190.2	104.4	85.7	153.7	67.9	163.9	44.4	35.9
2012	208.9	124.3	84.6	154.8	70.2	174.7	44.4	32.9
2013	214.4	131.0	83.4	152.6	69.2	183.6	43.3	30.8
2014	233.4	141.0	92.4	156.4	64.1	187.2	50.9	34.1
2015	251.5	156.1	95.4	164.2	68.8	195.5	49.5	32.3

Source: Estimates based on Central Bank, Ministry of Economy, Bicameral Commission, IMF and the Institute of International Finance.
Note: Public debt after 2005 includes holdouts.

3

Why Developing Countries Should Not Incur Foreign Debt

The Brazilian Experience

LUIZ CARLOS BRESSER-PEREIRA AND THIAGO DE MORAES MOREIRA

ABSTRACT

This chapter aims at addressing the macroeconomic difficulties imposed to middle-income countries that adopt a growth model based on foreign savings (or current-account deficits) in opposition to mainstream arguments that defend the existence of benefits for both borrowers (developing countries) and lenders (developed countries). To illustrate the theoretical arguments, we used empirical evidence from the Brazilian economy. These difficulties are not only associated to growth of foreign debt, which can lead to external financial crises, but also mainly to a causal relation between the current-account balance and the exchange rate. The accumulation of external deficits leads to a chronic overvaluation of the exchange rate. This macroeconomic dynamic, in turn, reduces the competitiveness of domestic producers in relation to foreign ones, which weakens domestic productive structures, condemning these economies to a low growth rate. Even when the external deficits are financed by foreign direct investments, there is another difficulty caused by remittances out of the country, which reduce national income and domestic savings, in particular when these investments contribute little to expansion of gross fixed formation, as verified in the Brazilian case. We note that in the last 70 years of Brazil's economy, the highest growth period (1947–72) was consistent with low levels of current-account deficits. From 1973 the pro argument of the benefits of foreign debt was definitely incorporated into economic policy. As a result, we observed an increase in external deficits, at the same time in which there was a slowdown in economic growth, including the occurrence of the debt crisis during the '80s and the need for external financial assistance in the end of the '90s and the beginning of the 2000s. More recently, although there is no interruption of foreign capital inflows, the negative effects of accumulation of external deficits must hinder a more robust economic recovery.

I. INTRODUCTION

Developing countries get indebted in foreign money because they are persuaded that they *need* foreign savings to grow. There is a growing literature showing that a growth-with-foreign-savings policy is a mistaken strategy: besides subjecting the developing country to cyclical financial crises, it discourages investment as it causes the long-term appreciation of the exchange rate. In this chapter we use the case of Brazil to reject the policy of growing with foreign savings. Not only because countries that get indebted in foreign money sooner or later will fall into balance of payment or currency crises – after which they become prisoners of a foreign debt that they are unable to pay – but also because, at least in the case of middle-income countries like Brazil that adopt a floating regime, the long-term appreciation of the local currency associated with the current-account deficit will reduce the competitiveness of the existing and potential competent business firms by reducing their expected profit rate, thereby blocking domestic investment.

Brazil has a long history of currency or balance of payment financial crises: 1930, the 1980s' foreign debt crisis, the 1998–99 currency crisis, which had a deleterious effect over the Brazilian economy. The suspension of the rollover of the foreign debt was in all cases the direct cause of such crises. In the second part of the twentieth century, particularly after the 1980s, multinational corporations spread all over the world financing current-account deficits, but these flows did not translate into higher growth of investment rates. In contrast, East Asian countries accepted foreign direct investments, but much less than Latin America and not to finance the current account, which was most of the time positive – and grew much faster.[1] What *should* we have learned? Essentially, that developing countries should *not* get indebted in foreign money, except in special cases; that they may receive foreign direct investments but not to finance deficits. Or, in other words, that they should pursue growth with domestic savings.

One of the major reasons why countries like Brazil grow at a slower pace than they might is the tendency towards cyclical and chronic overvaluation of the exchange rate that usually exists in developing countries. This structural tendency, in its turn, is fundamentally explained by accumulation of the current-account deficits. At the same time, these deficits incur in cyclical

[1] Between 1988 and 1992 privatization proceeds amounted to slightly more than $40 billion in Latin America and to $7.5 billion in East Asia according to the IBRD (*World Development Report* 1994, Oxford University Press, 1994, 105). The share of foreigners was 56 per cent and 2 per cent, respectively.

expansion of the foreign debt and often in cyclical currency or sovereign crises, which usually involve radical currency depreciation and, consequently, a strong increases in the risk perception, mainly of the external agents. Besides, the resulting high foreign debt burden turns into a major obstacle to growth, and governments get involved in negotiations with the creditors aiming at the restructuring of foreign debt – a painful 'confidence-building' process achieved on conditions often contrary to the national interest.

This book asks what we have learned from the foreign debt crises. Our response in this chapter is simply that developing countries should *not* get engaged in foreign indebtedness; that developing countries that already have means to domestically finance their investments should not incur current-account deficits. We have already learned that the accumulation of the external deficits can lead to sovereign crises, which can generate complex problems in terms of debt restructurings, as faced by the Brazilian economy. However, the idea here is not focusing on how to deal with foreign debt crises and the suffering of the indebted economies that have to deal with them, but rather focusing on the negative impacts of those deficits on growth, specifically the high rate of substitution of foreign for domestic savings that we observe in developing countries as a consequence of overvaluation of the exchange rate that is associated to the level of the current-account deficit.[2]

We know that this is not an easy path to follow. First, because it is apparently logical that capital rich countries transfer their capitals to developing countries', or, in other words, because current-account deficits represent 'foreign savings' that is supposed to finance additional investment. Second, because current-account deficits (and the exchange rate overvaluation) are associated with artificially high wages and other revenues and higher consumption, which makes them attractive to populist politicians on the left and on the right. Third, because rich countries have an interest in current-account deficits in developing countries, insofar as they legitimize the occupation of developing countries' domestic markets by multinational corporations. And, fourth, because developmental economists in developing countries have been, for long, unable to formulate logical and clear arguments to reject current-account deficits or the growth *cum* foreign savings policy.

[2] *See* L.C. Bresser-Pereira and Y. Nakano 'Economic growth with foreign savings?', *Brazilian Journal of Political Economy* 22, no. 2 (2003): 3–27; L.C. Bresser-Pereira and P. Gala 'Foreign savings, insufficiency of demand, and low growth', *Journal of Post Keynesian Economics* 30, no. 3 (2008): 315–34; L.C. Bresser-Pereira, E. Araújo and P. Gala 'An empirical study of the substitution of foreign for domestic savings in Brazil', *Revista EconomiA (ANPEC)* 15, no. 1 (2014): 54–67.

In recent years one of the authors of this chapter developed additional arguments against the attempt to grow by engaging in foreign debt. Current-account deficits imply an exchange rate that is overvalued in the long-term (instead of just being 'volatile') and make existing and potential local firms utilizing world state-of-the-art technology non-competitive. In this chapter we, first, summarize the main aspects of the critique of the growth *cum* foreign savings policy; second, we offer a brief history of Brazilian foreign debt, focusing on an analysis since 1973; and, third, we conclude by highlighting some worrying aspects of the Brazilian economy's current external situation.

II. A MISGUIDED GROWTH MODEL

The supposed need of developing countries to resort to foreign funds is an old mainstay of economics literature. Mainstream economics starts from the accounting macroeconomic identity between saving and investment and from the assumption that the availability of domestic savings stands as an important constraint against the expansion of investment, and comes to the conclusion that foreign financing is the solution to the problem. Insofar as a large share of middle-income countries, Brazil included, usually show low domestic saving rates, access to surplus funds in the form of foreign savings (equivalent to the current-accounts deficit) coming from developed, higher-income countries have been presented as a means to overcome the problems of limited domestic funds to finance investment.

But this view, aligned as it is with common sense (it would be only natural, after all, for rich countries to transfer capital to poor ones), is essentially misguided. Only in particular cases do foreign savings add to domestic ones and benefit developing countries. Starting in the early 2000s, several papers began to discuss the consequences for the Brazilian economy of a continued process of accumulating current-account deficits without that the rate of growth accelerated. We may point out a stream of essentially econometric studies that concluded that neoclassical current-account solvency models did not stand in the Brazilian case, that is, that the supposed boons of foreign debt were not found.[3]

From an alternative angle, also in the early 2000s, another group of Brazilian economists – including one of the authors of this chapter – began developing

[3] *See* F.A. Senna and J.V. Issler, 'Mobilidade de capitais e movimentos da conta corrente do Brasil: 1947–1997', *Estudos econômicos* 30, no. 4 (2000): 493–523; F. Rocha and S. Bender 'Present values tests of the Brazilian current account', *Revista Economia Aplicada* 4, no. 2 (2000): 203–22.

an approach based on classical developmentalism and post-Keynesian macroeconomics that became known as new developmentalism.[4] New developmental macroeconomics is a new theoretical approach based on the idea that the market is incapable of setting 'right' *macroeconomic prices*, in particular the foreign exchange rate and the profit rate of the manufacturing sector – the former becoming over-appreciated and the latter correspondently depressed for lengthy periods of time. The main causes explaining this tendency, which makes the country go from currency crisis to currency crisis, are Dutch disease and three habitual policies adopted by developing countries: the growth *cum* foreign savings policy, the use of the exchange rate as an anchor to control inflation and a monetary policy conducted by the central bank around a high level interest rate.[5] This chapter focuses on how the latter relates with the appreciation of the foreign exchange rate, as well as other macroeconomic developments.

For the new developmental macroeconomics, determination of the exchange rate in the medium run depends less on capital inflows and outflows (which do matter in the short run) than on the determination relationship between the current-account deficit and the exchange rate. The greater the current-account deficit, the more appreciated the foreign exchange rate. New developmentalism argues that a growth strategy for peripheral countries to embrace must not depend on foreign funds financing high current-account deficits. Instead, it must be based on domestic financing. The foreign financing that the accumulation of current-account deficits necessitates triggers a process of substitution of foreign for domestic savings, with negative consequences for investment and output growth. Furthermore, the continued expansion of foreign debt (or liabilities) increases the vulnerability to balance-of-payments crises. It is no surprise that the success of the developmental strategy adopted by dynamic Asian countries, beginning with Japan, was not based on absorbing foreign funds, but on generating current-account surpluses.

We therefore argue that there is a trend towards cyclic and chronic over-appreciation of the foreign exchange rate in economies that rely on the growth *cum* foreign savings policy. We emphasize that, before this new approach, econometric papers[6] indicated a positive relationship between foreign debt

4 *See* L.C. Bresser-Pereira 'A fragilidade que nasce da dependência da poupança externa', *Valor 1000* (September 2001): 34–38.

5 *See* L.C. Bresser-Pereira, J.L. Oreiro and N. Marconi, *Developmental Macroeconomics* (London: Routledge, 2014).

6 *See* D. Dollar, 'Outward-oriented developing economies really do grow more rapidly: evidence from 95 LDCs, 1976–85', *Economic Development and Cultural Change* 40, (1992):

and exchange rate appreciation, in addition to a negative relationship between an over-appreciated currency and growth. These studies lacked a theoretical foundation, however. The new developmental track sought to fill this gap, producing arguments for a deeper understanding of the causal links between the foreign exchange rate and economic development, particularly in economies that adopt the foreign financing strategy.

The focus on current-account deficits and the long-run over-appreciated foreign exchange rate to explain low growth is a relatively new element in the theoretical approach to development. According to the classical view of Prebisch and Furtado, peripheral countries experienced a structural foreign constraint, but the authors did not deduce from this constraint a need to control the foreign exchange rate, but simply to industrialize in order to overcome the constraint by means of high customs tariffs or multiple exchange rates.[7] Authors like Rodriguez and Thirlwall[8] picked up the foreign constraint problem, but also failed to deduce the need to make the foreign exchange rate competitive.

II.A. *Primary Income Remittances Abroad*

Adopting a strategy based on foreign financing has an impact on domestic demand. Given cheaper imports relative to domestic output as a result of the over-appreciated exchange rate, a significant share of capital inflows is dedicated to purchasing foreign consumer goods instead of investment goods. In other words, the strategy implies 'exchange rate populism', that is, it artificially raises consumption and discourages investment.

We must also consider the development of foreign financing on primary income flows and remittances. The main sources of financing of current-account deficits in the Brazilian economy include capital inflows as the so-called portfolio investments, foreign direct investment (FDI) and loans. In each of these cases the capital inflows – representing the acquisition of a Brazilian asset by a non-resident or even traditional loans – also imply future payments to its owners. In the case of bonds and loans, be they conventional or inter-company, funds outflows prevail as interest payments. For FDI and

523–44; O. Razin and S. Collins 'Real exchange rate misalignment and growth', *NBER Working Paper* no. 6147 (1997) Cambridge, MA.

7 *See* L.C. Bresser-Pereira and F. Rugitsky 'Industrial policy and exchange rate skepticism', Department of Economics FEA/USP, *Working Paper Series* 2016/08 (2016).

8 *See* O. Rodriguez, 'Sobre la concepción del sistema centro-periferia', *Revista de la Cepal* 3 (1977); A.P. Thirlwall 'The balance of payments constraint as an explanation of international growth rates differences', *Banca Nazionale del Lavoro Quarterly Review* 128 (1979): 45–53.

equity purchases, profits and dividends are prevalent. Therefore, the greater the foreign liabilities, the greater the flow of interest, profits or dividends payments.

These outflows are the main portion of the net income from abroad (NIA), which is the difference between payments made for the domestic use of foreign factors of production and payments received for the foreign use of domestic factors. It is therefore equal to the difference between gross domestic product (GDP) – the income made in the domestic territory – and the gross national income (GNI) – the income that remains in-country. Therefore, the greater the NIA, the lower the GNI. The GNI, in its turn, is a key variable in the consolidation of domestic saving (S_d), which is the difference between gross disposable income (GDI)[9] and final consumer spending (C).

$$GNI = GDP - NIA$$

$$GDI = GNI - UT$$

$$S_d = GDI - C$$

Therefore, growth based on the foreign financing strategy necessarily incurs increased transfers of income from the domestic economy abroad. These transfers *reduce* the national income and, therefore, domestic savings.

In any way, analysts generally argue that foreign financing by means of FDI should not be a concern from the angle of foreign vulnerability, and is even used as a positive economic indicator. This is due to the fact that direct investments are supposedly more closely linked to production than other essentially financial assets, such as shares, bonds, derivatives. This perception of the better 'quality' of direct investment, which may lead to mistaken conclusions regarding the situation of foreign accounts, explicitly emerges in the official statistics published by the Central Bank of Brazil, which uses the concept of 'foreign financing needs' calculated as the difference between the current account and FDI.

However, the presence of current-account deficits, regardless of the kind of capital flowing in through the financial account to finance them, is not in the country's best interest, and likewise implies exchange rate appreciation, discouragement of investment and the substitution of foreign for domestic savings. The interpretation might be different if FDI were to occur within a

[9] As the equation shows, the only difference between GDI and GNI lies in the so-called Unilateral Transfers (UT). The balances of these accounts, however, are of small shares of GDP, of approximately 0.1 per cent.

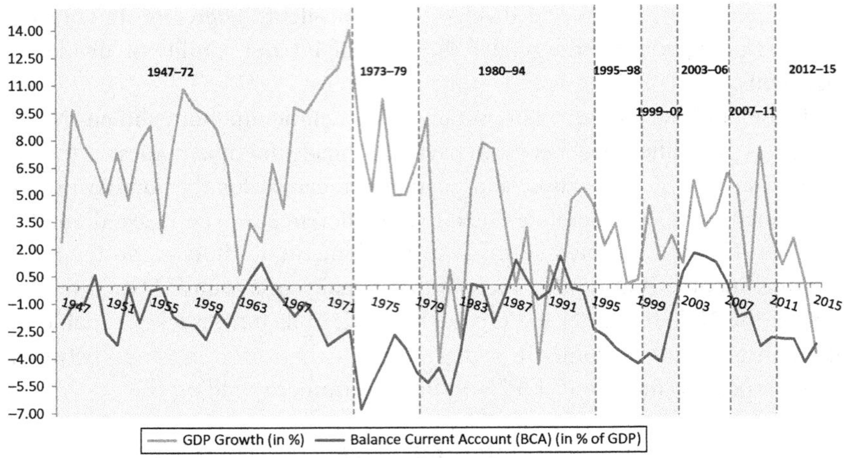

FIGURE 3.1 Real GDP growth (%) and balance current account (% of GDP).

context of brisk growth, where, given favourable profit expectations and high marginal propensity to invest, foreign savings would not substitute domestic ones. A similar effect would occur if FDI flows were associated with exports growth and thereby led to rising current-account balances, to a certain degree offsetting or even reversing income transfers abroad. In other words, when the correlation between the FDI (and other types of external capital) and the investment and exports growth is small (as verified in the Brazilian case), the substitution effect, which stimulates the foreign savings and restricts the domestic ones, is potentiated. The next section discusses to what degree history supports the new developmental theory, which claims the prevalence of the effect of substitution of foreign for domestic savings.

III. FOREIGN INDEBTEDNESS EVOLUTION

The current-account deficit is a determining factor in the evolution of the Brazilian foreign debt, here understood in its broad sense, including patrimonial debt. Figure 3.1 summarizes the evolution of Brazil's foreign debt since 1947, dividing it into several phases according to current-account changes, and therefore, capital flow changes for Brazil.[10] Besides the foreign balances, the graph presents the growth of the GDP. The Brazilian economy's main spurt of

[10] The Brazilian foreign sector's official database, elaborated and published by central bank, underwent important methodological changes over the course of this period in an effort to align with international standards. The latest base, called BPM6 and published in April 2015,

growth took place between 1947 and 1972, during which period the economy grew at an annual rate of 7.2 per cent.[11] Throughout this period, there was limited resorting to foreign savings, and domestic financing prevailed. The average current-account deficit in this period was 1.4 per cent of GDP.

The growth of GDP in this period was supported by the industrialization and urbanization processes, which induced much stronger growth of domestic demand (mainly private consumption and investment) than external demand or exports. Despite this performance of domestic demand, which does not generate external resources, the deficit in the current account, and therefore the need for foreign savings, was small. This is because accelerated growth of domestic demand was able to generate an expressive growth of domestic income, as suggested by GDP performance. In this sense, it is important to emphasize the macroeconomic consistency between the high level of economic growth and the low level of the current-account deficits, including verified in historical analysis of Brazilian external sector.

From 1973 we observe a major fall in growth of the economy to just 3.4 per cent a year, while the average current-account deficit increased to 2.2 per cent of GDP. The balances' increased volatility show periods of strong deterioration of the current account alternating with periods of its reduction and even of a small surplus.

Below, we present with a little more detail, although quite synthetically, the main factors/events that determined the dynamics of the external debt from 1973 to 2015, dividing the period in some intervals, as indicated in Figure 3.1.

1973–1979: Starting in the early 1970s, just after the 'Brazilian miracle' (1967–73) and the first oil shock (1973), the government's official position incorporated the notion that foreign debt was crucial to keeping up that pace of growth, finding theoretical support in neoclassical analyses and the multilateral institutions.[12] As a result, government policy began to encourage current-account deficits, which experienced an early major boost in 1973 due to the impact of the first oil shock on import expenditures.

only goes as far back as 1995. Therefore, for information from 1947 to 1994, the data used in this article correspond to the previous base of Brazilian foreign accounts, called BPM5.

[11] From now on, all data about the Brazilian external sector were extracted of the official database of the central bank. The data about GDP were extracted of the institution responsible by the System of National Accounts in Brazil that is the '*Instituto Brasileiro de Geografia e Estatística*' (IBGE).

[12] We emphasize the work of World Bank economists who used Prebisch's foreign constraint model to formulate the 'two-gap model'. For additional information, *see* H. Chenery and M. Bruno 'Development alternatives in an open economy: The case of Israel', *Economic Journal* (March 1962): 79–103.

The period from 1973 to 1979 is the only one that shows an expansion of current-account deficits simultaneously with the maintenance of high GDP growth rates. This combination helped support the thesis of the supposed benefits of foreign debt. But it is important to point out that rising foreign debt and the expansion of economic activity levels were explained by different processes, and no basis exists to argue for a causal link between the two.[13]

1980–1994: In 1980 the great foreign debt crisis, stemming largely from debt incurred in the immediately preceding years begins and leads the country to a major recession. Between 1989 and 1993, because of Brazil's lack of access to international credit, current-account deficits remained at low levels. A strong fiscal adjustment that began in 1981 helped this along and enabled a successful depreciation of the domestic currency in 1983, as well as retaining US dollars to honour debt service payments. In February 1987, Brazil declared a moratorium. In October of this year, Brazil's finance minister, Bresser-Pereira, proposed a plan to overcome the foreign debt problem, based on the securitization of the debt and the relative de-linkage between commercial banks and the IMF in the negotiations, which was rejected by the US Secretary of the Treasury, James Baker, but fully adopted by his successor, Nicholas Brady.[14]

1995–1998: Beginning in 1994–95, when the 1980s foreign debt crisis had already been addressed by the recessive adjustment, which lasted for close to ten years, and by the Brady Plan (1989), and when the Real Plan (1994) had already stabilized the country's high inflation, Brazil recovers its access to international credit,[15] and the government, forgetful of the poor outcomes of the indebtedness of 1973–80, understood that it was time to resume the growth *cum* foreign savings strategy.[16] In this context, neoliberal privatization reforms of the latter half of the decade helped to leverage those flows. Beginning in 1995, Brazil received even more expressive amounts of foreign funds via the financial account of the balance of payments. Capital inflows under this

[13] *See* P.C. Davidoff, *Dívida externa e política econômica: a experiência brasileira dos anos setenta* (São Paulo: Brasiliense, 1984).

[14] *See* L.C. Bresser-Pereira, 'A turning point in the debt crisis', *Brazilian Journal of Political Economy* 19, no. 2 (1999): 103–20.

[15] *See* M. Baer, 'Sistema financeiro internacional: Oportunidades e restrições ao financiamento do desenvolvimento', *Novos Estudos Cebrap* 42 (1995): 99–112; P.N. Batista Jr. and A.S. Rangel, 'A renegociação da dívida externa brasileira e o Plano Brady: avaliação de alguns dos principais resultados', *Caderno Dívida Externa* 7 (1994).

[16] For more details about the theoretical basis which supported the resumption of growth *cum* foreign savings strategy, *see* F.H. Cardoso and E. Faletto *Dependency and Development in Latin America* (Berkeley: University of California Press, 1979; original publication in Spanish, 1969).

account jumped from \$8.5 billion in 1994 to \$28.7 billion in 1995, and remained at levels near \$30 billion until 1998. Notwithstanding, the rates of investment and growth did not increase.

The profile of Brazil's foreign liabilities then undergoes a change. Although conventional debt contracts (loans from financial institutions or multilateral agencies) remained a relevant source of funds inflows, portfolio investments (in particular fixed-income securities and stocks), intercompany loans[17] and, above all, FDI increased as a share of foreign liabilities. On the other hand, reflecting the growth *cum* foreign savings policy and the resulting over-appreciation of the foreign exchange rate, the balance of current accounts once again showed rising deficits. It jumped from US\$1.2 billion in 1994 to approximately US\$18.7 billion in 1995, or from 0.3 per cent to 2.4 per cent[18] of GDP in a single year. Despite the negative effects of the currency over-appreciation on GDP growth and, therefore, on the growth of imports in the following years, the current-account deficit continued to increase as a result of the behaviour of the services balance (due mainly to increased international travelling) and income transfers abroad. These were decisive to cause the current-account deficit to reach 3.9 per cent GDP in 1998, equal to US\$33.9 billion. These macroeconomic dynamics based on the use of the exchange rate anchor as a means to control inflation proved to be unsustainable.

The international context was not also favourable for the stability of the growth model based on an appreciated exchange rate and on consumption, particularly because of the Asian crisis of 1997 and the Russian crisis of mid-1998. In this context, foreign debt continued to grow, rising from US\$159.2 billion to US\$241.6 billion between 1995 and 1998,[19] despite the previously mentioned diversification of liabilities. As a consequence of this increase, in the final quarter of 1998 foreign creditors suspended the foreign debt's roll-over, and a new financial crisis began. The effects were not more severe because the US government quickly directed the IMF to give Brazil financial support.

1999–2002: In the context of this financial crisis, the Brazilian government was forced to abandon the exchange rate anchor in early 1999, devaluing the rate of exchange. Then began the period in which the Brazilian government's official discourse upheld the so-called macroeconomic policy tripod, one of

[17] According to the official Balance of Payments accounting methodology used by the Central Bank of Brazil until 2001, inter-company loans were accounted for separately from FDI. Beginning in 2001, when the BPM5 base was published, these loans were included in the FDI.

[18] The two bases – BPM5 and BPM6 – yield the same results for current-account deficit as percentages of GDP.

[19] This includes inter-company loans in addition to loans from banks and multilateral agencies, and public and private debt bonds.

whose pillars was a floating exchange rate. The tripod also included inflation targeting and primary surplus targeting for public accounts. The new discourse assumed that the deteriorating foreign accounts and, consequently, the need for foreign savings, came as a result of lacking fiscal austerity, forgetting that the high current-account deficits that caused the crisis were the result of the government's formally adopted policy of growth *cum* foreign savings.

Thanks to the 1999 depreciation of the Brazilian Real and the world economy's good performance, exports show expressive growth. However, due mainly to income transfers abroad, the current-account deficit remained high and relatively stable from 1999 to 2001, at around 4 per cent of GDP. On the fiscal level, austerity was indeed put into practice, Anyway, in late 2002, within the context of a political crisis caused by the election of a left-wing presidential candidate, Luís Inácio Lula da Silva, creditors once again suspended foreign debt rollovers, the country entered a new balance of payments crisis and was once again rescued by the IMF. In this scenario, the exchange rate depreciation that began in 1999 took a brisk plunge.

2003–2006: Within the framework of two depreciations and the commodities boom, Brazil achieved current-account surpluses in this period. The main factors underlying the positive foreign trade flows and the reversal of the current-account deficit were, therefore, depreciations and the beginning of a lengthy cycle of rising international prices for the main Brazilian exports, that is, agricultural and metal commodities. This dynamic enabled a significant improvement to the Brazilian economy's terms of trade. The reversal of the foreign accounts that began in 2003, as in previous cases, was independent from fiscal indicators. By enabling massive inflows of US dollars, rising exports enabled current-account surpluses from 2003 to 2006, despite the intense appreciation of Brazil's currency.[20] Another highlight from this period includes the rising levels of international reserves (from US$49.3 billion to US$85 billion) and the reduction of the foreign debt (from US$235.4 billion to US$199.4 billion). In 2005, the Brazilian government settled its debt with the IMF, anticipating payments scheduled for later years. All of these indicators created a sense of euphoria and the (false) feeling that the foreign disequilibria were being corrected, creating a belief that the country was 'eliminating' its foreign vulnerability.

2007–2011: In this period, the Brazilian economy went back to showing increasingly high current-account deficits because of the huge currency

[20] In 2003, the annual average exchange rate was 3.08 R$/US$, down to 2.18 R$/US$in 2006.

appreciation that had been under way since 2003, once again confirming the trend to cyclic and chronic exchange rate over-appreciation. The Brazilian Real's appreciation continued to favour private consumption and harm domestic manufacturing. In this period, the exchange rate was far below the competitive, or 'industrial equilibrium', exchange rate – a central concept of the new developmental view.[21] Positive current-account balances were then reversed, and the foreign debt's downward path changed, but international reserves continued to grow exponentially.

Notwithstanding the negative effects of the financial crisis that erupted in late 2008, leading to a small (–0.3 per cent) retraction of GDP in 2009, the period was marked by accelerating GDP growth (4.2 per cent p.a., on average). This growth was founded on the expansion of commerce (averaging 4.9 per cent p.a.), pushed by private consumption (5.7 per cent p.a. expansion). A central element of this dynamic was the adoption of public policies fostering domestic demand, including that of real minimum-wage gains, tax exemptions/reductions for the purchase of durable consumer goods (particularly since 2009) and stimuli for increased individual credit.

Investment, too, showed marked average expansion in this period (9.3 per cent p.a.), by rising credits granted by the National Economic and Social Development Bank (*Banco Nacional de Desenvolvimento Econômico e Social* – BNDES). A breakdown analysis of investment shows, however, that this growth was largely due to increases in housing construction and automotive purchases (trucks in particular). Neither was a main driver of the manufacturing sector, which posted average annual growth of a mere 2.5 per cent. Construction expansion was largely based on the rising income and expanding credit of individuals. The purchase of vehicles, in its turn, was due largely to the rationale of commerce expansion, which in its turn was due far more to sales of imported goods than of domestically produced ones. In addition, the period was marked by ample international liquidity, low international interest rates (and an increasing spread relative to Brazil's domestic interest rates) and reduced perceived risk on the part of international investors. All of these elements enabled increased foreign capital inflows into the Brazilian economy, which were central to the previously discussed dynamic of appreciation of the domestic currency.

After a period of more intense foreign capital outflows, particularly in late 2008 as a result of the financial crisis, in 2009 significant foreign funds inflows

[21] According to development macroeconomics, the industrial equilibrium, or competitive, exchange rate is that which makes for competitive makers of tradable non-commodities using world state-of-the-art technology. *See* Bresser-Pereira, Oreiro and Marconi, *Developmental Macroeconomics*.

resumed for the Brazilian economy. After a balance of payments surplus of a mere US$3 billion in 2008, positive balances jumped to US$46.7 billion, US$49.1 billion and US$58.6 billion in 2009, 2010 and 2011, respectively. These surpluses helped maintain the rising path of international reserves, which rose from US$180.3 billion in 2008 to US$352 billion in 2011. This supposedly favourable outcome came at the expense of a marked increase in foreign debt, from US$240.5 billion to US$404.1 billion, despite the increased share of other forms of liabilities, in particular direct investment in capital and equity stakes. As a result, total foreign liabilities also expanded markedly, from US$889.3 billion in 2007 to US$1.47 trillion in 2011.

Although resumed GDP growth in 2010 and 2011 (of 7.5 per cent and 3.9 per cent, respectively) helped the consolidation of favourable expectations, the appreciation of the domestic currency[22] and the resulting loss of competitiveness for domestic output continued to severely weaken the Brazilian productive structure. In this period, commodity prices and terms of trade, after a brief drop in 2009, also remained favourable to the Brazilian economy, enabling successive surpluses on the balance of trade in goods. However, the expanding imports of services, added to profits, dividends and interest transfers, caused negative services and income balances, more than offsetting the balance of trade surpluses and causing a current-account deficit that reached 3 per cent of GDP by year end 2011.

2012–2015: This period was marked by stagnant Brazilian GDP. The world economy's pace of growth decelerates, starting in 2012, and the cycle of rising international commodity prices comes to an end. At first, the drop in commodity prices was slight, and they remained stable at still high levels until mid-2014. With the Central Bank of Brazil's sharp basic interest rate cut of 2012, the domestic currency finally depreciated. The average annual exchange rate rose to 1.95 and 2.16 R$/US$in 2012 and 2013, respectively. In addition to the fact that the devaluation was relatively timid compared to what was needed to stimulate the manufacturing sector, within the context of decelerating world trade and dropping international commodity prices, exchange-based stimuli to Brazilian exports proved themselves insufficient.

On the other hand, lower interest rates helped maintain the expansionary path of domestic demand, a growing share of which was met by imports, which continued to expand far in excess of GDP and deepened the manufacturing sector's crisis. Lower revenues from exports and rising imports were

[22] After a small devaluation in 2009, the exchange rate resumed marked appreciation and peaked, in average annual terms, in 2011 at 1.67 R$/US$.

decisive for maintaining high current-account deficits, which remained at levels close to 3 per cent of GDP.

Brazil's foreign situation began to deteriorate more abruptly after August/September 2014, when new and more expressive commodity price drops occurred. The retraction of exports in US dollars terms was expressive as well, helping the current-accounts deficit to reach its highest level since 1999 at 4.3 per cent of GDP, or US$104.2 billion. GDP, in turn, decelerated to a real growth of a mere 0.1 per cent. The deterioration of Brazil's international accounts was central to the confidence crisis that emerged in 2015, triggering a new and severe round of depreciation of the Brazilian currency,[23] even as the economic recession deepened, reducing GDP by −3.8 per cent. This recessionary adjustment reduced the current-account deficit to 3.3 per cent of GDP, or US$58.9 billion. It is worth emphasizing that this recession was not directly associated with a balance of payments crisis, as foreign debt rollovers were not suspended, and international reserves remained at high levels, at US $368.7 billion by year end 2015

The debt rollover, which helped prevent a more expressive drop in international reserves, was done under unfavourable conditions after the Brazilian economy lost its investment-grade status given by the main international risk ratings agencies. In addition, the maintenance of high FDI flows (of US $96 billion in 2014 and US$75 billion in 2015, in net terms), which also prevented a greater reserves loss, took place basically in response to the strong loss of market value of Brazilian firms, and to these firms' need to sell assets (or equity stakes) stemming from their high levels of foreign indebtedness. These flows, in their turn, have not stimulated an increase in the rate of investment, nor growth of the exporting sector, with funds largely set aside for debt payments.

IV. CLOSING COMMENTS

This chapter uses a historical analysis of foreign accounts to show the validity of the new developmental school of thought's theoretical arguments for the Brazilian case. The persistent accumulation of current-account deficits must not, under any circumstances, be named as a fundamental element for the creation of favourable macroeconomic conditions for sustained output growth. To the contrary, the causal link proposed here, which treats the absorption of foreign savings as the main determinant of a structural dynamics

[23] The average annual exchange rate went from 2.35 R$/US$ in 2014 to 3.33 R$/US$ in 2015.

of an appreciated exchange rate, tends to create severe economic frailty, particularly in terms of weakening of the productive tissue.

We have shown that, even where such frailties do not cause a balance of payments crisis, they can still constrain or hamper the dynamics of economic recovery. In other words, adopting a foreign financing strategy creates external constraints that limit output growth, even if a major foreign crisis does not occur.

In this sense, we emphasize two fundamental aspects of the current economic situation that are generally noted as indicative of supposed peace of mind vis-à-vis Brazil's foreign accounts: the maintenance of relatively high international reserves and/or foreign direct investment.

Although it prevents more significant international reserve losses, the greater stake of foreign capital reinforces foreign constraints. In addition to, once again, not being linked with strengthening potential exports or expanding productive investments, these funds can widen the channels for reducing national income by means of income transfers abroad. As a result, when the Brazilian economy recovers a more consistent growth path, it will be more difficult to achieve positive current-account balances, reinforcing the vicious cycle of exchange rate appreciation. In addition, firms have been rolling over their debt under far less favourable conditions than those found in previous periods, which should increase the interest payments flow, an element that equally reinforces the need for foreign savings.

Fighting the Brazilian economy's foreign constraints requires important macroeconomic policy management changes to recover the weakened productive tissue in such a manner as to enable it to generate foreign currency, reducing the need to absorb funds from abroad by means of rising foreign debt and/or liabilities. That is, relieving the foreign constraints against Brazil's economic growth requires generating current-account surpluses via trade flows. To this end, managing the exchange rate is indispensable for competitive domestic production, in addition to improved growth of the exporting sector, particularly as concerns goods and services with greater technology content. The decreased dependence on foreign funds via the financial account creates the conditions for financing growth with own funds.

Finally, we believe that the Brazilian experience is quite representative of what can happen to others' middle-income economies that already have a diversified productive structure and decide to adopt the growth with foreign savings strategy. This does not mean that multilateral institutions' initiatives, led by the most developed countries, in order to contribute to the financing for development of less developed countries mobilizing external funds, are not important. But, we believe that sustainable and autonomous development depends on the generation of a country's own resources for financing it. For that, developing countries need a strengthened productive structure, strong enough to stimulate the growth of domestic income and, consequently, domestic savings. As discussed, the dynamic of accumulation of current-account deficits (and growth of external debt) hinders consolidation of a more autonomous development process.

4

Ecuador's 2008–2009 Debt Restructuring

A Special Case?

ADAM FEIBELMAN

ABSTRACT

In late 2008, Ecuador launched a successful effort to restructure its external debt, the circumstances of which are unique in the recent history of sovereign debt restructurings. The country had a rocky history of debt repayment. In 1999, it became the first country to default on its Brady Bonds, which had been created to resolve the Latin American debt crisis of the 1980s. After debt restructurings in 1995 and 2000, the country had arguably sustainable levels of external debt. In 2006, Rafael Correa, running for president, promised to refuse to pay the country's debt if elected. After he was elected, Correa formed a public debt audit commission to evaluate debt incurred by the country over the previous three decades. The commission found that some of the country's bonds were illegitimate for various reasons, including unfair gains to private interests, oppressive terms in the bond contracts, and the fact that the country's debt burden was crowding out provision of basic public goods and services. In late 2008, the country defaulted on two of its bond issues. After the default, and amid global financial turmoil, as the price of those bonds dropped, the country began a programme of purchasing them through financial intermediaries. It then conducted a bond repurchase at 35 cents on the dollar, with an eventual participation rate of over 90 per cent. This episode represents a rare instance of a sovereign restructuring external debt in the absence of acute financial stress and an equally rare instance of a sovereign having obtained debt relief based, at least in part, on the express assertion of the illegitimacy of its obligations. After a number of years without accessing capital markets, Ecuador agreed to repurchase most of its remaining defaulted debt from the 2008 episode and was able to issue bonds again in 2014. Because of various factors, including the unique global financial context and the country's particular history of debt repayment, it is not clear whether one can draw any general lessons – regarding debt buy-backs or the viability of claims about legitimacy of debt, for example – from the 2008–09 episode.

I. INTRODUCTION

In late 2008, Ecuador launched a successful effort to restructure its external debt, the circumstances of which are unique in the recent history of sovereign debt restructurings. The uniqueness of Ecuador's experience is due to three related aspects of the episode. First, it was not premised on acute financial crisis or an unsustainable debt burden. Most outside observers have agreed that Ecuador's debt was burdensome but not unsustainable. Second, Ecuador's restructuring was expressly premised on a claim that the debt itself was illegitimate or odious. Third, it was conducted as a strategic default and bond repurchase rather than a bond exchange, the conventional approach to sovereign debt restructuring.

This chapter examines Ecuador's 2008–09 debt restructuring with emphasis on these aspects of the episode. It begins by discussing relevant background related to the country's financial and economic performance and its previous experience with debt restructuring. It then describes the role of President Rafael Correa, the chief instigator of the restructuring; the work of the public debt audit commission appointed by Correa to initiate the effort; the details of its default and repurchase of a portion of its external indebtedness; and the financial aftermath of Ecuador's actions. The chapter concludes that the restructuring secured a meaningful measure of debt relief and was thus strategically impressive. It is unclear, however, what broader lessons can be drawn from Ecuador's experience, especially regarding its decision to restructure sustainable levels of debt and its reliance on claims that its debt was illegitimate. This uncertainty is due in significant part to the fact that Ecuador's actions occurred in the pitch of a global financial crisis.

II. BACKGROUND

Ecuador's default and repurchase programme in 2008–09 was the most recent of a number of debt defaults and restructurings by the country stretching back to the 1980s. This history has earned Ecuador a reputation as one of the worst performing sovereign debtors.[1] The connection between the restructuring of 2008 and these

[1] L.C. Buchheit and G.M. Gulati, 'The Coroner's Inquest: Ecuador's Default and Sovereign Bond Documentation', (2009), working paper, at 2, available at http://papers.ssrn.com/scl3/

preceding episodes is direct and especially relevant in various respects. For one thing, at least some debt restructured in 2008 is traceable to these earlier crises and restructurings. Perhaps more important, as explained later in this chapter, the expressed rationale for the most recent restructuring rested in large part on the circumstances and nature of earlier debt and prior restructurings.

The modern history of Ecuador's rocky relationship with its foreign creditors begins in the early 1980s. The country had enjoyed an extended period of economic growth through the 1970s, spurred largely by expansion of the country's oil sector, and had enjoyed robust access to foreign capital markets, expanding its stock of external debt. Due to various factors, including the weakening of international oil prices, weather-related disasters and growing external indebtedness to cover fiscal deficits, the country had to reschedule debts to its external creditors – official creditors and private banks – in 1983–84. After another decline in oil prices in 1986, the country suspended its debt payments to its private creditors. Nonetheless, international banks and international financial institutions[2] continued to lend to the country, and by 1987, its external debt was around $10 billion.[3] The country again suspended payments on its external debt in 1987 in the aftermath of a major earthquake,[4] beginning a period of debt renegotiations with its external creditors, mostly foreign banks.[5]

In the early to mid-1990s Ecuador enjoyed a period of relative stability and growing capital inflows. Soon, however, the economy was overwhelmed by domestic political instability, lack of fiscal discipline, conflict with Peru, external shocks from financial crises in Latin American, and an increasing debt service burden. The country sought restructuring of its debt again in 1995, joining numerous Latin American countries in issuing Brady Bonds.[6]

After various failed efforts to address pervasive debt crises throughout Latin America during the 1980s, US Secretary of Treasury Nicholas Brady

papers.cfm?abstract_id=1470232; A.C. Porzecanski, 'When Bad Things Happen to Good Sovereign Debt Contracts: The Case of Ecuador' *Law and Contemporary Problems* 73 (2010): 251 ('[T]he sovereign has been in default for at least 109 out of the last 184 years.').

2 The IMF provided financial support to Ecuador in 1983–84; the World Bank extended the country loan in 1987 to fix a damaged oil pipeline.

3 *See* World Bank, World Debt Tables, 1996, Vol. 2.

4 Lydia Chavez, 'Ecuador Suspends Payment on Debt Following Quakes', *New York Times*, March 14, 1987, www.nytimes.com/1987/03/14/world/ecuador-suspends-payment-on-debt-following-quakes.html; L.I. Jacome H., 'The Late 1990s Financial Crisis in Ecuador: Institutional Weaknesses, Fiscal Rigidities, and Financial Dollarization at Work', (2012) IMF working paper, www.imf.org/external/pubs/ft/wp/2004/wp0412.pdf.

5 Jonathan Fuerbringer, 'Citibank Seizes $80 million in Ecuador Bank Deposits', *New York Times*, May 12, 1989, www.nytimes.com/1989/05/12/business/citibank-seizes-80-million-in-ecuador-bank-deposits.html.

6 Porzecanski, 'When Bad Things Happen', 252; Jacome, 'The Late 1990s', 8.

led a process of converting private bank loans to Latin American countries to tradable bonds, known since as Brady Bonds. Ecuador, like other Brady Bond issuers, exchanged these bonds for private bank loans at a discount. The bonds, featuring a menu of terms for creditors and collateralized with US securities held by Ecuador and the other issuing countries, allowed the banks to trade away some significant amount of their exposure to the debtors.

Despite the debt relief, economic conditions in the country continued to deteriorate, due largely to a reversal of capital inflows, limited access to international financial markets, unstable oil prices, growing domestic public debt, and increasing debt service burdens.[7] Then, a series of external shocks wracked the country, including disastrous flooding, plunging oil prices and the financial crises in Russia and across Latin America. The country experienced a full-blown banking and financial crisis beginning in the summer of 1998.[8] Due in large part to its attempt to support the banking sector, the crisis soon engulfed the government itself and caused its currency to collapse. In 1999, Ecuador stopped payments on debt to Paris Club members and to private foreign creditors,[9] becoming the first country to default on its Brady Bonds,[10] initiating a new round of contentious debt restructuring.

Ecuador's 1999 default came on the heels of a concerted effort by the official sector – other countries and international financial institutions, especially the IMF – to reduce its role in financing sovereign debt restructurings and bailing out private creditors.[11] The new expectation among global financial policymakers was that private creditors would face greater losses in sovereign debt restructurings, a significant challenge for a process based heavily on creditor consent. Ecuador, facing an acute need for debt relief, represented an important test case for the new resolve.

It met this challenge with an innovative and, to some observers, aggressive use of exit consents,[12] a strategy borrowed from commercial debt restructurings.

7 Ibid. During the second half of the 1990s 'Ecuador was able to access to international capital markets only once, in 1997' and domestic-held debt comprised 90 per cent of GDP in 1998. Ibid.

8 IMF, 'Sovereign Debt Restructurings and the Domestic Economy Experience in Four Recent Cases' (2002), www.imf.org/external/NP/pdr/sdrm/2002/022102.pdf.

9 Jacome, 'The Late 1990s', 23.

10 J.J. Cruces and C. Trebesch, 'Sovereign Defaults: The Price of Haircuts', *American Economic Journal* 5 (2013), online appendix 37, https://assets.aeaweb.org/assets/production/articles-attachments/aej/mac/app/2012-0058_app.pdf.

11 G.M. Gulati and L.C. Buchheit, 'Exit Consents in Sovereign Bond Exchanges', *UCLA Law Review* 48 (2000): 60–61.

12 Cruces and Trebesch, 'Sovereign Defaults' 73–74; ibid., fn 11.

Sovereign bonds, like corporate bonds, have long included provisions that allow a majority or super majority of creditors to amend terms other than payment terms, i.e. any terms that do not affect the amount or timing of payments due to bondholders.[13] (Provisions that allow for amendment of payment terms have long been common in bonds issued under English law and have become much more conventional since the recent global financial crises.) Examples of significant non-payment terms of sovereign bonds that might be altered through non-unanimous agreement by bondholders include waiver of sovereign immunity, submission to foreign jurisdiction and eliminating the requirement to keep the bond issuance listed on a stock exchange.[14]

The use of exit consents in a debt restructuring is possible when the restructuring is conducted through a bond exchange, as are almost all modern debt restructurings (Ecuador's restructuring of 2008–09 being a notable exception, as discussed later in this chapter). In an exchange, bondholders tender their old bonds and receive new ones that generally provide for changes in payment terms. Exit consents entail requiring creditors who agree to tender their old bonds to vote to change certain non-payment provisions before they exchange the old bonds with the issuing sovereign. This makes the old bonds less attractive to holders and less marketable. In this way, exit consents can significantly increase a debtor's leverage with holdout creditors to nudge them into participating in the bond exchange.

In its 2000 restructuring, with support from the IMF,[15] Ecuador required holders of its existing bonds to vote to eliminate a variety of significant provisions of those bonds, including the requirement that the bonds be listed on a public exchange, the covenant against negative pledges and the prohibition on Ecuador's purchase of its Brady Bonds during a payment default.[16] The new bonds that Ecuador issued and exchanged with Brady Bond holders also included provisions that were designed to avoid a subsequent restructuring or to protect bondholders in the case of a default.[17]

[13] Cruces and Trebesch, 'Sovereign Defaults' 65. [14] Ibid., 81–82.

[15] U. Das, M.G. Papaioannou and C. Trebesch, 'Sovereign Debt Restructurings 1950–2010: Literature Survey, Data, and Stylized Facts', IMF working paper, at 77 (2012), www.imf.org/external/pubs/ft/wp/2012/wp12203.pdf; Porzecanski, 'When Bad Things Happen', 254.

[16] IMF, 'A Survey of Experiences with Emerging Market Sovereign Debt Restructurings', at 15 (2012), www.imf.org/external/np/pp/eng/2012/060512.pdf; F. Sturzenegger and J. Zettelmeyer, 'Haircuts: Estimating Investor Losses in Sovereign Debt Restructurings, 1998–2005', IMF working paper WP/05/137, at 29 (2005), www.imf.org/external/pubs/ft/wp/2005/wp05137.pdf.

[17] Ibid. at 29 (noting provisions requiring Ecuador to conduct 'mandatory debt management' and to provide 'principal reinstatement' if it defaulted on the bonds); Porzecanski, 'When Bad Things Happen', 254–55.

Participating bondholders in the 2000 exchange were allowed to choose between two new bonds in the exchange, named Global Bonds, one issuance maturing in 2012 and another maturing in 2030.[18] A third Global Bond was issued in 2005, maturing in 2015. The 2000 episode effectively restructured over $6.5 billion in bond debt[19] with over 90 per cent participation rate among the eligible bondholders.[20] The overall haircut to bondholders in this restructuring has been calculated at around 38 per cent, but this figure incorporates varying haircuts to creditors depending on the bonds they held and the ones they chose.[21] The country subsequently restructured its debt to Paris Club members as well.[22]

Largely due to the use of exit consents, Ecuador's 2000 restructuring 'occupies a special place in the history of sovereign debt crises'.[23] Although exit consents have rarely been used as aggressively as Ecuador did in 2000, the move was viewed at the time as potentially unleashing a powerful tool for the unfair treatment of sovereign bondholders. It was criticized by investors as especially coercive[24] and reinforced Ecuador's reputation for having an ambivalent, occasionally antagonistic relationship with international financial markets.[25] The country was excluded from private international financial markets for the next half decade.[26]

In any event, however, the reduction in Ecuador's debt service burden, along with the stabilizing effects of 'dollarization' of the country's currency,

18 Sturzenegger and Zettelmeyer, 'Haircuts', 27.

19 Cruces & Trebesch, op. cit. (fn 10), at 106; IMF, *A Survey of Experiences with Emerging Market Sovereign Debt Restructurings*, op. cit. (fn 16), at 8.

20 Cruces and Trebesch, 'Sovereign Defaults', online appendix 37.

21 Ibid. at 32. Some bonds set to mature soon were exchanged at par while others took haircuts as low as 19 per cent and as high as 47 per cent. Sturzenegger and Zettelmeyer, 'Haircuts', 27–29.

22 IMF, 'A Survey of Experiences', 8.

23 J. Zettelmeyer, C. Trebesch and M. Gulati, 'The Greek Debt Restructuring: An Autopsy' working paper, at 2 (2013), http://scholarship.law.duke.edu/cgi/viewcontent.cgi?article=5343&context=faculty_scholarship.

24 F. Salmon, 'Belize Uses CACs – and Exit Consents!', (blog), Feb. 5, 2007, www.felixsalmon.com/2007/02/belize-uses-cacs-%E2%80%94-and-exit-consents/ (noting the backlash after Ecuador's use of exit consents). The restructuring deal rates slightly above average on one objective measure of coerciveness. Zettelmeyer, et al., 'The Greek Debt Restructuring', 60 (citing Enderlein, Trebesch and von Daniels (2012)).

25 Although recent case law in England, most notably the decision in Assénagon Asset Management v. Irish Bank Resolution Corp, [2012] EWHC 2090 (Ch) (London, High Court of Justice, Chancery Division), has set some limits on the enforceability of exit consents under English law, they appear to continue to be available as a restructuring tool.

26 C. Richmond and D. Dias, 'Duration of Capital Market Exclusion: An Empirical Investigation', working paper, at 2 (2009), http://faculty.las.illinois.edu/ddias/Marketaccess_0709_Richmond_Dias.pdf.

changes in political leadership, support from international financial institutions and rising oil prices[27] managed to resolve Ecuador's financial and economic crisis and turn its economy around in the early years of the new century.[28] Thereafter, the country was widely believed to enjoy sustainable, if still high, levels of external debt.[29]

III. CORREA'S CAMPAIGN AND COMMISSION

In 2006, Rafael Correa, an economist trained abroad who returned to serve as the country's Minister for the Economy, announced that he would be a candidate for president. A major platform of his populist, anti-elite campaign was a promise to refuse to pay the country's foreign creditors if elected. This promise was premised on three main claims. First, the large amounts of money spent on the country's debt service should instead be used to improve the country's basic services like health care and education. Second, the debts themselves had been incurred to unjustly enrich the country's oppressive leaders, its elites, and foreign creditors. And third, the terms of the debt contracts themselves were unfair.[30]

Correa was elected president in January of 2007 and in July of that year formed a public debt audit commission to evaluate the debt incurred by the country over the previous three decades.[31] The Commission was composed of officials from Correa's administration and other individuals with experience in debt-relief movements and organizations.[32] The presidential decree creating the Commission charged it with auditing the country's experience of incurring public debt between 1976 and 2006 'with the objective of determining its legitimacy, legality, transparency, quality, efficacy and efficiency', with consideration of legal, financial, economic, social, gender and ecological aspects.[33]

The Commission conducted a review of the available data about all of the country's outstanding commercial debt, debt to multilateral institutions

[27] Jacome, 'The Late 1990s', 8. [28] IMF, 'Sovereign Debt Restructurings', 20.

[29] Gulati and Buchheit, 'The Coroner's Inquest', 2.

[30] Porzecanski, 'When Bad Things Happen', 260–61.

[31] Internal Auditing Commission for Public Credit of Ecuador, 'Final Report of the Integral Auditing of the Ecuadorian Debt', 2008, www.jubileeusa.org/fileadmin/user_upload/Ecuador/Internal_Auditing_Commission_for_Public_Credit_of_Ecuador_Commission.pdf. *See also* Porzecanski, 'When Bad Things Happen', 261–65.

[32] Porzecanski, 'When Bad Things Happen', 262. Buchheit and Gulati describe the Commission as 'composed principally of local and foreign activists for third world debt cancellation'. Buchheit and Gulati, 'The Coroner's Inquest', 5.

[33] Internal Auditing Commission for Public Credit of Ecuador, 'Final Report', 8.

(especially the World Bank and the IMF), and bilateral debt, i.e. debt owed to other countries. This unique and public self-review covered the circumstances of the creation of those obligations, some of which often involved the restructuring of previous obligations; the relative returns to various counter-parties; their impact on overall debt service burdens; and the substantive terms of the underlying debt contracts.

In October of 2008, the Commission issued a report concluding that a significant portion of the country's external debt was illegitimate and did not warrant enforcement. It found that much of the country's borrowing and restructuring disproportionately benefitted elite and powerful interests in the country, its foreign lenders, and the international financial system. The Commission asserted that the country's Global Bonds were legally infirm because the country's leaders had ceded to oppressive terms such as waiving sovereign immunity and stipulating to foreign law.[34] Without claiming that the country's debt burden was unsustainable, it decried the burden for a country with significant public challenges, noting that service on the debt in 2007 was greater than public expenditure on health, 'social well-being', urban development and housing, the environment and education.[35]

The Commission also found that the amount Ecuador spent to service its external debt exceeded the amount that Ecuador had received from external lenders to begin with.[36] 'This proves', it wrote, 'that the commercial debt has not been a source of financing for the development of the country, but a perverse mechanism to pillage its limited resources.'[37] The Commission criticized the restructuring of Brady Bond debt for Global Bonds because it had been based on the Brady Bonds' nominal value when those bonds were trading at a lower price in the market.[38] It also criticized the fact that during the financial and banking crisis of 1999–2000, private commercial debt to external creditors had been taken over by the state with the encouragement of the IMF and thus became a public burden.[39] It proposed that the country default on nearly half – but not all – of its outstanding external debt.[40]

In sum, the Commission found, 'The continual flow of payments [to external creditors] shows that the public contraction of debts has not served as a financial source, but it has been a tool of resources pillage and submission to politics imposed by the multilateral organizations.'[41] The fact that most of

34 Ibid., 48–49. 35 Ibid., 14. 36 Ibid., 15. 37 Ibid. 38 Ibid., 16.

39 Ibid., 17–32.

40 O. Lienau, *Rethinking Sovereign Debt: Politics, Reputation, and Legitimacy in Modern Finance* (Cambridge: Harvard University Press, 2014), 217.

41 Internal Auditing Commission for Public Credit of Ecuador, 'Final Report', 11.

the aspects of Ecuador's public debt, when viewed objectively, were fairly common features of sovereign borrowing and sovereign debt restructuring, reflected that the Commission was essentially critiquing the underlying relationship between the country and the international financial system. As Odette Lienau puts it, the report 'in effect challenged the legitimacy of the international lending regime.'[42]

IV. DEFAULT AND REPURCHASE

Armed with the Commission's conclusions, Correa announced in late 2008 that the country would default on its Global Bonds maturing in 2012 and 2030, which it quickly did.[43] Notably, it did not default on its Global Bonds maturing in 2015, which were issued in 2005, or its debt to multilateral international financial institutions or domestic creditors. Along with its restructuring in 2000, this was a rare instance in which a sovereign debtor 'clearly discriminated' against external creditors as compared to domestic ones.[44]

Most observers at the time reacted with some mixture of incredulity and concern. As Mitu Gulati and Lee Buchheit have explained, 'It was the first time in modern history that a sovereign debtor had demanded that its external commercial creditors write off most of their claims . . . without advancing a plausible argument that financial distress warranted such extraordinary debt relief.'[45]

In their view, the features that bondholders presumed would protect them from a 'casual' default failed.[46] The country's default occurred a few weeks after the collapse of Lehman, when global financial markets were in acute crisis and investors were already reeling from losses and threats of worsening systemic instability. After Ecuador's default and amid the global financial turmoil, the value of the defaulted bonds dropped significantly, to below

[42] Lienau, *Rethinking Sovereign Debt*, 216.

[43] Buchheit and Gulati, 'The Coroner's Inquest'.

[44] Das et al., 'Sovereign Debt Restructurings', 54.

[45] Buchheit and Gulati, 'The Coroner's Inquest', 2. *See also* Porzecanski, 'When Bad Things Happen', 256–58 (noting that, at the time, Ecuador's 'public external debt was the least burdensome it had been in over three decades, relative to government revenues or to the gross domestic product (GDP). Moreover, the country's central bank held more freely disposable international reserves ($6.5 billion) than it had ever accumulated before.').

[46] Buchheit and Gulati, 'The Coroner's Inquest', 2 (noting 'the menacing prospect of legal enforcement of debt contracts, coupled with a fear of market exclusion and the prospect of a censorious raised eyebrow from the multilateral financial institutions').

30 cents on the dollar.[47] The country then began a programme of quietly purchasing the bonds through one or more financial intermediaries.[48]

In April of 2009, Ecuador conducted a formal repurchase programme for the defaulted bonds through a reverse auction with a floor of 30 cents on the dollar.[49] As part of its offer, Ecuador insisted that payments would not resume on bonds not tendered for repurchase. Ecuador also suggested that it could effectively control the votes of bonds purchased through its intermediaries before the exchange, raising the spectre of exit consents.[50] The repurchase eventually had a participation rate of 91 per cent at a buyback price of 35 cents on the dollar,[51] effectively restructuring $3.2 billion in debt.[52] In 2014, the country agreed to repurchase most of its remaining defaulted debt that had not been repurchased in 2009.[53]

Ecuador's actions may have been enabled by, and certainly shed light on, the weak legal obligations of the bond issue's trustee.[54] Among other things, a trustee of a bond issue acts on behalf of bondholders, who are generally numerous and unrelated, to correct their collective action problems and help resist potential abuse by the issuer. Reflecting this role, trustees of commercial bonds issuances under US law have a relatively strong fiduciary duty, pursuant to the Trust Indenture Act, upon a default by the issuer. Sovereign bonds, however, are not subject to this provision.[55]

The trustee for Ecuador's defaulted bonds did not exercise its discretion to accelerate the bonds nor did it take actions to challenge the repurchase at the arguably steep discount. Gulati and Buchheit argue that the trustee should have tried to thwart the repurchase, perhaps by attempting to attach the funds Ecuador intended to use for the repurchase. As they write, 'The trust indenture deprived the individual bondholders of their ability to pursue legal remedies on their own; they were thus wholly reliant on the trustee's vigilance

47 Ibid., 5 (noting that 'the bonds had been trading at or close to par as recently as end-2007').

48 Ibid. (noting rumours that Ecuador had enlisted two financial firms for this purpose); E. Levy-Yeyati, 'Debt Buybacks and Backdoor Restructurings: Can Greece Pull an Ecuador?', *Brookings Opinion* (July 29, 2011), www.brookings.edu/research/opinions/2011/07/29-greece-ecuador-yeyati.

49 Ibid.; Buchheit and Gulati, 'The Coroner's Inquest'.

50 Buchheit and Gulati, 'The Coroner's Inquest', 6.

51 Ibid., 9.

52 Cruces and Trebesch, 'Sovereign Defaults', 32.

53 B. Korby and C. Jenkins, 'Ecuador Sells $2 Billion in Return to Bond Market', *Bloomberg*, June 17, 2014, www.bloomberg.com/news/articles/2014-06-17/ecuador-plans-bond-market-return-today-five-years-after-default.

54 Buchheit and Gulati, 'The Coroner's Inquest', 7–12.

55 Ibid., 9; G. Pustovit, 'Sovereign Debt Contracts: Implications of Trust Arrangements for Financial (In)stability', (2016), 17 *European Business Organization Law Review* 41.

and enterprise to protect their interests.'[56] They propose that trustee would have been more vigilant if it had been subject to a strong fiduciary duty.

Despite the aggressive and unconventional aspects of Ecuador's default and debt repurchase, and its creditors' anger at the default, the country managed to garner grudging respect from many observers in the wake of its actions. As one prominent writer who was initially critical of the move put it: 'Somehow . . . this exchange offer was probably the most successful and least fraught debt restructuring in the history of Latin American sovereign defaults.'[57]

After its default and bond repurchases, Ecuador was shut out of private international financial markets for a number of years. But the country was able to continue borrowing from regional international financial institutions and from bilateral creditors, including China and Russia.[58] And it was able to return to private capital markets in 2014, issuing $2 billion in bonds with an interest rate of 7.95 per cent.[59] Subsequently, the country has issued three other bonds, most recently in the summer of 2016. The interest rate on this latest issue is over 10 per cent, reflecting significant deterioration of the country's economy after a major earthquake and historically low global prices for oil.[60] The interest rate on a previous issue in 2015 was 8.5 per cent.[61]

For a country with such a long history of debt misadventures that defaulted on its sustainable debt and essentially took advantage of creditors who were suffering through an acute financial crisis, it appears that Ecuador suffered only a 'relatively mild response' from the capital markets.[62] Sovereigns that restructure debt often suffer other costs, notably negative effects on their international trade.[63] This particular impact is difficult to assess for Ecuador's default and repurchase of 2008–09. The country did experience a significant drop in exports and terms of trade during the year following this episode, but both recovered to pre-default levels within the following years.[64] Furthermore, it is likely that the

[56] Buchheit and Gulati, 'The Coroner's Inquest', 8–9.

[57] F. Salmon, 'Lessons from Ecuador's Bond Default', (blog), May 29, 2009, http://blogs.reuters.com/felix-salmon/2009/05/29/lessons-from-ecuadors-bond-default/; Porzecanski, 'When Bad Things Happen', 14.

[58] Lienau, *Rethinking Sovereign Debt*, 220.

[59] Korby and Jenkins, 'Ecuador Sells $2 Billion'.

[60] A. Jaramillo and L. Pronina, 'Ecuador Offers $1 Billion of Bonds at Highest Coupon Since 2000', *Bloomberg*, June 25, 2016, www.bloomberg.com/news/articles/2016-07-25/ecuador-offering-dollar-bonds-at-highest-coupon-since-2000.

[61] N. Gill, 'Eight Defaults and 180 Years Later, Ecuador to Repay Bondholders', *Bloomberg*, November 18, 2015, www.bloomberg.com/news/articles/2015-11-19/eight-defaults-and-180-years-later-ecuador-to-repay-bondholders.

[62] Lienau, *Rethinking Sovereign Debt*, 220.

[63] Das et al., 'Sovereign Debt Restructurings', 61–62.

[64] IMF, 'Article IV Consultation – Ecuador', staff report (October 2015) at 24, www.imf.org/external/pubs/ft/scr/2015/cr15289.pdf. *See also* Porzecanski, 'When Bad Things Happen', 268

decline and recovery were largely due to the global financial and economic conditions and by the fact that Ecuador's primary export is oil. In any event, Ecuador's non-oil exports increased quickly if modestly after the default.[65] It is possible that Ecuador's exports and terms of trade would have been stronger after 2009 if it had not defaulted, but rough data do not suggest that the country suffered significant costs in this area as a result of the default and repurchase.

V. LESSONS?

As others have noted, Ecuador's 2008–09 sovereign debt episode is regarded as an 'exceptional case'[66] and any lessons one might draw from it are murky and ambiguous.[67] To be sure, this episode represents a rare instance, perhaps unprecedented in recent history, of a sovereign restructuring private external debt in the absence of acute financial stress. It expressly based its unilateral restructuring effort on claims that its debt was illegitimate, having fostered domestic corruption, included oppressive terms, and unreasonably benefitted foreign creditors at the expense of the country's citizens. The country lost access to financial markets for a period, but it was able to return to financial markets within five years. Furthermore, the length of Ecuador's exclusion from financial markets was likely affected by the global financial crisis and, in any event, it found some willing creditors in the meantime. It is possible, then, that Ecuador's experience could be a model for future sovereigns seeking to restructure their debt, casting promising light on strategic defaults, debt repurchases and claims of odious or illegitimate debt.

But each of these propositions loses some force upon closer inspection. It is possible, for example, that Ecuador's action reflects the strategic advantage and leverage that a defaulting sovereign has over its bondholders in general. But other sovereign debtors may have less leverage in this regard. As an initial matter, other countries that are more integrated with the global economy, or aim to be so,[68] will likely not have the latitude to play hardball with their external creditors. Furthermore, the fact that oil is the country's primary export may limit the broader impact of an aggressive posture towards its foreign creditors.

(noting that, in the immediate aftermath of the episode, 'the private sector in Ecuador was able to borrow much less from abroad after the default than it had borrowed before' relative to other countries in the region).

65 IMF, "Article IV Consultation" – Ecuador", at 24.

66 Das et al., 'Sovereign Debt Restructurings', 78.

67 Lienau, *Rethinking Sovereign Debt*, 215–22.

68 E. Borensztein and U. Panizza, 'The Costs of Sovereign Default', IMF working paper (2008), www.imf.org/external/pubs/ft/wp/2008/wp08238.pdf.

In other words, Ecuador may have been more willing than other sovereigns to forgo integration with the global economy to gain some debt relief.

In any event, the unique timing of Ecuador's action was crucial to the leverage it had over its foreign bondholders. Although it does not appear that Ecuador's officials anticipated this when they decided to default on their Global Bonds; that action occurred near the climax of the worst global financial crisis in many generations. It occurred just as investors were facing huge, systemically destabilizing losses and an uncertain environment going forward. Ecuador's offer to repurchase its bonds at a steep discount at that moment presumably seemed like a much more palatable deal to bondholders than it would under normal circumstances. It is certainly possible that Ecuador's strategy could have been successful under more normal financial market conditions, but it seems likely that it would have needed to offer more to repurchase its bonds or that the participation rate would be lower or both.

All of the forgoing is especially true with regard to Ecuador's particular approach of repurchasing its debt.[69] Such efforts are quite rare and, as noted earlier, most restructurings are conducted through bond exchanges.[70] For one thing, they are costly because the debtor has to have cash on hand to purchase the debt as opposed to swapping new promises to repay. Thus, they also tend to be premised on a significant decline in the market value of the sovereign's debt, which will be difficult and costly to achieve if the debt is not already trading at a steep discount. In Ecuador's case, for example, it required a disruptive default. More forbidding, in most cases, a sovereign's repurchases will inevitably increase its price and may end up providing less debt relief than other strategies. Thus, Ecuador's success with the repurchase appears to be due to a combination of factors that are uncommon for sovereigns needing debt relief: the country's sizable reserves on hand, its willingness to default and maintain a disruptive posture with creditors, buttressed by its historical reputation as a sovereign debtor, and an unfolding global financial crisis.

It is possible that Ecuador's experience also reflects the potential force of claims for debt relief based on the legitimacy of the underlying debt. There is growing appreciation by global policymakers and advocates that a high debt burden can crowd fiscal space and imperil social rights or well-being.[71]

[69] Yeyati, 'Debt Buybacks'.

[70] Ibid. (citing Panizza 2009; Sturznegger and Zettlemeyer 2008); Porzecanski, 'When Bad Things Happen', 267.

[71] United Nations, *Report of the Independent Expert on the Effects of Foreign Debt and Other Related International Financial Obligations of States on the Full Enjoyment of All Human*

Ecuador's effort was, at least initially, applauded by debt relief advocates as a promising approach to the problem of odious or illegitimate debt.[72] In recent years, a scholarly literature and some political movement around the world have emerged to advance a formal legal argument that illegitimate or odious debts of a government should not be enforceable.[73] This contemporary movement, sparked by the US administration's efforts to obtain debt-relief for post-Hussein Iraq, asserts that international law recognizes, or should recognize, a doctrine of odious debt. The components of such a doctrine provide that debts incurred by a government that are not designed to benefit its citizens, especially where proceeds are used to oppress those citizens, will not be enforceable if the creditors knew or should have known about the illegitimate purpose of the debt. Meeting resistance to the recognition of such a formal right, the movement has focused more recently on efforts, led by UNCTAD to advance principles of responsible sovereign lending and borrowing.

Correa's assertion that Ecuador was justified in refusing to pay debts that were illegitimate or unfair was celebrated by some proponents of this movement as the first time a government expressly based its claims for debt relief on the legitimacy of the underlying debts. In addition to signalling to creditors that the government was serious about a potential default, the work of Ecuador's public debt commission was clearly designed to bolster this rationale for the country's action. Its report can be understood as an elaborate effort to identify features of the county's debt that correspond to factors in the proposed legal tests for odious or illegitimate debt. In fact, Correa was careful to clarify at the time that the country was not claiming that the defaulted debt was entirely illegitimate, just largely so, and thus deserving of a haircut.[74]

Although they relied upon the nature of the debt as a rationale in defaulting on their Global Bonds, it is noteworthy that Ecuador's officials did not formally rely upon the nature or legitimacy of the underlying debt in seeking debt relief. They did not, for example, endeavour to seek any formal legal determination that the debt was discharged or unenforceable. This has at least two implications. First, it is not at all clear what weight Ecuador's claim of

Rights, Particularly Economic, Social and Cultural Rights (2015), www.un.org/ga/search/view_doc.asp?symbol=A/70/275.

72 Ibid., 218.

73 L.C. Buchheit, G.M. Gulati and R.B. Thompson, 'The Dilemma of Odious Debts', (2007), 56 *Duke Law Journal* 1201; M. Kremer and S. Jayachandran, 'Odious Debt', (2006), 96 *American Economic Review* 82.

74 Lienau, *Rethinking Sovereign Debt*, 218.

illegitimacy had on the process of their default and repurchases, on creditors' willingness to participate, or on the reaction of international financial markets. Second, even if it had some weight, it is not clear if this reflects anything about the viability or emergence of a legal doctrine that enables debtors to effectively discharge illegitimate or odious debt. It is theoretically possible, for example, that creditors and financial markets viewed Ecuador's action with some sympathy on ethical or moral grounds but that the country would not have prevailed with a more formal legal claim.

In fact, Ecuador's effort to claim that its defaulted debts were illegitimate or odious may have complicated the development of such a doctrine. Taking the Commission's report on its own terms, some aspects of Ecuador's public indebtedness it condemned certainly give cause for concern. The report reflects some questionable management of the country's economy, significant borrowing to fill fiscal gaps or to refinance existing obligations, and pervasively high level of debt-servicing requirements. Whereas these factors may suggest some degree of irresponsible lending and borrowing, they are shy of the kinds of circumstances that are usually cited as rendering sovereign debt dischargeable or unenforceable. Examples of such circumstances include outright theft of proceeds, proceeds used to abuse the population, and lending made with knowledge that it would have no benefit to the population. In its worst light, the circumstances of Ecuador's 'expansive understanding'[75] of what constitutes illegitimate debt seem to fall short of this.[76]

One of the primary challenges for any doctrine that would discharge odious or illegitimate debt is to carefully and predictably distinguish situations warranting discharge from those that do not. Ecuador's invocation of illegitimacy may muddy the waters or, worse, it may illustrate to perils of unleashing a formal doctrine of illegitimate or odious debt. However, it is also possible, as Lienau suggests, that Ecuador's action has indirectly advanced the notion of odious or illegitimate debt. According to her, '[the] insistence that Ecuador's case fails to correspond with the requirements of odious debt ideas . . . implicitly suggests that they might apply elsewhere.'[77]

Finally, it is difficult to determine how the country's unique and aggressive approach to obtaining debt relief in 2008–09 affected its experience after the default and repurchase. It did suffer a period of lack of access to financial

[75] Ibid., 222.

[76] Porzecanski, 'When Bad Things Happen'; A. Feibelman, 'Ecuador's Sovereign Default: A Pyrrhic Victory for Odious Debt?', (2010), 25 *Journal of International Banking Law and Regulation* 357.

[77] Lienau, *Rethinking Sovereign Debt*, 222.

markets, but this is a common result of sovereign debt restructurings. The interesting counter-factual question, then, is whether the country might have been able to return to financial markets earlier if it had followed a more conventional approach.

A few factors point towards a sceptical view of the proposition. It may be, for example, that Ecuador already had such a poor reputation as a sovereign debtor that it did not suffer a significant reputational harm from its actions. Or, perhaps, the high participation rate may suggest that the repurchase was simply not as coercive as some creditors claimed at the time. It also presumably helped Ecuador going forward that it did not default on all of its bonds, and especially not those bonds issued relatively recently. (In fact, the country repaid its Global Bonds issued in 2005 and maturing in 2015 when they were due and without any disruption in payments during the life of the bonds, the first time it had done so in almost two centuries.[78]) This may have sufficiently indicated the country's commitment to honouring its new obligations. Perhaps the country succeeded in building a plausible case for debt relief through the work of the public debt commission. Or, perhaps, none of these particular aspects of the restructuring were relevant but, *ex post*, after having significantly reduced its debt service burden, the country was simply an acceptable credit risk for future creditors, and this would have been true regardless of how it achieved the reduction.

VI. CONCLUSION

In sum, Ecuador's restructuring of 2008–09 may stand as evidence that, under certain circumstances, default and repurchases can be a viable approach to sovereign debt restructuring; that sovereign debtors need not reach the point of acute financial distress or crisis to successfully obtain debt relief; and that identifying and emphasizing inequitable aspects of the underlying debt can have an impact in such efforts. Ecuador may have fallen short of a viable legal claim for relief, but it is possible that it provided a template for future sovereigns with similar, if stronger, claims based on things like corruption, government oppression and lack of benefit to the citizenry.

It appears, however, that many aspects of the episode were unique and highly circumstantial. To begin with, the approach depended on the country having enough reserves to conduct the repurchases without dangerously depleting them. It also depended on the willingness of the country's leaders

[78] N. Gill, 'Eight Defaults'.

to follow an aggressive path and, perhaps, on the country's poor reputation of debt repayment to make its commitment to the programme credible. It is also possible that the country benefitted from timing and the bad luck of its bondholders who were suffering through a global financial crisis. In any event, this episode shows that sovereigns are generally able to obtain credit even after aggressive restructurings. International financial institutions and bilateral creditors will often step in when private financial markets are forbidding.

5

Greece: An EU-Inflicted Catastrophe*

KUNIBERT RAFFER

To service its debt burden would require Greece to operate as a quasi slave economy, running a primary surplus of 5 per cent of GDP for years, purely for the benefit of its foreign creditors.

Financial Times, 26 January 2015

It's uncontroversial that debt relief is necessary and I think that nobody has ever disputed that. The issue is what is the best form of debt relief within our framework, within our legal institutional framework.

Mario Draghi, *Guardian*, 16 July 2015

ABSTRACT

Greece is a striking example of how politicians can mess up a simple and easy-to-solve problem, purporting to 'rescue' an insolvent sovereign and transforming a minor problem into outright catastrophe. Greece's debt burden has increased substantially since 'rescue' started, her GDP has shrunk sizeably, avoidable damages have been inflicted on Greece's people and economy, taxpayers in other euro-member states and the private sector. Future capital market access for euro-countries may be damaged. The European Central Bank was brought into the delicate position of a bad bank, even a public 'vulture'. Future speculation against euro-countries may have been encouraged. Democracy and human rights were two main casualties of EU debt 'management'. Technically unfounded fears about the survival of the common currency had been triggered. A good part of taxpayers' money illegally used for Greece's 'bailout' is definitely lost. The FT defined Greece as a 'quasi slave economy' run for the benefit of its (official) creditors. Inflicting more damages seems technically impossible. Draghi's statement

* For useful comments I am indebted to J.P. Bohoslavsky and J.K. Galbraith.

that it has been 'uncontroversial that debt relief is necessary and nobody has ever disputed that' raises questions this chapter will discuss. If so, why was debt relief not implemented in 2010, which would have been in the best interest for anyone but some speculators and EU functionaries? Why does the Troika still shun this necessary solution at the cost of violating basic human rights? Why did the Troika increase the debt overhang, creating more phantom debts? Who has benefitted from that strategy? This chapter will discuss these issues, also showing which avoidable damages have been illegally inflicted on Greece by the EU. It will very briefly compare Greece with other insolvent countries and advocate Raffer's model of sovereign insolvency as the best and necessary solution.

I. INTRODUCTION

If there were a prize for the 'most unsuccessful and catastrophic debt management', the EU's actions in Greece would most certainly carry the day. Official creditors, especially the EU, have snatched defeat from the jaws of victory, successfully turning a small problem into catastrophe.

During and not least because of the Troika's interventions, real GDP fell by 26 per cent.[1] The OECD finds 'raised poverty' and an increasing 'share of the population at risk of poverty'[2] – with anchored poverty (relative to its pre-crisis income level) almost tripled in 2013, 'the sharpest increase across OECD countries.' Youth unemployment has increased dramatically during the crisis to over 50 per cent; unemployment is at about 25 per cent. The Troika made central government expenditures on fighting unemployment decrease by 29.8 per cent between 2009 and 2013. 'Cuts in social expenditure undermine the ability of the State to guarantee basic economic and social rights.'[3] The previous UN independent expert already highlighted these concerns on impacts of austerity measures on the enjoyment of human rights. They persist today. According to Eurostat[4] the ratio debt/GDP worsened from about 120 per cent (2009) to about 180 per cent (2014); gross external debt was 184.1 per cent in 2014 according to the OECD. Harsh austerity measures

[1] OECD, *OECD Economic Surveys: Greece* (Paris: OECD, 2016), 12. [2] Ibid., 14.

[3] J.P. Bohoslavsky, *Report of the Independent Expert on the effects of foreign debt and other related international financial obligations of States on the full enjoyment of all human rights, particularly economic, social and cultural rights on his mission to Greece*, UN, 2016, A/HRC/31/60/Add.2, 14.

[4] Eurostat, 'General government gross debt – annual data'; 176.9 for 2015 according to this EU source. http://ec.europa.eu/eurostat/tgm/table.do?tab=table&init=1&language=en&pcode=teina225&plugin=1

had no visible positive effect, on the contrary depressing living conditions of most people below the minimum human rights and international treaties on human rights demand.

Unashamedly violating the 'no bailout clause' initially necessary to lure some parliaments into ratifying the treaty,[5] the Troika managed to increase Greece's debt burden substantially,[6] shrink her GDP sizeably, inflict avoidable damages on the Greeks and their economy, taxpayers in other euro-member states and the private sector. People continue to die in Greek hospitals because easily available medicines cannot be bought under the Troika's diktat. At least one ray of hope, sumptuous and luxurious hospitality of EU politicians during Greece's presidency of the EU Council could be assured.

The Troika seems unaware of Draghi's 'uncontroversial' necessity of debt relief, which 'nobody has ever disputed'. The IMF keeps mentioning EU resistance to a haircut. Obviously, Draghi's statement is at severest odds with facts. Early on, many people from the banking community thought debt reduction inevitable.[7] All EU politicians outside Greece, especially in Germany, that had benefitted from Greece's generously forgiving debts in 1953 and still owes contractual debts to Greece, have opposed it ferociously.

According to the *WSJ*, eurozone taxpayers will have to take losses on their governments' Greek debts of 30 per cent of GDP to reach the old debt targets of below 110 per cent of GDP, €53.1 billion would be lost in addition to more bailout cash through 2020, if Greece were only able to achieve a budget surplus of 2.5 per cent of GDP over the medium term; with growth shocks debt could well be twice GDP in 2017.[8]

5 The Court of Justice of the EU (*nomen est omen*) did not see the unconditional prohibition of Art 125 violated because it was 'indispensable for the safeguarding of the financial stability of the euro area as a whole and subject to strict conditions'. http://curia.europa.eu/juris/document/document.jsf?text=&docid=130381&pageIndex=0&doclang=en&mode=req&dir=&occ=first&part=1&cid=454620 Fortunately, the European Convention on Human Rights is not under this Court's jurisdiction. Its Art 3 (Prohibition of Torture) remains absolute, thus even torturing 'subject to strict conditions' or to save the stability of the Eurozone remains a violation of human rights.

6 In euros the picture looks somewhat better, but debt was still slightly higher in 2015 than in 2009; ibid.

7 Cf. K. Raffer, 'Turning a Small Problem into Catastrophe: The Case of Greece', in *The Eurozone Crisis and the Future of Europe: The Political Economy of Further Integration and Governance*, eds. D. Daianu, G. Basevi, C. D'Adda and R. Kumar, (Basingstoke: Palgrave Macmillan, 2014), 154–70.

8 I. Talley, 'Greece's Debts: The Numbers', *Wall Street Journal*, July 3, 2015 http://blogs.wsj.com/briefly/2015/07/03/greeces-debt-the-numbers/.

> Greece's public debt has become highly unsustainable. . . . The financing need through end-2018 is now estimated at Euro 85 billion and debt is expected to peak at close to 200 percent of GDP in the next two years, provided that there is an early agreement on a program. Greece's debt can now only be made sustainable through debt relief measures that go far beyond what Europe has been willing to consider so far.[9]

Gross financing needs may rise to levels 'well above what they were at the last review (and above the 15 percent of GDP threshold deemed safe) and continue rising in the long term'.[10]

Probably frustrated by the EU, the IMF meanwhile asked quite outspokenly not to make the IMF responsible for what Greece (under pressure) and the EU have concocted. In contrast to the EU, which demands a primary surplus of 3.5 per cent contrary to the IMF's advice, the Fund 'warned that this would generate a degree of austerity that could prevent the nascent recovery from taking hold'.[11] For the Fund, which 'did not call for additional measures to achieve a higher surplus' 1.5 per cent would suffice: 'Greece does not need more austerity.' The IMF thinks 'that these cuts have already gone too far, but the ESM program assumes even more of them'. Briefly, 'Greece's *debt is highly unsustainable and no amount of structural reforms will make it sustainable again without significant debt relief*.'[12] Naturally, the IMF also demands reforms, acknowledging, though, that they alone cannot solve this crisis.

This catastrophic aggravation of Greece's debt crisis caused by EU 'rescue' must be judged against the background of €240 billion channelled to Greece by EU bailouts (or rather via Greece to other, real beneficiaries), and two private debt reductions of over €100 billion; in total more than Greece's 'debt mountain' (€340 billion) in 2015.

Mallien and Watzlawek[13] computed the costs until 2014: two rescue packages (€240 billion), debts vis-à-vis the ECB (€122 billion), one private sector haircut (€100 billion; debt buy-back, €31.8 billion, not included), EU transfers (structural and agricultural funds: €40 billion), Greek instruments bought by

[9] IMF, 'Greece: An Update of IMF Staff's Preliminary Public Debt Sustainability Analysis', July 14, 2015, at 1, www.imf.org/external/pubs/ft/scr/2015/cr15186.pdf.

[10] Ibid., 2.

[11] M. Obstfeld and P.M. Thomsen, 'The IMF Is Not Asking Greece for More Austerity', December 12, 2016, https://blog-imfdirect.imf.org/2016/12/12/the-imf-is-not-asking-greece-for-more-austerity/#more-15842.

[12] Ibid. (stress added).

[13] 'Bundestag stimmt Griechenland-Hilfe zu; Die Rechnung, bitte', *Handelsblatt* (Germany) November 30, 2012; Eurostat shows (19 June 2016) a slightly higher (provisional) GDP for 2014 (177,5B).

the ECB (€30 billion) add up to €532 billion, over three times Greece's GDP (€173 billion). Including the third bailout in 2015 (€85 billion) and the buyback adds another €116.8 billion. Financing a 50 per cent haircut totally by taxpayers would have cost 60 per cent of GDP in 2010, which was 330.57 billion.[14] Half – which might have sufficed – would have been some 165.3 billion, much less than public money wasted.

Such lousy 'management' poses questions: how was this possible, who is primarily culpable (apart from Greece amassing debts and faking data with connivance of other euro-countries) and most important *cui bono*? It must be recalled that Greece openly admitted fudging euro entry shortly after joining,[15] which was publicly known at this time.[16] If the Maastricht criteria were actually as important, even necessary as publicly purported, and not just a means firmly to install neoliberal, anti-Keynesian policies,[17] the EU would not have tolerated this. Instead, nothing was done and the crisis could continue to build up.

The Greek tragedy is not described once again in detail (there already exists a cottage industry on that), nor the many recurrent 'crises' when official creditors threatened not to disburse new funds, a silly spectacle continuing to this day. They always did, as not disbursing would have meant recognising losses. This chapter will discuss the main issues and lessons emerging from this crisis:

- Over-optimism, more appropriately misinformation of decision-makers
- the public sector's faults
- *cui bono?*

II. OVER-OPTIMISM – A TRADITIONAL TRICK TO AVOID TIMELY AND PROPER SOLUTIONS

Overly optimistic assumptions about recovering growth and debt sustainability paved the way to catastrophe in Greece. Guzman and Heymann[18] showed

[14] According to Eurostat, 'General government gross debt'.

[15] 'Greece admits fudging euro entry', *BBC News*, November 15, 2004, http://news.bbc.co.uk/2/hi/business/4012869.stm.

[16] Cf., e.g., A. Little, 'How "magic" made Greek debt disappear before it joined the euro', *BBC News*, February 3, 2012, www.bbc.com/news/world-europe-16834815. A London investment house employee is quoted, advising her clients that government statistics 'did not reflect reality'.

[17] Cf. K. Raffer, 'Is a Revival of Keynes's Ideas Likely? (Some Comments on Chapters by Gerald M. Meier and Sir Hans W. Singer)', in *John Maynard Keynes – Keynesianism into the Twenty-First Century*, ed. S. Sharma (Cheltenham: Elgar, 1998), 116–27.

[18] M. Guzman and D. Heymann, 'Macroeconomic Crises: An Overview of Experiences and Some Analytical Issues', YSI-EBRD Workshop, Warsaw School of Economics, 2014.

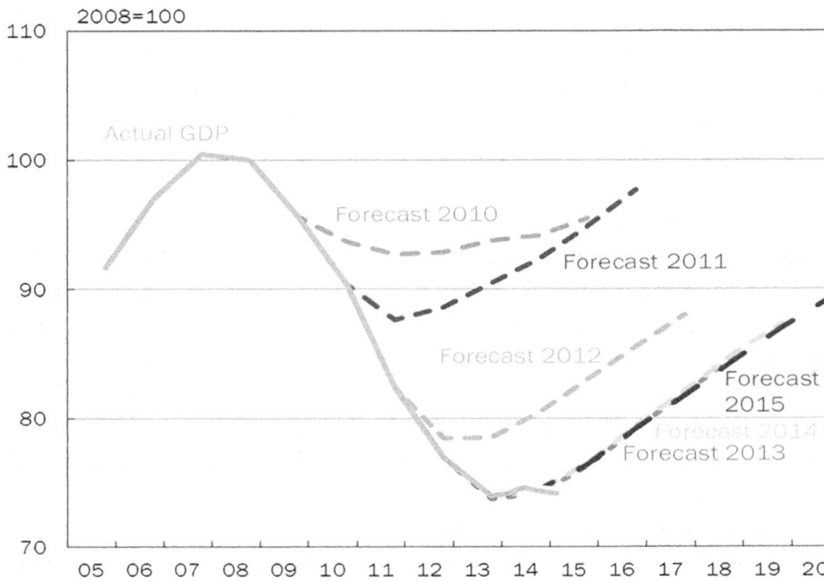

FIGURE 5.1 Greece's real GDP: comparison of the real evolution with IMF forecasts.
Source: Sinn, 2015.

IMF projections over the crisis years continuously markedly better than actual growth until October 2013 for Greece, Ireland, Italy, Portugal and Spain. An updated, similar graph by Sinn (Figure 5.1),[19] proved his trend to continue: over-optimistic forecasts continue to upturn GDP-projections radically while actual GDP falls. Greece has become a failed state. Optimism is alive and kicking: 'the economy is projected to grow again in the course of 2016 and 2017, but a full recovery will take time.'[20]

Over-optimism is usual with the IMF: 'Overoptimism appears to be a feature of most large IMF-supported programs.'[21] It is helpful for official

[19] Hans-Werner Sinn, *The Greek Tragedy* (CESIfo-Forum: Munich, 2015), 10.
[20] OECD, *OECD Economic Surveys*, 10.
[21] IMF, IEO, *Evaluation Report, The IMF and Recent Capital Account Crises: Indonesia, Korea, Brazil*, 2003, www.imf.org/external/np/ieo/2003/cac/index.htm, 30, cf. for more quotes K. Raffer, *Debt Management for Development – Protection of the Poor and the Millennium Development Goals* (Cheltenham: Elgar, 2010; paperback 2011), 206; re Europe, see the IEO's devastating report: IMF, 'The IMF and the Crises in Greece, Ireland, and Portugal: An Evaluation by the Independent Evaluation Office', 2016, e.g. 'IMF-supported programmes in Greece and Portugal incorporated overly optimistic growth projections' (p. viii, p. 49, cf. also p. 30), which supported wrong decisions. Quite logically, 'staff did not assess the risks associated with the underlying projections' either. 'In contrast, it appears that many of the post-Lehman

creditors wishing to avoid, or rather postpone (eventually it cannot be avoided) *the only* possible solution, debt reduction. Undue 'optimism' makes parliamentary consent, if needed, easier. The EU also simply blocked the economically proper solution the IMF thought adequate: debt reduction.[22]

Eurozone-Parliaments have been misled to believe that the crisis was less pronounced. Facts make it difficult to believe that this happened unintentionally. Based on what (considering the long and officially documented history of over-optimism) one may have to call intentional misinformation, Parliaments allowed themselves to be pushed into agreeing to 'rescue packages', saddling taxpayers with the bill. Publicly optimistic, the IMF formulated: 'Because the IMF did not assess Greece's debt to be sustainable with high probability, the framework required an upfront debt reduction.'[23] But it went on financing a programme it considered highly probable to fail, presenting optimistic forecasts, stating that Greece could return to capital markets in 'more than 18 months', possibly 'sooner than that'.[24]

Logically, fiscal multiplier estimations were also overoptimistic. In 2012 the IMF admitted: 'multipliers underlying growth projections have been too low'[25] – 'about 0.5'.[26] When many countries adjust together multipliers are closer to 1, the IMF contends, seeing this as one of the 'reasons for avoiding abrupt adjustments'. It goes on: 'sharp expenditure cutbacks or tax increases can set off vicious cycles of falling activity and rising debt ratios, ultimately undercutting political support for adjustment'.[27] The 'historical record for public debt reduction suggests that a gradual, sustained approach supported by structural changes offers the best chance for success within today's constraints'. It forced the very opposite on Greece.

Eichengreen and O'Rourke estimated a fiscal multiplier 'in the range of 1.6',[28] roughly three times the value on which 'optimistic' policy measures

crisis programs *outside* the euro area were designed with more realistic assumptions' (stress in o.) than the 'overly sanguine' assumptions for euro-countries, especially Greece. 'More realistic projections' the IMF contends, would have allowed better crisis management.

[22] IMF, IEO 'The IMF and the Crises in Greece, Ireland, and Portugal', 16 ('decision not to seek debt restructuring at the outset was the preferred choice of a majority (by voting power) of the IMF membership'). Obviously other advanced economies' supported the EU.

[23] IMF, 'IMF Survey: IMF Reforms Policy for Exceptional Access Lending', 2016, www.imf.org/external/pubs/ft/survey/so/2016/POL012916A.htm

[24] IMF, 'Transcript of a press Briefing by Caroline Atkinson, Director, External relations Department, IMF', May 6, 2010, www.imf.org/external/np/tr/2010/tr050610.htm.

[25] IMF, *World Economic Outlook, October* (IMF: Washington DC, 2012), 41. [26] Ibid., 43.

[27] Ibid., 21.

[28] B. Eichengreen and K.H. O'Rourke, 'Gauging the multiplier: Lessons from history', October 23, 2012, www.voxeu.org/article/gauging-multiplier-lessons-history.

had been based. Harsh austerity did more harm than officially foretold. 'Optimism' that had proved so helpful in convincing sceptic lawmakers and the public to agree to Greece's 'rescue' (properly: bank and speculator bail-out) was unfortunately not the only important official sector contribution to the crisis.

III. THE PUBLIC SECTOR'S GREAT CONTRIBUTION TO THE CRISIS

The public sector, especially the EU, has contributed fundamentally to causing and deteriorating the crisis. Official signalling, especially the Basel Norms, significantly shaped the perception of riskless lending to euro-countries. Consequently, pre-crisis years show a clear tendency towards a unispread market for sovereign Euro-debts. The European Commission admitted that from the 'introduction of the euro until 2007, spreads on European government bonds moved in a narrow range with little differentiation between countries.... Public debt from any euro area country was broadly considered as good as the best among them ... risks were significantly underestimated.'[29] The EU helped reinforce that mistake. Its present policy of buying sovereign instruments is again driving down interest rates for problem countries such as Italy. Is there a desire to create a new crisis?

Hannoun[30] (Deputy General Manager of the BIS) highlights three components of official disaster production:

- capital weights of zero pursuant to Basel I for OECD-countries, modified to countries with ratings from AAA to AA- by Basel II – 'the chairman of the IASB is said to have gone so far as to call this the "biggest accounting scam in history"'.[31] To do Basel II justice: it would have been a minor brake to lending. But the EU Capital Requirements Directive removed this brake, 'exempting' EU-member states from proper risk assessment. Sovereign exposures carried zero risk weights within the EU if denominated and funded in the sovereign's domestic currency.
- the ratio of government bills and bonds forming a substantial part of the liquid assets, required in the newly established liquidity coverage ratio, could be seen as incentivizing banks to hold sovereign debt

[29] European Commission, *European Financial Stability and Integration Report 2011*, Brussels SWD 103 final, 2012, 8.

[30] H. Hannoun, 'Sovereign risk in bank regulation and supervision: Where do we stand?', BIS, 26 October 2011, www.bis.org/speeches/sp111026.htm, p. 11.

[31] Ibid.

- the EU-exemption from the large exposure regime for highly rated sovereigns, from the 25 per cent of equity limit

Bona fide private creditors were misled to invest in dubious Euro-members' bonds anointed with 'risklessness', a clear regulatory failure if not worse. Banks were literally pushed into these sovereign instruments. Soros pointed out that the ECB treated sovereign debts of all euro-countries as riskless, accepting them at its discount window on equal terms, corroborating the perception of equal risklessness.[32] Regulatory measures induced banks to hold too high amounts of euro-member-country debts. This worked particularly perniciously in the case of weaker members, combining officially declared 'no risk' with more fun, those few extra basis points. The dire consequences of this fundamental regulatory blunder are now felt all over euroland. It is uniquely important in Greece, where government, not private debts caused the crisis. This is a regulatory original sin, a brilliant example of policy encouraged or caused crashes, as the Asian Crisis, Iceland, Cyprus or Chile 1982. Apparently, regulators have refused to learn.

Significant sovereign debt exposures of EU banks were one link between sovereign debt troubles and concerns about the stability of the banking system. Too low interest rates and purported absence of risk certified both officially and by rating agencies (as in the case of US subprime instruments) boosted lending to Eurozone problem debtors, a scenario that could well be repeated by the ECB's large-scale purchases of government bonds, a policy meanwhile even extended to private corporations by the corporate sector purchase programme.

When the clearly foreseeable and officially produced Greek crisis finally broke, official surprise, obviously feigned, was the currency of the day. Immediately and against economic evidence, the EU stated that euro-countries could not go bankrupt, pouring money into Greece veiled by the slogan of solidarity with the Greeks. Decision makers knew that most money went immediately to foreign banks.

Greece's debt crisis started at a ratio debt-GDP of 120 per cent, 'rescuers' managed to drive this ratio up to some 180 per cent (the IMF estimating close to 200 per cent likely). This speaks for itself. Logically, 'earlier projections' had predicted a 'peak in debt – at 177 percent of GDP in 2014',[33] while: 'By 2022, debt is now projected to be at 170 percent of GDP, compared to an estimate of

[32] G. Soros, 'How Germany can avoid a two-speed Europe', *Financial Times*, March 21, 2011.

[33] IMF, 'Greece: An Update of IMF Staff's Preliminary Public Debt Sustainability Analysis', *Country Report No. 15/186*, 2015, 2

142 percent of GDP projected in our published DSA'. Optimism rather than realism continues to subordinate solutions to political whims[34] of politicians personally immune from legal and financial, even political consequences.

A quick cut in 2010 would have solved the problem relatively painlessly. If it had triggered problems for some banks (mainly French and German, but also Cypriot), misled by the EU to buy Greek instruments, these countries could have established national bank saving programmes (in Cyprus also with EU support), preferably modelled after the US TARP that, unlike EU-programmes, was quite profitable for the Treasury. However, if things can be made worse, the EU is not the one to miss this 'opportunity'. Personally absolutely free from any real accountability, EU-politicians do not have to vouch for what they do. Destroying Europe does not mean losing large salaries and pension benefits.

By accepting Greece as a euro-member in spite of obviously faked statistics, inducing private capital to invest in Greece and delaying insolvency (a delict in all municipal laws, unfortunately not internationally) the public sector has destroyed the very foundations of law and what Greek politician's mismanagement over many years had left of the Greek economy.

IV. CUI BONO? CUI MALO?

The next question is who benefitted and who suffered. Obviously, 'normal' people not inviting decision makers to sumptuous dinners did not benefit.

Data contradict official newspeak that breaking the law (no-bailout-clause) benefitted 'the Greeks':

- ATTAC:[35] 'At least 77.12%' of programme resources went to the financial sector
- Varoufakis:[36] 'more than 90 per cent' to this sector; he asserts that he had opposed this 'enormous new loan by European taxpayers' in early

[34] See, e.g., IMF, IEO 'The IMF and the Crises in Greece, Ireland, and Portugal', 7 ('2002 framework for exceptional access was modified to allow exceptional access financing to go forward', to allow channelling money to Greece; 'the modification process departed from the IMF's usual deliberative process whereby decisions of such import receive careful review', obviously to please the EU).

[35] ATTAC 'Background material, Three years of Greek bail-out: 77% went into the financial sector', (no year), www.attac.at/fileadmin/_migrated/content_uploads/backgroundmaterial_bailout_english.pdf.

[36] Y. Varoufakis, 'Genug mit dem toxischen Schwarzen-Peter!', IPG, 26 March 2015, www.ipg-journal.de/rubriken/europaeische-integration/artikel/genug-mit-dem-toxischen-schwarzen-peter-856/.

2010, when Greece was unable to service her debts vis-à-vis French, German, and Greek banks, a 'cynical shift of private losses off the banks' books onto the shoulders of the most vulnerable citizens of Greece'.

- The *Washington Post* noted that loans 'have gone almost entirely either to cover interest payments or repay past loans; only 11 percent has actually gone to Greece's government'[37]
- According to the Truth Committee on Public Debt established in April 2015 by a decision of the President of the Hellenic Parliament 'Approximately 10% of the bailout programme was used to finance the budget'[38] during 2010–15.
- Rocholl and Stahmer's[39] most recent study shows: 'only €9.7 billion or less than 5% of the total amount of €215.9 billion being distributed in the 1st and 2nd programme were not used for debt-related payments and bank recapitalizations and thus directly contributed to the Greek fiscal budget.'

Briefly, 'almost none of the huge amount of money loaned to Greece has actually gone there . . . Greece has gotten but a pittance, but it has paid a high price to preserve these countries' banking systems.'[40] According to all estimates, 'Solidarity with the Greeks', politicians' justification for the illegal bailout, is most obviously at severest odds with the truth. Taxpayers and parliaments deceived by politicians showed solidarity, but with speculators and banks, not 'the Greeks'. Adding the FT's analysis of the Greek slave economy one cannot but conclude that Greece was made to suffer to save bankers' boni, while duping real payers (taxpayers in 'rescuing' countries), claiming everything would be repaid.

Sheltering the financial sector including speculators at taxpayers' cost is *the* common feature of the 'euro-crisis'. In Ireland, e.g., the IMF had 'initially favored a haircut of roughly 50 per cent, a proposal which gained the Irish government's full support. But the ECB opposed this approach on the grounds that it might disrupt the flow of wholesale funding to other

37 H. Meyerson, 'In Greek crisis, Germany should learn from its fiscal past', *Washington Post*, January 28, 2015.

38 Truth Committee on Public Debt, *Preliminary Report*, 2015, www.hellenicparliament.gr/UserFiles/f3c70a23-7696-49db-9148-f24dce6a27c8/Report_web.pdf, p. 22.

39 J. Rocholl and A. Stahmer, 'Where did the Greek bailout money go?', ESMT White Paper WP–16–02, ESMT, Berlin, 2016.

40 J.E. Stiglitz, 'Europe's Attack on Greek Democracy', 2015, www.project-syndicate.org/commentary/greece-referendum-troika-eurozone-by-joseph-e–stiglitz-2015-06?barrier=accessreg.

Eurozone banks.'[41] The ECB prevailed. As in Greece: 'Concern about cross border euro area spillovers was the main argument against a bailin'.[42] Routinely, Euro area banks have been sheltered. But 'evidence is not clear ... Irish (senior unsecured) bank bonds traded at the time at levels consistent with clear anticipations of a principal hair-cut, reflecting that some burden sharing was anticipated by bondholders and markets.'[43] Thus, investors had already adjusted to expected losses as the market mechanism requires, when the EU stepped in and saved them, shifting the costs on Irish taxpayers in the very same way the EU acted in Greece. One difference remains, though: Greece will not be able to repay, not least due to the way the Troika mismanaged her crisis. Also, unlike Ireland Greece's government had high debts when the crisis started. Taxpayers of 'rescuing' countries will have to foot a substantial part of the bill. Irresponsible politicians will get off scot-free without having to pay for the damages they caused. Understandably, 'many in Ireland question why Irish taxpayers should be the ones covering the cost of addressing such euro area wide concerns'[44]. One may assume many Greeks to do the same.

Greece's 'rescue' operation also indirectly affected non-Greek taxpayers negatively. Steil and Walker[45] show that by shifting debt onto official (EU) shoulders 'France has actually managed to reduce its total Greek exposure (sovereign and bank) by €8 billion'. Italy's and Spain's exposures to Greece skyrocketed.

Taxpayers' money was also poured lavishly into the pockets of the pariahs of capital markets. 'Vulture funds stand to make a fortune from a second Greek bailout after buying hundreds of millions of euros of distressed sovereign debt in the past few months.'[46] Robert Marquardt, founder of Signet, a fund of hedge funds, saw the Greek crisis as 'certainly a great chance to make money', taxpayers' money, of course, because the price offered was too high given

[41] B. Eichengreen, 'The Irish Crisis and the EU from a Distance', 2015, p. 7, www.imf.org/external/np/seminars/eng/2014/ireland/pdf/Eichengreen_IrishCrisisEU.pdf; cf. IMF, IEO 'The IMF and the Crises in Greece, Ireland, and Portugal', 44, 'the IMF staff's judgment was that senior unsecured creditors of Irish banks should be bailed in, but this position was overruled by the European partners'. Like in Greece, 'the IMF's largest advanced economy shareholders' supported the EU's bailout agenda.

[42] IMF, 'Ireland: Ex Post Evaluation of Exceptional Access under the 2010 Extended Arrangement', 2015, 28.

[43] Ibid. [44] Ibid., 29.

[45] B. Steil and D. Walker, 'Greece Fallout: Italy and Spain Have Funded a Massive Backdoor Bailout of French Banks', Council on Foreign Relations, 2015, www.cfr.org/blog-post/greece-fallout-italy-and-spain-have-funded-massive-backdoor-bailout-french-banks.

[46] Philip Aldrick, 'Vulture funds to profit from a second Greek bailout', *The Telegraph*, June 25, 2011.

circumstances. The December 2012 buyback brought about some debt relief, although its announcement triggered a significant rise in bond market prices. Prior to the announcement new Greek bonds traded at about 28 per cent of face value.[47] 34 per cent were paid, knowing that many hedge funds had bought Greek debt at less than 15. Voluntary buybacks, Zettelmeyer *et al.* showed, tend to benefit creditors, in the form of higher market values of debt, rather than the debtor country, as 'economists had been pointing out for some time'.[48]

The authors think that there would have been 'more effective ways of using the extra financing even from the narrow vantage point of reducing Greece's debt burden – in particular, by conducting the buyback at a negotiated price that would not have distributed the buyback induced appreciation of Greek bonds back to investors.'[49]

Summing up, 'timing, execution, and design left money on the table from the perspective of Greece, created a large risk for European taxpayers, and set precedents – particularly in its very generous treatment of holdouts – that are likely to make future debt restructurings in Europe more difficult.' One may also say more profitable for those unduly privileged by EU-politicians. 'Partly as a result, it will be hard to repeat a Greek-style restructuring elsewhere in Europe should the need arise.'[50] Those deciding on Greece were exceptionally generous to creditors: 'Bondholders were offered an exceptionally large cash sweetener, in the form of highly rated EFSF notes – worth 15 percent of the "old" bond's face value', the largest cash sweetener ever offered in sovereign debt restructurings (aside from outright cash buybacks). The 'average cash sweetener across 180 debt restructurings since 1975 amounted to only 3.6 percent'.[51] Public money was wasted on the financial sector including 'vultures', as everywhere in eurozone debtor countries. Thanks to the EU, the so-called eurocrisis proved a wishing table cum gold-donkey all in one for some. This proves with utmost clarity that some form of holding politicians financially (and criminally) accountable for damages they inflict on the public is sorely needed. Only Iceland did so.

One might assume 'solidarity with the Greeks' to include supporting any sensible effort to save money. Not so: Greece's military spending declined briefly when the crisis broke, bouncing back quickly. Greece's military expenditures were traditionally at least double of the Eurozone and OECD averages. Reductions to these averages would have saved 2.6 per cent of GDP

[47] J. Zettelmeyer, C. Trebesch and M. Gulati, 'The Greek Debt Restructuring: An Autopsy', working paper 13–8, Peterson Institute for International Economics, Washington DC, 2013, 30.
[48] Ibid. [49] Ibid., 34. [50] Ibid., 3. [51] Ibid., 26.

annually. Spending only 1.7 per cent (EU average) over 1992–2012 would have produced enormous savings: 'No other area has contributed as heavily to the country's debt mountain. If Athens had cut defence spending to levels similar to other EU states over the past decade, economists claim it would have saved around €150bn – more than its last bailout.'[52] Main arms exporters (Germany and France) exerted pressure in favour of lucrative exports, while insisting on severe cuts in pensions and social expenditures, as *The Guardian* reported. Though eventually cut, defence expenditure per head remained above the Eurozone average.

Even in cases of corruption, where German penal courts had convicted people, contracts had to be 'honoured'. The fines paid were cashed by Germany, the damage remained Greece's.

The press[53] reported obstinate rumours that importing arms had been made a precondition for 'rescue' loans. This was officially denied; nevertheless, a very interesting aspect of 'rescue' and 'solidarity' operations.

Interests other than the country`s own seem to prevail with privatization. It is general knowledge that selling under duress does not yield good prices. Nevertheless, Greece is forced to sell quickly, with predictable results. Greece had agreed with her creditors in 2011 that sales of state assets would generate €50 billion. €3.2 billion were realized through 2015.

Logically, Greece is again 'expected to miss 2016 privatization target'.[54] Buyers struck a gold mine, being able to buy Greece's family silver for a song. One example: 14 profit-making Greek regional airports went to Fraport AG at €1.23 billion; the other 30 airports with losses remained Greek property. *Die Zeit* quotes the Greek Minister of infrastructure, calling this a model never before implemented in Europe and 'more in line with a colony than with an EU-member.'[55]

Where some few profit, others usually loose. Greece is a prime example. Poor Greeks had to shoulder the costs, but also taxpayers of other

[52] Helena Smith 'German "hypocrisy" over Greek military spending has critics up in arms - Athens' fondness for weaponry, and willingness of Germany and France to feed it, under fire as Greece struggles with debt crisis' , *Guardian* (19 April, 2012), www.theguardian.com/world/2012/apr/19/greece-military-spending-debt-crisis

[53] E.g. Gerd Höhler, 'Kein Geld für Pensionen – aber für Panzer', *Handelsblatt* (17 January 2012) www.handelsblatt.com/politik/international/griechenland-ruestungsauftraege-als-gegenleistung-fuer-hilfskredite/6077224-3.html

[54] N. Stamouli, 'Greece Expected to Miss 2016 Privatization Target', *WSJ*, December 8, 2015, www.wsj.com/articles/greece-expected-to-miss-2016-privatization-target-1449595718.

[55] 'Griechische Regierung erlaubt Fraport Übernahme von Regionalflughäfen', *Die Zeit* (Germany), www.zeit.de/wirtschaft/2015-08/griechenland-fraport-regionale-flughaefen-uebernahme.

euro-countries that will lose money illegally bailing out the financial sector. Even the private sector itself has (as a block) lost more money due to damages inflicted by unaccountable EU-politicians compared with a quick solution. Protecting private sector creditors was officially another main goal at the beginning. Due to EU-mismanagement, the private sector (highly speculative funds, e.g., exempted) lost more than economically necessary, although some (speculative) private actors were indeed able to profit. The collapse of Cypriot banks was largely a result of the private sector's haircut without considering possible contagion. The EU could have avoided it. Rather than 'protecting the private sector' the EU inflicted grave damages on it taken as a whole. So-called rescue operations have inflicted damages on nearly anyone except speculators and politicians claiming to have saved the Euro, Europe or (like James Bond) simply the world.

The effects on the Greeks are described in detail by the UN's Independent Expert:[56] social protection expenditure witnessed cuts by 21.3 per cent (2009–13), while it increased by 8.4 per cent in the Eurozone. Even Portugal (+9.1 per cent) and Spain (+6.8 per cent) fared better than Greece. Public health expenditures fell by 42.5 per cent. Admitting the need for reform, Bohoslavsky concluded 'the excessive austerity in the public health care sector literally killed first nurse and doctor before treating the patient.'[57] The number of persons considered severely materially deprived, has nearly doubled (2010: 11.6 per cent; 2014: 21.5 per cent, Eurozone average: 7.3 per cent). In 2014 32.9 per cent lived in households unable to keep their homes adequately warm (2010: 15.4 per cent).[58] Official information on the number of homeless does conveniently not exist. Briefly, 'Social and economic rights have been denied in a widespread manner … individuals are ultimately denied … the enjoyment of core essential minim levels of social, economic and cultural rights that States have to protect in all circumstances … austerity measures implemented since 2010 contributed significantly to this outcome.'[59]

Human rights obligations enshrined in international treaties have been violated in Greece in favour of the lemon squeezer principle. The EU even violated its own treaties, such as the EU Charter of Fundamental Rights.[60] The EU chose not to observe human rights and the Rule of Law in order to allow private profits of some few actors.

Especially in Greece official 'rescue'-lending has prolonged and worsened the crisis, pushing debts to 180 per cent of GDP, postponing and increasing

56 Bohoslavsky, *Report of the Independent Expert*, 9f. 57 Ibid., 11. 58 Ibid., 17.
59 Ibid., 18. 60 Ibid., 7.

eventually unavoidable haircuts. After six years the crisis is not over, but the situation is worse than when it started. The illegal and economically absurd bailout of speculators rather than Greece has already afflicted would-be 'rescuers' themselves. A quick haircut, would have contained losses (not least of the budgets of those illegally bailing-out speculators) and spared the Greeks unnecessary hardship.

Unlike other creditors, the ECB was allowed to get away scot-free. Its claims were not subjected to PSI. Not without justification a private sector participant at a conference at Columbia University called the ECB an 'official vulture'.

Last but not least, the EU has rolled democracy back further. Weisbrod argues that the ECB could have easily stopped the crisis, a crisis of bad policies, as it eventually did in July 2012, but 'for the ECB and its allies ... the crisis was an opportunity: to force the weaker Eurozone governments to institute "reforms" that their electorates would never vote for.'[61] The obvious failure and perniciousness of Troika-policies made many economists see 'the true nature' of the debt drama as 'about power and democracy much more than money and economics.'[62] Neoliberal policies had to be enforced, which could only be done by overriding democracy and purported 'European values' such as human rights. It is interesting to note that a proposal denied to Greece was adopted a few months later for Ukraine.[63] Economics cannot explain this, politics can. Rodrik[64] already interpreted debt crises as opportunities seized by orthodox economists for a 'wholesale reform of prevailing policies', the chance 'to wipe the slate clean and mount a frontal attack on the entire range of policies in use', irrespective of whether these were the reason for the crisis (e.g. in Greece) or not (e.g. Ireland, Spain).

When Papandreou proposed a referendum in 2011, EU-pressure, especially by France and Germany, stopped it. Pressure was again exerted when the second referendum was to take place in 2015. The ECB kept the existing cap on the Emergency Liquidity Assistance, Greece's funding lifeline, increasing pressure on Greece. Recently, after a referendum in the Netherlands that could not be squashed, Rebecca Harms, head of the Green in the EU-Parliament, demanded a ban on referenda. The Parliament's President saw it necessary to fight for the 'project of civilization', meaning the EU

61 M. Weisbrod, *Failed* (New York: Oxford University Press, 2015), 39, *see also* pp. 44ff.

62 Stiglitz, 'Europe's Attack'.

63 Y. Varoufakis, 'Greek Debt Denial: A Modest Debt Restructuring Proposal and Why It Was Ignored', in *Too Little, Too Late, the Quest to Resolve Sovereign Debt Crises, eds.* M. Guzman, J.A. Ocampo, and J.E. Stiglitz (New York: Columbia University Press, 2016), 95.

64 D. Rodrik, 'Understanding Policy Reform', *Journal of Economic Literature* 1, XXIV (1996): 17.

without democratic referenda.[65] Apparently they both concur with Juncker: 'Of course, politicians should obey the will of the people as much as possible, if in doing so they continue respecting European agreements.'[66] People may decide whatever they want, as long as they decide what their 'leaders' want.

This anti-democratic bias is built-in. The first blueprint of a European Economic Community with a Council composed of representatives of member states, and committees for trade, agriculture etc., even a European currency union with a central bank in Germany (though no European Parliament, not even without full parliamentary powers) was part of the 'New Order', Nazi plans for Europe after the War.[67] Worried about its propaganda effect the British government asked Keynes to prepare an attractive counterproposal, Bretton Woods. In contrast to the usual untruth that the EU was designed after 1945 as a peace project, plans already there were implemented, not seldom by people, who had been involved in drawing them up before 1945. The 'debt crisis' seems to be used as a possibility to converge to the original, again under German leadership.

V. THE WRITING ON THE WALL

In spite of asserting 'considerable misgivings about Greece's debt sustainability'[68] the IMF approved an exceptionally large loan to Greece in 2010. It had to 'depart from its established rules on exceptional access' because 'euro partners had ruled out debt restructuring and were unwilling to provide additional financing assurances'.[69] Such indulging docility has been uncommon outside Europe: strongly and justifiably doubting the programme's success the Fund nevertheless obliged the EU. Unlike in Uruguay (2002), Jamaica (2011), and Iceland 'Ex ante debt restructuring was not attempted ... debt restructuring had been considered by the parties to the negotiations but had been ruled out by the euro area.'[70] Or, 'An upfront debt restructuring would have been better for Greece although this was not

65 'Nach Nein der Niederländer: Grünen-Abgeordnete lehnt EU-Volksabstimmungen ab', *Spiegel* (Germany), April 8, 2016.

66 Interview in *Spiegel* March 11, 2013, www.spiegel.de/spiegel/print/d-91464871.html.

67 J. Laughland, *The Tainted Source, the Undemocratic Origins of the European Idea* (London: Little Brown & Company, 1997), 5; K. Raffer and H.W. Singer, *The Economic North-South Divide: Six Decades of Unequal Development* (Cheltenham: Elgar, 2002), 1f. One of the authors, Sir Hans, was a contemporary witness.

68 IMF, 'Greece: Ex Post Evaluation of Exceptional Access under the 2010 Stand-By Arrangement', 2013, 32; cf. also IMF, 'The IMF and the Crises in Greece, Ireland, and Portugal', 46 ('absence of a high probability for sovereign debt sustainability').

69 Ibid. 70 Ibid., 27.

acceptable to the euro partners.'[71] According to Varoufakis, the IMF was 'even more militant than I regarding the importance of a straight write down (including in terms of net present *and* face values)'[72]. One possible lesson to be learned presented under the heading 'Avoiding undue delays in debt restructuring' is:

> Earlier debt restructuring could have eased the burden of adjustment on Greece and contributed to a less dramatic contraction in output. The delay provided a window for private creditors to reduce exposures and shift debt into official hands. This shift occurred on a significant scale and left the official sector on the hook.[73]

Knowingly and against its own appraisal, the IMF participated in a solution that damaged its own client and member in clear violation of the most basic good governance and Rule of Law principles. The present 'refugee' crisis further increases Greece's financial burden.

Once it has become totally clear that taxpayers' money is lost, the main objective is to delay recognition, ignoring the writing on the wall. Apart from political (budgetary) reasons, undemocratically administering the debtor is apparently wanted. An open haircut (of face value) is opposed, but Official Sector Involvement has already taken place. Interests were lowered, maturities stretched, interest rates for bilateral credits (Greek Loan Facility) cut, the EFSF Guarantee Commitment Fee cancelled, a ten-year moratorium of interest payment to the EFSF conceded, ECB-profits on Greek instruments are to be refunded to Greece. Official creditors expressed readiness to stretch maturities and cut interests further. Anything goes but a clear haircut to a sustainable level, or 'letting Greece off the hook'. Thus the Greek tragedy will go on in order to conceal EU-mistakes and the EU's political agenda. Maybe, someone will pick up an IBRD-recommendation, 'concessional interest rates and a repayment period of 125 years, including 65 years of grace',[74] or a '"bullet" option' with an interest rate of 0.0001 per cent preferably until 2300 to keep Greece captive. In any case, Greece's suffering will be prolonged, but eventually reality will have to be faced, losses will eventually have to be recognized.

VI. CONCLUSION

Greece is a prime warning against letting unaccountable public officials determine crisis management, against undue and antidemocratic political

[71] Ibid., 28. [72] Varoufakis, 'Greek Debt Denial', 86. [73] IMF (2013), 33.

[74] IBRD, *Global Development Finance* (vol. 1), (Washington, DC: IBRD, 2000), 171.

interference, and an ardent case in favour of a market solution: a sovereign insolvency procedure to abolish the unjustified difference between countries and other debtors.[75] As the official sector usurps more and more power in debt crisis management, it becomes mandatory to introduce meaningful liability norms for politicians, preventing them from knowingly inflicting damage. Iceland has shown the way by indicting responsible decision-makers – a commendable and remarkable first step on which to build – but financial damage compensation still remains a desideratum.[76] Comparing Greece with Iceland shows that democratic structures can more easily overcome debt crises. It also shows how much damage unaccountable and irresponsible politicians can inflict.

75 Obviously, the author recommends this model: K. Raffer (2016) 'Debts, Human Rights, and the Rule of Law: Advocating a Fair and Efficient Sovereign Insolvency Model', in *Too Little, Too Late, the Quest to Resolve Sovereign Debt Crises*, eds. M. Guzman, J.A. Ocampo and J.E. Stiglitz.(New York: Columbia University Press, 2016). 253–69.

76 Cf. Raffer, *Debt Management for Development*, 228ff.

6

Grenada: A Small Island Developing State Needs New Ways Out of Its Debt

JÜRGEN KAISER

ABSTRACT

Grenada is a small island developing state (SIDS) in the Eastern Caribbean which has been driven into over-indebtedness by a combination of structural weaknesses and external shocks. The small size of the island's economy and its limited diversification met with the shocks of the cessation of the EU banana trade preferences and hurricane Ivan in 2004. Due to these factors, Grenada has hardly ever had an unproblematic external debt level throughout its recent history. It defaulted, however, only in 2013 after long and futile attempts to keep its debt service payments on schedule. Grenada is indebted to multilateral, private and official bilateral creditors. Bilaterals outside the Paris Club and private bondholders agreed to reduce their claims on Grenada after lengthy negotiations. Multilaterals insisted on their 'exempt creditor status' and refused to contribute to debt relief. The Paris Club finally added insult to injury, when it amended its rescheduling without any debt reduction with a 'comparability of treatment' clause and a mock 'hurricane clause'. The concessions reached leave Grenada with a debt stock of more than 90 per cent of GDP and it takes again over-optimistic growth assumptions by the IMF to presume that the country has left its debt crisis behind. A remarkable development, though, was the broad and forceful participation of civil society in the debt negotiation process. The interventions of the influential Conference of Churches in Grenada led to a far more balanced economic reform programme than is common among highly indebted countries under pressure from the IMF and other creditors.

I. SPICE ISLE AND THE ORIGINS OF GRENADA'S DEBT PROBLEMS

Like most of its Caribbean neighbours Grenada's debt problems have two origins: (1) its character as a small and extremely vulnerable economy and (2) the change in the EU's banana preference system, which undermined what used to be the major export business model of many Caribbean countries after World War II.

Regarding the former, the vulnerability is the result of a hardly diversified economy with an extraordinary dependency on imports on the one hand and its exposure to natural disasters on the other. The probability of a hurricane striking Grenada in any given year is 8.9 per cent.[1]

Despite such challenges, Grenada and her neighbours managed to have their economies grow on the back of the EU preference system, which favoured fruit imports from former colonies through the 1960s and 1970s. With the further development of the common market and its opening to broader trade liberalization, the EU abandoned the preference system and exposed Caribbean producers to the competition of far bigger and more cost-effective competitors in Central and South America. Within a few years bananas lost their position as the major hard currency source of the Grenadian economy and could not be substituted for, until tourism gained more strength in the 1990s. However, tourism, mostly from the United States and Canada is a volatile income source, too, as drastic reductions in arrivals after 9/11 and through the global financial crisis in 2008 demonstrated. Like many peers, the Grenadian authorities filled the income gaps through loan taking.

II. DEBT INDICATORS IN THE CRUCIAL PHASE OF 2012–2015

At the beginning of 2012 Grenada's external and public debts approached critical thresholds.

End-2012, on the eve of its partial default Grenada's external debt stood at EC$ 2328.58 million, of which EC$ 420.88 million were domestic and EC$ 1497.96 million external debt. Annex 1[2] shows the absolute amounts of Grenada's public debt expressed in EC$; with 1 US$ = 2.71 EC$. These data are not always coherent with data published by the World Bank in IDS. In the following we refer to data by the government of Grenada, unless indicated otherwise.

EC$ amounts have been published in greater detail by the government of Grenada for end-2013. They are shown in Annex 2.

Of course, a debt problem does not manifest itself in absolute debt or debt service amounts, but in an eventual disproportion between the debt and the

[1] IMF, *Caribbean States: Challenges of High Debt and Low Growth*, WDC, 2013, 7.

[2] 'The case of Grenada', presentation by Minister of the Economy Oliver Joseph to the Civil Society Workshop 'Putting Insights into Practice' St George's, May 23, 2013.

economic capacities of the country in question. The most common indicators have given reason for concern since the beginning of the decade:

- Public debt to GDP end-2012 stood at 110 per cent.[3]
- Public Debt Service due[4] was EC$ 456m in 2013 or 41 per cent of total public expenditure or slightly more than 100 per cent of total non-grants revenue.[5]
- Grenada was then considered as being at 'high risk of debt distress' under the regular assessment, which the IMF conducts for most low-income countries (LICs).[6] Grenada is being included in the LIC-DSA list, although it is an upper-middle-income country (UMIC), due to its status as an IDA-blend country and because it also is eligible for borrowing from the IMF's concessional window, the Poverty Reduction and Growth Trust (PRGT).
- All of Grenada's external payment obligations are owed or guaranteed by the state. Therefore external debt equals public external debt. With only 22 per cent of all public debt being domestic Grenada is relatively more indebted to external creditors than peers such as Jamaica and other nations in the Eastern Caribbean.[7] The key for solving Grenada's debt sustainability problems therefore lies clearly in its relations to external rather than to domestic creditors.
- Grenada's export-income based indicators have been quite high, too. Debt stock to exports has been hovering around 300 per cent ever since 2008. Total external debt service to exports has been kept mostly below 15 per cent because of the relatively strong average grant element of the external debt stock. The 2013 partial default then reduced the debt service (paid) ratio even further.

Early 2013 Grenada defaulted on a US$ 193 million bond due in 2025 and some local debt. It has been considered as being in default ever since.

Figure 6.1[8] illustrates the shares of each creditor category before the debt relief operation of 2014–15.

3 Ibid.; IMF, *Macroeconomic Issues in Small States*, WDC, 2013, 24.

4 Not necessarily identical to debt service actually paid.

5 H.E. Prime Minister Keith Mitchell (2013): Budget Speech 2013.

6 www.imf.org/external/pubs/ft/dsa/dsalist.pdf, last visited September 5, 2013.

7 UNDP, *Achieving Debt Sustainability and the MDGs in Small Island Developing States*, New York, 2010, fig. 19.

8 Ministry of Finance Grenada, *Debt Sustainability Assessment*, 2013.

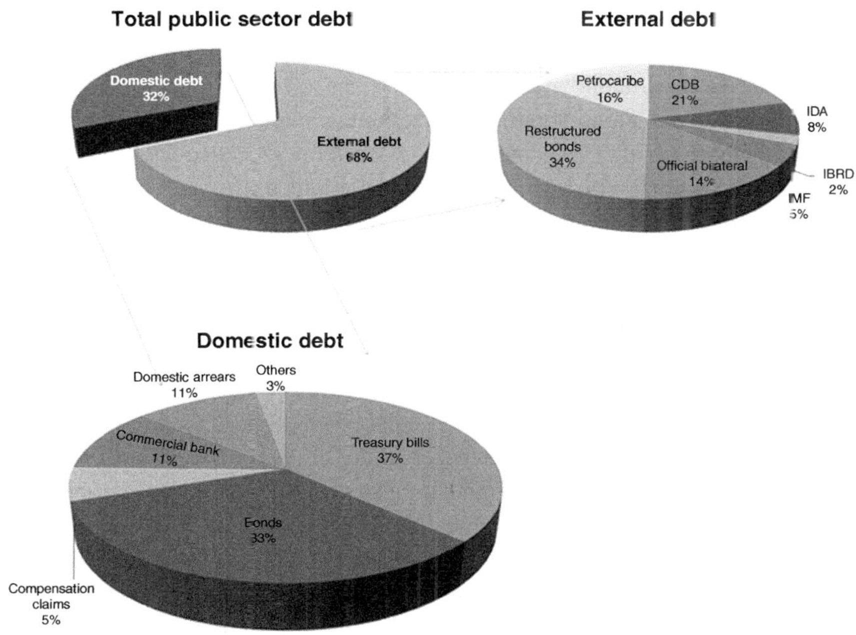

FIGURE 6.1 The shares of each creditor category before the debt relief operation of 2014–2015.

III. THE DEBT RESTRUCTURING 2013–2016

At the beginning of the decade it became more and more obvious that Grenada would not be able to restore debt sustainability by traditional austerity and bridge lending from multilateral sources, because the debt overhang was already too severe. The authorities consequently had to explore ways and means to obtain debt relief through the complicated landscape of traditional negotiation fora.

III.A. *Some Debt Categories Are Restructured, Others Are Not*

As a middle-income country, Grenada never became eligible for any comprehensive debt reduction scheme, like HIPC/MDRI. All it was conceded was a US$ 16 million rescheduling under classic terms (i.e. without any relief element) from the Paris Club in 2006. That agreement included a 'goodwill clause', which under a series of conditions signalled the Club's willingness to again look at Grenada's debt, but then under the 'Evian Approach', which means: without any predefined upper or lower threshold of an eventual treatment.[9] The effect of that non-concessional restructuring of just a minor part of the overall US$ 437 million external debt of Grenada on the island's debt sustainability was negligible.

The envisaged Evian treatment was then granted by the Paris Club in November 2015,[10] after the country had been more than two years in default, and after bondholders had agreed to an exchange with a relief element of roughly 50 per cent and the more important official creditors – notably Taiwan – had provided relief in about the same extent. With this background the Paris agreement turned out to be a cruel hoax for Grenada: de facto 'Evian' meant the same 'classic' restructuring conditions as the earlier agreement, which was implemented when Grenada was still not in default and debt indicators were still substantially lower. 'Classic' in this case meant that the US$ 8 million out of a Paris Club stock of claims of US$ 11 million, which were actually negotiated, were not reduced but were rescheduled at the original interest rates. As these were far higher than today's extremely low global interest rates, this rescheduling even turns out to be an attractive investment for the creditors.

Adding insult to injury, this time the Club provided, with much fanfare, a 'hurricane clause', which the debtor indeed had requested. However, the clause did not allow for any immediate cessation of payments in the case of a natural disaster, as one might have expected, but only signalled the Club's willingness to again negotiate with the Grenadian authorities should the island be sufficiently damaged by another hurricane – something Grenada, of course, could have requested any time or even enforced through a simple unilateral stop of payments.

In sum, Grenada managed to negotiate three different agreements with its external creditors – each of them ad-hoc and without any specific link to the others, except for the somewhat weird Paris Club agreement (described previously). Most strikingly, what is missing from the whole negotiation process, however, was any coherent definition of debt sustainability as a target for debt restructuring. Rather, the bondholder and Taiwan agreements reflected more or less what seemed realistically recoverable to creditors, who were certainly more insightful and cooperative than their counterparts in Paris.

9 Paris Club, 'Debt treatment – May 12, 2006', www.clubdeparis.org/en/traitements/grenada-12-05-2006/en. For the specificities of the Evian Approach, see www.clubdeparis.org/en/communications/page/evian-approach.

10 The Paris Club is an informal forum for renegotiating debt owed to OECD member and a few other sovereigns. For more information see its website at www.clubdeparis.org. For a critical assessment of its role and record, see J. Kaiser, 'Debt Management à la Louis XVI: A short promenade through the Programme and Practice of the Paris Club', 1999, www.erlassjahr.de/english/debt-management-a-la-louis-xiv518.html.

III.B. *The (Non-)Definition of Debt Sustainability in the Restructuring Context*

The big innovation in sovereign debt management, which the multilateral HIPC initiative by the G7, respectively the IMF and the World Bank, had brought about in 1995–96 was that for the first time debt relief was not tailored through a series of individual negotiations with private creditors and unrelated to this, a treatment up to predefined and often totally unrealistic debt relief thresholds of the Paris Club. Instead, a sustainable debt level was defined by IFIs, which subsequently was the target of a comprehensive debt relief operation. Any existing external debt beyond that threshold had to be cancelled one way or another.

At the beginning of the HIPC process in 1995–96 this new comprehensive process was undermined by unrealistic definitions of these debt sustainability targets. Consequently debt relief for those severely indebted sovereigns, which still qualified, was minimal. This changed at the Cologne G8 summit in 1999 when debt thresholds were substantially lowered. Additionally, the possibility to top-up relief, in cases where circumstances had changed, was introduced at the Kananaskis G8 summit in 2002.

Grenada as a non-HIPC never had any realistic debt sustainability calculation considered as the target or at least the starting point for any comprehensive process. This does not mean that nobody tried to define sustainable debt levels for Grenada. The Eastern Caribbean Central Bank (ECCB) has established a sustainable debt level of 60 per cent of GDP[11] as an orientation for all its members, and most participants in Grenada's restructuring process after 2012 would agree that this was a realistic magnitude.

Several authors have explored the growth-enhancing effects of external debt, and the unsurprising result was that the growth curve related to the level of external debt shows three segments: importing capital from abroad supports growth, as long as the overall level of indebtedness is low. From a certain level onward the marginal positive growth effect starts to diminish, and beyond a tipping point an additional dollar of debt is not growth enhancing, but, – due to the debt overhang effect – actually reduces growth.

Where exactly this tipping point is to be located, is, of course, controversial among academics, governments, international financial institutions and civil society. HIPC was the extraordinary case, where an inflexible upper limit was defined and mandatorily linked to debt relief. After some countries had

[11] Indeed the same debt/GNI ratio which the EU defines as an upper limit for its members.

received still insufficient relief through the scheme, while others, in hindsight, were seen as having been treated 'unnecessarily generous' it was evident that no single limit can serve all cases in a uniform way. Consequently, some authors like Reinhart and Rogoff had advocated a relatively high ceiling of 90 per cent, while others calculated with much more caution.

Other authors had identified substantially lower threshold values, such as a 'tipping point' at 35 to 40 per cent and a diminishing marginal value added by additional debt at half this level.[12]

The most relevant paper on the basis of this concept for the Grenadian case is, however, Greenidge et al. (2012).[13] The authors analyze debt distress episodes not on a global scale, but in the Caribbean, and they specifically show that here at debt levels lower than 30 per cent of GDP, increases in the debt to GDP ratio are associated with faster economic growth. The positive effect on growth diminishes rapidly as debt rises beyond 30 per cent of GDP, and beyond 55 per cent of GDP debt becomes a drag on growth.[14]

Greenidge et al. relate their findings to the regional specifics: '*Compared to Reinhard and Rogoff . . . a much lower threshold was found for the Caribbean region because of its small size and lack of physical resources* (. . .). *Therefore, in order to achieve faster and sustained growth paths, government in conjunction with the private sector need to present more innovative ideas and rehash some of the current policies for the region.*'

Table 6.1 provides an overview of both the general debt indicators and Caribbean-specific indicators plus the level of necessary relief they would have implied at the onset of the Grenadian default.[15]

As we can see, none of the calculation with the exception Reinhart/Rogoff considers less than a reduction of roughly one-half as sufficient for the restoration of debt sustainability. In order to reach this, a roughly 50 per cent reduction of the whole debt stock would have been the obvious option. Whereas in theory maturities extensions and interest reduction like other forms of debt service reductions could do the job as well, it seems plausible that a fresh start from Grenada's extreme high stock level, a nominal haircut would be the most effective instrument, in order to restore the island's economic capacities. The agreements with Taiwan and private bondholders

[12] C.A. Pattillo, H. Ward and L.A. Ricci, 'External Debt and Growth', IMF working paper 02/69 (2002).

[13] G. Greenidge et al., 'Threshold Effects of Sovereign Debt Service: Evidence from the Caribbean', IMF working paper 12/157 (2012).

[14] IMF, 'Caribbean States: Challenges of High Debt and Low Growth', 2013, 29.

[15] The table and surrounding data are taken from J. Kaiser, 'Debt Sustainability in Grenada. Challenges for Overcoming the Present Crisis', paper prepared for UNDP, September 2013.

TABLE 6.1 *Debt Sustainability Thresholds and Their Implications for Grenada*

Concept	Indicator	Actual level (%)	Sustainable level (%)	Suggested debt reduction in %
HIPC Comparability	EDT/XGS	296.4	150	48
Debt Sustainability Framework	TDS/XGS	13.3	15	–
Debt Sustainability Framework	Public Debt Service/Revenue	103	20	81
London Debt Accord	TDS/XGS	13.3	3.4	75
'Natural Debt Limit'	Public Debt/GNI	101.2	6.3	95
Debt-Growth Nexus according to Greenidge et al.	Public Debt/GNI, maximum marginal growth effect	101.2	30	71
Debt-Growth Nexus according to Greenidge et al.	Public Debt/GNI tipping point	101.2	55	45
Debt Growth Nexus according to Reinhart/Rogoff	EDT/GNI	73.8 (2011)	60	23

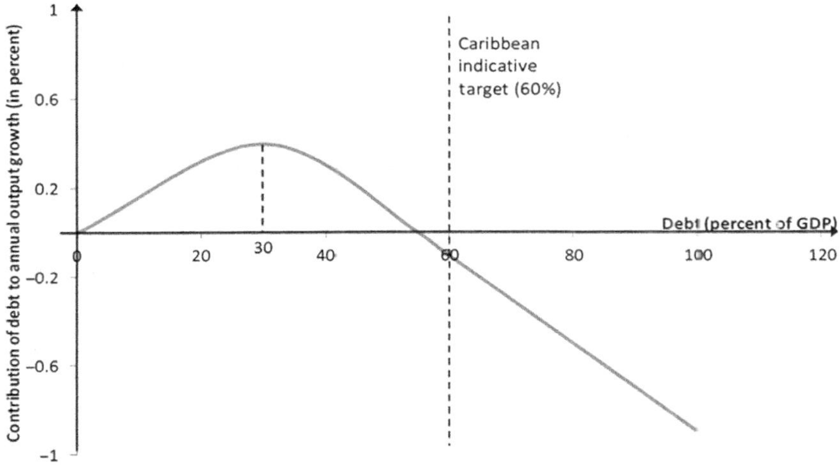

FIGURE 6.2 Stylized shape of the threshold effects of public debt on growth.

broadly complied with this target, whereas the Paris Club's did not, and the multilateral creditors never seriously considered to participate in the effort. Thus, the target debt level was never reached in the end. Instead the combined effects of the private and non-Paris-Club creditors' concessions reached about 20 per cent of Grenada's debt stock.

III.C. *The Inescapable Threat of Austerity*

Traditionally, small countries such as Grenada have been expected to exhaust all options for improving their capacity to pay before creditors were willing to provide debt relief. Consequently, the first choice is to make more domestic resources available for debt service, as also expressed by the Prime Minister in the context of the current crisis.[16] So the 2013 budget has saved all in all EC$ 60 million over the 2012 budget. This however falls short of the 3.5 per cent of GNI,[17] which the IMF at the same time has considered as necessary in order to just stabilize the public debt ratio.

Recent positions taken by the government of Grenada have confirmed that its internal efforts to mobilize domestic resources will be through expenditure cuts rather than through raising taxes.[18] An additional element would be the reduction of labour costs to enhance competitiveness. This relates to both wages and labour regulations.[19]

However, there is broad agreement that from present debt levels, which are more serious than ever in the country's history, Grenada will not be able to return to debt sustainability by its own efforts. The government instead has joined academics, analysts and even the IMF itself, who – particularly after the most recent Greek experience – have warned against the unwanted implications of an austerity policy. Despite dramatic austerity measures being taken – particularly on the expenditure side – Greece has failed to regain debt stability, mostly because the impairment of growth through such measures has been way beyond the expectations upon which the IMF had based its programme in this European country. The limitations of austerity as an approach to overcome Grenada's debt problems has been clearly expressed

[16] Prime Minister Keith Mitchell, Budget Speech 2013.

[17] Amounting to about EC-$73 million based on the 2011 GNI. IMF: 'Macroeconomic Issues in Small States and Implications for Fund Engagement', February 20, 2013, fig. 13.

[18] The IMF has pointed out that Grenada is having a below-average tax rate, which would give it some leeway to raise more taxes. However the Mitchell government has excluded tax rises categorically. Instead measures such as the Investment for Citizenship program are being considered, which are strongly criticized by civil society.

[19] IMF, 'Grenada: Third Review under the Extended Credit Facility', November 2015, 27.

by the Prime Minister in his 2013 budget speech, where he stated: '*Government recognizes that raising tax rates in a depressed economic situation is not smart economics.*'[20]

This point was then reinforced by some observers:

> Former IMF representative to Ireland Ashoka Mody has expressed his critical view on austerity as an instrument to restore debt sustainability in a paper for the Brussels-based think tank Bruegel: 'There was not one single historical instance where austerity policies have led to an exit from heavy debt burden.'[21]

Even more focused on the situation in the Caribbean, the IMF itself reveals that fiscal consolidation has a fairly negative track record in the region.[22] In the extreme, St Luca has undergone eight episodes of fiscal consolidation, none of which was a success – defined as a 5 percentage point reduction of the debt/GDP indicator below the level prior to the start of consolidation – after four years. Grenada's own track record is somewhat better with three successes after eight episodes. Still, it is disappointingly weak given the social costs which are regularly associated with fiscal consolidation. One of the most recent unsuccessful episodes was the cut in public expenditure, including capital expenditure by 4.5 per cent by 2010–11 over 2008–09.[23] Its effect on the rising debt indicators was negligible.

III.D. *The Fragmented Process and Its Outcome*

By April 2016 the debt relief process came to a formal close with the following results:

> The overall debt stock was reduced by about 20 per cent through the combined effects of the agreements for the 2025 international bonds and the agreement with Taiwan – way below the reductions considered necessary in any of the analytical works cited earlier. Additionally the exchange of the EC dollar 2025 domestic bonds held by the

[20] Prime Minister Keith Mitchell, Budget Speech 2013.

[21] J. Crosbie, Former IMF Official Warns Austerity Could Be 'Self-Defeating' for Ireland, *The Irish Times*, July 21, 2013, www.irishtimes.com/business/former-imf-official-warns-austerity-could-be-self-defeating-for-ireland-1.1470669. See the link to the full Bruegel paper there.

[22] See table 2 on p. 19 in IMF 'The Challenges of Fiscal Consolidation and Debt Reduction in the Caribbean', November 2012, 17.

[23] UNICEF, 'Prioritizing Expenditure for a Recovery for All: A Rapid Review of Public Expenditures in 126 Developing Countries', August 27, 2010.

National Insurance Scheme (NIS), provided for no haircut, but a limited cash flow relief in favour of the state budget.

The relief was reached through a 50 per cent reduction only applied to two segments of the total debt stock:

- US$ 193 million in bonds, on which the country had defaulted in 2013 through a framework agreement reached with bondholders in early April 2015;[24]
- the bilateral official claims held by Taiwan's Exim bank; an agreement on the outstanding US$ 36.6 million was reached in January 2015. It implied a repayment period of 15 years with three years of grace and a 7 per cent coupon. It ended a litigation which the creditor had started in New York two years before.

Both arrangements implied some novelty:

- in the form of a 'hurricane clause', which turned out to be not very efficient however (see preceding text);
- the payments to private bondholders were formally backed by a part of the income from the country's controversial 'citizenship by investment' program.[25]

As a result of the relief efforts, the IMF expects Grenada's debt-to-GDP ratio to fall from 107 per cent in 2013 to 90 per cent end-2016.[26] The ECCU sustainability threshold of 60 per cent is expected to be reached by 2021 – absent any negative shocks, which could eventually distort the smooth year-on-year 2.5 per cent real growth expectation until 2021.[27]

[24] News release of the Grenadian Ministry of Finance and Energy, April 8, 2015. As the defaulted 2015 bonds were traded at 33 per cent of face value in November 2015, the 50 per cent haircut would allow distressed debt specialists, such as vulture funds, even a handsome profit; *see* 'Spice Island Is a Case Study in Debt Traps', *Financial Times*, November 20, 2014.

[25] CBI schemes are presently being introduced by a number of Caribbean and other small island states, led by pioneer St Kitts and Nevis. Civil society has been very critical of the islands' citizenships being sold to people qualifying through nothing else but their wealth. Moreover the scheme would only be attractive as long as Caribbean citizenships allow visa-free entrance into the US and/or the EU. Once cases of f.i. financing of terrorism, money laundering, illegal capital flight, etc. become known in those places, it is unlikely that the free access and with it the attractiveness of the CBI programs are to persist.

[26] IMF, 'Grenada: Third Review under the Extended Credit Facility', November 20, 2015, 8.

[27] IMF, 'Grenada: Debt Sustainability Analysis', November 20, 2015.

III.E. *No Comprehensive Process*

The negotiations between the Grenadian authorities and the island's creditors lacked all the features of a rule-of-law-based approach, which Jubilee Grenada (see next paragraph) had hoped would lead to a more lasting and sustainable solution:

- Negotiations took place with each individual creditor. Some completely stayed out of any restructuring; the suggested comprehensive process never took place.
- Although Jubilee had hoped for a consideration of the preliminary work it had done with regard to the necessary haircut, the suggested independent assessment of the need for debt relief has never been commissioned.
- Decisions were taken with each individual creditor group on an ad-hoc basis and first of all in line with these creditors' individual readiness to make concessions. No impartial mediator, for whom Jubilee and its international partners had lobbied, has ever been involved.

As a result, Grenada continues to be considered as a country 'in debt distress' by the IMF.[28]

IV. CIVIL SOCIETY INVOLVEMENT AND THE 'HOME-GROWN' PROGRAMME

When the Eastern Caribbean moved into the focus of the global Jubilee movement after 2010, Grenada was already in dire straits. Sovereign debt had thus far not been a major topic for Grenadian civil society. However, particularly the churches in Grenada readily saw the connection between an unbearable debt and some passages in the old and new testaments which guided the churches' social teaching. Therefore, with some catalytic support from the global Jubilee movement, members of the Catholic and Protestant churches formed a local Jubilee committee, which quickly became a competent counterpart to the government. Ultimately, the Minister of the Economy was invited to chair it.

Jubilee Grenada's efforts to instigate the government to insist on a fair and transparent negotiation process with its creditors and through this to obtain a relief at least in line with the ECCB target, was unsuccessful. However, it was successful in influencing the design of the 'home-grown' adjustment

[28] IMF, list of Debt Sustainability Analyses of countries with low income and small island developing states as visited April 7, 2016, www.imf.org/external/pubs/ft/dsa/dsalist.pdf.

programme, which Grenada had to present to the IMF in order to (1) clear badly needed disbursements from the multilateral lender, and (2) produce in any credible way the option to ensure the necessary savings in the state budget. Both sides, the government of Grenada as well as Jubilee, claim that the dialogue in the Jubilee committee under the chairmanship of Minister of the Economy Oliver Joseph was instrumental in avoiding the polarization between rich and poor which often has been the result of adjustment programmes designed under the IMF model. In particular this referred to the design of the income tax reform and some parts of the country's energy policy.

V. SOME DEBATES TRIGGERED BY THE GRENADIAN CASE

Grenada's debt was restructured at times when global crises suggested reforms to the existing sovereign debt management schemes. Whereas individual cases therefore always need to be seen in the context of such broader debates, there are two aspects which are of particular relevance for Grenada, and where the country case and the global reform debate have been interlinked: the natural limit and vulnerability and the quest for a (valid) hurricane clause.

V.A. *The Natural Debt Limit*

Even seemingly 'neutral' and 'objective' commonly used debt indicators can hide looming crisis situations by suggesting that even high debt levels are still manageable. The Caribbean at large is being treated by the International Financial Institutions as the upper-middle or even high-income countries which they statistically are. With the all too common mix of national pride and IFI technocracy a general consensus is built that 'we are not Africa'. However, the situations in very small states can be far more volatile, even when plain indicators are identical, than even in low-income countries' in sub-Saharan Africa. Ecological vulnerability, the limited size and diversity of the domestic economy and limited domestic capital formation contribute to the specific vulnerability of small island developing states (SIDS).

The probability of a hurricane striking Grenada in any given year is 8.9 per cent.[29] On average 1 per cent of Caribbean GDP is destroyed every year through natural disasters.[30] In Grenada, however, the average annual

[29] IMF, 'Caribbean States: Challenges of High Debt and Low Growth', February 2, 2013, 7.

[30] S. Acevedo, 'Debt, Growth and Natural Disasters: A Caribbean Trilogy', IMF working paper 14/125 (2014), 4.

direct losses are 9 per cent.[31] Grenada and her neighbours have repeatedly tried to insure themselves in one way or another against such catastrophes. The enormous amount of potential destruction which may result from Caribbean hurricanes, however, has prevented any market-based scheme so far – even when it had been considered by financially more powerful institutions like the Caribbean Development Bank. This infeasibility of a classical market-based 'insurance' solution leaves the country with the only option of building up financial buffers if it does not want to exclusively rely on ad-hoc external aid in cases of disruptions through natural disasters.

Even if the search for an insurance scheme has failed to provide the country with some reliable fiscal backing, it has given rise to an important and promising proposal with regard to defining debt sustainability.[32]

At a recent Caribbean high-level forum in Port of Spain a group of authors affiliated to the IMF – but not in any official capacity – has developed the concept of a 'natural debt limit'. Besides the normal parameters of defining debt sustainability they have taken the huge variations of those parameters – as reflections of the volatility of income and economic conditions at large – into account. From there they have created a formula for defining how much debt any of the islands which form part of their panel could 'naturally' carry without running the risk of a debt crisis.

Grenada, St Vincent and Dominica stand out as countries which can only sustain a very low debt/GDP level due to the vulnerabilities of their economies, but are still absurdly over-indebted: the front-runner Grenada has a 16.1 times higher debt level than the country can actually sustain, because the natural debt limit is at an extreme low of 6.3 per cent of GNI.

Though Amor-Yartey et al.'s calculations certainly are on the extremely cautious side of speculation over the economic future of SIDS, they are an essential corrective to the de facto negligence of the specific vulnerabilities in the islands' economies in traditional DSAs.

V.B. *Vulnerability and the Quest for a (Valid) Hurricane Clause*

As a formal insurance scheme had turned out not to be politically and economically feasible, Grenada requested the inclusion of 'hurricane clauses'

[31] T. Haque et al., 'Addressing Debt Vulnerabilities of Small States: The Potential Role of New Financial Instruments', World Bank (2016), 12.

[32] Ch. Amo-Yartey et al., 'The Challenges of Fiscal Consolidation and Debt Reduction in the Caribbean', IMF working paper 12/275 (November 2012): Box 6, 23.

into its debt restructuring agreements with her creditors, thus 'externalizing' the considerable risk to some degree to creditors.

The Paris Club in its November 2015 agreement responded seemingly positive by including a hurricane clause. However, its meaning was far off any effective crisis insurance: the clause only allows Grenada to negotiate with Paris Club creditors in the case of a hurricane of an unspecified magnitude. This, however, is something the authorities would have been free to do anyway.[33] Neighbouring Dominica has now been offered the same kind of crisis response, months after hurricane Erica destroyed 93 per cent of GDP last August. It can be expected that Grenada's neighbour will be provided with the same meaningless language in the agreed minutes.

Unlike Dominica, however, Grenada has lost annually more through natural disaster damage between 1980 and 2015 than it was able to gain through the nominal growth of its economy. Whereas the latter was 3.3 per cent on average, the average yearly loss through natural disasters (notably the devastation through hurricane Ivan in 2004, of course) in this longer-term perspective was 4.4 per cent.[34]

At the World Bank/IMF annual meetings 2015 in Lima, two additional proposals were made by intergovernmental organizations in order to deal with the Caribbean islands' extreme vulnerability:

- The World Bank suggested a debt buy-back scheme for particularly vulnerable SIDS, financed through contributions from rich member countries.[35]
- The UN Economic Commission for Latin America and the Caribbean (ECLAC) suggested a scheme for multilateral debt relief with the aim of establishing a common 'Resilience Fund'.

Although welcomed in the region and by civil society, neither proposal seems to have gained much traction since the Lima 2015 annual meetings.

33 The hurricane clause in the private debt exchange is somewhat more helpful, as it allows for the deferral of current payments in the case of a hurricane which caused damage beyond US$ 15 million. Whereas still this does not imply any debt stock reduction – the deferred debt needs to be repaid later and will accrue interest in the meantime – it is still more helpful than the Paris Club clause, because it allows for immediately retaining resources in the country, with the need for any further bureaucratic measures by creditors.

34 Moody's Investor Service, 'Caribbean Sovereigns: The Silent Debt Crisis', February 2016, 11.

35 World Bank, 'A Comprehensive Debt Framework for Small States', presentation during the 2013 Small States Forum.

VI. TWO, THREE, MANY GRENADAS ...

The 2012–15 process in Grenada has demonstrated how difficult it is for a poor nation with fewer than 100,000 inhabitants, to gain innovative treatment of its external debt problem – even as the limitations of traditional approaches are obvious and alternatives clearly visible.

However, Grenada is not alone. Six out of the ten most indebted low- and middle-income countries are small island developing states. All in all seven of the comparably sized small island developing states in the Eastern Caribbean have one or several (mostly several) indicators in a critical range – with a strong deteriorating trend.[36] Dominica after 'Erica' may be the next in line for a restructuring, but Antigua and Barbuda or Barbados may even overtake it. It therefore makes sense to think of a more collective response and innovation to a threat which is shared by almost everybody in the region.

So far, innovation within sovereign debt workouts has been considered either on the global level, i.e. towards a scheme which would eventually encompass any sovereign with payment problems, or it has sought individual solutions for individual countries. Though both levels continue to be of essential importance, not much progress has been achieved since the outbreak of the 'Third World Debt Crisis' in the early 1980s. The debt problems of a relatively homogenous group of small island developing states in the Caribbean and beyond may therefore be seen as an opportunity to consider a third level of reform, which would allow debtor and creditors to implement necessary reforms without first reaching a global consensus or confining themselves to individual country solutions without precedence effects for others. The precedence for such an approach, which could be implemented for either the Eastern Caribbean or the community of all in all 50 small island developing states and territories (SIDS) worldwide, is the Heavily Indebted Poor Countries (HIPC) initiative.

From 1996 onwards the HIPC initiative served to provide broad-based and far-reaching debt relief to a group of up to 42 poor and severely indebted countries in Africa and Latin America. When it was introduced, it provided rules, benchmarks and procedures to reduce eligible countries' external debt. Its key elements were

36 erlassjahr.de, 'Global Sovereign Indebtedness Monitor 2016', 2016, http://erlassjahr.de/wordpress/wp-content/uploads/2016/04/Debt-Report-2016-Global-Sovereign-Indebtness-Monitor.pdf.

- the qualification of countries based on their debt levels, plus a sufficiently low per capita income, plus a few less transparent criteria enforced by influential creditors;
- a fixed, but later adapted timeline of economic reform and debt relief implementation;
- predefined debt sustainability indicators as targets for debt relief;
- the principled participation of all creditors in the relief effort.

HIPC's strengths were:

- HIPC was based on a broad consensus that for a certain group of countries 'something had to be done';
- HIPC credibly addressed creditors' fears of too broad-based debt relief scheme;
- equal treatment of comparable cases was broadly achieved.[37]

However the scheme also had its weaknesses. They need to be avoided when a group approach for SIDS is being developed. This requires some innovation in the design of the initiative:

- HIPC had to be reformed and extended a few times (HIPC-I, HIPC-II, Topping-up, MDRI) because the benchmarks in the original initiative of 1996 were unrealistic, and procedures were not flexible enough in the face of outright insolvency in some HIPCs.
- Buy-in to the initiative was limited among some creditor groups, notably private and non-Paris-Club members on the official side.
- Its access criteria were not always coherently applied.[38]

So, what can be learnt from HIPC's strengths and weaknesses is first of all that debt relief needs to be rules-based, and that those rules need to be set by an institution that is not biased to either the debtor or any creditor side.

[37] This changed, when HIPC was supplemented by the Multilateral Debt Relief Initiative (MDRI) in 2005, which led to the cancellation of almost all remaining debt outstanding to the most important multilateral creditors. This 'sweeping' approach provided (finally) for a sufficient degree of debt relief in most affected countries; however, it was a deviation from coherent and uniform debt sustainability targets, which had been the basis of the original HIPC-Initiatives, as some countries benefitted absolutely and relatively more than others.

[38] An example for the positive deviation was the inclusion of (then) LMIC Cote d'Ivoire into the initiative, when important creditor France felt that the original proposal was inappropriately favouring English-speaking African countries; an example for the negative deviation is the exclusion of Nigeria, which was eliminated from the HIPC-list when its democratization at the beginning of the last decade no longer allowed the exclusion of the formally qualified heavyweight debtor with the argument of its notoriously poor governance.

A Heavily Indebted Small Island Developing States (HISIDS) initiative should therefore build on the strengths and avoid the weaknesses of the HIPC initiative:[39]

- HISIDS would be open to all member states of the SIDS group; of these, however, some would not need it anytime soon – just like some HIPC-eligible countries never took recourse to the debt relief it offered. The decision to avail oneself of a debt workout is always the respective government's.
- Its logic would be to provide a debt relief option (*not* a compulsory debt restructuring) for a narrow and predefined group of countries potentially suffering from similar economic challenges and structural weaknesses, from regular natural disasters, to the breakdown of tourism income due to the world financial crisis. In that sense it would not be a one-off cancellation effort addressing a crisis of the time like HIPC, but a relief option, that could be invoked under clearly defined circumstances. As such it would respond to Caribbean states' repeated call for a working 'insurance scheme' against natural disasters.
- Debt relief needs to be comprehensive, but not by trying to force every creditor into a scheme developed by a competing creditor such as the IMF/WB, but by giving everybody a place at the negotiation table.
- Individual debt relief decisions are to be based on an impartial assessment of the problem, rather than one by a creditor such as the IMF or the World Bank.
- In order to conclude on a debt restructuring where warranted, the framework can allow for ad-hoc mediation or binding arbitration. It should ideally start with the former and move on to the latter, if informal processes such as mediation do not lead to results which are acceptable to everybody.
- The framework serves as a 'safeguard' procedure which can only be triggered by each individual debtor government once it has decided that it needs a debt restructuring. The safeguard approach seems particularly appropriate for SIDS, as – different from most HIPCs of the time – debt problems are less the result of imminent structural weaknesses of individual SIDS' economies, but the result of specific but frequent external shocks, such as natural disasters.

Such a scheme would obviously not lead to any immediate debt relief, but it would provide a reliable and calculable crisis response, once it has to be triggered by a regional government.

[39] Cf. a similar, not further elaborated proposal by G. Hurley, 'Financing for Development and Small Island Developing States: A Snapshot and Ways Forward', UNDP & UN-OHRLLS discussion paper (2015), 2.

Annex

TABLE 6.2 *Grenada's debt profile before the default*

	2011	2012
Central Government	1,866.75	1,918.84
Total Domestic	378.66	420.88
Treasury Bills	220.3	259.39
Bonds	22.51	57.49
Loans	55.61	31.44
Other	80.24	72.56
Total External	1,488.09	1,497.96
Bonds	768.39	768.39
Loans	719.7	729.57
Government Guaranteed	346.08	409.74
Total Public Sector Debt	2,212.83	2,328.58

TABLE 6.3 *Individual creditors to Grenada in May 2013.*

Government of Grenada – Bilateral Debt as of May 31, 2013	
Creditor	EC$ Balances as at May 2013
EXIM Bank (Taiwan)	88,500,000 (est)
Libya	13,500,000
Algeria	1,653,750
UK/Grenada – Paris Club Debt Agreement	7,197,931
EXIM Bank USA/Grenada – Paris Club Agreement	7,918,611
Government of Trinidad & Tobago Bonds US$ 16.5M 2005–30	46,750,370
Credit Facility-Caisse Francaise De Develop (French)	7,190,297
	165,520,662

7

Iceland: A Human Rights-Sensitive Approach to Deal with Financial Crises

JUAN PABLO BOHOSLAVSKY[1]

ABSTRACT

This chapter is based on the country mission report the author presented to the UN Human Rights Council in March 2015. On the one hand, it assesses to what extent Iceland fulfilled its obligations to secure economic, social and cultural rights in the aftermath of its recent banking crisis. Though Iceland managed the crisis better than many other countries and responded overwhelmingly in compliance with its international obligations, certain gaps that should be addressed are identified. On the other hand, it identifies several good practices on how States facing a financial crisis can prevent and/or minimize negative human rights impacts in the context of economic adjustment programmes. International organizations and other countries can learn from the particular path chosen in Iceland, which included protecting its core social welfare system, tax progressive reforms, efforts to ensure citizens participation in the decision-making process and endeavours to establish political, administrative and judicial accountability.

I. INTRODUCTION

This book is about learning lessons. This is why the Icelandic case is highly relevant and worth researching: in several ways this country dealt with the financial crash and banking collapse of 2008–09 in unique ways with unique outcomes.

[1] The author wishes to extend his gratitude for the comments to the drafts of this paper and the generous material, information, insights, critiques and questions received from Martín Guzmán, Rachael Lorna Johnstone, Þórólfur Geir Matthíasson, Kunibert Raffer, Sigurbjörg Sigurgeirsdóttir, Margrét Steinarsdóttir and Gunnar Theissen.

In my capacity as United Nations Independent Expert on Foreign Debt and Human Rights I conducted an official visit to Iceland in December 2014. The purpose of the visit was twofold: to assess the extent to which Iceland had fulfilled its obligations to protect economic, social and cultural rights in the aftermath of its financial banking crisis; and to identify good practices that other governments could adopt to prevent negative human rights impacts in the context of financial crises and economic adjustment programmes. The country mission report, on which this chapter is based, was presented and discussed by the Human Rights Council in March 2015.[2]

The structure of the chapter is as follows. In Section II the causes of the boom years, the financial crash and the rebuilding of the banking sector are explained. In Section III the measures implemented to shelter the welfare state and the pertinent budgetary data are presented. Section IV describes the most important and unique Icelandic responses to the crisis, including taxation and fair distribution of losses, targeted debt relief programmes, the work of the Special Investigative Commission of the parliament, the reform of banking supervision, the investigations of the Office of the Special Prosecutor, the participation of citizens and the degree of accountability of those responsible for the crisis and its consequences. In Section V the lessons that might be learned from the good (and also some bad) practices in Iceland are proposed. Section VI discusses whether the Icelandic experience can be useful in other contexts. Finally, in Section VII some concluding remarks are presented.

Just one caveat: although the Icelandic case might teach us a great deal on the moral and psychological driving forces that can push an entire country into a financial boom and crash, as well as the systemic risks of deregulating the banking industry,[3] this chapter only tries to identify *good practices* on responding to financial and banking crises.

II. THE BANKING COLLAPSE

The majority of Iceland's banks were privatized between 1991 and 2004, and a floating exchange rate was introduced. Icelandic banks expanded rapidly during the 2000s owing to a combination of uncontrolled risk taking, a strong Icelandic currency exchange rate and very favourable conditions on international financial markets, which enabled them to provide an ample credit supply at low interest rates. The country became one of the richest countries

[2] A/HRC/28/59/Add.1, March 20, 2015.

[3] *See generally* G. Johnsen, *Bringing Down the Banking System: Lessons from Iceland* (Basingstoke and New York: Palgrave Macmillan, 2014).

in the world. From 2003, the public Housing Financing Fund was allowed to provide loans to cover up to 90 per cent of the market value of a house, below a certain ceiling. Commercial banks entered the mortgage loan market, frequently offering better terms than the government and aggressively expanding their consumer lending, which resulted in Icelandic households being among the most heavily indebted in the world.[4]

By 2008, Iceland was one of the most over-banked economies in the world, with its banks holding assets to a value ten times that of the country's GDP.[5] Early warnings of the crisis by foreign analysts in 2006 where largely ignored.[6] Icelandic triple-A rated banks were already facing liquidity problems, but continued to grow, offering clients abroad, mainly in the United Kingdom of Great Britain and Northern Ireland and the Netherlands, attractive interest rates on presumably secure deposits. The bubble continued to grow until the fall of Lehman Brothers Holdings Inc. when tightening conditions led the gross foreign debt burden of Icelandic banks to rise from 43 per cent of GDP in 2002 to over 700 per cent of GDP in October 2008, which resulted in the collapse of all three major Icelandic banks — Glitnir, Kaupthing and Landsbanki.

On October 6, 2008, the Icelandic parliament passed Emergency Act No. 125/2008, authorizing the Financial Supervisory Authority to take control of the three large banks. Crisis management emphasized the need for uninterrupted domestic banking operations and three new banks — Islandsbank, Arion Bank and Landsbankinn — were established to take over the domestic activities of the three collapsed banks. The State became a majority owner of Landsbankinn and a minority owner of the other two banks. The government injected share capital into the three new banks and several smaller financial institutions and took over losses at a combined cost of roughly one third of GDP for 2008. Although foreign investors bore the bulk of the cost of the Icelandic banking collapse, the amount invested by the State to recapitalize the Icelandic Central Bank and to cover the losses from the takeover of Icelandic financial institutions has been estimated at ISK

4 E. Bergmann, *Iceland and the International Financial Crisis* (Basingstoke and New York: Palgrave Macmillian, 2014); Johnsen, *Bringing Down the Banking System*; S. Sigurgeirsdóttir and R. Wade, 'From Control by Capital to Control of Capital: Iceland's Boom and Bust, and the IMF's Unorthodox Rescue Package', *Review of International Political Economy* 22, no. 1, (2015), 103–33; T. Tjörvi Ólafsson and K.A. Vinisdóttir, Household's Position in the Financial Crisis in Iceland, Central Bank of Iceland, working paper no. 59 (June 2012).

5 Central Bank of Iceland, 'Economy of Iceland', Reykjavik, September 2014, 29.

6 Iceland, 'Report of the Special Investigation Commission', Reykjavik, 2010. See, for example, Carsten Valgreen et al., 'Iceland: Geyser Crisis', Danske Bank, March 21, 2006.

348 billion–393 billion, an amount almost equivalent to the annual worth of taxes paid by Icelanders.[7]

In November 2008, following a steep depreciation of the Icelandic krona, the government introduced capital controls to stabilize the currency and prevent excessive capital outflows. Shortly thereafter, Iceland applied to the International Monetary Fund (IMF) for emergency financial aid and was granted a US$ 2.1 billion loan under a two-year standby programme. The adjustment programme implemented jointly with IMF was rather unorthodox in the light of previous IMF adjustment programmes;[8] it included stabilizing the currency through the introduction of capital controls, rebuilding the banking sector and addressing the public deficit through a combination of tax increases and expenditure cuts, while keeping the country's social protection system largely untouched.

The rebuilding of the banking sector and the protection of core social expenditure from cuts required borrowing by the government. Whereas in 2007, the central government debt was 43 per cent of GDP, it reached 109 per cent of GDP in 2013. The main reasons for the increase of public debt were the shifting of private debt — mainly by banks — into public debt and the depreciation of the krona, as 33 per cent of the central government debt was denominated in foreign currency.[9]

III. SHELTERING THE WELFARE STATE

The emergency legislation approved by parliament in October 2008 and subsequent adjustment policies were based on the principle that socialization of the losses of the banking collapse should be avoided as much as possible. Savings in deposit accounts in Iceland were secured for customers and given preference over other claims, including those by international institutional investors. The debt of many local businesses was written off to a large degree to ensure that economically viable businesses and related workplaces would survive. The devaluation of the Icelandic krona helped export-driven demand, in particular in the fishing industry, and contributed

7 T. Matthiasson and S. Davidsdóttir, 'State Costs of the 2008 Icelandic Financial Collapse', *EconoMonitor*, December 5, 2012, www.economonitor.com/blog/2012/12/state-costs-of-the-2008-icelandic-financial-collapse/.

8 An interesting question is why the IMF decided to do so. It could have been that the IMF truly trusted the Icelandic government to be able to sort the crisis out on its own way, and/or that the IMF was in a rather weak position as it had not many clients at that moment. *See* S. Sigurgeirsdóttir and R. Wade, 'From Control by Capital', 1–31.

9 Central Bank of Iceland, 'Economy of Iceland', 70.

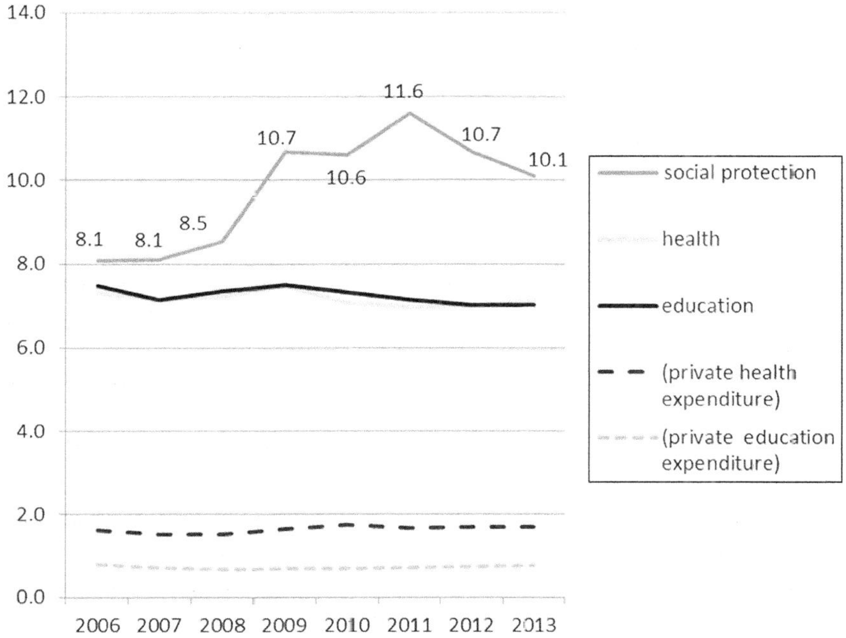

FIGURE 7.1 General government expenditure on social protection, health and education (in percentage of GDP).
Source: Statistics Iceland, general government finances 2013, 23 September 2014.

to a tourism boom. However, workers, in particular those in the construction industry, suffered a heavy blow.[10]

The government elected in 2009 should be commended for sheltering core social expenditure against cuts. While overall government revenues fell as a consequence of the economic crisis, the State made a strategic decision to maintain the percentage of the budget for health care and education, and even increased social protection expenditure from about 8.5 per cent of GDP in 2008 to above 10 per cent of GDP during the first four years after the banking collapse (see Figure 7.1).[11]

Public health expenditure decreased from 7.22 per cent of GDP in 2008 to 6.99 per cent of GDP in 2012, with only a limited shift of health-care costs from public coverage to the pockets of individuals. Private health-care expenditure

[10] This also explains the spike in unemployment amongst Polish men who were heavily employed in this sector.

[11] On how economic, social and cultural right were negatively affected by the crisis, and the governmental measures taken to minimize these effects, see the report A/HRC/28/59/Add.1.

grew by 13 per cent between 2008 and 2012, but remained moderate and, so far, has not exceeded 19.7 per cent (2010) of total health expenditure.

Measured as a percentage of GDP, overall public education expenditure was only moderately reduced, while private expenditure for education increased by about 12 per cent after the banking collapse.

As the economy contracted by about 8 per cent between 2008 and 2010, it should be noted that, in real terms, painful cuts were made to public health services and education. Compared to 2007 expenditure, funds spent in 2013 on public health care and education were 7.2 per cent and 8.3 per cent lower, respectively (see Table 7.1). Most of the cuts in the health sector, however, were made strategically, focusing on decreasing hospital costs, postponing investments in hospital infrastructure and the acquisition of new equipment, and reducing pharmaceutical costs. Outpatient services were largely spared cuts. In the education field, primary schools were hardest hit by cuts, while pre-primary and tertiary education institutions suffered less.

Research conducted so far indicates that the banking collapse had only limited impact on the health of the population. Studies have identified slightly higher stress levels among women, in particular unemployed women, and students with middle levels of income or education. However, the crisis seems to have reduced smoking, heavy drinking, consumption of sugared soft drinks and fast food, and resulted in better sleeping behaviour.[12] And happiness increased by 5 per cent in the adolescent population from 2000 to 2010 despite the economic crisis.[13]

The sharp increase in government spending in 2008, compared to 2007, reflects the cost of recapitalizing the Central Bank of Iceland and the new, downsized domestic branches of Icelandic banks (see Table 7.1, Economic affairs row). By 2013, overall government spending had returned roughly to pre-crisis levels. However, the State had to borrow to cover the costs of the banking collapse, which resulted in the significant increase in public debt service, the main reason for the growth in overall spending on general public services, as debt service is currently responsible for about 60 per cent of the expenditure under this category. In 2013, debt service accounted for

[12] See Christopher MacClure, 'Mental Health and Health Behaviours Following an Economic Collapse. The Case of Iceland', (2014) PhD dissertation, University of Iceland; also Tinna Ásgeirdóttir et al, 'Was the Economic Crisis of 2008 Good for Icelanders? Impact on Health Behaviours', *Economics and Human Biology* 13, (2014): 1–19.

[13] Dora Gudmundsdóttir et al., 'How Does the Economic Crisis Influence Adolescents' Happiness? Population-Based Surveys in Iceland in 2000–2010', *Journal of Happiness Studies* 17, no. 3 (2016): 1219–34.

TABLE 7.1 *Change in general government expenditure (2007–2013), total and selected subcategories (at 2013 prices, in ISK millions)*

	2007	2008	2009	2010	2011	2012	2013	Change (2007–13)
Total expenditure	810,010	1,121,026	915,781	912,646	853,380	838,613	827,904	2.2%
General public services (total)	108,420	127,786	179,940	159,101	150,087	160,229	156,029	30.5%
Executive and legislative organs	7,861	7,842	6,384	6,086	6,159	6,228	6,647	–18.3%
Debt service	49,135	64,477	117,344	93,615	86,682	94,745	92,004	46.6%
Public order, safety and justice	27,264	26,753	29,366	23,491	30,626	26,171	26,619	–2.4%
Economic affairs (total)	112,417	378,653	113,762	125,011	106,683	88,729	88,836	–26.5%
Road, water and air transport	65,434	76,875	56,266	46,147	38,704	39,194	44,032	–48.6%
Housing and community amenities	9,337	10,013	8,938	43,978	6,284	20,243	11,476	18.6%
Social protection (total)	161,812	172,914	201,684	197,055	207,295	194,964	188,973	14.4%
Unemployment	4,490	7,101	30,520	28,901	27,319	22,835	16,792	73.3%
Disability pensions	41,313	45,894	48,690	48,065	52,453	52,000	53,659	23.0%
Old age pensions	42,238	43,404	39,746	37,197	45,973	45,996	47,011	10.2%
Family and children	48,867	49,141	49,809	48,248	43,057	41,614	44,713	–9.3%
Housing	11,477	13,120	17,376	18,568	25,384	19,864	13,414	14.4%
Social exclusion	5,263	6,026	6,994	7,675	7,895	7,711	7,950	33.8%
Health care (total)	150,068	153,860	149,020	138,823	136,834	136,866	140,054	–7.2%
Pharmaceutical products	10,216	12,132	12,762	10,959	10,245	9,268	8,218	–24.3%

(continued)

TABLE 7.1 (*continued*)

	2007	2008	2009	2010	2011	2012	2013	Change (2007–13)
Hospital services	74,900	75,720	72,454	66,014	64,306	65,854	68,208	−9.8%
Nursing and convalescent home services	26,208	25,672	24,135	23,600	24,027	23,464	24,092	−8.8%
General medical services	16,324	16,744	15,521	15,324	15,431	15,384	16,178	−0.9%
Education (total)	155,492	163,192	153,735	147,635	145,244	141,976	143,537	−8.3%
Pre-primary	15,262	16,783	16,174	14,922	15,016	14,265	14,532	−5.0%
Primary	51,488	52,453	48,691	46,658	47,737	44,506	45,594	−12.9%
Secondary	46,654	48,224	45,858	42,693	43,226	43,072	43,266	−7.8%
Tertiary	33,967	37,164	35,024	35,027	31,577	32,095	31,986	−6.2%

Source: Statistics Iceland, general government total expenditure by functions, 1998–2013.

11.1 per cent of all State expenditure, which meant that, compared to the pre-crisis years, fewer funds were available to cover other public costs.

Spending on public order, safety and justice was reduced only slightly (by 2.4 per cent), while cuts were strongest in the area of road, water and air transportation infrastructure (by 48.6 per cent). It should be noted that the executive and legislative branches also made efforts to save costs.

Social protection spending peaked during the period from 2009 to 2012 when Iceland witnessed historically unprecedented rates of unemployment. Funds for rental subsidies and to combat social exclusion were also augmented. Government spending on disability pensions grew, owing to the increase in beneficiaries.[14] Public expenditure on old age pensions also registered an upward trend after 2011. Only spending on family and child benefits was reduced as stricter income-based eligibility criteria for accessing benefits were imposed.

While unemployment in Iceland increased to about 10 per cent in 2009 and 2010 (this meant a tenfold increase in the country), it never reached the unprecedented levels seen in other European countries trapped in a debt crisis. Active labour market programmes, training and the opening up of secondary schools and universities to unemployed persons prevented a much larger part of the population from ending up out of work or without training. The policies were largely successful, with the number of long-term unemployed dropping from about 2,500 persons in 2012 to around 1,000 job seekers by the end of 2014.

The government provided assistance to companies to keep their staff, with reduced working hours and subsidized salaries. Social partners agreed on wage restraint to safeguard employment in the aftermath of the crisis, but decided to increase the minimum wage to protect low-income workers. Instead of shortening the duration of unemployment benefits, the government temporarily extended unemployment benefits to a maximum duration of four years, preventing a much larger proportion of the unemployed from having to depend on social security benefits as a last resort.

It was not only the smart and more targeted use of funds that ensured that core social and economic rights remained protected, but also the willingness of society — in particular the overwhelmingly female workforce in the health and education sectors — to work unpaid overtime, accept a salary freeze and use resources more efficiently. As the Working Group on the issue of

[14] There was not a sudden increase in disabled persons owing to the crisis (though perhaps a slight increase in stress-related mental health issues). Yet, disabled people perhaps found it harder to get work or stay in work and so were referred to disability pensions rather than unemployment benefits.

discrimination against women in law and practice stressed in 2014, such gender imbalances caused by the financial crisis in Iceland need to be corrected.[15]

Welfare Watch, one of the new innovative bodies formed in early 2009, is an independent consultative body, comprising more than 35 representatives of key ministries, municipalities, social partners and civil society, many of whom are also working at the grass-roots level. Welfare Watch was established to monitor the social impact of the crisis, provide advice to State institutions and coordinate targeted interventions on the ground. It managed to spread the message that, during the crisis, the weakest in society should be protected. The watchdog submitted several reports with recommendations to the government, as well as one to the parliament.

In 2015, it put forward additional recommendations on how to address and guarantee the rights of persons suffering multiple forms of deprivation. They included more specific and fair support to low-income families with children; review of minimum living standard payments to ensure that payments to individuals, families and families with children in need of social financial support are high enough; secure housing for everyone, especially long-term housing for families with children;[16] and ensure that low income families and those who live in poverty should be able to make use of the social services available to them, among other initiatives.[17]

IV. OTHER UNIQUE ICELANDIC RESPONSES TO THE CRISIS

IV.A. *Taxation and the Distribution of Losses*

Iceland's adjustment programme strongly emphasized increasing revenue generation through taxation, while focusing to a lesser extent on public expenditure cuts. The reintroduction of a progressive income tax system helped to shelter the most vulnerable groups from the effects of the crisis. In addition, the flat tax on capital income was increased and a wealth tax was temporarily introduced to generate revenue. The only regressive tax measure was a 1 per cent increase in the value added tax, from 24.5 to 25.5 per cent. On the whole, social benefits were directed to lower-income households, mainly by cutting maternal and

[15] See A/HRC/26/39/Add.1, September 16, 2014.

[16] The government has already adopted a legislation to the effect of ensuring more availability of social housing, higher rent benefits to low income families and more equal footing between tenants and homeowners.

[17] Welfare Watch, 'Skýrsla Velferðarvaktarinnar Tillögur um aðgerðir til að vinna bug á fátækt' (Reykjavík, 2015), www.velferdarraduneyti.is/media/rit-og-skyrslur-2015/Skyrsla_Velferdarvaktar_Jan2015.pdf.

parental leave entitlements.[18] Disposable income fell across the entire society. The poorest 20 per cent of the population in Iceland lost around 9 per cent of their disposable income between 2008 and 2010. In contrast, 10 per cent of the wealthiest households that had accumulated assets during the boom years of the bubble economy seem to have lost 38 per cent of their income – it would be interesting to see to what extent these assets flew to tax heavens.[19] Social transfers and taxation policies reduced inequality in Iceland significantly. This is against what usually happens in financial and debt crises.[20] They also helped to stabilize internal demand, as the citizens with lower incomes spent a much higher percentage of their funds on goods and services.[21]

IV.B. *Targeted Debt Relief*

The cost of servicing loans shot up for both companies and households; so did arrears. The government passed in 2009 a comprehensive debt relief programme which provided standardized and objective thresholds to apply for. Mortgages in excess of 110 per cent of fair value of a house were written down – yet some *caveats* remained regarding income wealth. If a family was not able to repay a loan of 110 per cent of fair value, to change to a cheaper house was ultimately possible. Finally, a fresh start was facilitated by legally establishing that claims against bankrupt individuals expire two years after bankruptcy (instead of four years).[22]

There was also a debt relief programme for businesses. Firms had their debts written down to the present value of expected cash flow or the fair value of physical assets. These write-offs, aimed at cleaning out unviable firms and adjusting the balance sheets of viable ones, contributed to rebuild trust and contain unemployment.[23]

[18] This also had a gender impact, as women started taking more of the shared leave and some men did not even take their full untransferable allowance.

[19] S. Erlanger, S. Castle and R. Gladstone, 'Iceland's Prime Minister Steps Down Amid Panama Papers Scandal', *New York Times*, April 5, 2016, www.nytimes.com/2016/04/06/world/europe/panama-papers-iceland.html?_r=0.

[20] See the report A/HRC/31/60, January 12, 2016.

[21] *See* S. Ólafsson, 'The Icelandic Way Out of the Crisis: Welfarism, Redistribution and Austerity', Social Research Centre, University of Iceland, working paper no. 1 (2012); and B. Martorano, 'Is It Possible to Adjust "with a Human Face"? Differences in Fiscal Consolidation Strategies between Hungary and Iceland', UNICEF, Office of Research working paper WP-2014-No. 03 (May 2014).

[22] *See* T. Matthiasson and S. Davidsdottir, 'Five Years on: Myths and Lessons from Post-Collapse Iceland – and the Eurozone Debt Crisis Seen from the North', Institute of Economic Studies, W13:09, University of Iceland, 2013.

[23] T. Matthiasson, 'The Icelandic Response to the Collapse of the Financial Sector in October 2008', Institute of Economic Studies, W13:01, University of Iceland, 2013.

In June 2010 the Supreme Court ruled that foreign currency indexed loans that were offered by Icelandic banks to many clients for buying vehicles and houses were illegal, violating laws designed to protect borrowers from exchange rate risks. This reduced debts further.

IV.C. *Special Investigative Commission of the Parliament*

In December 2008, the Icelandic parliament set up a Special Investigation Commission to investigate and analyse the processes leading to the collapse of the three main commercial banks. The Commission was co-chaired by a supreme court judge, the parliamentary ombudsman and an academic expert. The Commission submitted a detailed report to parliament in April 2012 in which it outlined the responsibilities of entities and individuals, including bankers, politicians and governmental officials in charge of supervising the financial and monetary systems. From December 2009 to September 2010, a Parliamentary Review Committee scrutinized the report.

On 28 September 2010, the parliament unanimously adopted a resolution providing for the review of existing legislation, including the Constitution of the Republic of Iceland, Act No. 4/1963 on Ministerial Responsibility, and legislation relating to financial markets and their operations. Yet, although some of the previously mentioned legislation has already been reviewed and revised, to date, many of the laws have not yet been amended in order to prevent the recurrence of a similar crisis.

On 28 September 2010, parliament also adopted a resolution to initiate legal proceedings against former Prime Minister Geir Haarde, before the High Court of Impeachment. Resolutions against three other ministers failed to receive a sufficient majority in parliament and therefore they could not be examined by the High Court of Impeachment. The former prime minister was cleared by the High Court of most of the charges, but sentenced for failing to call emergency meetings, as provided for under the Constitution. He has appealed to the European Court of Human Rights where his case is still under consideration.

IV.D. *Reform of Banking Supervision*

The Special Investigative Commission also noted the failure of supervisory authorities to foresee the crisis. In its report, it concluded that the Financial Supervisory Authority (FME), the institution that bore the main responsibility for monitoring the activities of the banks, had not grown in proportion to the banks, and its practices had not kept up with the rapid change in banking practices. Failings of FME included insufficient expertise to carry out its statutory supervisory tasks, as well as a lack of assertiveness when it discovered that regulated entities did not comply with applicable laws or regulations. In response to violations of the law, only written comments were provided to the relevant financial corporations; the issues were not examined through the proper legal channels, nor did the authorities try, in a decisive way, to prevent the collapse and to reduce the size of the balance sheets of Icelandic banks, after 2006. The Special Investigative Commission also detailed the failure of the Board of Governors of the Central Bank of Iceland and the Ministers responsible to inform each other appropriately or to act adequately on information indicating that urgent action was required. It concluded that, in addition to the former Prime Minister, the Ministers of Finance and Business Affairs, the Director General of FME and three Governors of the Central Bank had shown negligence.[24] In addition, FME staff were frequently recruited from their supervisory functions directly into more lucrative jobs in financial institutions whose operations they were previously required to supervise, thereby undermining the ability of FME to perform its functions.

In the aftermath of the crash, the government implemented a range of reforms aimed at enhancing the supervisory capacities of FME.[25] FME also assisted in the investigation of 205 cases relating to alleged violations prior to the 2008 banking collapse, referring 103 cases of bankers to the Office of the Special Prosecutor for further action.[26]

Iceland should implement the recently passed European banking legislation in order to further strengthen the system of banking supervision.[27] The Financial Stability Council, composed of representatives of the Ministry of Finance, the Central Bank and FME, seeks to adequately monitor the macro-financial situation of the country in order to make timely decisions. As the Parliament played a crucial role in identifying the causes of the financial

[24] Iceland, Report of the Special Investigative Commission, 'Causes of the Collapse of the Icelandic Banks – Responsibility, Mistakes and Negligence', chapter 21, (Reykjavik, 2010), www.rna.is/media/skjol/RNAvefurKafli21Enska.pdf.

[25] See, for example, 'Future Structure of the Icelandic Financial System', report of the Minister of the Economy to the Althingi (March 2012), 63–77, 101–02.

[26] Iceland, Annual Report of the Financial Supervisory Authority (FME) 2013 (Reykjavik, 2013), 9.

[27] On the preparatory work being undertaking by the financial Icelandic authorities for the transposition of European Union regulations and directives into national laws and regulations, Acts that will be transposed into Icelandic law include Regulation (EU) No. 236/2012 on short selling, Regulation (EU) No. 648/2012 on OTC derivatives (EMIR), Regulation (EU) No. 596/2014 on market abuse (MAR), Directive 2014/65/EU and Regulation (EU) No 600/2014 on markets in financial instruments (MiFID2/MiFIR) and Regulation (EU) No. 909/2014 on central securities depositories (CSDR). *See* 'Annual Report of the Financial Supervisory Authority 2015', (Reykjavik, 2015), 16–18.

crisis, one would think that it should play a role in the Financial Stability Council, either by including a parliamentary representative on the Council or by ensuring citizens' oversight of the Council through a parliamentary committee.

IV.E. *Office of the Special Prosecutor*

The capacity of the judicial system to scrutinize criminal financial and economic conduct was inadequate in comparison to the size of Iceland's international banking operations. Parliament passed Act No. 135/2008 establishing the Office of the Special Prosecutor to investigate alleged criminal conduct, before and during the banking collapse, relating to the financial undertakings of the Icelandic financial institutions, including the activities of their owners. Since 2011, the Office has also been tasked with investigating economic crimes and tax evasion. The Office deals with complex cases, involving many suspects, witnesses and a huge amount of documentation relating to alleged fraud, embezzlement, market manipulation and insider trading. In 2012, it had up to 110 staff supporting its investigations; staffing and funds have been reduced since then. As of 1 December 2014, 184 cases relating to the banking collapse had been investigated by the Special Prosecutor, including 27 cases, involving 62 individuals, prosecuted by district or higher courts, six cases ruled on by the Supreme Court and 35 cases still under investigation.

The efforts of the Special Prosecutor to combat impunity for economic crimes and ensure justice in relation to alleged criminal conduct before and during the banking collapse is commendable and will hopefully promote law-abiding behaviour in the financial sector. However, individuals who have been under investigation, and the lawyers representing them, expressed concerns, including about telephone tapping of privileged telephone conversations between suspects and their lawyers.[28]

IV.F. *Participation of Citizens and Accountability*

In the aftermath of the banking collapse, Icelandic citizens took to the streets and protested in front of the Parliament building. The government resigned and parliamentary elections were held in early 2009, which brought a new coalition to power until April 2013. Many citizens had, however, lost

[28] *See* J. Sigurdsson and D. Juliusson, 'Hriktir i studum rettarrikis?', *Timarit lögfraedinga* 64, no. 2, (2014): 105–68.

trust in the established political and public institutions and new forms of citizens' participation emerged.

For the first time in Icelandic history, referenda were held on the question as to whether and to what extent the government should pay back deposits by foreigners in Icesave, a branch of the former Landsbanki. As most of the concerned savers in the United Kingdom and the Netherlands were covered by national banking guarantees, individuals residing in those countries were protected up to their national guarantees from losing all their deposits, which indeed led to a harsh legal and diplomatic battle of these two countries against Iceland.

After the banking crash, there was a huge turnover in senior management at the Financial Supervisory Authority and the Central Bank of Iceland, to a large degree through resignations. However, there appear to have been hardly any sanctions in relation to any criminal or non-criminal aspects of negligent behaviour on the part of officials. Administrative, civil or criminal sanctions against government officials appear to have been limited to the trial of the former Prime Minister and one government official who was accused of insider trading. While the efforts to hold bankers accountable are remarkable in the light of modern financial history, a comprehensive attempt to ensure accountability in the public sector appears to be lacking. Furthermore, there are no regulations prohibiting high-level civil servants or Members of Parliament from being immediately re-employed in certain positions in the private sector. Post-employment restrictions have been repeatedly recommended in Council of Europe evaluation reports.[29]

In 2012, the Council of Europe identified shortcomings in relation to the independence and impartiality of the judiciary in Iceland.[30] The system for appointing judges could be further strengthened to ensure absolute independence of the judicial branch from executive influence. A more sophisticated domestic legal framework, establishing the duty of public officials to protect the public interest and outlining the consequences of breaches of that duty would contribute to creating the right incentives for ensuring public accountability.

[29] Council of Europe, Second Evaluation Round, Addendum to the Compliance Report on Iceland (Greco RC-II (2006) 10 E Addendum), February, 19 2009, paras. 14–18; and Council of Europe, Fourth Evaluation Round, Corruption prevention in respect to members of parliament, judges and prosecutors, Evaluation Report – Iceland (Greco Eval IV Rep (2012) 8E), March 22, 2013, paras. 59 and 60.

[30] Council of Europe, Fourth Evaluation Round, paras. 74, 75, 83, 84, 94 and 160.

V. LESSONS LEARNED

V.A. *Good (and Also Some Bad) Practices*

Several good practices can be identified. First, the government tried to reduce the negative impact of the banking collapse on its citizens by sheltering their deposits; restructuring and dividing the failed banks into smaller entities to serve the local citizens and economy; introducing capital controls, as needed; and debt relief for companies and private households (which promoted growth and sustained economic activity without putting at risk the balance sheets of the financial sector),[31] including the establishment of a Debtors' Ombudsman.

The government also responded to the financial and economic crisis by sheltering vulnerable groups through expanding social protection spending, promoting temporary part-time work, formulating active labour market policies[32] and granting a temporary expansion of entitlement to unemployment benefits; instead of implementing front-loaded austerity measures – which would have worsened the crisis – adjustment policies focused on increasing government revenue through the reintroduction of progressive income taxation, a wealth tax and higher corporate taxes. Yet, the renters were much worse off, not least because the owners of the houses they rented upped the rent to cover mortgage payments.

Although practically every citizen suffered losses, the cost of the collapse was distributed in an overwhelmingly fair manner, with stronger protection for low-income groups, while the wealthy, who are not at risk of falling below the minimum levels of enjoyment of social and economic rights, experienced a much higher drop in their disposable income.[33] Inequality within Icelandic society decreased. While unemployment rose, it never reached the catastrophic levels experienced by other European countries affected by financial crises.[34] Iceland reduced poverty among the elderly and, more particularly, among elderly women, by increasing the government-guaranteed minimum pension.

[31] Matthiasson and Davidsdottir, 'Five Years On', 13.

[32] This has been a great advantage of the Icelandic economy when it comes to adjusting to economic recessions, i.e. the fact that Icelandic workforce is considered to be very flexible.

[33] This higher drop in disposable income was due to a number of causes: tax and benefits policies, losses of the value of financial assets and reduced dividend payments, and bonuses and compensation schemes in banks and financial firms removed after the crisis in 2008.

[34] It must be said that a high number of foreign workers left. There was also a leap in emigration of Icelanders, specially in health services, to some European countries.

Welfare Watch is worth mentioning as an innovative response to the financial crisis. The watchdog can be credited for having improved collaboration between government departments, local authorities and civil society in tackling the social impact of the crisis and for enhancing citizens' participation. Its work resulted in improved social monitoring and targeted interventions by the authorities and welfare organizations. Welfare Watch also helped to spread the message to the public authorities and society at large that nobody should be left behind as a consequence of the banking collapse.

Iceland should also be credited for initiating a comprehensive analysis and official acknowledgment of the causes of the banking collapse by the Special Investigation Commission, which was established by the Parliament. In addition, serious efforts were made to combat impunity for economic crimes in the financial sector through the establishment of the Office of the Special Prosecutor.

In terms of bad practices from which it is also possible to learn lessons, the banking collapse helped raise public awareness about whatever might constitute signs of public misbehaviour, and stressed the importance of democratic accountability and legal accountability. Yet, though the effort to hold bankers accountable is something remarkable, there has been an extremely low degree of accountability of those governmental officials in charge of supervising the banking industry. This may help in understanding the continuously growing use of offshore accounts in tax havens in Iceland and the resignation of the Prime Minister in 2015 when a scandal broke after the Panama papers revealed that he and his wealthy wife had set up a company in the British Virgin Islands.[35]

As explained in Section III, the public order, safety and justice sectors were barely affected by cuts. This shows, also in the case of Iceland, that there is in practice an implicit and disturbing hierarchy of human rights – to the detriment of economic and social rights – when implementing austerity measures.

V.B. *Can the Icelandic Experience Be Useful in Other Contexts?*

In order to assess whether the lessons learned in Iceland could be fruitful for other countries, first of all, certain particularities should be considered. Before the banking crisis, Iceland enjoyed, in comparison with other countries, particularly high levels of realization of social and economic rights. The country ranked very high on the Human Development Index, had one

[35] Erlanger, Castle and Gladstone, 'Iceland's Prime Minister Steps Down'.

of the lowest infant mortality rates in the world, enjoyed unemployment levels below 2 per cent and had a high degree of gender equality, despite persistent pay gaps.

The government of a country similar to Iceland may find it easier to respond in a human rights–compliant manner to an economic shock when it can still depend on significant revenues, a modern infrastructure and well-equipped, mostly functioning public institutions with well-trained officials.

Iceland was able to rely on its social welfare system, which proved largely capable of absorbing the shock of the economic crash. Before the crisis, a social security benefit of last resort was already in place to guarantee some basic protection to all. Iceland also had a guaranteed minimum old-age pension and other social benefits that could be adjusted to respond to the crisis. The Icelandic experience underlines the critical role that a comprehensive social security net can play in protecting economic, social and cultural rights in the event of an economic downturn.

The economic crisis was largely rooted in one sector, which helped the response. Furthermore, Iceland had a track record of responsible public debt management and was therefore able to take on new debt to recapitalize its Central Bank, downsize its financial institutions and expand its social spending in response to the crisis. Instead of Iceland engaging in a policy of internal devaluation, the sharp fall of the krona helped the country to come out of the economic crisis through export-driven demand and a tourist boom.

With a population of 320,000, the country is small, with strong interconnections. It has an active civil society, well-rooted democratic traditions, a high degree of trade union organization, a long tradition of collective bargaining and conflict resolution through dialogue and compromise and a public administration that is overwhelmingly willing and competent to respond to its citizens' needs. In response to public discontent after the banking crisis, the government resigned, which opened the way for early elections, and referenda were held to allow citizens to express their views on certain decisions. There was increased dialogue with and among citizens.

Of course, countries with fewer resources and/or with part of the population not being covered by social security nets (even during boom years) will find it more difficult to follow the Icelandic path. Yet, this case shows that there are always policy choices on how to advance economic decisions in line with human rights law. There are human rights duties that must be respected even during crisis times: measures need to be justified, be proportionate, be applied in a non-discriminative manner and should include fiscal measures that mitigate inequalities, including through progressive taxation and fighting tax avoidance and evasion. And they should only be introduced after the most careful consideration of all other less restrictive alternatives; and participation of those affected must be ensured.[36]

Despite the particularities outlined earlier, bigger and less developed countries with more complex problems can learn from the policy responses of the government of Iceland and cherish the value of having a social security net in place to ensure a basic protection floor for all. Of course, those countries must adopt and adjust solutions to meet their particular needs and circumstances.

Accountability and transparency are two principles that make the public discussion around the crisis more informed, robust and democratic. Their implementation does not depend on resource availability but on political will.

International financial institutions can also learn from the successful implementation of the adjustment programme in Iceland, which included capital controls, sheltering the social welfare system from cuts and a strong focus on revenue generation and redistribution through taxation policies. The efforts of the IMF to consult extensively with public institutions and interest groups, including extra-Parliamentary groups, improved the design and public acceptance of programmes. However, economic, social and cultural rights failed to feature more explicitly in the agreed adjustment programme.[37]

VI. CONCLUDING REMARKS

Iceland managed the financial crisis better than many other countries and responded overwhelmingly in compliance with its international human rights obligations, yet particularly the most vulnerable were hit stronger by the crisis. Although certain gaps still need to be addressed,[38] this chapter has rather focused on good practices that might be useful for other countries.

[36] See letter dated May 16, 2012, from the Chair of the Committee on Economic, Social and Cultural Rights addressed to States parties to the International Covenant on Economic, Social and Cultural Rights (ICESCR); and more recently the Statement by the Committee on Economic, Social and Cultural Rights on Committee on Economic, Social and Cultural Rights Public Debt, Austerity Measures and the (ICESCR), June 24, 2016.

[37] *See* H.O. Ágústsson and R.L. Johnstone, 'Practising What They Preach: Did the IMF and Iceland Exercise Good Governance in Their Relations 2008–2011?', *Nordicum-Mediterraneum* 8, no. 1 (2013), http://nome.unak.is/wordpress/08–1/c48-article/practicing-what-they-preach-did-the-imf-and-iceland-exercise-good-governance-in-their-relations-2008–2011/

[38] Of particular concern has been access to affordable and appropriate housing with secure legal tenure for the less affluent, especially given the fact that many homeowners have lost their own homes, and have entered the rental market. In particular young persons with children have found it difficult to find affordable accommodation, more in the report A/HRC/28/59/Add.1. *See* also R. Johnstone, 'Myths and Legends of Contemporary Iceland', (2014) VII Annuaire International des droits de l'Homme, LGDJ, 2014, 473.

The largely human rights–compliant response to the financial crisis was not only an outcome of conscious policy decisions, but was also a reflection of the responsible behaviour of social partners, a vibrant civil society, committed and competent civil servants and individuals engaged in their communities and working towards the common good. It seems that the idea that development is not only about shared growth but also about shared losses in society[39] inspired some of these policies.

International organizations and countries facing similar situations can learn from the particular path chosen by Iceland, which included protecting its core social welfare system, meaningful debt relief, efforts to ensure citizens' participation in the decision-making process and endeavours to establish political, administrative and judicial accountability.

39 A. Sen, *Development as Freedom*, (Oxford: Oxford University Press, 1999).

8

Indonesia's 1997–1998 Economic Crisis

A Teachable Case Wasted

MANUEL F. MONTES

ABSTRACT

The 1990s Asian financial crisis swept through the economies that had been built reputations as being successful globalizers. Thus, it would have been very difficult to make the case that the crisis could only be attributed to domestic shortcomings and policy mistakes. Nevertheless, the dominant narrative of the crisis expressed by Western observers, which became the basis of policy reform programmes for debt distressed countries, left external factors blameless and assigned the primary responsibility to national explanations. Indonesia experienced the greatest economic reversals from the crisis. The political dislocation included the fall of the long-ensconced authoritarian Suharto regime. In leaving external factors blameless, the crisis response programme became obsessed with domestic governance failings and untimely deregulation and liberalization reforms, distracting attention from the causes that could have been remedied by immediately effective policy actions. A swift and thoroughgoing banking sector reform behind a wall provided by capital controls would have been a proper response, but the former was considered too late and the latter was never even a gleam in the eyes of policy authorities. Indonesia's subsequent recovery, as in the case of neighbouring East Asian countries, owed much more to the rapid deterioration of investor sentiment in other regions, beginning with the Russian payments crisis of August 1998 which halted the haemorrhaging of hot money flows out of the region.

I. INTRODUCTION

The widespread economic distress from the Asian currency and financial crisis triggered by the devaluation of the Thai baht on 2 July 1997 shook the foundations of global economic governance. But these foundations, and the dominant political interests buttressing them, stood firm enough to withstand the intense reform proposals the grave crisis generated. At the start of the crisis, few observers expected the economic debacle and political upheaval that engulfed Indonesia in 1997–98. When it became the turn of the eurozone countries to experience the same rigors in the wake of the 2007–08 North Atlantic economic crisis, many lessons from the Indonesian experience could have been applied to avoid or mitigate European distress. Indonesia's experience was the rehearsal for many of the events and policy choices in the eurozone crisis, taking the sad song of Indonesia's experience and making it better – by making it sadder still.

This chapter presents an analysis of Indonesia's 1997–98 economic crisis. Because the Indonesian and the East Asian crises elicited numerous accounts, including by this author,[1] this analysis will be an interpretation-with-hindsight of those studies.

The axis of the debate sparked by the Indonesian (and the East Asian) crisis has revolved around whether its causes and policy solutions should be assigned to the domestic sphere or to international institutions and policies. With hindsight, both arenas played a key role in the crisis, and it is quite important to accurately define these roles – and how they impelled or interacted with the other sphere.

With hindsight it is, for example, possible to say that domestic lessons from the Indonesian crisis were ignored in the practice of financial liberalization in the United States and Europe in the lead-up to the subprime crisis of 2007–08 and the ensuing financial adversities in European credit markets. But in the case of Indonesia in particular and developing countries in general, private hazards, treacherous rules and domineering political and economic interests, which preclude many policy choices, located in the international sphere have proved decisive. In the context of potentially harsh external environments, analyses[2] that emphasize domestic sources take the risk of forgetting that

[1] M.F. Montes 'Private Deficits and Public Responsibilities: Philippine Responses to Capital Inflows,' (1997) in *Papers and Proceedings of the International Symposium on Macroeconomic Interdependence in the Asia-Pacific Region* (Economic Research Institute, Economic Planning Agency, Government of Japan), March 1997, 409–60; M.F. Montes, *The Currency Crisis in Southeast Asia Updated Edition* (Singapore: Institute of Southeast Asian Studies, 1998); and M.A. Abdusalamov and M.F. Montes 'Indonesia: Reaping the Market' (1999) in *Tigers in Trouble: Financial Governance, Liberalisation and Crises in East Asia*, ed. K.S. Jomo (London: Zed Books Ltd., 1998).

[2] Such as that elaborated in G. Corsetti, P. Pesenti and N. Roubini 'What Caused the Asian Currency and Financial Crisis?,' *Japan and the World Economy*, 11 (1999): 305–73.

domestic contexts everywhere, even in developed countries, have their own political and economic failings. However, developed countries have the advantage of a greater scale of resources and policy power (including the capacity to suspend the rules) to overcome adverse external shocks.

Under this eclectic view, reforms would be required both in domestic and international policy. Indonesia and other East Asian countries undertook significant domestic reforms (including those not relevant to the problem at hand) but the track record of reform is not as positive on the international side. This chapter seeks to contribute to understanding the tortured and frustrating manner by which learning takes place (or does not take place) in setting the international rules and financial governance from debt crisis episodes.

The next section, the second, provides a condensed narrative of events in the Indonesian crisis. The third section discusses two key analytical components of crisis responses – the financial sector collapse and austerity. The final section is on lessons learned and not learned from the Indonesian crisis.

II. BRIEF NARRATIVE OF EVENTS

On 14 August 1997, after weeks of speculative selling, Indonesia uncoupled the rupiah from its dollar peg and allowed it to float. Figure 8.1 traces the dramatic fall in the value of the rupiah. By October the rupiah had dropped from \$1 = Rp 2,400 in early August to \$1 = Rp 4,000, and the Jakarta stock market index had fallen by almost 30 per cent, from just over 700 to under 500. With its end-1996 \$18 billion reserve declining quickly and no end in sight, the government invited the IMF in September to begin negotiating a precautionary facility.[3] In October the negotiations started on a regular programme as conditions continued to deteriorate.

On 31 October, a \$37 billion financial support programme with the IMF joined by the World Bank and the Asian Development Bank was announced. After initially strengthening, rupiah selling restarted at a faster pace, through the open capital account through which portfolio-motivated funds had rushed into Indonesia in the previous four years. These channels also provided the facilities for selling the rupiah short. Portfolio investors tested their scepticism in the market over the ability of President Suharto's government to fulfil the IMF programme, which became the main indicator of public policy and economic

[3] See p. 47 in J.S. Djiwandono 'Ten Years after the Asian Crisis: An Indonesian Insider's View,' in *Ten Years After: Revisiting the Asian Financial Crisis*, ed. B. Mucchala, (Washington, DC: Woodrow Wilson International Center for Scholars, Asia Program, 2007), 39–52.

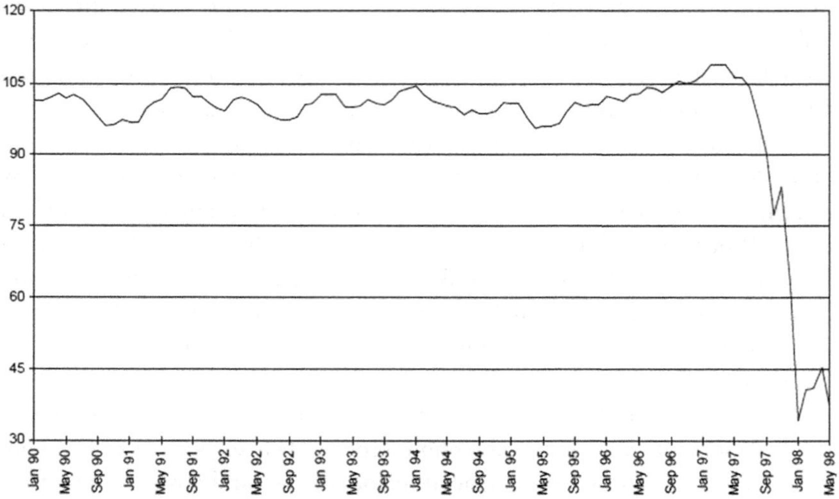

FIGURE 8.1 Real Effective Exchange Rate Index, January 1990–May 1998 (1990 = 100).
Source: Nasution, 2000, Figure 2.

prospects. Thus began the saga of the series of seven memoranda[4] of economic and financial policies in 1998 – dated 15 January,[5] 10 April, 24 June, 29 July, 11 September, 19 September, 19 October, 13 November – as the government and IMF sought to play catch-up with negative portfolio sentiments in the currency markets by tinkering with agreed targets and conditionalities.

A prior action commitment of the 31 October IMF programme saw the closure of 16 banks. It was an attempt to send the signal to portfolio investors that Indonesia would address its banking sector problems faster than Thailand. The immediate material impact was a credit crunch as the then governor of the Bank Indonesia ('BI,' the Indonesian central bank) describes it: 'the bank closures did not just fail to bring back market confidence, they actually instigated bank runs and brought the entire banking sector near total dissolution.'[6] Market sentiment turned more negative after an announcement that

4 Partly in parallel to changes in the national leadership, in 1999, three more memoranda were signed: 16 March, 14 May, 22 July; there were four memoranda in 2000: 20 January, 17 May, 31 July and 7 September; two in 2001; and three in 2002.

5 The 15 January programme with the initial list of structural reform obligations was signed in public by President Suharto with managing director Michel Camdessus pictured to his right with his hands akimbo in approval. Because of the rapid deterioration of conditions, ironically this programme was never brought up for approval by the IMF Executive Board.

6 Djiwandono, 'Ten Years after the Asian Crisis.'

no further banks would be closed, apparently at the behest of the president.[7] This announcement implied the loss of monetary control if the central bank needed to continue to bail out other banks.

In December, the US credit rating agency Moody's downgraded Indonesia's credit rating to junk bond status. In January 1998, Hong Kong-based Peregrine Investments, Asia's largest private investment bank with a large portfolio of loans to Indonesia, filed for bankruptcy. As the economy and exchange rate continued to collapse and the number of non-performing loans in banks' balance sheets began to soar, the ability of the domestic private sector to service its external liabilities in a situation in which hot money stopped flowing inward came into question.

Driven by the judgement of portfolio investors of the 15 January programme, the value of the rupiah plunged to $1 = Rp 10,000 by end-January from $1 = Rp 5,005 at end-December 1997. With the removal of state subsidies, prices of basic food staples surged by as much as 80 per cent. The re-election of President Suharto in March was the occasion for a new memorandum in April,[8] but did not restore confidence in the currency markets. This memorandum contained seven appendices, detailing obligations on monetary and interest rate policies; budgetary support for vulnerable groups; enterprise reform and privatization; 'structural reform'; corporate debt restructuring; bankruptcy and judicial reforms; and an appendix ominously labelled 'MATRIX' that summarized in 117 rows the promised policy reforms, target dates and status. In 1998, the content of IMF programmes were confidential and not officially published, though they could be surreptitiously shared. The word 'matrix' became the talisman of Indonesian economic policy discussions and the country's prospects for economic recovery.

Many of the structural reforms resonated with those accepted by debt-distressed eurozone countries. For Indonesia, these reform obligations, many already included in the January programme, were spelled out in great detail, including:

- Eliminating the administrative retail price for cement
- Expanding medium-term tariff reductions to include chemical and metal products and from 1 January 1999 on steel imports with a medium term target of a maximum 10 per cent tariff on all chemical and metal products

7 *See* IEO-IMF (Independent Evaluation Office of the International Monetary Fund), 'The IMF and Recent Capital Account Crises: Indonesia, Korea, Brazil,' Washington DC: International Monetary Fund, 2003, 14.

8 IMF, 'Indonesia – Supplementary Memorandum of Economic and Financial Policies,' Jakarta, April 10, 1998.

- Eliminating all restrictions on foreign investment in retail trade, wholesale trade and investment in palm oil plantations
- Abolishing the monopoly of the state trading agency, BULOG, over the importation and distribution of essential food items so that it now faces private sector competition
- Eliminating export taxes on a wide range of products – including leather, cork, ores and waste aluminium products – and, for environmentally sensitive products, substituting 'resource rent taxes' for export taxes
- Eliminating all other types of export restrictions, such as quotas, by the end of three years, except for health and security reasons, as well as time-bound, temporary measures introduced in the event of occasional domestic shortages
- Abolishing all import restrictions on new and used ships

These bullets exemplify the lengthy and detailed nature of the government's obligations. In the midst of popular protests, political contestation and the flight of capital of ethnic Chinese business families frightened by the revolutionary situation, these reforms amounted to trying to fix Indonesia's engine of growth while in mid-air and an abiding faith in the development efficacy of ramping up liberalization-privatization-deregulation development strategies in any circumstance. A technocratic coterie, an important subsection of the country's elite with Western educations and strong international links, played an active role in supporting these reform items even before the onset of the crisis. This group could not evaluate objectively the practical feasibility of these reforms[9] in 1998. IMF staff saw the onset of the crisis as 'an opportunity to assist the reformist economic team in carrying out financial sector reform and deregulation,'[10] which had been identified as priorities in IMF evaluation reports.

The justification for including extensive structural conditionality was reportedly[11] the perceived necessity to 'restore confidence,' presumably with investors. In its analysis,[12] the IMF's Independent Evaluation Office called the extensive structural agenda 'ill advised,' in retrospect, and instead advised future programmes 'to concentrate on macro-critical' areas. Further, the report presented the lesson that '[T]he crisis should not be used as an opportunity to seek a long agenda of reforms with detailed timetables just because leverage is high, even though such reforms may be beneficial to long-run economic efficiency.'[13]

[9] *See* IEO-IMF, 'The IMF and Recent Capital Account Crises.' On page 77 of the report, the independent evaluation office report cites a speech by Boediono (2001) that takes the position that government capability was not a binding constraint in implementing the reforms.
[10] Ibid., 13. [11] Ibid., 42. [12] Ibid. [13] Ibid., 50.

This lesson appears to be unlearned, based on many structural elements of the eurozone adjustment programmes after 2010.[14]

In Indonesia in 1998, as well understood by portfolio currency traders, the detailed and elaborate programme could not have been implemented even by a sincerely reformist government within the programme time frame. Moreover, the government had been forced to agree to the list whose elements were targeted at reducing the privileges of the supporters of the Suharto regime.

How did IMF staff learn to impose trade conditionalities? The long lists appear to have been grabbed off the shelf of the Jakarta office[15] of the World Bank, with World Bank staff taking a lead role in the drafting of the structural conditionalities[16] of the programme.

The IMF evaluation report[17] interprets Mr Suharto's last period as president as a case of non-implementation of, if not outright resistance to, programme obligations. After losing the support of his parliamentary allies in the wake of public unrest and riots, Mr Suharto resigned on May 21 after 31 years in power. In accordance with the constitution, Vice President B.J. Habibie became president. Mr Habibie, a 'protégé of Mr Suharto' had 'no political base' and a 'reputation as a big spender.'[18] Mr Habibie would serve as president until 20 October 1999, overseeing the rest of the crisis period. The April programme had already begun to relax fiscal austerity ceilings. The June programme restored food and fuel subsidies. On 23 September 1998, the Paris Club agreed to reschedule $4.2 billion of sovereign debt.

Private investment collapsed by 33 per cent in 1998, quite at variance with the IMF programme projection of less than one percentage point decline for 1998. Indonesian GDP fell by 13.1 per cent in 1998 (Table 8.1) instead of growing at the IMF-projected 5 per cent. Twenty million Indonesians fell below the poverty line from the combination of job losses and inflation. The national investment ratio, averaging 30 per cent since 1990, fell to 17 per cent in 1998 and 11 per cent in 2000 (Table 8.1) and recovered only to below 25 per cent in the 2000s.

The economic albatross continued to be the external liabilities of the private sector and the absence of resources to service foreign currency

14 Many of the reforms had been long advocated by Indonesian economic reformers and supported by the IMF and World Bank staff. See D. Rodrik, 'Understanding Policy Reform,' *Journal of Economic Literature* XXXIV no. 1 (1996): 9–42, on how such reform lists have become in IMF structural adjustment programmes.

15 Mucchala, 'Ten Years after the Asian Crisis,' 9.

16 IEO-IMF, 'The IMF and Recent Capital Account Crises,' 79.

17 Ibid., 82.

18 A. Nasution 'The Meltdown of the Indonesian Economy: Causes, Responses and Lessons,' *ASEAN Economic Bulletin* 17, no. 2 (2000): 148–62.

TABLE 8.1 *Basic macroeconomic indicators*

	1990	1991	1992	1993	1994	1995	1996	1997	1998	1999	2000	2001	2002
GDP growth rate (%)	9	8.9	7.2	7.3	7.5	8.1	7.8	4.65	−13.1	0.8	4.9	3.6	4.5
(in % of GDP)													
Trade balance	1.60	1.70	2.93	2.99	1.15	−1.33	−0.62	−0.28	9.75	8.08	10.52	8.27	6.30
Current account	−2.82	−3.65	−2.17	−1.33	−1.58	−3.18	−3.37	−2.24	4.29	4.13	4.84	4.30	4.00
Investment rate	30.7	31.6	30.5	29.5	31.1	31.9	30.7	31.8	16.8	11.4	22.2	22.5	21.4
Savings rate	29.4	23.2	24.5	30.1	30.7	29.0	28.6	29.9	23.8	14.3	27.4	23.7	18.9
Gov't Fiscal Balance	0.4	0.4	−0.6	0.4	2.0	3.0	2.3	0.2	−1.7	−2.5	n.a.	n.a.	−0.3
Domestic credit to private sector	48.09	47.25	45.53	48.98	51.94	53.53	55.47	60.85	53.24	20.59	19.91	20.29	21.28

Source: Author's calculations, source of basic data: World Bank Development Indicators and IMF financial statistics.

obligations under the reign of hot money flowing out. What was needed was a period to 'land the airplane' to carry out repairs to the engine of growth. A bank-restructuring agency installed with the January 1998 programme began to help restart domestic credit markets.

The scale of currency outflows began to wane and exchange rates stabilized not just for Indonesia but also throughout the region starting from September 1998[19] because of the series of external financial crises well prompted by the East Asian crisis: the Russian payments crisis (21 August), New York stock exchange and Brazilian stock market sell-off (10 September), Japan stock market sell-off (17 September), collapse of Long-Term Capital Management hedge fund (23 September), sell-off in stock markets in New York and Europe (24 September), Brazilian austerity package (27 October), outsized IMF standby package for Brazil (13 November). On 3 October, Japan announced a $30 billion aid package for Southeast Asia. On 5–8 October, the IMF and the World Bank held a joint plenary session to debate the global economic crisis, sending a possible signal that the global financial system cannot be held blameless for the East Asian crisis and that domestic reform is not a sufficient policy response. The G7 communiqué of 30 October announced a commitment to contain current and future crises.

As distinctly as it swooped into East Asia in 1997, the crisis slinked away on little cat's feet at the end of 1998 and coaxed the so-called V-shaped recovery in Thailand and the Republic of Korea. For Thailand and the Republic of Korea economic recovery occurred within the year that the Russian crisis broke out – thus a V-shaped pattern. (This is not to minimize the human dislocation the crisis inflicted on these countries in a period of about nine months.) In Indonesia, the recovery took the so-called U-shaped path, with the exchange rate beginning to appreciate and the debt overhang falling strongly in 1999 (Table 8.2) and growth coming back to around 5 per cent in 2000 (Table 8.1), thus a recovery period of two years.

If a new widespread currency and financial crisis erupts in the developing world in 2017, it could only further distress a weakened global financial system. A reversal of the direction of portfolio-driven flows as the East Asian economies experienced in their favour at the end of 1998 is unlikely.

[19] See M.F. Montes and V. Popov, *The Asian Crisis Turns Global*, (Singapore: Institute of Southeast Asian Studies, 1999) and G. Corsetti et al., 'What Caused the Asian Currency and Financial Crisis?'

TABLE 8.2 *Indicators of external stability*

	1990	1991	1992	1993	1994	1995	1996	1997	1998	1999	2000	2001	2002
Total reserves (mos. of imports)	3.1	3.3	3.3	3.4	3.2	2.9	3.5	3.0	5.2	6.1	5.3	5.7	6.3
External debt stock (% GNI)	64.0	71.6	72.2	58.7	62.6	63.4	58.3	65.1	168.2	117.4	95.6	92.3	74.3
External debt stock (% of exports of goods, services, primary income	235.1	238.3	231.5	214.3	234.0	229.4	222.4	209.4	266.9	262.9	196.6	204.0	190.8
Short-term debt (% of reserves)	128.6	138.2	157.3	144.2	146.1	174.2	166.2	187.9	85.2	73.2	73.9	71.3	55.0
Short-term debt (% of exports of goods, services, primary income)	37.5	42.9	47.5	43.2	42.2	47.9	55.6	50.5	35.4	34.7	29.7	30.9	26.3

Broad money to reserves ratio (%)	5.4	5.0	5.1	5.5	6.0	6.6	6.2	6.9	2.4	3.0	3.0	2.9	2.9
Official exchange rate (rupiah per US dollar	1842.81	1950.32	2029.92	2087.10	2160.75	2248.61	2342.30	2909.38	10013.62	7855.15	8421.78	10260.85	9311.19

Source: Author's calculations, source of basic data: IMF Financial Statistics.

III. CAUSES, CRISIS RESPONSES AND CONSEQUENCES

Before the 1997 crisis, the Indonesian economy grew strongly (Table 8.1), propelled by investment spending which was in turn fuelled by the strong growth in external borrowing and domestic credit. Despite the high level of growth, current account deficits (Table 8.1) were within what would normally be deemed sustainable levels.[20] As in other Asian countries which were export-oriented and strove mightily to lean against[21] currency appreciation, there was a noticeable but not extravagant case of currency appreciation after 1995 (Figure 8.1). The overall fiscal balance was in surplus after 1992 (Table 8.1). The external debt stock had declined from its 1991 levels (Table 8.2), after the government applied part of its privatization proceeds to repaying foreign debt. Inflation was slightly higher than the low rates in other East Asian economies.

III.A. *Private External Debt and the Financial System*

The IMF was aware of weaknesses in the banking system. This was at the root of the Indonesian crisis, as it was in Thailand and the Republic of Korea: the disassembling of a sound domestic financial system by rapid portfolio inflows.[22] A July 1996 board discussion urges Indonesian authorities to address weaknesses[23] in the banking system, while celebrating the country's open capital account. Thus, the function of private external borrowing as creator of banking system vulnerabilities was laid firmly in domestic policy[24] and was not associated with the open capital account.

In hindsight, the IMF provided figures that indicated 'the stock of private foreign debt increased rapidly from about US$38 billion in 1995 to US$65 billion just before the crisis and US$82 billion at the end of 1997';[25] of this amount, short-term private debt amounted to $33 billion. The rapid granting of banking licenses financed by resources on offer from external sources

[20] *See* also M.F. Montes (1998), *The Currency Crisis in Southeast Asia*, for other Southeast Asian economies Spring 1998d.

[21] *See* M.F. Montes 'The Ungainly EMU and the Flailing Geese,' *The NIRA Review*, (1998), 16–19.

[22] For Indonesia, *see* Abdusalamov and Montes, 'Indonesia: Reaping the Market.'

[23] *See* page 151 in S. Radelet and J. Sachs 'The Onset of the East Asian Financial Crisis,' in *Currency Crises*, ed. P. Krugman (Chicago: The University of Chicago Press, 2000), 105–53.

[24] Abdusalamov and Montes, 'Indonesia: Reaping the Market.'

[25] IEO-IMF, 'The IMF and Recent Capital Account Crises,' 61.

overtook the increase in capability[26] to effectively supervise a rapidly expanding sector – from less than 100 banks in 1988 to 240 banks when the crisis broke out.

As the Indonesian government itself had initiated in August 1997, a brisk but high-cost restructuring of the domestic banking sector (along the lines undertaken by Sweden in 1992[27] and the Roosevelt bank holiday measure in the United States of 6–10 March 1933) would have been a logical focus. The first IMF programme in November 1997, including the initial version of the 15 January programme, did not have a strong bank-restructuring component. But this problem was eventually recognized. The 45 per cent breaching[28] of the base money target by December 1997 could be traced to liquidity provided to banks experiencing bank runs and such liquidity injections had exchange rate impacts. Unless done swiftly with adequate resources, a Swedish-style programme might have been difficult with the Indonesian-style open capital account of 1997, when runs[29] on banks financed flights to safety to the US dollar by wealthy Indonesians and corporations.

In a discussion[30] on capital controls early in the crisis, in October 1997, between IMF staff and Indonesian authorities, government officials considered these infeasible and its practice a potential source of corruption. It was an unlikely time to seriously consider ways and means to make capital controls feasible when the IMF staff themselves were seeking a mandate from the International Monetary and Financial Committee at the September 1997 annual Bretton Woods meeting in Hong Kong to begin working with member economies on capital account liberalization.

It would take 15 more years for the IMF to take an 'institutional view'[31] to begin to tolerate capital account regulation[32] but only for macro-prudential reasons. Macro-prudential regulations would have mitigated Indonesia's

[26] *See* K.S. Jomo 'What Did We Really Learn from the 1997–98 Asian Debacle?' in Muchhala, *Ten Years After*, 21–22.

[27] Montes, *The Currency Crisis in Southeast Asia*.

[28] IEO-IMF, 'The IMF and Recent Capital Account Crises,' 14–15.

[29] A related debate is the provision of deposit insurance and whether to introduce a blanket deposit insurance in the midst of a crisis. Djiwandono, 'Ten Years after the Asian Crisis' suggests that such a measure would not have applied to large deposit holders and would not have changed the scale of runs on banks.

[30] IEO-IMF, 'The IMF and Recent Capital Account Crises,' 72.

[31] IMF, 'The Liberalization and Management of Capital Flows: An Institutional View,' (Washington, DC: IMF, 2012).

[32] While member states have the sovereign right to impose capital controls, IMF's institutional view came after the Iceland programme in which the IMF tolerated the capital controls authorities imposed after the 2008 collapse of its banking system.

bank-based imbalances. However, these regulations would have been irrelevant to corporate external debt, accumulated outside banking channels, which were a significant proportion of Indonesian external debt and eventually required a rollover adjustment including some protection from exchange rate risk for foreign creditors in September 1998.

One often-used argument in 1997 against capital controls was that Singapore's financial centre is physically in the north-western edge of Indonesian territory making it difficult to police transactions; in 2016, when Internet connections are used for such transactions it would be a magnitude easier to police these transactions. The debate suggests that unilateral capital controls could be ineffective without some minimal level of international cooperation and thus some participation by the IMF and other international mechanisms. The difficulties arising from European attempts to regulate 'naked shorts' independently of the US and UK authorities are a current example.

The most cogent counter example to the short shrift given to the possibility of applying capital control policies in both the actual Indonesian programme and its evaluation was the much less socially costly[33] crisis programme of Malaysia in the same period. Malaysia had a similar physical disability to that of Indonesia: the Singapore financial centre is located at its southern tip. It can be argued that Malaysia's disability was even greater because of the existence of an officially operating offshore centre trading in Malaysian ringgit physically located in Singapore. Malaysia's capital controls proved effective in creating the domestic fiscal and monetary space to combat the crisis. Among other policies, capital controls included (1) on foreign institutions and persons, a one-year moratorium from the purchase date on repatriation of proceeds from the sale of equity shares; (2) restrictions on transfers of ringgit funds in external accounts held by non-residents; (3) prohibition on ringgit loans to non-resident banks and stock-broking firms; (4) prohibition on foreign loans for residents and resident companies; and (5) except for trade payments, a ceiling of ringgit 10,000 on Malaysian residents for payments to foreign parties or on foreign investment.

The Indonesian 1997–98 programme implemented by the IMF and the government coddled the private sector by keeping the capital account open while the same private sector did not perform on domestic investment spending that was needed to prevent an economic collapse. Admittedly, this all took place in the midst of a political succession struggle but it can be

[33] *See* M. Khor, 'The Malaysian Experience in Financial-Economic Crisis Management: An Alternative to the IMF-Style Approach,' (2005) Third World Network, Penang.

argued that this is an insufficient excuse for the technical inattention to logically needed capital controls.

III.B. *Austerity in Indonesia, 1997–1998*

A much-debated issue is whether Indonesia's IMF programme(s) exacerbated the crisis by imposing unduly constricting fiscal and monetary ceilings. The programme evaluation[34] admits that for a capital account crisis, the initial austerity was logically inappropriate. However, the report provides adequate evidence that in legal terms – in the terms in which the programmes were written – fiscal austerity was not unduly strict beginning with the 15 January 1998 programme. In the case of monetary policy, the series of IMF programmes imposed tight monetary policy targets without raising the policy rate.[35]

The 15 April 1998 programme raised the allowable public deficit from 1 per cent of GDP to a deficit of 4.7 per cent. The actual 1998 deficit was 2.1 per cent, an outcome more contractionary than allowed by the programme.[36] From the IMF point of view, the shortfall was associated with failure to meet expenditure targets on the part of the government (for example, there were no pre-existing social safety net programmes that would have automatically increased public spending). With no government bond market, government had no recourse to non-inflationary finance and the rate of spending was tightly matched to revenues.

As mentioned earlier, the shortfall in growth came from the collapse in private investment. Having borrowed in foreign currency before the crisis, corporations (that had not gone bankrupt as a result) found themselves heavily indebted from the unexpectedly sharp fall of the rupiah. The public sector could not ramp up investment quickly enough to take advantage of unused fiscal space.

In the case of interest and monetary policy, these were already tight when IMF entered the scene, except for the emergency liquidity provisions to banks experiencing large deposit withdrawals. The programme(s) sought to continue this stance. As mentioned earlier, the agreed monetary ceiling was being breached by these liquidity provisions, and these had implications for capital flight and exchange rate fragility. At the same time, it is likely that in the specific context, higher interest rates would not have noticeably reduced the scale of capital flight as long as the rest of the world had not yet begun

34 IEO-IMF, 'The IMF and Recent Capital Account Crises.'

35 Ibid., 87–88.

36 Ibid., 67.

experiencing its own financial difficulties. In the situation, the tight monetary policy could be seen as a suitable compromise to the well-known Mundell-Fleming trilemma, if imposing capital controls was out-of-bounds as it was for the IMF and Indonesian authorities.

Many analysts[37] immediately after the crisis, emphasizing the domestic origins of the crisis, argued strongly against[38] the feasibility and desirability of capital controls.

IV. LESSONS LEARNED AND NOT LEARNED

This section attempts to distil some (interrelated) key policy lessons from the 1997–98 Indonesian crisis and discuss the extent to which these lessons have become pertinent in the eurozone and the incipient developing country payments crises. Word limit restrictions preclude an extended treatment of each of these areas.

IV.A. *Domestic versus External Causes?*

The financial stampede into the region, especially after Mexico's so-called Tequila crisis can mainly be attributed to poorly regulated international financial markets. The World Bank[39] had been particularly active in accelerating capital account liberalization in the region. At the very end, the V-shaped recovery, made possible by the emergence of financial crises elsewhere, belied the importance of domestic causes of the crisis, even as there were plenty of institutional weaknesses that were dredged up during the crisis to make this argument.

To address international vulnerabilities, Asian countries have built up international reserves. In 1997, it could be argued that Indonesia's reserves were strongly adequate when measured against short-term debt, money supply, and exports (Table 8.2). Building up reserves greater than three months of imports is a lesson learned for developing countries. East Asia has

37 Corsetti et al., 'What Caused the Asian Currency and Financial Crisis?'

38 *See* also S. Fischer 'Exchange Rate Regimes and Crisis Prevention in Emerging Economies,' comments for delivery at the 4th Annual Conference of the Brookings-Wharton conference on Financial Services, Washington, DC, January 12, 2001.

39 The thinking in the World Bank advocacy of capital account liberalization is embodied in the papers of the staff during the period, including: S. Claessens and T. Glaessner. 'The Internationalization of Financial Services in Asia,' (1998) World Bank Policy Research working paper no. 1911 World Bank, Washington, DC, April; G. Caprio and P. Honohan, *Finance for Growth: Policy Choices in a Volatile World*, (Oxford: Oxford University Press, 2001).

the advantage that because it is able to run current account surpluses, its reserves are mostly earned, not borrowed.

IV.B. *Currency versus Financial Crises*

Analysts that emphasize the domestic causes of the crisis point to the financial reasons for the sudden stop in financing experienced by Thailand, then Indonesia. The reality is that with liberalized capital accounts, currency crises are an intimate companion of domestic financial crises in developing countries; only developed countries have the luxury of decoupling domestic financial crises from their payments and trade sector. Booms which cause currency appreciation are as perilous as busts: a lesson learned and thus the need for policy space for exchange rate setting. In Indonesia the bust led to a severe devaluation, which imposed banking and corporate financial distress.

In Indonesia, there was a policy debate on installing a currency board beginning in January 1998 in an attempt to decouple currency policy from financial policy. Aside from being rejected by major countries and international institutions, it appeared untimely in the midst of the crisis, and the straitjacket it would impose on future monetary policy would not justify its use in the long-term.

IV.C. *Bailing In versus Bailing Out the Private Sector*

The Indonesian financial crisis was a private sector crisis, on both the creditor and debtor sides. Lesson learned but no action: The Asian crisis provoked the IMF's proposal for a sovereign debt restructuring mechanism (SDRM), which did not prosper. In 2014–15, there was a UN General Assembly process to establish a legal framework over sovereign debt resolution[40] which was resisted by developed countries and has stalled because it has lost Argentina's moral leadership in this effort with the election in November 2015 of an opposition party that prioritized reconciling with holdout hedge funds. In the wake of the 2007–08 crisis, US and European governments took the same action as in Indonesia in 1997 – rescue of the banks and impose the costs on taxpayer resources.

The Indonesian crisis involved banks on both sides and Indonesian corporate borrowers on the debtor side. At the current conjuncture, bond

[40] United Nations, 'Basic Principles on Sovereign Debt Restructuring Processes,' (A/RES/69/319) (2015), New York, September 10, 2015.

instruments have become the dominant type of international finance for developing countries. Recent outcomes on Argentina's debt restructuring, in which non-cooperative holdout bondholders have been allowed outsized returns, have undermined market-based restructuring processes.

IV.D. *Fixed Rates versus Floating Exchange Rates*

A debate on which exchange rate regime would be more appropriate in a global economy with potentially volatile swings in portfolio investment (as happened before the 1994 Mexican crisis) broke out in the run-up to the Asian crisis and after it. IMF policy suggestions before the Asian crisis verged on requiring public sector deficit adjustment in response to changes in private capital flows. This would have imposed[41] its own instability in the domestic macroeconomy.

Because portfolio-driven private capital flows are by nature volatile, Akyuz[42] argues that both exchange rate regimes impose their own instabilities. If, for example, exchange rates in East Asia had been allowed to float when inflows were excessive, the result could have easily been further currency appreciations. Private capital flow surges bring up the paradoxical situation[43] as characterized this way: 'if a country is successful because it has undertaken all kinds of reforms, has its fiscal accounts in order and is growing and attractive, then it receives large capital inflows. These inflows give rise to an appreciation of the currency and, after some time, a current account deficit emerges. When the current account widens, there is a perception of risk and then anything can turn market sentiment around.'

This suggests that the issue is not whether to fix or float but how unfettered private capital flows will be. This is the argument in favour of capital controls and capital account regulation. As discussed earlier, in the Indonesian case, the inability to regulate capital movements undercut monetary policy and could have undercut fiscal policy except that in actual practice fiscal policy was already overly contractionary on its own.

In the absence of a rules-based international debt restructuring, the ability to impose capital controls could be indispensable – as Iceland and Cyprus

[41] Montes, "Private Deficits and Public Responsibilities...".

[42] Y. Akyuz, 'On Financial Instability and Control,' in Reforming the International Financial System Crisis Prevention and Response, *ed.* J.T. Teunissen (FONDAD: The Hague, 2000), 164–77.

[43] Quoted in Teunissen, *Reforming the International Financial System*, 184.

recently demonstrated. In the case of Iceland, the domestic polity decided to impose it; in the case of Cyprus, the EU commission imposed it.

IV.E. *Good Governance, Transparency and Rule of Law*

It appears that the lack of transparency is an explanation and an increase in it a solution to all problems encountered by economists. Then US Treasury Secretary Larry Summers had a four-word explanation[44] for the totality of the East Asian crisis – 'generally accepted accounting principles' – which he considered as the most powerful driver of capital market development in the United States. As crisis countries, Indonesia, Thailand, Malaysia and Korea became the poster children of bad governance until the Russian payments crisis began in August 1998.

Bad governance became the most popular and internationally preferred explanation for the Indonesian crisis, which was seen as particularly apropos because of the stranglehold on economic policy of the waning Suharto presidency. However, the bad governance explanation can distract attention from the causes over which immediately effective policy actions can be applied. After the crisis, well-meaning research and advocacy projects to improve transparency in government and the corporate sector proliferated in East Asia. Singh and Zammit[45] suggest that, in the end, the US model of corporate governance was being held up as the model. If so, within half a decade of East Asian reform efforts, the US model of corporate governance led to the subprime crisis of 2007–08.

V. FINAL REMARKS

Writing in 2016, the tragedy of Indonesia's economic crisis in 1997–98 is that many of its elements were replayed in the eurozone in the wake of the 2007–08 North Atlantic financial crises. We see a replay of the Indonesian programme's policy choice to bail out private creditors, forgetting the bailing-in lesson from that period. The reliance on governance-as-explanation and as venue for conditionality was also played out in the Greek programme. Rapid

[44] PBS.org 'Interview with Lawrence Summers,' April 24, 2001, www.pbs.org/wgbh/commandingheights/shared/minitext/int_lawrencesummers.html (accessed November 28, 2015).

[45] *See* A. Singh and A. Zammit 'Corporate Governance, Crony Capitalism and Economic Crises: Should the US Business Model Replace the Asian Way of "Doing Business?"' *Corporate Governance* 14, no.4 (2006): 220–33.

deregulation and privatization were key elements the Indonesia programme, as they were in subsequent programmes, even after the Indonesian programme lesson that these were untimely efforts.

The Indonesia experience demonstrated that these approaches, even if they are socially costly and not apropos to the payments problem at hand, do not materially harm the international network of creditors. Thus, there appears to be no constituency for a thoroughgoing reform of the system of international finance.

9

The Irish Sovereign Debt Crisis Post-2009

A Lesson on Why Countries Should Never Enter into Unsustainable Currency Unions

PHILIP PILKINGTON

ABSTRACT

Prior to the financial crisis of 2008 Ireland tended to run fiscal surpluses and have low government debt-to-GDP. But after the banking system blew up as a Minskyian property bubble unwound government debt skyrocketed as the government absorbed private sector debts. From a sectoral balances perspective what effectively occurred was that the government sector forced the private sector into borrowing by running public budget surpluses. When the private sector debt became unsustainable it was then forced back onto the public balance sheet. The Irish government was forced into backstopping the debt that had originated in the banking system. We now have clear evidence that public officials were effectively forced into accepting the debt by European and international institutions and threatened when they indicated possible non-compliance. Because the Irish central bank had been stripped of its money-issuing capacity the Irish government was placed in a position of powerlessness where it had to concede to any and all demands lest the economy be starved of liquidity and brought to a standstill. At the same time, the rise in interest rates on government bonds that triggered the sovereign debt crisis would never have occurred had the Irish central bank retained its money-issuing capacities. The Irish sovereign debt crisis was generated by Ireland's adherence to the European monetary union's neoliberal policy stance, as enshrined in documents like the Maastricht Treaty, together with their ceding control over money-issuance to non-elected, centralized authorities. Today there is the possibility that some of this debt might be written down but without an aggressive turn towards expansionary fiscal policy far outside of Maastricht Treaty limitations, full employment is unlikely to be achieved. The most rational path for Irish policymakers to undertake would be a managed exit from the single currency accompanied by a temporary peg to either the British sterling or the US dollar.

I. INTRODUCTION

Between 2010 and 2012 Ireland suffered from a sovereign debt crisis that required a bailout by the European Central Bank, the International Monetary Fund and the European Commission. The bailout was a direct result of a major banking crisis in Ireland that had begun in 2008. This banking crisis was a result of two related historical dynamics. First of all, Ireland had trapped itself in an unsustainable and misguided monetary arrangement with other European countries. Secondly, its government and authorities had stoked a housing bubble in order to run high-income growth policies together with a fiscal surplus.

In what follows we will provide the full macroeconomic context for the events that occurred in Ireland in those years. We will investigate the institutional dynamics that allowed these events to take place. We will then examine the Irish government's response first to the banking crisis and then to the bailout that resulted from it. We will argue that the bailout would not have been required had Ireland not locked itself into a misguided monetary union. Finally, we will discuss whether the best actions moving forward entail debt forgiveness given to Ireland by its partners or whether Ireland should undertake a managed exit from the monetary union.

II. THE SEEDS OF THE CRISIS

In order to properly understand the sovereign debt crisis that occurred in Ireland between 2010 and 2012 we must first understand the structural problems that were inherent in the Irish macroeconomy in the run-up to this crisis. These structural problems had deep roots in the failure of the reform programme adopted by Ireland in the 1980s and 1990s.

The reform of the Irish economy that resulted in the so-called Celtic Tiger is often thought to have taken place in the 1980s. In fact, this is not true. Ireland's main problem in the post-war era was that of low productivity growth. This low productivity growth was countered through the use of industrial and education policy in the 1960s and 1970s. These supply-side reforms led to an enormous burst of productivity growth which eventually allowed Ireland to catch up with the rest of the developed world.[1] All of this was assisted by subsidies from the European Union.

[1] K. Whelan, 'Ireland's Economic Crisis: The Good, The Bad and The Ugly', (June 18, 2013) Bank of Greece, www.karlwhelan.com/Papers/Whelan-IrelandPaper-June2013.pdf.

In the 1980s Ireland suffered from a heavy burden of public sector debt-to-income – 110 per cent + – and high interest rates on this debt of over 10 per cent. The Irish central bank was unable to lower these high interest rates as in a world of universally high interest rates this would have put major downward pressure on the Irish punt which was at that time trying to maintain its inclusion in the European Monetary System (EMS), which Ireland had joined in December 1978.[2] This led to a neoliberal policy of austerity being imposed in Ireland in the 1980s to try to rein in public debt – this policy would later be credited with the emergence of the Celtic Tiger.[3]

The myth that the austerity imposed in the 1980s had given rise to the Celtic Tiger had substantial effects on Irish economic policy in the 1990s and 2000s. In the 1990s and 2000s the Irish government prioritized running fiscal surpluses. But in-line with the sectoral balances identity we know that if a government accumulates net assets this will result in an accumulation of net liabilities on the part of the other sectors. The identity is derived, simply, from national accounting identities and runs as such:

$$(G-T) = (I-S) + (X-M + \textit{Net Financial Assets})$$

Where $(G-T)$ is the government balance, $(I-S)$ is the domestic private sector balance and $(X-M + \textit{Net Financial Assets})$ is the current account. As we can see, for the government to run a surplus either the domestic private sector must run a deficit or the external sector must run a surplus, or some combination of both. We can further disaggregate the domestic private sector into the household and firm sector as such:

$$(G-T) = (I_h-S_h) + \left(I_f-S_f\right) + (X-M + \textit{Net Financial Assets})$$

Where (I_h-S_h) is the domestic household sector and $\left(I_f-S_f\right)$ is the domestic firm sector. Figure 9.1 lays out the sectoral balances of Ireland from 1991 to 2014. Note that we have included a disaggregation of the private sector where data is available, otherwise we have simply included the aggregate private sector.

As we can see, beginning in 1997 the Irish government ran a fiscal surplus. Since the balance on the current account could not supply sufficient assets to cover this surplus, the domestic private sector was forced into deficit. We can also see from the data between 2002 and 2008 that this deficit fell on the

2 J. Kelly, 'The Irish Pound: From Origins to EMU', (2003) *Irish Central Bank Quarterly Bulletin*, www.centralbank.ie/docs/default-source/consumer-hub-library/the-irish-pound-from-origins-to-emu.pdf?sfvrsn=2

3 S. Kinsella, 'Is Ireland Really the Role Model for Austerity?', (2011) *UCD Geary Discussion Paper Series*, https://core.ac.uk/download/files/153/6273821.pdf.

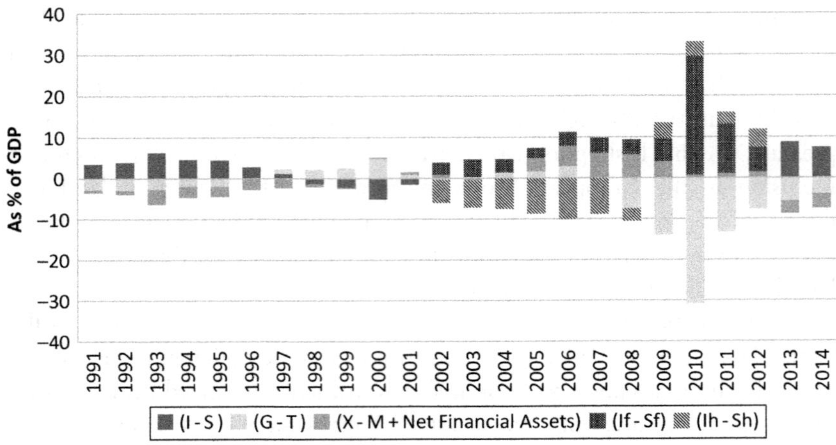

FIGURE 9.1 Ireland sectoral balances.
Source: The Irish Department of Finance; the Central Statistics Office; and Eurostat. Note that the current account in the diagram is flipped to give the presentation symmetry and make it more readable; we can think of this as 'foreign net saving' or as the capital account.

domestic household sector. We thus know that the Irish government sector surplus was being maintained by the household sector, generating ever more debt.

The manner in which this manifested itself in the real economy was quite straightforward. In this period an enormous housing bubble was generated in Ireland which was driven by excessive bank lending to the private household sector. Figure 9.2 plots inflation-adjusted Irish house prices over this period.

As we can see, up until 1996 inflation-adjusted house prices in Ireland were roughly stable. But after this they rose precipitously. This coincided exactly with the government running its fiscal surpluses. We can thus say that the domestic household deficit that we see in Figure 9.1 which was allowing the government sector to run a fiscal surplus was the result of a massive wave of bank lending to households. This massive uptick in lending was in turn being driven by a house price bubble.

At the same time Irish employment growth was being driven by a huge boom in construction expenditure. As house prices spiralled ever upwards, property developers borrowed and built large amounts of properties which they hoped to sell for very high prices to households that would take on increasing levels of mortgage debt. This led to a boom in construction employment, which allowed Ireland to bring down its historically high unemployment rate. Figure 9.3 plots the weighted contribution to employment growth by sector.

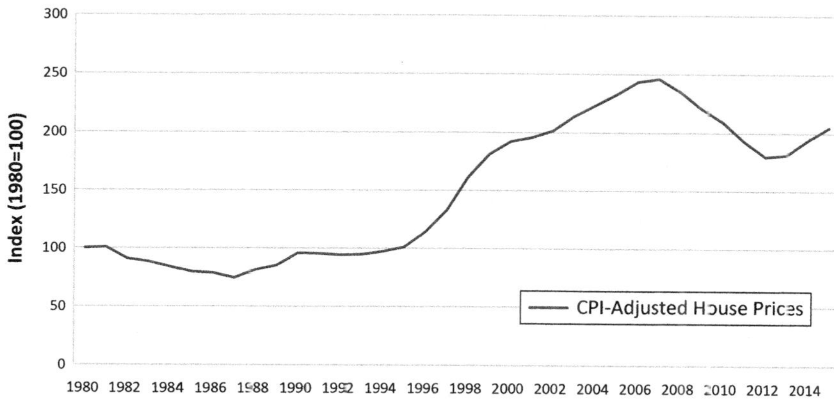

FIGURE 9.2 Ireland inflation-adjusted house price index.
Source: Oxford Economics and CSO.

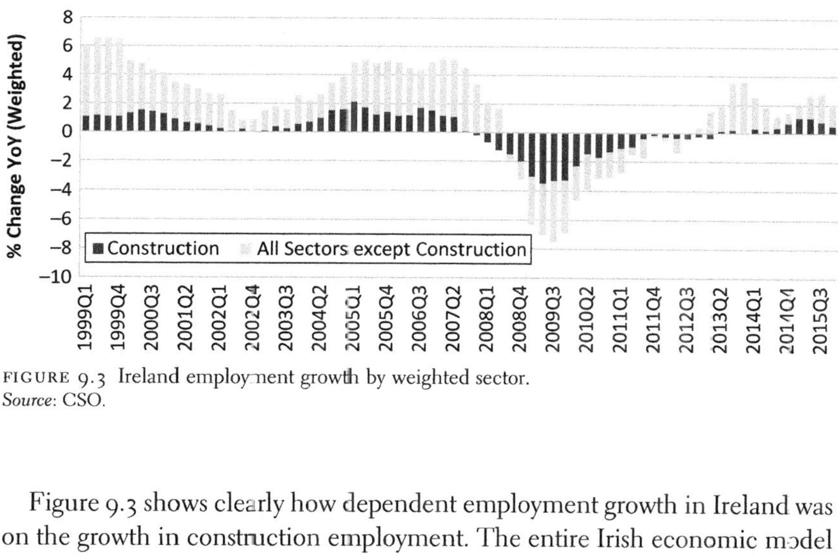

FIGURE 9.3 Ireland employment growth by weighted sector.
Source: CSO.

Figure 9.3 shows clearly how dependent employment growth in Ireland was on the growth in construction employment. The entire Irish economic model had become reliant on the property market and the real estate boom.[4]

4 Many commentators seem to think that the Irish model relies heavily on its low corporate tax rate. On the face of it, however, there appears to be little evidence of this. The profits that are washed through Ireland earn the Irish people – beyond a small number of accountancy and law firms – very little income. The data also suggests that Irish growth was soaring prior to the cutting of the corporate tax rate and, when the tax rate was cut, growth did not improve to any noticeable extent. (M. Taft, 'Low Corporation Tax Rates Do Not Boost Growth', Unite's Notes on the Front, http://notesonthefront.typepad.com/politicaleconomy/2014/11/there-are-a-

The model was supposed to deliver high rates of income and employment growth together with fiscal surpluses. The only way that this could be achieved was through a huge run-up in household debt-driven expenditure.

These dynamics were not widely understood at the time. Some commentators argued that there was a housing bubble in Ireland but they did not understand that the model of high income and employment growth with fiscal surpluses required a housing bubble or some other means to ensure that households or firms loaded up on debt. To this author's knowledge no one in Ireland at the time acknowledged that, in fact, the only way to run a truly sustainable economic model based on high income and high employment growth without burdening the private sector with debt was for the public sector to run substantial deficits. This is still not recognized today which accounts for Ireland's obsessive attempts to rely on unrealistic assessments of export growth potential.

In 2007–08 house prices began to collapse (Figure 9.2) and construction employment began to contract (Figure 9.3). These forces took the wind out of the sails of the Irish economy and it slipped into recession. It is only in this context that the banking crisis and sovereign debt crisis that followed can be understood.

III. THE MELTDOWN

As we have already seen the Irish model of high economic and employment growth while running fiscal deficits was predicated on the private sector taking on increasing levels of debt. This was done mainly through the advance of mortgage lending, but was also done through the expansion of other types of credit that were typically tied to the property market. Figure 9.4 and Figure 9.5 provide a breakdown of private credit expansion relative to GDP.

As we can see, the Irish growth model relied on massive outlays of household mortgage credit and business credit tied to real estate. Acceleration in these credit metrics is strongly correlated to rising house prices. These correlations are shown in Table 9.1.

Household mortgage credit growth was roughly following house price growth while business real estate credit growth was lagging house price growth by a year. As house prices collapsed, credit growth dried up and the Irish economy ground to a halt. It was at this point that the Irish government began to realize how dependent they were on the housing bubble and the industries

number-of-reports-that-ministers-have-travelled-to-the-us-in-order-to-reassure-investors-following-the-closure-of.html).

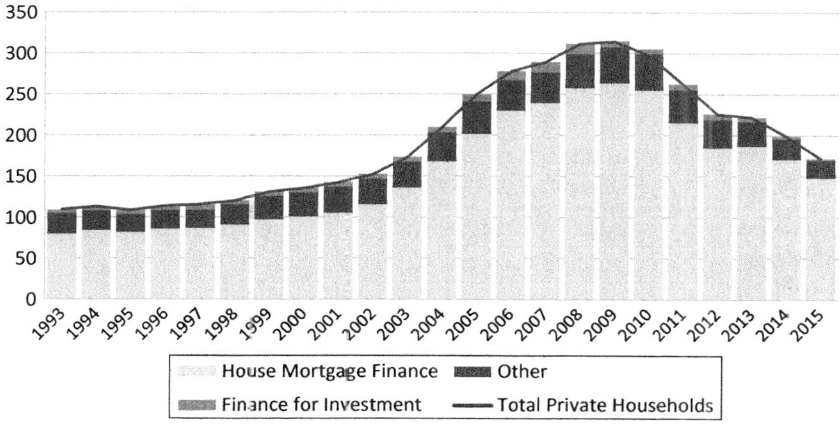

FIGURE 9.4 Irish private household debt as % of GDP.
Source: Irish Central Bank.

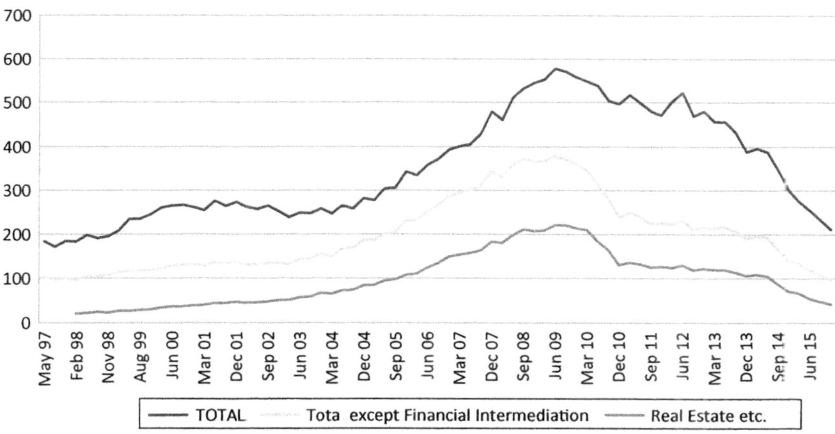

FIGURE 9.5 Irish private business debt as % of GDP.
Source: Irish Central Bank.

that were deriving their revenue sources from the construction industry for tax receipts. As shown in Figure 9.6 tax revenues collapsed completely in 2007–08.

This collapse in tax revenue, together with the collapse of economic growth and the rise in unemployment claims, would have been enough to create large government deficits. But because Ireland had been running a fiscal surplus for a number of years its government debt-to-GDP was only around

TABLE 9.1 *House price growth vs. credit growth.*

Metric	Correlation Coefficient	P-Value	Correlation Coefficient (w/ House Price Growth Leading By One Year)	P-Value (w/ House Price Growth Leading By One Year)
Household Mortgage Credit Growth vs. House Price Growth	0.5663	0.0000534***	0.5673	0.012935**
Business Real Estate Credit Growth vs. House Price Growth	0.3464	0.000081***	0.5207	0.001889***

Source: Irish Central Bank and author's own calculations.

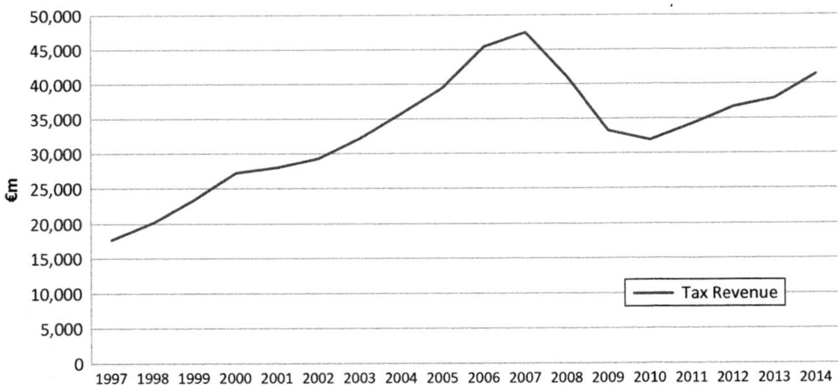

FIGURE 9.6 Tax revenue.
Source: CSO.

23.9 per cent in 2007. This means that the deficits that would have followed would probably not have provoked a sovereign debt crisis. It was the banking crisis that followed on from the collapse in the housing market that paved the way for the sovereign debt crisis that followed.

The banking crisis emerged as Irish banks extended massive amounts of credit to property builders and speculators – this credit expansion can be seen in Figure 9.4. This credit was extended on the basis of very lax credit standards. Banks often extended loans to property speculators who had already made money on the property market and were levering up their already extensive property portfolios. The mania got so intense that speculative Irish money poured into Eastern Europe – with small buyers and large firms speculating in property markets in the likes of Poland.[5]

The most infamous of the banks was Anglo Irish. Anglo Irish specialized in property development and was known for its buccaneering culture. The bank expanded its loan book at roughly 20 per cent per year, with its assets growing from €26 billon in 2003 to €97 billion in 2007 – some 49 per cent of Ireland's 2007 GDP. Though Anglo Irish was the most egregious example of lending excesses it was not alone. Nationwide Building Society went from a small-time mortgage lender to a property development bank with €14 billion in loans on its book – some 7 per cent of Irish GDP. Allied Irish Bank, one of Ireland's main high street retail banks, grew its property-related loans from €16 billion in 2004 to €47 billion in 2007 – or 24 per cent of Irish GDP – which represented half of the €81 billion it held in customer deposits.[6]

During the property bubble these banks sought to attract foreign capital through international bond issuance. In 2003 these bond issuances were around €15 billion – or around 10.4 per cent of GDP – but by 2007 they had risen to around €100 billion – or over 50 per cent of GDP.[7] Not only did this represent a far more unstable source of financing for the banks when the property markets finally crashed, but it would also introduce an important political element into the mix that would subsequently become important: because many of these bonds were held by European banks in different countries these bonds would ultimately threaten the stability of the banks in other European countries, thus raising the difficult question of who would take financial responsibility for the situation.

Why then did the authorities not realize what was going on? During the property boom numerous economists publicly highlighted the dangers inherent in the property boom. They even managed to get substantial coverage in the media, making television appearances and debating other economists – typically representatives of the property sector. Some of these economists even went as far as to highlight the danger that the property bubble posed for the viability of the banks. For example, in an *Irish Times* article from September 2007 entitled 'Banking on Very Shaky Foundations' the economist Morgan Kelly wrote:

5 'Foreigners Abandon Polish Property Market', *The Financial Times* (London), January 3, 2011.

6 Whelan, 'Ireland's Economic Crisis'. 7 Ibid.

> While mortgage lending has slowed since the middle of last year, lending to builders and developers continues to grow rapidly and now stands at almost €100 billion, an increase of €20 billion on last October. To put this in perspective, €20 billion is twice the market value of Bank of Ireland shares; while €100 billion is the approximate value of all public deposits with retail banks. Effectively, the Irish banking system has taken all its shareholders' equity, with a substantial chunk of its depositors' cash on top, and handed it over to builders and property speculators.[8]

Those highlighting these problems at the time in Ireland, however, were stigmatized by leading figures in the media and even by senior politicians. Then Taoiseach Bertie Ahern – the most senior member of government at that time – said in a now famous remark that he did not understand why economists and others who were talking down the economy 'don't commit suicide'.

Meanwhile some of those who were promoted to senior regulatory positions had affiliations with groups that favoured extreme free market/deregulatory policy approaches.[9] This was reflected in the culture of deregulation and 'hands-off' monitoring at the Irish central bank at the time. In 2010, after the crash, the Ministry of Finance commissioned a retrospective study by the central bank to try to figure out what had gone wrong. The report concluded, among other things, that the root causes of the irresponsible deregulatory laxity were:

> 1 A regulatory approach which was perceived to be excessively deferential and accommodating; insufficiently challenging and not persistent enough…
> 2 An under-resourced approach to bank supervision that, by relying on good governance and risk-management procedures, neglected quantitative assessment and the need to ensure sufficient capital to absorb growing property-related risks.
> 3 An unwillingness by the [financial regulator] to take on board sufficiently the real risk of a looming problem and act with sufficient decision and force to head it off in time (p 16).[10]

Interestingly, while the report did admit that many of its policy decisions were 'not based on any quantitative calculations or analysis'[11] it also concluded that

[8] M. Kelly, 'Whatever Happened to Ireland?', *CEPR Discussion Papers*, May 2010, http://cepr.org/active/publications/discussion_papers/dp.php?dpno=7811.

[9] M. Kelly, 'Banking on Very Shaky Foundations', *The Irish Times* (Dublin), September 7, 2007.

[10] P. Honohan, 'The Irish Banking Crisis: Regulatory and Financial Stability Policy', (2010), *Irish Finance Ministry*, www.bankinginquiry.gov.ie/The%20Irish%20Banking%20Crisis%20Regulatory%20and%20Financial%20Stability%20Policy%202003-2008.pdf.

[11] Ibid.

the lack of regulatory supervision had nothing to do with the fact that many of the senior banking executives were politically well-connected. The report reached this conclusion based on the fact that 'none [of the central bank officials] that were interviewed during the investigation agreed with this proposition'.

> While it is easy to imagine that senior management of [the financial regulatory board] might have instinctively and almost unconsciously shied away from aggressive action to restrain politically connected bankers and developers during a runaway property boom, no evidence has been presented that this was the case.[12]

The report did not state, however, whether a psychoanalyst was present during the interviews to detect 'unconscious' motivations on the part of senior management.

IV. FROM BANKING CRISIS TO SOVEREIGN DEBT CRISIS

The lack of preparedness on the part of the authorities manifested itself when those authorities sought to contain the effects of the crisis. Although much information is now publicly available on the response to the crisis from an official inquiry that took place in 2015 it is still unclear exactly what the motivations of those making the decision were.

The best account of the decision to backstop the Irish banking system by the government is the written account recently released by ex-department chief Kevin Cardiff. Cardiff provides us with a narrative of confused government officials meeting with various bankers. He claims that the bankers had little impact on the decision and that 'their interventions had only added colour to the picture of the situation that had already been available to us'.[13] Cardiff argues that the reason that the government decided to provide such a substantial and total guarantee to the failed Irish banks was because they feared a bank-run triggered by a default of Anglo Irish on its commitments.

> In the absence of significant official intervention, a failure of Anglo to meet any of its obligations would trigger events of default on many of its borrowings, so billions of euro would become payable immediately. Anglo's depositors would lose access to their money and the bank would close its doors. Depositors, large and small, would rush to take funds from the other banks,

[12] Ibid.

[13] K. Cardiff, 'How I Remember the Night of the Bank Guarantee', *The Irish Times* (Dublin), February 15, 2016.

> and international investors would withdraw from Ireland as much as they could. The resulting recession would be unprecedented and the damage to the Irish economy and society would be long term and devastating. So, in other words, there was never a realistic option for the authorities to step back from the situation and 'let the banks take the hit'. A decision was required and the approach most favoured in the meeting was turning out to be that of granting broad guarantees to all of the significant Irish banks.[14]

While we have no doubt as to the accuracy of Cardiff's narrative the threat seems to have been much overblown. The government could have realistically undertaken any number of different actions. For example, they could have simply guaranteed the Anglo Irish depositors but nothing else. Or they could have declared an extended bank holiday while they undertook a more fine-grained analysis of the situation and consulted with neutral advisors – perhaps some of those that had expertise in banking crises. The reader gets a distinct impression from Cardiff's narrative that the politicians and regulators simply did not understand what they were doing. Eichengreen points out that the Irish blanket guarantee was not in keeping with standard EU and IMF practice which would have favoured a large haircut for bondholders.[15]

Once the bank guarantee was in place the government undertook an extended policy of attempting to deny the true scale of the problem. At first, the government was desperate to convince the public – and the bond markets – that the banks did not suffer from solvency problems. They hired independent consultants at PriceWaterhouseCoopers (PWC) to run stress tests on the banks' balance sheets. The report that PWC wrote reads rather oddly today. The analysts state that 'under the PWC highest stress scenario, [Anglo Irish's] core equity and tier 1 ratios are projected to exceed regulatory minima' but they then go on to write that this 'highest stress scenario represents a downside risk but not necessarily the worst case scenario'.[16]

By September 2010, however, the true scale of the problem had become publicly known. A 'final estimate' revealed that Anglo Irish alone would cost the Irish state €30 billion or around 18 per cent of the country's GDP. The bank was recapitalized by providing it with a form of government bond called a 'promissory note' that would make cash payments over the course of a number of years. Due to accounting standards set down by Eurostat, these

[14] Ibid.

[15] B. Eichengreen, 'The Irish Crisis and the EU From a Distance', (2015), IMF Working Paper, www.imf.org/external/np/seminars/eng/2014/ireland/pdf/Eichengreen_IrishCrisisEU.pdf.

[16] PriceWaterhouseCoopers, 'Project Atlas – Anglo Irish Bank Corporation PLC', (2009), PriceWaterhouseCoopers, www.finance.gov.ie/sites/default/files/Anglopwc.pdf.

promissory notes were recorded as part of Ireland's government borrowing for that year, thus leading to the record fiscal deficit that can be observed in Figure 9.1.[17]

It was at this point that the Irish banking crisis became a sovereign debt crisis. Other countries – such as the United States and the United Kingdom – had bailed out parts of their banking systems and were running substantial fiscal deficits in the face of the recession but they did not suffer an increase in interest rates on their government bonds. This is because these countries issued their own currency and their government bonds were denominated in this currency. For this reason the interest rates on these bonds are effectively set by the central banks in those countries. If markets attempt to bid down the price of these bonds, thus causing their interest rates to rise above the policy target rate set by the central bank, then the central bank will simply create new reserve balances (i.e. new money) and buy up this debt in order to hit their target interest rate. Bond market participants are aware that this is the case and thus rarely speculate against the central bank.

The Eurozone monetary system suffered from its inception from a fatal flaw in that the bonds issued by various countries were never backstopped by a money-issuing authority. For this reason the interest rates on various government bonds are ultimately dictated by the bond markets. Economists from the Modern Monetary Theory (MMT) school of thought had long been pointing out this fatal flaw and had been highlighting that it would lead to a sovereign debt crisis in the event of an economic crisis or serious recession in the region.[18]

This is precisely what would later transpire, and Ireland, with its enormous absorption by the government of private banking debt, would get caught in the trap. Figure 9.7 plots the spreads of various 10-year government bonds against the interbank interest rate ruling in that country. We have included Japan, as this country had world record levels of sovereign debt-to-GDP throughout this period but maintained its ability to issue its own currency.

As we can see, the predictions made by the MMT economists came to pass. Due to Ireland giving up its ability to issue its own currency, sovereign debt yields blew out in mid-2010 as markets started to question the solvency of the Irish state itself. Meanwhile, after an initial mild increase in 10-year sovereign bond yields in other countries that had bailed out their banks – such as the United States and the United Kingdom – these yields gradually trended lower.

[17] Whelan, 'Ireland's Economic Crisis'.

[18] W. Mosler, 'Rites of Passage', (2001) Epic Coalition, www.epicoalition.org/docs/rites_of_passage.htm.

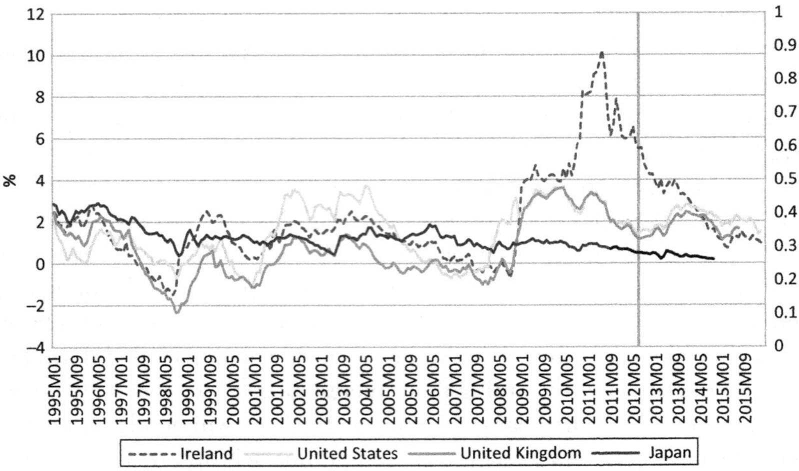

FIGURE 9.7 Ten-year bond spread over interbank interest rate.
Source: CSO, Bank of England, Federal Reserve of St. Louis, OECD, Bank of Japan and author's own calculations.

At this point the Irish government was forced to enter into negotiations with what became known as the Troika – which included the International Monetary Fund (IMF), the European Central Bank (ECB) and the European Commission (EC) – to avail of a bailout in order to assuage the bond markets. Since the banking inquiry took place in 2015 we now know that the Irish government was largely cajoled by the institutions into accepting the bailout.[19] Kevin Cardiff testified that:

> At the moment we entered [the bailout], we were pushed quite hard. We knew who was doing it; we knew what they were saying. In other cases the pressure came indirectly via some misinformation, anonymous media briefings, reportedly coming from official sources which acted to accelerate market pressure and create enormous pressure on Ireland to enter the EU/IMF programme quickly.[20]

This is corroborated by letters released by the ECB that showed that then-president Jean-Claude Trichet 'forced Dublin to seek a bailout in late 2010'. Letters between Trichet and then-Finance Minister Brian Lenihan stated that the ECB would cut off liquidity to the Irish banks if Ireland did not accept the

[19] The IMF favoured debt relief but the austerity package was general consensus.
[20] 'Irish Banking Crisis Inquiry: Ireland Was 'Pushed' Into Bailout', *BBC*, June 18, 2015.

bailout.[21] This would have had the effect of starving the entire country of funds and would probably have led to bank-runs as it later did when the ECB used this policy in Greece after the election of the anti-austerity SYRIZA party in 2015.[22]

The bailout procedures led to yields on Irish sovereign debt falling slightly but it was only after the ECB committed to the backing of its money creation capacity that yields normalized to global market levels. This commitment is highlighted in Figure 9.7 by the grey vertical line which is when the now famous 'whatever it takes speech' was given by ECB president Mario Draghi. Shortly after this speech was given the ECB announced a policy entitled Outright Monetary Transactions (OMT) which effectively committed the ECB to buy sovereign debt directly in the secondary markets if there was a crisis. Bond markets understood this signal and subsequently moved to bid Irish yields down to levels similar to the rest of the world. Ireland returned to the international bond markets in the summer of 2012.[23]

V. FROM BAILOUT TO AUSTERITY TO THE RE-EMERGENCE OF GROWTH

The full backing by the ECB, which has unlimited money-issuing capacity, succeeded in driving down Irish government yields. The ECB, however, insisted that the OMT is contingent on countries enforcing austerity programmes. This is a very different stance from a central bank in a country that issues its own currency where the elected government is typically thought of as senior to the central bank. In the eurozone it appears that due to odd institutional structures the elected governments are subordinate to unelected central bankers. ECB board member Benoît Cœuré sums the ECB position as such in a 2013 speech:

> Even if the ECB were to decide – at its full discretion – to buy bonds via OMTs, governments would have to continue their reform efforts as required by the respective ESM programme and by IMF involvement. Otherwise, they would simply become ineligible for OMTs. Hence, no reforms, no OMTs.[24]

[21] 'ECB Threatened to End Funding Unless Ireland Sought Bailout', *The Financial Times* (London), November 6, 2014.

[22] 'Markets Set for Turmoil as Greece Hurtles towards Financial Collapse and Capital Controls', *Daily Telegraph* (London), June 28, 2015.

[23] C. O'Sullivan, 'Ireland's Return to the Bond Market', (2012), *Public Policy Ireland*, www.publicpolicy.ie/wp-content/uploads/Irelands-return-to-the-bond-market.pdf.

[24] B. Cœuré, 'Outright Monetary Transactions, One Year On', (2013) speech at CEPR, www.ecb.europa.eu/press/key/date/2013/html/sp130902.en.html.

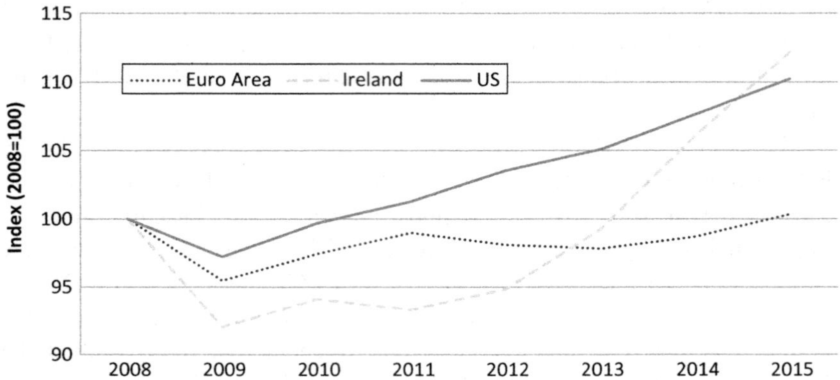

FIGURE 9.8 Annual GDP/GNP growth rates.
Source: AMECO and Federal Reserve Bank of St. Louis.

These austerity policies have dramatically slowed growth in the eurozone and have led to the debt-to-GDP ratios of many countries actually rising rather than falling. They have also contributed to increases in poverty and inequality in the countries where they have been implemented.[25] Ireland, however, performed remarkably well in growth terms in 2014 and 2015 and this has led to it catching up with the United States in growth terms. Figure 9.8 shows these growth rates expressed as indices.[26]

This chart suggests that while the adoption of austerity in the rest of the Euro Area has proved disastrous for growth this has not been the case in Ireland. After a few years of very negative growth, Ireland has experienced very rapid growth that has allowed it to catch back up with economies like the United States that did not engage in austerity.

The reason for this is because Ireland is a small open economy with strong trading ties to the United States and the United Kingdom. When these economies began to recover Ireland was able to increase its exports substantially. This export-led growth strategy is the reason that despite these very high rates of income growth, employment growth has remained relatively muted – as can be seen in Figure 9.3 – and unemployment remains

[25] Oxfam, 'A Cautionary Tale: The True Costs of Austerity in Europe', (2013), Oxfam briefing paper no. 17, www.oxfam.org/sites/www.oxfam.org/files/bp174-cautionary-tale-austerity-inequality-europe-120913-en_1.pdf.

[26] Note that real GDP metrics are used for the Euro Area and the United States, while GNP is used for Ireland. This is because Ireland has large profit transfers overseas that are counted in GDP metrics and are somewhat misleading. That said, if real GDP were used for Ireland here the story would be much the same.

stubbornly high at 8.4 per cent as of April 2016, and this in spite of mass migration out of the country after the crisis.

Another problem is that this employment growth seems to be unevenly distributed. Much of it is concentrated in the mid-east around the capital (Dublin) with the midlands, the south-west and the south-east deemed as 'blackspots' by a recent trade union survey.[27] Another problem is that the Irish recovery seems strongly dependent on economic growth in the rest of the world, which, at the time of writing, is beginning to look very shaky as the credit cycle turns and crises break out in China and the emerging markets.

VI. DEBT FORGIVENESS OR EUROZONE EXIT?

Some have proposed that forgiveness on some of its sovereign debt would be a just and equitable means to rebalance the Irish economy and return it to a sustainable growth footing. Given the evidence we have outlined earlier there is little doubt that such forgiveness would be just. As we have shown, the reason that the Irish sovereign currently finds itself so indebted is due to a failure on the part of policymakers to understand the implications of a bank guarantee followed by a cajoling on the part of international institutions to accept bailouts that saddled the Irish government with bank debt so that other countries did not have to deal with this. In the interest of fairness alone there is a strong case that Ireland should have much of this debt forgiven – particularly any debt that is currently held by European institutions.

But beyond this there are questions as to how such debt forgiveness would positively impact the Irish economy. Such forgiveness can only prove effective to the extent that the space opened up is used to increase government borrowing and expenditure thus ensuring higher employment and income growth. For this reason any forgiveness of Irish sovereign debt should only be discussed in conjunction with an expansionary fiscal policy that promotes full employment in Ireland.

The problem here is that Ireland seems 'locked in' to the austerity culture that has swept Europe. In 2012 the Irish Finance Ministry was offered a means by which to fund expanded fiscal expenditures based on innovative new financial instruments called 'tax-backed bonds'. These new instruments would have allowed the Irish government to drive down interest rates on their sovereign debt without recourse to bailouts or central bank programmes based

[27] NERI, 'Quarterly Economic Observer Spring 2015', (2015), Nevin Economic Research Institute, www.nerinstitute.net/download/pdf/nerispring2015qeo_compressed.pdf?issuusl=ignore.

on policy conditionality. They worked on the principle that including a clause that allowed the bonds to be used to repay tax in the event of default, thereby giving these bonds a 'money good' status that would be recognized by investors. Despite the fact that this was during the depth of the downturn in Ireland and no prospects of growth were on the horizon, the Irish government rejected the proposal based on a legal argument that the authors subsequently showed was spurious.[28]

This seems to suggest that Ireland has been engulfed by the culture of austerity that has taken over the eurozone; a culture that one author has argued was akin to 'groupthink' as discussed in the psychological literature.[29] For this reason any debt forgiveness given to Ireland would likely not result in increased fiscal expenditure and would thus have little actual economic impact. While debt relief would certainly be a step forward it would not put the Irish economy on a sustainable footing. The next time a recession came around the economy would be plunged back into austerity and the economic cycle would continue to be amplified – with grim social and economic results. Ireland would thus be reduced to a proverbial cork in the ocean, floating precariously in the world economy and subject to particularly violent cycles.

As we have discussed, the root of the problem lies in the fact that Ireland does not have the capacity to issue its own currency. If it could it would have no problem running both counter-cyclical fiscal policies and activist fiscal policies aimed at buttressing household savings ratios and full employment. If Ireland had followed these policies in the late 1990s and had stamped out property speculation through targeted tax increases, the Celtic Tiger would likely have continued right up until the present day. Even if Ireland had followed its misguided macroeconomic policies in that period, if it had been able to issue its own currency it could have undertaken its bank bailouts through its central bank without having to worry about its government balance sheet – as happened in the United States and the United Kingdom.

Ireland is in a unique position among the countries that were subject to bailouts during the debt crisis in that it runs consistent and healthy current-account surpluses. For this reason it is assured that a reissued Irish pound/punt would probably trade at high valuations and the Irish Finance Ministry would have discretion in choosing its value. If the government is concerned about short-term speculative pressures, the new currency could be temporarily

28 P. Pilkington, 'The Continued Relevance of Tax-Backed Bonds in Post-OMT Europe', (2013), The Levy Institute of Bard College, www.levyinstitute.org/pubs/pn_13_10.pdf.

29 B. Mitchell, *Eurozone Dystopia: Groupthink and Denial on a Grand Scale* (Edward Elgar, 2015).

pegged to either the British sterling or the US dollar. This would not prove difficult as at the time of writing Ireland has some €2.94 billion worth of foreign exchange reserves. Such a peg would constrain Irish macroeconomic policy, however, and thus should only be undertaken for a short period. After the issue of the new currency the peg should be announced for a fixed period – for example, for a period of 12 to 18 months – and de-pegging should occur on this pre-specified date.

VII. CONCLUSION

The Irish example is a fascinating one for those seeking to learn from sovereign debt crises. First of all, Ireland was not a classical sovereign debt crisis insofar as the crisis was not generated through systematic overspending by the public sector. Rather it was generated by chronic *underspending* by the public sector, which generated a shortfall of aggregate demand that then needed to be 'plugged' by rapid and unsustainable private sector borrowing in order to maintain reasonable levels of economic growth. Secondly, Ireland's subsequent public financing problems are the result of the fact that it is part of a highly dysfunctional monetary union. Countries that issue their own currencies and have central banks with money-issuing capacity cannot and do not have issues financing their public borrowing, as their central bank always acts as a backstop. In Ireland this is not the case because a currency is issued by a centralized institution in Europe (the ECB) over which the Irish government has minimal influence and consequently this institution does not feel compelled to answer to the needs of the Irish people.

Other countries can learn significant lessons from the Irish case. First of all, if a country runs a current account deficit then, by identity, its private and public sector combined must also run a deficit. Allowing the private sector to run a deficit typically results in large-scale debt accumulation by the private sector that ultimately results in a financial and economic crisis. If a country finds itself running a current account deficit – or even if the private sector in a country wishes to save a substantial amount of financial assets – the government's default position should be to run deficits to offset these claims on financial assets. Secondly, and following from this point, countries should never lock themselves into monetary unions or currency arrangements that constrain their ability to finance their borrowing. The former include all monetary unions where the money-issuing authority is not accountable, formally or informally, to the government. The latter include hard currency pegs and foreign-denominated borrowing by public or private sectors. Such arrangements ensure that in a crisis scenario when financial markets panic, the government of the country must reach out to others outside their borders and control for monetary resources to mitigate the crisis. Ireland provides an objective lesson in why this can be damaging, not just to national sovereignty and pride but also to the economy.

Debt forgiveness for the Irish government would be a welcome development but it would not be sufficient to regain economic stability in a dysfunctional monetary union. Debt forgiveness would merely provide a small amount of fiscal space for the Irish government equivalent to the amount currently spent on interest payments. But it would not extricate the country from the institutional arrangements that prevent it (1) from pursuing a balanced fiscal policy targeting growth and sustainability and (2) from intervening to prevent systemic private and public borrowing crises. For these reasons, Ireland should immediately negotiate a gradual, managed exit from the single currency with the relevant institutions. The case for remaining in the currency union is non-existent; the case for a managed exit is incontrovertible. In the timeless words of Franklin Roosevelt, the Irish people have nothing to fear but fear itself – and if they do not take action themselves history will likely take action for them; with all the mess that then becomes inevitable in such circumstances.

10

Short-Term Capital Controls and Malaysia's Fast Recovery after the East-Asian Crisis

MARION PIRCHER

ABSTRACT

This chapter shows in detail the remedies used by Malaysia during the East-Asian Crisis, which helped the economy to recover quickly leading to a V-shaped recovery. Being part of the so-called East-Asian Miracle, Malaysia suffered from the outbreak of the East-Asian Crisis in 1997 and was hurt by sharp currency depreciations and massive capital outflows. As opposed to the view of the IMF, which explained the main problem of the East-Asian Crisis by macroeconomic fundamentals and institutions, it is widely recognized that the crisis had been caused by a set of factors such as high capital inflows, capital account liberalization, currency and maturity mismatches and the exchange rate system. The involvement of the private sector and the resulting credit crunch (i.e. banks unwilling to rollover short-term credits as currency downturns put pressure on domestic corporate sectors) during the crisis necessitated specific crisis remedies. Unlike other crisis-hit economies in the region (e.g. Indonesia, Korea, Thailand), Malaysia was not going to call-in the IMF and followed its own policy strategy which was to impose capital controls on short-term outflows. Malaysia opted therefore for monetary policy autonomy and stable exchange rates in order to restore tranquillity in the economy, which are considered 'unorthodox' policies. Capital controls combined with fixed exchange rates gave the Malaysian authorities policy autonomy which resulted in macroeconomic stimulation and the restructuring of the banking and corporate sector. The policies adopted by Malaysia are considered successful and the result was a fast and V-shaped recovery of the economy (in contrast to a U-shaped recovery that Indonesia, for instance, experienced).

I. A SHORT OVERVIEW OF THE EAST-ASIAN MIRACLE

In the 1990s East Asia experienced a 'rise and fall' in the international financial community: the rise was the so-called East-Asian Miracle[1] while the fall of the region came in 1997–98 due to the experience of the East-Asian Crisis. A more detailed view shows that the East-Asian Miracle was in fact not a miracle, as economic growth was long-term – characterized by the decision to stick to specific economic policies only if they seemed to be beneficial to their economies. Growth and development in the East Asian region were the highest in the world for the period of 1965 to the mid-1990s. In this period, economic growth and transformation were high.

During the late 1980s until the mid-1990s the so called Washington Consensus[2] influenced policy choices in East Asian countries. The Washington Consensus describes the shared ideas of the US Treasury and the Washington-based Bretton Woods institutions, the IMF and the World Bank, on appropriate universal economic policies. They emphasized during this period the need for free markets, free trade, free capital mobility and a limited government. The fears of these institutions regarding macroeconomics were external shocks as the oil price shock (in 1973, 1979), the commodity price shock (1986), two deep recessions in OECD countries (1975, 1982) and the debt crises in developing countries (1982–83). The World Bank began to implement this neoclassical orthodoxy with their 'structural adjustment lending' programmes which could be seen as a variation of the IMF 'conditionality' (lending respectively financial assistance was conditional on fulfilling certain policy measures).

As proposed by the 'Washington Consensus' the East Asian countries opened their current accounts, being therefore relatively open compared to other developing countries. Furthermore, these countries opened their capital account gradually, starting in the late 1980s, too. Therefore, the East Asian countries experienced a sharp increase of capital flows where structure and time of capital flows changed from long-term in the late 1980s to huge amounts of short-term capital flows (bank loans and portfolio flows) until the outbreak of the crisis in 1997. The structure and change in composition

1 World Bank, *The East Asian Miracle: Economic Growth and Public Policy* (New York: Oxford University Press, 1993).

2 J. Williamson, 'What Washington Means by Policy Reform' in *Latin American Adjustment: How Much Has Happened?* ed. J. Williamson (Washington DC: Institute for International Economics, 1990).
J. Williamson ed., *The Political Economy of Policy Reform* (Washington DC: Institute for International Economics, 1994).

TABLE 10.1 *Currency movement and depreciation (in local currency per US dollar) during first weeks of East-Asian Crisis*

	July 2, 1997	End-September 1997	Rate of depreciation (%) from July 1997 to September 1998
Philippine peso	26.38	43.80	66.10
Indonesian rupiah	2,341.92	10,638.30	354.30
Thai baht	24.40	38.99	59.80
Malaysian ringgit	2.57	3.80	47.80
Korean won	885.74	1,369.86	54.70

of capital flows were crucial not only for Malaysia but for the overall region, too. Furthermore, crisis management in Malaysia, i.e. policies available for the resolution of the crisis, was mainly driven by the behaviour and structure of capital flows and influenced strongly the success of crisis resolution.

II. A SHORT DESCRIPTION OF THE EAST-ASIAN CRISIS IN 1997

The East-Asian financial crisis was almost unexpected, as 'traditional' economic indicators showed no vulnerability: high GDP growth rate, relative low inflation and indebtedness of governments. In early 1997 the East-Asian financial crisis began to spread from Thailand to the whole region within a few weeks. On 2 July 1997 the Thai baht was devalued by the Bank of Thailand and in August 1997 its neighbours, Malaysia, Indonesia and the Philippines, had substantially devalued their currencies[3] as can be seen in Table 10.1.

After the collapse of the Thai baht, perception of foreign investors changed and Malaysia was involved in the crisis from the beginning, i.e. from 14 July 1997. The currency fell rapidly from RM/US$ 2.48 in March 1997 to RM/US$ 2.57 in July and RM/US$ 3.77 at year-end of 1997. In order to defend the ringgit in mid-1997, Bank Negara Malaysia (BNM) increased short-term interest rates with a peak of the overnight and seven-day interbank rates at 50 per cent and 35 per cent in July 1997.

However, since this intervention did not help to stabilize the currency, BNM abandoned the defence and therefore the outflow of foreign reserves

[3] S.D. Sharma, *The Asian Financial Crisis: Crisis, Reform and Recovery* (Manchester: Manchester University Press, 2003).

was halted. The rally against the currencies continued and in early January 1998 the ringgit fell to an all-time low of RM/US$ 4.88, recovering thereafter in April 1998 to RM/US$ 3.73 and falling again to RM/US$ 4.20 in August 1998. The stock market tumbled as well and investors began selling stocks on Kuala Lumpur Stock Exchange (KLSE) as concerns about the economy and the exchange rate grew. In January 1997, the Composite Index of KLSE was 1,216.7 points, and it fell to 594.4 points in December 1997, i.e. it halved in about one year. In August 1998, the Composite Index was even lower, at 302.9 points, and market capitalization was only RM200 billion compared to RM826 billion in January 1997. On 2 September 1998, the exchange rate was fixed at RM/US$ 3.8 and capital controls on short-term capital outflows were introduced.

The debate on the causes of the East-Asian crisis is both wide and varied and there are many opinions regarding the reasons. A detailed discussion on the causes of the crisis would be beyond this chapter. Theoretical models, i.e. so-called third-generation crisis models,[4] show that macroeconomic fundamentals were not the main cause of the crisis in East Asia as claimed by the IMF. Nowadays, it is widely recognized that the crisis was not caused by 'bad' macroeconomic fundamentals, but that the East-Asian Crisis was a kind of 'liquidity' crisis, as it affected the liquidity of the private sector, although there is some disagreement about the details. Furthermore, the discussion on the causes of the crisis shows that there might not be one single factor but a set of different factors leading to the crisis: inflows of capital increased the fragility of the corporate and banking crisis to changes of expectations; problems within the institutional sector in the different countries like weaker regulations on banking supervision or incentives of foreign banks to invest in emerging market countries (e.g. Basel core standards); currency

[4] P. Aghion, P. Bacchetta and A. Banerjee, 'A Simple Model of Monetary Policy and Currency Crises', *European Economic Review* 44 (2000): 728–38; P. Aghion, P. Bacchetta and A. Banerjee, 'Currency Crises and Monetary Policy in an Economy with Credit Constraints', *European Economic Review* 45 (2001): 1121–50; P. Aghion, P. Bacchetta and A. Banerjee, 'A Corporate Balance-Sheet Approach to Currency Crises', *Journal of Economic Theory* 119 (2004): 6–30; R. Chang and A. Velasco, 'Financial Fragility and the Exchange Rate Regime', (1998) 6469 *NBER Working Paper*; R. Chang and A. Velasco, 'Financial Crises in Emerging Markets: A Canonical Model', (1998) 98–10 *Federal Reserve Bank of Atlanta Working Paper*; L.F. Céspedes, R. Chang and A. Velasco, 'Balance Sheets and Exchange Rate Policy', (2000) 7840 *NBER Working Paper*; P. Krugman, 'Balance Sheets, the Transfer Problem, and Financial Crises', in *International Finance and Financial Crises: Essays in Honor of Robert Flood*, eds. Peter Isard, Assaf Razin and Andrew K. Rose (Norwell Massachusetts: Kluwer Academic Publishers, 1999); P. Krugman, *Analytical Afterthoughts on the Asian Crisis* (Mimeo: MIT, 1999); P. Krugman, 'Crises: The Next Generation?', draft prepared for Razin Conference, Tel Aviv University, March 25–26, 2001.

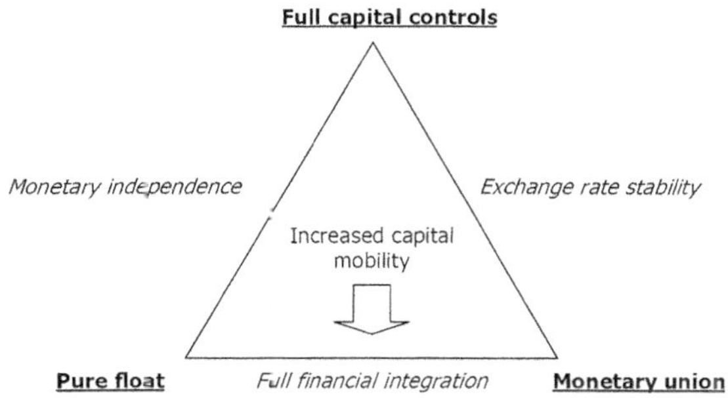

FIGURE 10.1 Impossible trinity.
J.A. Frankel, 'No Single Currency Regime Is Right for All Countries or at All Times', (1999) 7338 *NBER Working Paper*.

and maturity mismatches, i.e. low incentives of corporations to hedge against their currency risk and the liberalization of capital flows in the late 1980s and 1990s; and finally, a currency system which neglected the standard textbook description of the 'trilemma' in open economies and seemed to work well.

III. POSSIBLE REMEDIES

Domestic policies at disposal are based on the so-called trilemma in open economies, which includes the trade-offs in exchange rate, monetary policies and capital mobility. A graphical representation of the choices of the trilemma can be found in Figure 10.1. This figure shows on the three corners of the triangle the three policy instruments in an open economy (full capital controls, pure float and monetary union) while on the three sides of the triangle the three goals are listed: monetary independence, exchange rate stability and full financial integration. Capital mobility increases by moving from the top to the bottom of the triangle. Policymakers can only choose to pursue two policies contemporaneously, i.e. monetary independence and exchange rate stability, which leads to full capital controls, or monetary independence and full financial integration leading to a pure float and lastly, exchange rate stability and full financial integration, which lead to a monetary union. Any combination of all three policies cannot be reached at the same time and will create instability in the system.

Before the onset of the East-Asian Crisis, Malaysia began to liberalize the capital account in the late 1980s and had a managed float as a currency regime. According to economic theory Malaysia had at disposal three policy options: (1) move to a floating exchange rate, (2) establishing a monetary union with other countries in the region or a currency board and (3) imposition of capital controls. Although the discussion on the imposition of capital controls is controversial, Malaysia adopted capital controls on short-term capital flows. Therefore, and according to theory, Malaysia could enjoy the benefits of monetary policy autonomy and stable exchange rates.

IV. ACTIONS TAKEN BY MALAYSIA

During the crisis the exchange rate fluctuated widely. The fixing of the ringgit to the US dollar became effective on 2 September 1998 at RM/US$ 3.8. During the period between the outbreak of the crisis and the introduction of controls on capital outflows the stream of capital reversed sharply: from inflows to outflows. Portfolio capital, which is highly mobile, was the main source of capital flight. This increased not only the pressure on exchange rates but as well on the stock market exchange, which plunged around 80 per cent, i.e. the Malaysian stock market plunged from almost 1,300 in February 1997 to a low of 262 in early September 1998, and only in 2007 did the Kuala Lumpur Composite Index (KLCI) return to its pre-crisis level.

The major problems in Malaysia were mainly due to capital flows from portfolio investment, as the economy was not exposed to large foreign debt of its banking system, as was the case of Thailand, Indonesia and Korea. Therefore, Athukorala argues that Malaysia was 'able to "muddle through" without an IMF-sponsored rescue package'.[5]

IV.A. *The First Stage of Policy Response*

Soon after the outbreak of the crisis, Prime Minister Mahathir stated that the crisis was due to currency speculators and blamed especially George Soros for putting Malaysia into the crisis. Prime Minister Mahathir continued the complaints about currency speculators during the IMF and World Bank annual meetings in Hong Kong in late September 1997. In his speech he stated that 'currency trading is unnecessary, unproductive and immoral' and that it should be 'stopped' and 'made illegal', and continued at the Annual Asia-Pacific Economic Cooperation (APEC) summit on 18 November 1997 in Vancouver and the Commonwealth Heads of Government Meeting in Birmingham in the same month.[6] During this early stage and until the

[5] P.-C. Athukorala, *Crisis and Recovery in Malaysia: The Role of Capital Controls*, (Cheltenham: Edward Elgar Publishing Limited, 2001), 63.

[6] Ibid., 63–64; K.S. Jomo, 'Malaysia's September 1998 Controls: Background, Context, Impacts, Comparisions, Implications, Lessons', (March 2005) G-24 Discussion Paper Series, no. 36, 7.

imposition of capital controls and the fixing of the exchange rate, the downward pressure of the ringgit was external, and the political rhetoric of Prime Minister Mahathir and policy measures put even more pressure on the exchange rate. Therefore, the foreign exchange reserves of Malaysia depleted rapidly and improved significantly only after the imposition of capital controls.[7]

At this early stage sponsored share purchases by the government were introduced which decreased confidence in the Malaysian government and economy. On 3 September 1997, the prime minister announced that funds from the Employees Provident Fund (EPF) would be used to prop up share prices by buying stocks from Malaysian shareholders and not from foreigners at a premium above prevailing prices. The result of these actions was that local and foreign investors regarded it as a possibility of getting rid of Malaysian shares.[8] Furthermore, it was seen as a bailout facility designed to save 'cronies' from disaster, although the fund was never properly institutionalized as announced, and government officials later denied its existence.

On 5 December 1997, finance minister Anwar announced a policy package, the so-called White Paper:[9]

- Cut of government spending by 18 per cent;
- Postponing indefinitely all public sector investment projects which were still in the pipeline, stopping new overseas investment by Malaysian firms, freezing new share issues and company restructuring, and cutting salaries of government ministers by 10 per cent;
- Bank Negara Malaysia increased its three-month intervention rate from 7.55 per cent to 8.7 per cent, reduced the default period for classifying a loan as a non-performing loan by banking institutions from six months to three months and increased the inter-bank lending rate from the pre-crisis level of 7.6 per cent to 8.7 per cent in December 1997 and to 10 per cent in January and 11 per cent in February 1998.[10]

This repressive package was considered to please mainly foreign financial interest and did not recognize the gravity of the crisis and its possible causes.[11] In the news media the new package was labelled as 'IMF policy

[7] Jomo, 'Malaysia's September 1998 Controls', 4–5.
[8] Athukorala, *Crisis and Recovery in Malaysia*, 64–65.
[9] NEAC, 'White Paper: Status of the Malaysian Economy', Kuala Lumpur, National Economic Action Council, April 6, 1999, box 1, 25–26.
[10] Athukorala, *Crisis and Recovery in Malaysia*, 65; Jomo, 'Malaysia's September 1998 Controls', 9–10.
[11] Jomo, 'Malaysia's September 1998 Controls', 9.

without IMF'.[12] The following period was characterized by the underlying conflict between Prime Minister Mahathir and Finance Minister Anwar on how to manage the crisis and causing a state of policy paralysis.

On 7 January 1998, the National Economic Action Council (NEAC) was set up acting as a consultative body for the government and 'to chart its own course of action, instead of following IMF's prescription'.[13] Prime minister Mahathir was the chair of the NEAC and as executive director, Daim Zainuddin, a former finance minister, was called in. The exchange rate reached its historic intra-day low of RM/US$ 4.88 on that day and the media interpreted the step of Dr Mahathir and the call in of Daim Zainuddin as a 'calculated plan to sideline Anwar Ibrahim from the policy scene'.[14]

During the following months the contractionary monetary and fiscal policies announced and introduced in late 1997 were reversed in an ad hoc manner. Therefore, BNM reduced the statutory reserve requirement from 13.5 per cent to 10 per cent in February 1998 and to 8 per cent in July 1998, arguing that it was necessary to 'avoid a recession-deflation spiral'.[15] Furthermore, the three-month, inter-bank intervention rate was reduced in three steps from 11 per cent to 9.5 per cent in August and government expenditure was restored, and some large, halted projects were reactivated.[16]

On 23 July 1998, the National Economic Recovery Plan (NERP) prepared by the NEAC was launched inasmuch as a policy blueprint, but failed to include precise policy measures.[17] In May 1998, the Malaysian authorities introduced an institutional framework for recapitalizing troubled banks and resolving mounting corporate distress by setting up an asset management company, Pengurusan Danaharta Nasional Berhad (Danaharta), to acquire and manage non-performing loans (NPLs) from banks. In July 1998, a banking and corporate recapitalization company, Danamodal Nasional Berhad (Danamodal), was established aiming at recapitalization of financial institutions whose capital adequacy ratio had fallen below 9 per cent. In August 1998, the Corporate Debt Restructuring Committee (CDRC, a joint public and private sector steering committee) was established in order to facilitate the restructuring of corporate debts through out-of-court settlements between debtors and creditors. These three institutions were introduced to deal with

[12] FEER (Far Eastern Economic Review), 'Malaysia: Hit the Brake', December 18, 1997, 14–15.

[13] Government of Malaysia, 'Economic Survey – 1999', Kuala Lumpur, Ministry of Finance, 1999, 9.

[14] Athukorala, *Crisis and Recovery in Malaysia*, 66.

[15] BNM (Bank Negara Malaysia), 'Annual Report of the Board of Directors for the Year Ended 31 December 1998', Kuala Lumpur, BNM, 1999, 4.

[16] Athukorala, *Crisis and Recovery in Malaysia*, 66. [17] Ibid.

the rising problem of bad debt of the financial system and corporate distress. The three institutions had difficulties getting the required funds Therefore, BNM had to continue intervening in the banking and the corporate sector to prevent an increasing liquidity squeeze caused by the share market crash and capital outflow.[18]

In August 1998, the economy already had entered into recession and in contrast to the other crisis-affected countries there seemed not to be any signs of achieving currency and share price stability. Output as well as employment declined, while the inflation rate peaked at 6.2 per cent in June 1998. The impact of the collapse of output and the crash of the property market increased NPLs in the banking system, aggravating the situation and resulting in a 'flight to quality' of deposits from smaller to large well-managed banks from the fourth quarter 1997 onwards.[19]

Banks changed strategy, too: instead of issuing new loans, loan recovery was reinforced, creating a credit crunch, which had an impact on domestic consumption and investment. Growth of net outstanding bank loans (in nominal terms) decreased from about 26 per cent per annum during the five years preceding the crisis to 9 per cent during the year ending July 1998. Annual rate of growth of money supply (M3) declined from 18.5 per cent at the end of 1997 to 4.4 per cent by August 1998.[20]

Additionally, asset prices declined even more, recovery in the export market did not show up and investor confidence weakened. External reserves of the country decreased to very low levels despite the massive import contraction in the depressed economy.[21] The large capital outflows did not improve the foreign reserve position of the current account that was in surplus due to the recession and in contrast to the experience of the four IMF-programme countries (Thailand, Indonesia, the Philippines and Korea). Widening current account surpluses boosted international reserves, preventing further exchange rate collapse.[22]

One characteristic of capital flight from Malaysia since early 1998 was that about 25 to 35 billion ringgit flew to Singapore at the height of the crisis in mid-1998.[23] This had been caused by attractive money market rates of

[18] Ibid., 67. [19] Ibid., 68. [20] Ibid. [21] Ibid., 68–69.

[22] World Bank, *Recovery in Asia* (Washington, DC: World Bank, 1998).

[23] M. Ariff (1999), 'The Financial Crisis and the Reshaping of the Malaysian Economy: Trends and Issues', (1999, unpublished paper, Kuala Lumpur: Malaysian Institute of Economic Research).

S. Tripathi, B. Dolven and F. Keenan, 'Some Pains, Some Gains', *Far Eastern Economic Review*, September 17, 1998, 51–52; IMF, *International Capital Markets: Developments, Prospects and Key Policy Issues* (Washington, DC: IMF, 1999).

20 per cent to 40 per cent in Singapore (compared to 11 per cent in the domestic market) combined with a weakening exchange rate of the ringgit. This arbitrage position put pressure on domestic interest rates in Malaysia and therefore politicians became concerned about the 'internationalization' of the national currency, which was considered a new threat to economic stability and monetary policy autonomy.[24] Demand for offshore ringgits and the build-up of offshore ringgit deposits increased the vulnerability of the Malaysian currency and undermined the effectiveness of monetary policy.[25] Furthermore, in the early and mid-1990s massive portfolio capital inflows had transformed the capital market in Malaysia. Foreign investors held an estimated one-third of the stock of the largest 100 companies of the KLCI and were involved in short-term transactions and speculation. Local institutions were generally too small in comparison and took generally more long-term stock positions. Malaysia was very attractive for foreign fund managers and therefore they probably played a key role in the phenomenon of 'contagion', which involves cross-border investment trends.[26] Herd behaviour was especially dangerous for Malaysia being exposed more to portfolio flows than to private creditors.

IV.B. *Turning Around Policies – the Introduction of Capital Controls*

During the second half of 1998 policy choices available to the Malaysian government were very limited. The Malaysian government followed a strategy of monetary and fiscal expansion in order to fight recession and let the exchange rate fluctuate. Therefore, in theory, the exchange rate could have gradually stabilized as the economy recovered from the recession by introducing expansionary macroeconomic policies and corporate and banking restructuring. But the ringgit remained under attack and market sentiments and confidence was not restored due to policies differing from those proposed by the IMF and being 'unorthodox'. Furthermore, they were considered to rescue some politically connected corporations and banks. Additionally, downgrading of Malaysia's credit rating by international credit rating agencies was depleting market confidence and the planned sovereign bond issue in August 1998 in the United States and Europe, which should have

[24] Athukorala, *Crisis and Recovery in Malaysia*, 71.
[25] BNM (Bank Negara Malaysia), *The Central Bank and the Financial System in Malaysia* (Kuala Lumpur: BNM, 1999), ch. 14.
[26] Jomo, 'Malaysia's September 1998 Controls', 5–6.

raised US$ 2 billion for the implementation of the banking sector restructuring programme had to be postponed.[27]

At this stage Malaysia's government had two possibilities:

1 Calling in the IMF and adopting similar policies like those applied in Thailand, Indonesia or Korea;
2 Introducing capital controls in order to increase the influence of domestic policies and to speed up recovery.

Although the IMF had adopted a contractionary policy strategy in the region at the beginning, it had changed the strategy by the second half of 1998 to a more expansionary macroeconomic policy. Market sentiment was not very favourable as there was less constraint for Malaysia to undergo structural reforms when not calling in the IMF.[28] Some authors argue that Malaysia was not eligible for IMF support even if it wanted to seek such support because of its relatively strong balance of payments position and its relatively lower foreign debt,[29] although the actual practice of the IMF is to give assistance to member countries in the event of an economic crisis and not necessarily in a balance-of-payments crisis.

The key point against calling in the IMF was that the Malaysian leadership did not want to change the Malaysian policy practice of having distortionary policies like the New Economic Policy, which had established intimate links between business and government, stabilizing the economy. Therefore, any new policy was weighted against the potential negative effect on the socio-political stability of the country.[30] Therefore, the leadership changed its approach to deal with the crisis, and policies applied thereafter could be explained by the 'impossible trinity' of open economies as discussed previously. The social equilibrium and its stability in Malaysia played an important role in choosing capital controls, i.e. Malaysia is sociopolitically more fragile than more socially homogenous countries like Thailand and Korea.

In Malaysia, capital controls were already used before September 1998, i.e. in the period of 1993–94 when BNM successfully used capital controls on inflows without experiencing adverse effects on Malaysia's long-term prospects for attracting foreign investment. On 30 July 1997, just two weeks after the speculative attack on the ringgit, the prime minister gave a hint that the government might use capital controls as a possible policy alternative.[31]

[27] Athukorala, *Crisis and Recovery in Malaysia*, 73. [28] BNM, *Annual Report*, 5.
[29] Ibid.; NEAC, 'White Paper: Status of Malaysian Economy', 1.
[30] H. Crouch, 'The Asian Economic Crisis and Democracy', *Public Policy* 11, no. 3 (1998): 39–62.
[31] FEER (Far Eastern Economic Review), 'Thus Spoke Mahathir', September 18, 1997, 65.

TABLE 10.2 *Currency movement and depreciation (in local currency per US dollar) during first weeks of East-Asian Crisis*[32]

Transactions subject to control	Transactions not subject to control
Ringgit-denominated transactions with non-residents	Current-account transactions ➔ Trade transactions denominated in foreign currency
Outflow of short-term capital ➔ One-year withholding period until 30 August 1998, ➔ A three-tier tax (10%, 20%, 30%) on profit remittance between September 1998 and February 1999, ➔ A 10% tax on profit remittance since February 1999	Repatriation of profits to Malaysia, interests, dividends, capital gains and rental income from FDI and similar forms of ringgit assets owned by non-residents
Import and export of ringgit (carriage on person)	
Export of foreign currency by citizen (carriage on person)	General payments by residents including those for education abroad
Outflow of Malaysian investment abroad	FDI inflows and outflows

The introduction of capital controls began with the ban of offshore trading of shares of Malaysian companies effective from 31 August 1998 and therefore the over-the-counter share trading in the central limit order book (CLOB) market in Singapore was effectively frozen. On 1 September 1998, comprehensive controls over short-term capital flows were introduced and on 2 September 1998 the exchange rate was fixed at RM/US$ 3.80. The fixing of the exchange rate was equivalent to a mild appreciation of the ringgit from the average level of the previous three months (around RM/US$ 4.18) but it represented a 35 per cent depreciation against the pre-crisis level of about RM/US$ 2.5.

The capital controls on outflows banned trading in ringgit instruments among offshore banks operating in Malaysia and stopped Malaysian financial institutions from offering domestic credit facilities to non-resident banks and stockbrokers. The ringgit was banned as an invoicing currency in foreign trade and legal tender on all ringgit deposits outside the country with effect from 30 September 1998, too. Furthermore, a 12-month withholding period was

[32] Athukorala, *Crisis and Recovery in Malaysia*, 77.

introduced on repatriation proceeds (principal and profit) from foreign portfolio investment and restrictions on overseas investment by residents exceeding RM 10,000, and a limit of RM 1,000 on Malaysian overseas travellers was imposed.

Table 10.2 summarizes the policies introduced in September 1998 in Malaysia. The goal of the capital controls was to limit short-term capital flows; selling of shares of portfolio investors became more difficult and this should result in an alleviated pressure on the exchange rate. Long-term capital flows were not under control as well as import and export trade, which was exempted from controls. Profit remittances and repatriation of capital by foreign investors continued to remain free of control.

Summarizing, the policies were aimed to:[33]

⇒ Kill the offshore ringgit market: this was done by forbidding the transfer of funds into the country from externally held ringgit accounts, except for investment in Malaysia or for the purchase of goods in Malaysia.

⇒ Close off access by non-residents to domestic ringgit sources: this was reached by banning ringgit credit facilities.

⇒ Shut down the offshore market in Malaysian shares: the CLOB in Singapore was closed.

⇒ Obstruct speculative outward capital flows: Malaysian residents needed prior approval to invest abroad in any form, and exports of foreign currency by residents for other than valid current account purposes were limited.

⇒ Protect the ringgit's value and raise foreign exchange reserves: the export proceeds had to be repatriated within six months.

⇒ Insulate monetary policy from the foreign exchange market: the authorities imposed a 12-month ban on outflow of external portfolio capital on the principal while interest and dividend payments could be freely repatriated.

In the following period, capital control policies were changed and relaxed:

- In early February 1999, the original 12-month holding restriction on portfolio investment was replaced by a system of repatriation levy. This repatriation levy identified two sets of repatriation levy: on funds which

[33] I. Rajaraman, 'Management of the Capital Account: A Study of India and Malaysia' in *UNCTAD Management of Capital Flows: Comparative Experiences and Implications for Africa* (New York and Geneva: United Nations, 2003), 109–83.

entered the country before 15 February 1999 a three-tier levy to the principal was to be applied (the capital value) for the retaining period of these funds in the country. On funds which entered the country after 15 February 1999 a two-tier levy was imposed on the repatriation of profits and not applicable on the principal: 30 per cent on profit made and repatriated within one year, and 10 per cent on profit repatriated after one year. On 21 September 1999, the two-tier levy on profit repatriation was replaced by a 10 per cent levy. On 27 October 2000, the authorities announced that profit earned from foreign portfolio investments in the country for a period of more than one year was exempted from this levy. On 1 January 2001, the 10 per cent levy on capital gains repatriated after investing in Malaysia for more than one year was effectively removed.

- On 26 February 2000, the KLSE and the Singapore Stock Exchange reached an agreement on the transfer of the shares trapped in the CLOB market to the Malaysian stock exchange and allowed trading to resume.[34]

The change of the capital controls policy by exchanging the one-year moratorium on portfolio capital with an exit tax was mainly interpreted by the financial press as a major backsliding from the original capital controls. The change was introduced in consultation with key players in the capital market[35] and it was a pragmatic revision of the former capital control policy to only one element of the comprehensive controls in order to manage capital inflows in the recovery phase. The tax on profit repatriation from portfolio investment, together with the restrictions in place on foreign short-term bank borrowing, was intended to discourage excessive reliance of Malaysian corporations on volatile foreign capital.[36] The ringgit offshore market was destroyed by this policy package and exchange rate controls limited access to the ringgit for non-residents, preventing the re-emergence of an offshore ringgit market.

The fixed peg of the ringgit to the US dollar was removed on 21 July 2005. At the same time Chinese authorities announced that they allowed appreciating their own currency. These two announcements implied that the economic environment in and outside the region changed. Therefore, Malaysia moved to a managed float, based on a currency basket consisting of the currencies of its major trading partners. In the months after this change, the ringgit appreciated slightly with respect to the US dollar (from RM/US$ 3.8 to

34 Athukorala, *Crisis and Recovery in Malaysia*, 78; Jomo, 'Malaysia's September 1998 Controls'.

35 'New Measures Aim to Rekindle Foreign Investment: Malaysia Eases Fund Flows', *International Herald Tribune*, February 9, 1999.

36 Athukorala, *Crisis and Recovery in Malaysia*, 78–79.

almost RM/US$ 3.7). The offshore ringgit market did not re-emerge, i.e. its internationalization was banned.

V. THE ROLE OF CAPITAL CONTROLS IN THE ECONOMIC RECOVERY OF MALAYSIA

Looking at history, the imposition of capital controls is not as new as it seemed in 1998, as capital controls were imposed before for example by Chile and Malaysia. These capital controls were on inflows whereas the 1998 experiment of Malaysia was to impose controls on outflows. Whereas there is more agreement that temporary capital controls on inflow are beneficial for the recovery and stabilization of an economy, there is much more controversy on temporary capital controls on outflows. Therefore, the capital controls introduced in September 1998 in Malaysia are considered to be an 'unorthodox' step (i.e. 'orthodox' policies were promoted especially by the IMF and other institutions). Although there is a huge literature on the effectiveness and advantages and disadvantages of capital controls on inflows[37] and empirical studies,[38] the topic of capital controls on outflows has received more attention consequently after its imposition in Malaysia. The result of analyses on capital controls is rather mixed depending on sampling and methodology used.[39]

In the case of Malaysia, the proponents of the success of the capital controls on outflows argue that the economic and stock market decline came to a stop

[37] E.g. J. Williamson, 'Comments and Discussion on Cooper (1999): 'Should Capital Controls Be Banished?', *Brookings Papers on Economic Activity* 1 (1999): 130–38; P.J. Montiel, 'Managing Economic Policy in the Face of Large Capital Inflows: What Have We Learned?', document presented at Private Capital Flows to Emerging Markets after the Mexican Crisis, Institute for International Economics (Vienna: Österreichische Nationalbank, 1995); M.P. Dooley, 'A Survey on Academic Literature on Controls over International Capital Transactions', (1995) 5352 NBER Working Paper; R.N. Cooper, 'Should Capital Controls Be Banished?', *Brookings Papers on Economic Activity* 1, (1999): 89–141; S.C. Saxena and K. Wong, 'Currency Crises and Capital Controls: A Selective Survey', (1999), Discussion Papers, Department of Economics, University of Washington.

[38] E.g. R.B. Johnston and C. Ryan, 'The Impact of Controls on Capital Movements on the Private Capital Accounts of Countries' Balance of Payments: Empirical Estimates and Policy Implications', (1994) 94/78 IMF Working Paper; Dooley, 'A Survey on Academic Literature'; G. Epstein, I. Grabel and K.S. Jomo, 'Capital Management Techniques in Developing Countries: An Assessment of Experiences from the 1990's and Lessons for the Future', (2003) working paper no. 56, Political Economy Research Institute, University of Massachusetts Amherst; S. Edwards, 'Exchange Rate Regimes, Capital Flows and Crisis Prevention' in *Economic and Financial Crises in Emerging Market Economies*, ed. Martin Feldstein (NBER, Chicago: The University of Chicago Press, 2003), 31–78.

[39] N. Magud and C.M. Reinhart, 'Capital Controls: An Evaluation', (2006), 11973 NBER Working Paper.

soon after the controls were implemented.[40] Opponents argue that the reversals have been more pronounced in the rest of the region. The empirical study of Kaplan and Rodrik[41] suggests that there is strong evidence that the controls had a positive effect on the economy as they provided some room to breathe for domestic monetary and financial policies. For these reasons, they permitted a faster recovery than by implementing the orthodox IMF policies.

A further advantage of the controls on capital outflows was that the Malaysian government was able to finance the deficits through issuing Malaysian government securities. The funds financing the deficit came mainly from domestic borrowing (86 per cent, mainly from the centrally controlled Employees Provident Fund and other saving funds) and the remainder was externally (concessionary long-term credit from multilateral sources); therefore, Malaysia remained a net creditor to the IMF throughout the crisis period.[42]

Kaplan and Rodrik,[43] as well as Epstein et al.,[44] also argue that the Malaysian government reached their goal of eliminating the offshore ringgit market by the implementation of the policy package in 1998; therefore, the targets of these policies were reached. On the other hand, a leading Malaysian neo-liberal economist, Thillainathan, argued that in spite of the huge amount of ringgit held abroad (around RM25–30 billion) the speculative offshore market was very thin; Thillainathan failed to provide further evidence.[45] Jomo[46] argues that the imposition of capital controls might have contributed to cronyism and corruption. Additionally, Jomo[47] argues that the policy package is generally recognized as being comprehensive and cleverly designed to limit foreign exchange outflows and ringgit speculation by non-residents as well as residents, but at the same time not affecting foreign direct investors. Furthermore, BNM effectively enforced the measures, and its success is often attributed to Malaysian conditions, i.e. the adequacy of its

[40] E. Kaplan and D. Rodrik, 'Did the Malaysian Capital Controls Work?', (2001) 8142 NBER Working Paper; K.S. Jomo, *Malaysian Eclipse* (London: Zed Press, 2001); G. Palma, 'The Three Routes to Financial Crises: The Need for Capital Controls', (2000) CEPA Working Paper Series III, no. 18; R. Dornbusch, 'Malaysia's Crisis: Was it Different?', in *Preventing Currency Crises in Emerging Markets*, eds. S. Edwards and J.A. Frankel, (Chicago: The University of Chicago Press, 2002), 441–60.

[41] Kaplan and Rodrik, 'Did the Malaysian Capital Controls Work?'.

[42] Athukorala, *Crisis and Recovery in Malaysia*, 79.

[43] Kaplan and Rodrik, 'Did the Malaysian Capital Controls Work?'.

[44] Epstein et al., 'Capital Management Techniques'.

[45] Jomo, 'Were Malaysia's Capital Controls Effective?', in *After the Storm: Crisis, Recovery, and Sustaining Development in four Asian Economies*, ed. K.S. Jomo (Singapore: Singapore University Press, 2004), 182.

[46] Jomo, *Malaysian Eclipse*.

[47] Jomo, 'Malaysia's September 1998 Controls', 12.

foreign exchange reserves, its lower exposure to foreign debt and strong economic fundamentals.

The preceding discussion shows that the fast recovery of Malaysia after the East-Asian Crisis can be attributed to the introduction of capital controls in combination with other policy measures. Capital controls on short-term capital outflows as imposed by Malaysia in 1998 eliminated pressure on the economy (e.g. elimination of offshore ringgit market, limiting the rise of overnight interest rates) and gave the policymakers room for the introduction of other policy measures (e.g. restructuring of financial sector), leading to a fast recovery.

Nevertheless, a generalization of the experience of Malaysia cannot be drawn. As in the case of Malaysia in 1998, which introduced controls on short-term capital outflows for a predefined time period, a thorough understanding of the crisis is needed in order to isolate the type of controls needed and the duration of capital controls. Furthermore, both type and duration should be clearly announced with their introduction. Therefore, the Malaysian experience shows that capital controls on short-term capital outflows are an option for policymakers in a crisis situation.

11

Sovereign Debt

Lessons from the Mexican Experience

OSCAR UGARTECHE AND RODRIGO DELGADO*

ABSTRACT

A new borrowing cycle began after the 2008 financial crisis using bonds as instruments under the conception of low interest rates. This was true for six years, but in December 2015 interest rates began to rise in the United States, leading to a potentially difficult situation, particularly for emerging economies that do not have regional central banks to purchase their problem debts.

New debts include sovereign borrowing, state and municipal borrowing and interbank and private borrowing. This brings forth various issues: the first is the risk quality of the various bonds. The three major credit risk analysis firms separate each and every one as if they did not have the same country balance of payment support. The hypothesis is that different sub-national states have different credit ratings leading to expensive borrowing. The second issue relates to the construction of the total amount of the national debts. Using Mexico as an example, we shall attempt to review how the national debt is constructed, how the sub-national debts are included and how private international debts are taken into account. The hypothesis is that the total national debt is understated. Finally, the problems and limitations created to countries that have FTAs concerning how to manage their debts in case of default will be reviewed using Mexico as an example. FTAs have a clause that treats defaults as a violation of the contract. The clause that restricts default management gives precise instructions as to how to reorganize debts. This has far-reaching consequences at the time of debt negotiations. What debts are affected by this clause and how they are treated differently from

* The authors wish to thank Raúl Esqueda for his valuable assistance with the data.

other debts is something to be explored in the Mexican case. The hypothesis is that there are negotiation restrictions for future debt problems.

Between the 1980s and the first decade of the twenty-first century, debt instruments changed, and so have institutions. During the post-war period up to 1990 the common debt instrument in international operations were floating rate notes (FRN), defined as a variable interest, long-term debt instrument. The sovereign loan market was the euromarket, the agents were commercial banks, and the euromarket operated through syndicated loans for larger operations. After the 1990s, the euromarket operates with bonds, the agents are investment banks and creditors have turned into investors changing the debt management mechanisms. This chapter seeks to review the case of Mexico both for its historical value of the 1982 default and the 1995 crisis resolution as well as for its size as a new, emerging large capital market.

The hierarchy of the international financial architecture became manifest when problems emerged in Zaire, Jamaica, Turkey and Peru starting in the second half of the 1970s with a combination of rising interest rates and decreasing commodity prices; the IMF led the negotiations and set conditionality. This paved the way for Club of Paris and London Club settlements. The Paris Club reunited all G7 creditor countries with bilateral loans. Next in line came the London Club of private bank creditors managed by a steering committee which effectively negotiated with the debtor government in representation of all private banks. In addition, multilateral lenders had to rethink how to proceed to face the increasing risk. This led to the shift from project-based lending to policy-based lending in 1985.[1] The shift in instruments and markets since the 1980's debt crisis has led to the need of new negotiation mechanisms.

This chapter is divided in six parts: firstly, a review of the Mexican debt crisis and its management during the 1980s; this is followed by a review of the opening of the capital account in the 1990s and the emergence of new debt instruments in local currency; thirdly, a revision of the three stages of debt management after 1990; fourthly, a review of the new debt of states and municipalities and their importance; fifth an analysis of short-term capital flows that result from the previous sections; and finally some concluding remarks and lessons learnt from this case.

[1] P. Mosley, J. Harrigan and J. Toye, *Aid and Power: The World Bank and Policy-Based Lending* (Routledge, London, 1991).

I. THE MEXICAN DEBT CRISIS

The debt crisis appeared in the late 1970s and peaked in 1982 as a consequence of the rise in interest rates and volatility in commodity prices, which affected simultaneously all commodity-exporting countries.[2] The size of the debt against GDP (TD/GDP) was in the 50 per cent range.[3]

Mexican Finance Minister Silva Herzog announced on 12 August 1982 that the country would default given the impossibility to meet its debt payments on that day. This was the breaking point of the bank credit cycle that began in the early 1960s. What followed was the nationalization of private banks and the establishment of tight exchange controls in order to prevent their bankruptcy and possible bank runs. Immediately after came the private debt default and only multilateral loans were paid. To handle this,

> [I]n August 1982, Western central banks, at the behest of the US government and Federal Reserve Chairman Paul Volcker, arranged an unprecedented USD 1.5bn loan to Mexico, additional to USD 2bn in cash (oil prepayments and agricultural credits) from the US government. In essence, Mexico received USD 3.5bn in official loans to relieve immediate cash needs, but only a 90-day rollover of the principal.[4]

This is relevant because it gave the IMF time to prepare a major standby loan with the conditions it wanted Mexico to meet. Conversations with the IMF also began in early August 1982, before the default. The IMF viewed itself as 'crisis manager' and officials were concerned with crisis containment given the international consequences if not handled properly. In September, a brief workout plan was presented to Mexico which followed the measures accordingly while the international assistance package was organized and disbursed. In December, the 90-day rollover came due and Mexico had to meet those payments.[5] By then, a proper IMF standby loan had been organized and conditionality was signed.

The initial official response from Western governments in September did not prevent other countries from defaulting, as the international economic climate was the same for all, but Mexico followed a different path than the others to handle the problem. After the first 90-day rollover of principal, the IMF approved a US$3.8 billion loan to the Mexican government.

2 A. Clem, 'Commodity Price Volatility: Trends during 1975–84,' (June 1995) *Monthly Labor Review*, 17–21.

3 C. Reinhart and K. Rogoff, *This Time Is Different: Eight Centuries of Financial Folly* (Princeton University Press, 2009).

4 K. Brinke, 'The Mexican 1982 Debt Crisis,' 2013 Rabobank Economic Research, https://economics.rabobank.com/publications/2013/september/the-mexican-1982-debt-crisis/.

5 J. Boughton, 'The Mexican Crisis: No Mountain Too High?,' in *Silent Revolution: the International Monetary Fund, 1979–1989*, IMF, 2001, 281–318.

The effects of those conditions were a 50 per cent peso devaluation, inflation soared to over 100 per cent and GDP growth turned negative as a result of reduced consumption and investment.

In total, Mexico had three IMF programmes during the 1980s: one from December 1982 to December 1985, another from 1986 to 1988 – related to the Baker Plan – and the last one from 1989 to 1993 – related to the Brady Plan. These agreements are related to three bank debt restructurings. This was a small number compared to Ecuador, Brazil, and other countries, which were closer to five IMF programmes and five debt rescheduling agreements between 1981 and 1990.[6]

By the end of 1985 the grim outlook for Mexico was that it would have to meet payments for over $9.6 billion per year. This pushed both creditors and the country to a multi-year negotiation where debt paybacks were reduced to $1.1 billion.[7] The Baker Plan was announced in September 1985, soon after President Garcia of Peru had announced the 10 per cent of exports payback policy to what was then perceived as a dead end, with GDP dropping in debtor countries, banks with lending fatigue and debtor governments suffering adjustment weariness. The Baker Plan announced at the G7 meeting in Seoul in September 1985 by Secretary of the Treasury Baker focused on additional lending against structural reforms and a new role for the World Bank with policy-based lending.[8] 'Operationally, the main advantage to the Fund from the Baker Plan was that it provided a systematic channel for catalyzing resources from other creditors at a time when the Fund's own net financial contribution would inevitably be declining.'[9] The country that used the Baker Plan most was Mexico, which began its market-led structural reforms before 1988.[10]

The failure of the Baker Plan (1985–88), where only two countries out of 15 possible candidates used it extensively, was followed by the Brady Plan. The end of the debt crisis came through the Brady bonds in 1989, an idea that had bounced around in Latin America between 1984 and 1987.[11] Again,

6 O. Ugarteche, *Arquitectura Financiera Internacional: una Genealogía 1850–2010*, 2014, IIEC UNAM, Ch. 5.

7 J. Boughton, 'Growth, the Elusive Goal: 1985–87,' in *Silent Revolution: the International Monetary Fund, 1979–1989*, IMF, 2001, 415–76.

8 C. Bogdanowicz-Bindert, 'The Debt Crisis: The Baker Plan Revisited,' *Journal of Interamerican Studies and World Affairs* 28, no. 3 (1986): 33–45, www.jstor.org/stable/165706.

9 J. Boughton, 'Growth, the Elusive Goal: 1985–87,' in *Silent Revolution: the International Monetary Fund, 1979–1989*, IMF, 2001, p. 424.

10 M. Monteagudo, 'The Debt Problem: The Baker Plan and the Brady Initiative: A Latin American Perspective", *The International Lawyer* 28, No. 1 (1994): 59–81.

11 L.C. Bresser-Pereira, 'A Brazilian Approach To External Debt Negotiation,' paper presented to the XIV Latin American Studies Association International Congress, New Orleans, March 1988, published in *LASA Forum* 19, no. 4 (Winter 1989): 1–7.

it would be Mexico to make use of this before it entered the third IMF agreement. In December of 1987 Mexico reached a deal with J.P. Morgan whereby

> The Mexican government extended an offer to the banks to exchange up to $20 billion in outstanding loans for negotiable bonds. The bonds would be sold to the banks at a discounted price to be determined by auction, but the principal would be guaranteed by the U.S. Treasury. To implement that guarantee, the treasury issued zero-coupon bonds with 20-year maturities, to be held in custody by the Federal Reserve Bank of New York.[12]

This mechanism worked well and was later refined by Secretary of the Treasury Brady in what is known as the Brady Plan, which allowed for debt reduction. One answer to the risk issue was a US Treasury guaranty.[13] This way the emerging country bond market came into being and with it a new role for credit rating agencies and the new Emerging Market Bond Index (EMBI).

The return of bonds opened the need for new and deeper sovereign risk analysis and active credit rating agencies with a much more specialized definition of yield curves. Since the change in instruments, emerging markets like Mexico have proven to have learnt from the experience that external restriction matters and issue local currency bonds. (See Figure 11.1.) Jeanneau and Tovar from the BIS have argued that

> In recent years, however, domestic bond markets have constituted a growing source of financing for Latin American economies and of portfolio allocation for global investors. This has called into question the view that countries in the region cannot borrow in local currency at longer maturities, sometimes referred to as the 'original sin' hypothesis. The expansion of these markets has reflected a conscious effort by the authorities of most countries to reduce their vulnerability to adverse external shocks.[14]

The rules of the game changed, allowing new short-term treasuries issued in pesos to be purchased by foreign investors. The property of foreign owners of Mexican peso denominated debt instruments come under the terms of

[12] J. Boughton, 'Debt Denouement, 1987–89' in *Silent Revolution: the International Monetary Fund, 1979–1989*, IMF, 2001, 490.

[13] J. Sachs, 'Making the Brady Plan Work,' *Foreign Affairs*, Council on Foreign Relations 68, no. 3 (1989): 87–104; W. Cline, 'International Debt Re-Examined,' 1995, Peterson Institute of International Economics, Washington DC; R. Buckley, 'The Facilitation of the Brady Plan: Emerging Markets Debt Trading from 1989 to 1993,' *Fordham International Law Journal* 21, no. 5 (1997): 1802–89.

[14] S. Jeanneau and C. Tovar, 'Latin America's Local Currency Bond Markets: An Overview,' BIS Papers, no. 36 (2007), 46.

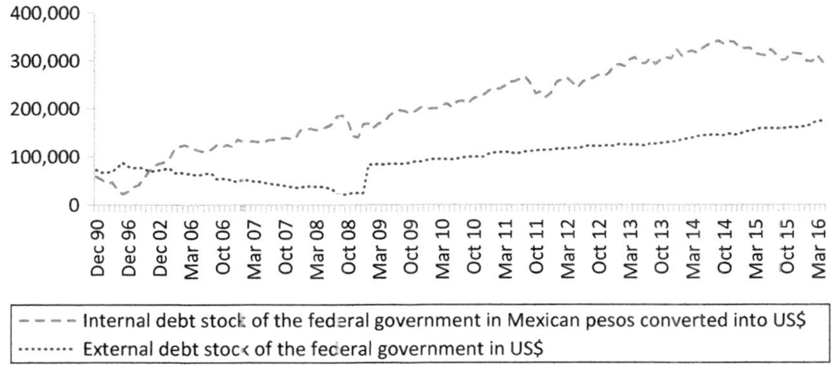

FIGURE 11.1 Total Mexican debt (in US dollars).
Source: Secretaría de Hacienda y Crédito Público.[15]
http://finanzaspublicas.hacienda.gob.mx/es/Finanzas_Publicas/Estadisticas_Oportunas_de_Finanzas_Publicas

NAFTA, and the Pacific Alliance. They define, in case of default, how investors will recover their portfolio investments.

II. AFTER THE 1990S

The Brady Plan came with the third IMF adjustment programme that required the opening up of domestic financial markets to foreign investments and the total deregulation of the Mexican financial sector. The domestic instrument was the 1989 Law on the Promotion of Mexican Investment and the Regulation of Foreign Investment.

This was modified to encourage foreign portfolio investment, and two years later, in 1991, Treasury securities (CETES, Certificados de la Tesorería) issued by the federal government were made available to foreign investors. This meant the total opening of the capital account of the balance of payments. *De facto*, the government freed the capital account and generated new financial investment channels into the country. Between 1989 and 1994, foreign portfolio investment grew twentyfold, from under $351 million to $28.9 billion and then shrunk to $8 billion, as a result of high political risk after the Zapatista Army uprising in Chiapas on New Year's Day, the assassination of presidential candidate Colossio in March 1994, the presidential elections in August 1994 and the assassination of the secretary general of the

[15] http://finanzaspublicas.hacienda.gob.mx/es/Finanzas_Publicas/Estadisticas_Oportunas_de_Finanzas_Publicas.

TABLE 11.1 *Foreign investment portfolio in Mexico 1989–1994 (in millions of dollars)*

FOREIGN INVESTMENT PORTFOLIO IN MEXICO 1989–1994 (millions of dollars)							
	1989	1990	1991	1992	1993	1994	1989–1994
Stock market	493	1,995	6,332	4,783	10,717	4,088	28,484
Securities in national currency	–	–	3,406	8,147	7,406	-2,225	16,734
Securities in foreign currency	-142	1,376	3,015	5,111	10,797	6,324	26,491
Total portfolio investment	351	3,371	12,753	18,041	28,920	8,197	71,633

Source: Banco de México (Mexico´s Central Bank) and Ernesto Zedillo, Government's first report, statistical annex, Mexico, September 1995 in Lecuona (1996).

government party Mr Ruiz Massieu in September. The new president was sworn into office on 1 December 1994. (See Table 11.2.)

There was also higher economic risk due to a rise in US interest rates. The 10-year Treasury note yield rose from 5.61 per cent to 7.33 per cent between January and May. Other factors involved were the appreciation of the peso by 23 per cent during the 1991–1994 period, and a massive fiscal deficit of 5 per cent of GDP. The president leaving office, Salinas, warned bankers that the exchange rate ceiling would be lifted when the new president would be sworn in.

A third element is the debt profile. With international reserves of US $12.4 billion, there was a $28 billion short-term debt contracted to 182 days, to be paid in pesos at a nominal interest rate of 34.55 per cent. One-third of this was in foreign hands.[16]

The exchange crisis was triggered on 19 December 1994, by the presence of the Zapatista Army in six townships in Chiapas and the blocking of roads. Investors began to reduce their positions in Mexico with its immediate effect on international reserves.

Since the official exchange rate was overvalued by November 1994 and currency speculators bet it would come down, a massive depreciation happened on 19 December, when the exchange rate jumped from 3.60 to 7.50 pesos for US dollars. This was quickly contained with a $48 billion loan

[16] S. Schmidt and R. Rivera, 'La doctrina del shock en México: los cambios estructurales / II,' *Revista Forbes*, Mexico, Invitado Forbes, Economía y Finanzas September 15, 2015.

package from the US Treasury, as the volumes of dollars in cash and speed required by Banco de Mexico where faster and greater than what the IMF procedures allowed for.

The rescue package led by the US Treasury's Exchange Stabilization Fund (ESF) in January 1995 loaned Mexico $12 billion[17] from a total package of $48 billion. The IMF lent $17.8 billion in a standby credit signed 23 January 1995, plus $10 billion from the Bank for International Settlements and $3 billion from private commercial banks. The reason for this order of agreements, according to Schwartz,[18] was speed, as the Exchange Stabilisation Fund needs solely the initiative of the Secretary of the Treasury and the approval of the President in order to withdraw the funds.

Lustig[19] states that the $48 billion package was seven times larger than the 1982 rescue package in real terms and that the US contribution was three times larger. The disbursement speed of the funds allowed for a quick turnaround of the Mexican reserve position, a restoration of confidence, the stabilization of the peso exchange rate and a return to the markets by April 1995.

Since 1996, states and municipalities issue their own bonds independently.[20] The effect has been that there is now credit risk analysis for every state and municipality of Mexico. This is done by the big three – Moody's, S&P and Fitch's – plus a local firm, H.R. Ratings.

Eichengreen and Hausman[21] argued that the *original sin* of emerging markets was that they could not issue debt in their own currency having to assume exchange risk in addition to credit risk. Mexico starting from January 2000 shows that most bond issues are launched in local currency, and that foreign investors assume the exchange risk. Mexican peso bonds are issued by state and municipal governments as well as by the federal government. What triggered the change was the reduction in January 2000 of US interest rates.

[17] A. Schwartz, 'Money, Credit, and Banking Lecture, from Obscurity to Notoriety: A Biography of the Exchange Stabilization Fund,' *Journal of Money, Credit and Banking* 29, no. 2 (1997): 135–53.

[18] Ibid.

[19] N. Lustig, 'Mexico in Crisis, the U.S. to the Rescue: The Financial Assistance Packages of 1982 and 1995,' *UCLA Journal of International Law and Foreign Affairs* 2, no. 1 (1997).

[20] Ley Federal de Deuda Pública, Diario Oficial de la Federación of 27 April 2016. Before the reform it was Ley General de Deuda Pública, Diario Oficial de la Federación, December 31, 1976.
The change of 1996 included that each State issued its own public borrowing law for itself and its municipalities. They were published in the Diario Oficial del Estado, August 31, 1996.

[21] B. Eichengreen and R. Hausmann, 'Exchange Rates and Financial Fragility,' NBER Working Paper 7418, 1999.

III. DEBT MANAGEMENT

Between 1990 and 2015 there are three distinct periods in terms of debt management: the first period was between 1990 and 1994 when the overvalued fixed floating exchange rate was left free to float with an open capital account, which ended in December 1994 in what is referred to as the first twenty-first century financial crisis.

The second stage after the crash was between 1995 and 2008 when new bonds were issued mostly in local currency with a major participation of foreign bondholders and total debt was reduced .to 17 per cent of GDP.[22] This new stage started with the recovery of creditworthiness in April 1995 and the return to the markets and ended in August of 2007, when the US financial crisis hit the country. The third stage covers from the 2007 start of the crisis to date. The impact of the 2008 crisis was cushioned by the swap line between the Banco de Mexico and the US FED, signed 29 October 2008.[23] This reciprocal currency arrangement was to run until 30 April 2009; but was extended until 1 February 2010. The exchange rate depreciated by 40 per cent between January 2008 and March 2009, from 10 pesos to the dollar to 14.64 pesos. The run against the peso was stopped through the use of the swap line which was drawn upon in April 2009. This intervention led to an exchange rate revaluation which then stabilized at an average of 12.20 pesos between 2009 and 2014. As a result of this external shock, counter-cyclical policies were applied and fiscal policy went from neutral to expansionary with large public borrowing.

In two years, 10 per cent of GDP of net new debt was contracted to finance public spending, as agreed at the London meeting of the G20 in March 2009. The federal government debt doubled from $40 billion in June–September 2009 to $82 billion in the last quarter of 2015 partially as a result of those counter-cyclical policies and after 2012 partially due to the losses from *Petroleos de México* (PEMEX), as oil prices came crashing down (see Table 11.2).

However, as counter-cyclical policies were reduced drastically after 2010, the question is why the debt grew from 17 per cent of GDP in 2007 to over 42 per cent of GDP in 2015 (Table 11.2). This opens the issue of tax revenues and State-owned firms. The public sector debt statistics and the *Secretaría de Hacienda y Crédito Público* include the local currency and external debt of public enterprises such as *Petróleos de México*, PEMEX; the *Comisión Federal*

[22] O. Ugarteche, 'Fuentes de financiamiento públicos e indicadores internacionales: la evidencia latinoamericana reciente,' *Economía UNAM* 5, no. 13 (2008) : 128–40.

[23] Banco de Mexico, 'Measures Implemented by the Federal Government and Banco de México to Preserve the Financial Stability,' 2010, www.banxico.org.mx/dyn/sistema-financiero/material-educativo/intermedio/%7B92EBEAEF-8C40-98C6-0313-253626159A4F%7D.pdf.

TABLE 11.2 *Gross external debt of the federal government long term*

Available period	Jan–Mar 2002 to Jan–Mar 2016
Frequency	Quarters
Amount	Balances
Units	Millions of Dollars
Date	14 August 2016
Jan–Mar 2002	59,883.0
Jan–Mar 2003	60,417.2
Jan–Mar 2004	59,286.7
Jan–Mar 2005	60,464.7
Jan–Mar 2006	56,865.2
Jan–Mar 2007	41,071.7
Jan–Mar 2008	41,761.4
Jan–Mar 2009	39,633.4
Jan–Mar 2010	48,196.0
Jan–Mar 2011	57,001.9
Jan–Mar 2012	64,338.8
Jan–Mar 2013	67,203.5
Jan–Mar 2014	73,914.1
Jan–Mar 2015	81,784.4
Oct–Dec 2015	82,588.3

Source: Banco de México. Posición de deuda externa bruta. Clasificación por reside http://finanzaspublicas.hacienda.gob.mx/es/Finanzas_Publicas/Estadisticas_Oportunas_de_Finanzas_Publicasncia.

de Electricidad (CFE), the electric utility firm, and also states and municipalities. The *Banco de Mexico* statistics refer only to the external debt and includes the private sector, both banking and non-banking.

Private firms include banks, which have borrowed $10 billion in long-term loans between 2009 and December 2015, and non-banking institutions. These include State-owned firms plus privately held companies, both multinational firms and domestically held firms. These have the largest burden of external debt growth during the 2008 and 2015 period. They borrowed heavily starting from January 2009 and have almost doubled the amount of external debt, from $100.1 billion in December of 2009 to $189.2 billion in December 2015. (See Table 11.3.)

TABLE 11.3 *Gross external debt of other sectors (non-financial)*

Available period	Jan–Mar 2002 to Jan–Mar 2016
Periods	Quarters
Amounts	Balances
Units	Millions of Dollars
Date	14 August 2016
Jan–Mar 2002	68,508.9
Jan–Mar 2003	64,893.8
Jan–Mar 2004	63,169.6
Jan–Mar 2005	61,660.9
Jan–Mar 2006	60,460.0
Jan–Mar 2007	68,686.5
Jan–Mar 2008	75,449.1
Jan–Mar 2009	100,137.5
Jan–Mar 2010	104,337.8
Jan–Mar 2011	116,564.7
Jan–Mar 2012	126,899.3
Jan–Mar 2013	138,229.6
Jan–Mar 2014	168,312.5
Jan–Mar 2015	181,186.0
Oct–Dec 2015	189,191.9

Source: Banco de México Posición de deuda externa bruta. Clasificación por residencia.

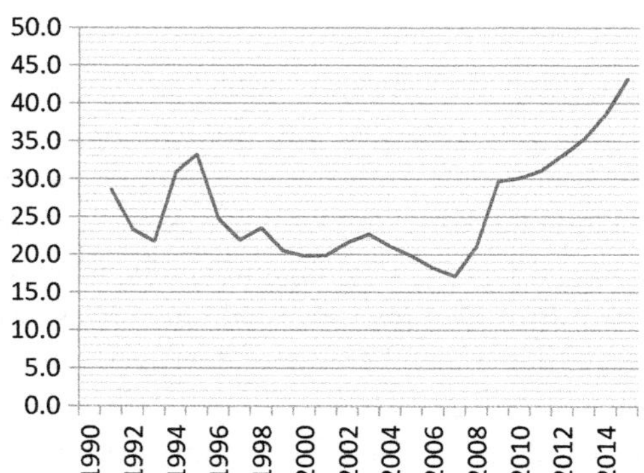

FIGURE 11.2 Total public debt as % of GDP (dollar and peso obligations).
Source: Secretaría de Hacienda y Crédito Público.
http://finanzaspublicas.hacienda.gob.mx/es/Finanzas_Publicas/Estadisticas_Oportunas_de_Finanzas_Publicas

IV. STATES AND MUNICIPALITIES

The states plus Mexico City (CDMX), which is a state on its own right, borrow domestically. The total amount borrowed is not very significant in GDP terms on a national level. It was a meagre 1.7 per cent of national GDP in 2008. The analysis changes when the states are analysed in terms of their own state GDPS. The definition of GDPS is state GDP. The most indebted state in terms of its own economy is Chihuahua, in 2015 having jumped from the eleventh place to first place (Table 11.4). Something similar happens with Quintana Roo and Coahuila pointing to a peculiarity in their debt policy.

The rise of some states with massive new debt in terms of their GDPS does not reflect a problem for the national economy, as they do not add more than 1.42 per cent of national GDP between 2008 and 2015. The debt of all states in terms of national GDP added together represents a meagre 3.1 per cent of national GDP. This means the problem of the rising total national debt levels observed earlier is not explained by the states and their municipalities, in spite of the spectacular rise in debt levels in three states: Chihuahua, Quintana Roo and Coahuila. Table 11.4 shows the states that have borrowed most heavily between 2008 and 2015 in terms of total GDP and it is clear that none of them have done so very heavily in national terms. The one that borrowed the most in terms of national GDP was Nuevo Leon followed by Coahuila, Chihuahua and Veracruz. These four alone reflect 0.8 per cent of GDP, which is more than half the total debt rise of 1.42 per cent of all 32 states added together between 2008 and 2015.

It can be concluded that state governments borrow not only for long-term capital investment projects but also for short-term current expenditure. State debt, called sub-national debt in Mexico, does not include the federal government.

Short-Term Capital Flows

The opening of the capital account after the 1988 crisis led to a surge in portfolio investments, namely from US investment banks. Palma[24] and Mussachio[25] argued that the main characteristic of the first financial crisis of the twenty-first century is centred around the movement of short-term capital

[24] J.G. Palma, 'How the Full Opening of the Capital Account to Highly Liquid and Unstable Financial Markets Led Latin America to Two and a Half Cycles of Mania, Panic and Crash,' in M.H. Wolfson and G.A. Epstein (eds.), *The Handbook of the Political Economy of Financial Crises* (Oxford: Oxford University Press, 2013).

[25] A. Musacchio, 'Mexico's Financial Crisis of 1994–1995,' Harvard Business School Working Paper, no. 12–101, May 2012.

TABLE 11.4 *Debt levels ranked by GDPS by state 2008 and 2015 and per cent change*

	Political Party	States ranked by debt levels 2015	Debt/GDPS 2015	Political Party	States ranked by debt levels 2008	Debt/GDPS 2008	Change Debt/ GDPS
1	PRI	Chihuahua	8,9	PRI	Sonora	3,5	5,4
2	PRI	Quintana Roo	8,5	PRD	Chiapas	3,4	5,1
3	PRI	Coahuila	6,6	PRI	México	3,1	3,5
4	PVEM	Chiapas	6,0	PRI	Oaxaca	2,5	3,6
5	PRI	Nayarit	5,5	PRD	Michoacán	2,4	3,1
6	IND	Nuevo León	5,2	PRD	Ciudad de México	2,2	2,9
7	PRI	Veracruz	5,0	PRI	Durango	2,2	2,8
8	M. Ciud.*	Oaxaca	4,8	PRI	Nuevo León	2,1	2,7
9	PRI	Sonora	4,5	PRI	Nayarit	2,0	2,6
10	PRD	Michoacán	4,3	PAN	Aguascalientes	1,9	2,4
11	PRI	Zacatecas	4,0	PRI	Chihuahua	1,8	2,1
12	PAN	Baja California	3,7	PRI	Sinaloa	1,8	2,0
13	PRI	Durango	3,6	PAN	Baja California	1,7	1,8
14	PRI	Colima	3,2	PRI	Puebla	1,7	1,6
15	PRI	México	2,6	PAN	Jalisco	1,6	1,0
16	PRD	Morelos	2,6	PRI	Colima	1,5	1,0
17	PRD	Ciudad de México	2,5	PRI	Quintana Roo	1,5	0,9
18	PRI	Tamaulipas	2,5	PRI	Veracruz	1,5	1,0
19	PRI	Jalisco	2,3	PRI	Hidalgo	1,3	1,0

20	PRI	Hidalgo	2,2	PAN	San Luis Potosí	1,3	0,9
21	PAN	Sinaloa	2,1	PRD	Guerrero	1,0	1,1
22	PAN	Baja California Sur	1,8	PAN	Querétaro	0,9	0,9
23	PRI	Aguascalientes	1,6	PAN	Guanajuato	0,8	0,8
24	PAN	Puebla	1,6	PAN	Baja California Sur	0,8	0,8
25	PRI	San Luis Potosí	1,3	PRD	Zacatecas	0,7	0,6
26	PRI	Guerrero	1,1	PRI	Tabasco	0,6	0,5
27	PAN	Guanajuato	1,0	PRI	Coahuila	0,5	0,5
28	PRI	Yucatán	0,9	PRI	Yucatán	0,4	0,5
29	PRD	Tabasco	0,8	PRI	Tamaulipas	0,4	0,4
30	PAN	Querétaro	0,5	PAN	Morelos	0,4	0,1
31	PRI	Campeche	0,2	PRI	Campeche	0,0	0,2
32	PRI	Tlaxcala	0,0	PAN	Tlaxcala	0,0	0,0

Source: INEGI.

flows. This led to the need of a stabilization fund intervention more than a debt negotiation which solves liquidity problems in times of foreign exchange crises derived from major short-term capital outflows. Since then it led to a major financial innovation at the IMF referred to as a Flexible Credit Line (FCL). 'It has no ongoing (ex post) conditions and no caps on the size of the credit line,'[26] which makes it an emergency liquidity instrument.

Mexico's first FCL arrangement was approved on 17 April 2009; renewed on 25 March 2010; 10 January 2011; 30 November 2012, 26 November 2014 and finally 27 May 2016. The most recent one almost triples the initial one in SDRs. In US dollars it quadruples from US$20 billion to $88 billion.[27] The size of the short-term capital flows into and out of Mexico has made evident that there is volatility in debt-related instruments. As the weight of short-term capital flows in the balance of payments grow, its total national liabilities become more significative. All new pluri-lateral agreements, such as TPP, NAFTA and the Pacific Alliance, include clauses related to workout solutions only for these new short-term instruments. They do not refer to long-term debt.

The quarterly international investment position in the balance of payments of these foreign short-term portfolio investments in the Mexican markets add up to US$445.8 billion in the last quarter of 2015, making them 27 per cent larger than FDI and larger than sovereign long-term borrowings (see Table 11.5). Debt instruments (public and private) are nearly 75 per cent of all foreign portfolio investments. The stocks of money market instruments within the debt instruments category, mostly CETES, are larger than long-term sovereign bonds issued in the last quarter of 2015, making the category very important for sovereign debt negotiations in spite of its short-term nature. These refer to the portfolio investment category of NAFTA and Pacific Alliance treaties.

V. LESSONS LEARNT AND CONCLUSIONS

To conclude, the preferential treatment Mexico receives from the US Treasury makes it different from other countries in the world. The Treasury intervention both in the last quarter of 1982 and the first quarter of 1995, injecting liquidity are expressions of this special treatment. This can be due to

26 www.imf.org/external/about/lending.htm.

27 www.banxico.org.mx/publicaciones-y-discursos/publicaciones/mexico_-arrangement-under-the-flexible-credit-line/%7B0095FED5-DCA0-8836-0A25-2128CF51B053%7D.pdf.

TABLE 11.5 *Mexico short-term capital flows (in thousand USD)*

I Q 1995	$(7,355,114)	I Q 1999	$1,805,318	I Q 2003	$2,867,980	I Q 2007	$1,349,796	I Q 2011	$14,170,748	I Q 2015	$8,295,028
II Q 1995	$(3,832,578)	II Q 1999	$5,170,531	II Q 2003	$(312,227)	II Q 2007	$4,436,714	II Q 2011	$9,453,422	II Q 2015	$10,015,038
III Q 1995	$(248,467)	III Q 1999	$3,571,819	III Q 2003	$(2,118,970)	III Q 2007	$2,704,037	III Q 2011	$11,062,243	III Q 2015	$1,883,959
IV Q 1995	$1,721,178	IV Q 1999	$1,425,320	IV Q 2003	$2,568,842	IV Q 2007	$4,774,929	IV Q 2011	$7,825,936	IV Q 2015	$182,764
I Q 1996	$1,558,048	I Q 2000	$3,687,288	I Q 2004	$2,705,619	I Q 2008	$4,211,943	I Q 2012	$24,971,268	I Q 2016	$12,005,817
II Q 1996	$2,224,306	II Q 2000	$588,715	II Q 2004	$(3,128,053)	II Q 2008	$5,826,117	II Q 2012	$9,041,040	I Q 2015	$8,295,028
III Q 1996	$9,168,310	III Q 2000	$(521,394)	III Q 2004	$3,365,952	III Q 2008	$547,122	III Q 2012	$24,283,897	II Q 2015	$10,015,038
IV Q 1996	$408,336	IV Q 2000			$(5,149,675)	IV Q 2004	$2,062,817	IV Q 2008			
							$(6,007,962)	IV Q 2012	$23,545,712	III Q 2015	$1,883,959
I Q 1997	$2,693,912	I Q 2001	$3,610,487	I Q 2005	$5,350,122	I Q 2009	$(1,176,277)	I Q 2013	$13,074,720	IV Q 2015	$182,764
II Q 1997	$6,823,450	II Q 2001	$321,591	II Q 2005	$1,434,578	II Q 2009	$1,034,933	II Q 2013	$(291,099)	I Q 2016	$12,005,817
III Q 1997	$(3,125,275)	III Q 2001	$(496,534)	III Q 2005	$328,180	III Q 2009	$7,740,694	III Q 2013	$18,412,145		

(continued)

TABLE 11.5 (*continued*)

IV Q 1997	$(1,419,582)	IV Q 2001	$(506,260)	IV Q 2005	$(52,442)	IV Q 2009	$7,688,452	IV Q 2013	$19,922,930		
I Q 1998	$3,115,130	I Q 2002	$2,474,842	I Q 2006	$3,314,720	I Q 2010	$10,372,966	I Q 2014	$10,600,062		
II Q 1998	$(309,015)	II Q 2002			$(3,648,150)	II Q 2006	$609,055	II Q 2010	$6,259,530	II Q 2014	
	$23,680,524										
III Q 1998	$(3,113,726)	III Q 2002			$(1,385,965)	III Q 2006	$(8,947,619)	III Q 2010	$10,222,923	III Q 2014	$2,823,711
IV Q 1998	$1,261,930	IV Q 2002	$888,644	IV Q 2006	$5,146,113	IV Q 2010	$11,204,262	IV Q 2014	$9,974,477		

Source: Banco de México, Balanza de pagos.
Note: Outflows in parenthesis. All other inflows.

TABLE 11.6 *Stocks of quarterly international investment position (in thousands of USD)*

	Jul–Sep 2015	Oct–Dec 2015
Foreign investment in Mexico	966,675,935.3	961,879,543.4
Foreign direct investment	355,421,019.8	356,896,382.0
Foreign portfolio investment	458,252,008.1	455,852,054.9
Foreign investment (equity)	134,522,220.4	134,145,841.2
Foreign investment (debt instruments)	323,729,787.7	321,706,213.7
Money market	127,160,394.7	123,298,495.2
Securities issued abroad public sector	113,692,100.0	115,202,600.0

Source: Banxico. Sistema de información económica. Balance of payments.
Period: Jan–Mar 2009 to Jan–Mar 2016, quarterly, thousands of US dollar, stocks. Last consulted 29 August 2016.

its very major size, to its proximity to the United States and the fear of some political backlash if the problem were not treated quickly and properly.

The Mexican case in the 1980s demonstrates that with a reasonable total debt/GDP ratio, what strangles the economy is the debt service/exports ratio. In this sense, a country with a normal debt level (50 per cent of GDP) turned into a country with a serious debt problem when interest rates rose dramatically between 1979 and 1981 and the debt service/exports ratio rose. This in turn led to a refinancing which resulted in a rise of the debt/GDP ratio.

Private sector debt was very important in the Mexican case and though it was reduced from nearly half of all debt service in the 1970s, it was still nearly 20 per cent of all debt service in the early 1980s. The Mexican federal government nationalized this debt and refinanced it together with the public debt while the private sector received the benefits of not having a US dollar debt anymore and paid it back at the fixed exchange rate of 1982 over a ten-year period.

During the 1980s Mexico signed three IMF standby agreements: December 1982, January 1986 and January 1989. Two of these were accompanied by a debt reduction scheme: the Baker Plan in 1986 and the Brady Plan in 1989. This country was the first to make use of the Baker Plan. 'Even though it was Mexico's plight which necessitated the Baker Plan, it was, at least on paper, formulated as a more generalized solution to the debt crisis.'[28]

[28] M. Mohanty, 'Strategies for Solution of Debt Crisis: An Overview,' *Economic and Political Weekly* 27, no. 9 (1992): 465–76.

> First, the Baker Plan recognised that debt was not a short-term liquidity problem but at least a medium term growth problem. Second, by committing the money of multilateral lending agencies towards resolving the problem, it implicitly accepted that creditor country governments had a responsibility towards solving the crisis. Third, institutionally, much greater emphasis was placed on the World Bank as the leading agency, as opposed to the IMF in the earlier phase.[29]

There were 17 targeted countries but overall two received 75 per cent of the private funds available, Mexico and Brazil. Those two account for 55 per cent of multilateral loans between 1985 and 1987. According to Vasquez,[30] the Baker plan was unable to provide the proper incentives for developing countries to introduce consistent market reforms, or for banks to supply new money that would finance such reforms.

In the late 1980s Mexico was also the first to make use of the Brady Plan.[31] This was followed by another 15 countries, including Argentina, Bolivia, Brazil, Bulgaria, Costa Rica, Dominican Republic, Ecuador, Jordan, Nigeria, Panama, Peru, Philippines, Poland, Uruguay and Venezuela.

The Brady Plan allowed for a return to the bond markets following a scheme Mexico had tried in December 1987 and Brazil had discussed earlier. Mexico did not discuss it but managed to make the scheme work on a small scale in 1987 and later under US Treasury guidance in 1989. This allowed for a return to the bond markets while bank lending effectively disappeared. The scheme consisted of buying the debt at market price and then issuing bonds for that amount to finance the purchase. It is a refinancing with a debt reduction component. What allowed for the issuance of the Brady bonds was the US Treasury guarantee.

There is more exchange rate volatility after the Mexican capital account was opened than before, as the 1994–95 crisis showed. That rescue was made quickly by the US Treasury using first the Treasury's exchange stabilization fund and only then the IMF. This was due to the speed required to stop a negative capital flow. IMF procedures were slow.

The lesson on the lack of quick response by the IMF to reversals in capital flows was to introduce in 2009, a flexible credit line. The Mexican credit line has quadrupled in size since its creation in 2009 and is now $88 billion, as a

29 Ibid.

30 I. Vasquez, 'The Brady Plan ad Market-Based Solutions to Debt Crises,' *Cato Journal* 16, no. 2 (1996): 233–43.

31 S. van Wijnbergen, M. King and R. Portes, 'Mexico and the Brady Plan,' *Economic Policy* 6, no. 12 (1991): 13–56.

precautionary fund available to countries with a positive article IV assessment in the most recent consultation. Only three countries have signed agreements to use this line, Colombia, Poland and Mexico.

Short-term capital flows have become very important for the country and these are invested in short-term Treasury bills. They make the foreign exchange rate very volatile as it appreciates or depreciates with the direction of the flows, which is determined in the international exchange rate market and by the interest rate, and margin differentials between US dollars and pesos. From April 1995 onwards, net new borrowing has been done mostly in Mexican pesos and using Treasury certificates (CETES) in the Mexican market. This is a major change from the *original sin*. Government bonds issued in the Mexican capital markets attract foreign buyers and have grown under relatively stable exchange rates leading to high levels of international reserves between 1996 and 2008. At the same time, private borrowers have borrowed heavily abroad doubling the national external debt given extremely low US and European interest rates. The framework to deal with private debt and with foreign investors in the Mexican capital markets is defined in the NAFTA agreement. Long-term sovereign debt is not considered in the NAFTA agreement nor in the Alliance for the Pacific treaty.

The size of the Mexican private sector external debt must be taken into account in case of any major balance of payments shortfall, as the federal government in the end guarantees the availability of foreign exchange to these firms.

After the 2008 US financial crisis, total Mexican debt grew given the Mexican government borrowed heavily due to counter-cyclical policies agreed to by the G20 and also to private borrowing given the drop in US interest rates.

A new element is that after Mexico underwent financial deregulation during the 1990s, states and municipalities started to borrow independently from the Mexican federal government. Risk measurement for them is provided by the big three credit rating agencies plus an independent Mexican agency for these new borrowers, which also issue bonds and borrow from multilateral banks. The weight of those debts is small thus far in terms of national GDP but has grown in some cases in terms of their own state GDP.

The debt of publicly held firms *Petróleos de Mexico* (PEMEX) and *Comisión Federal de Electricidad* (CDE) is important and has bearing on the Mexican national credit rating. They either generate income in favour of the federal government or receive a subsidy, in case of losses. The fall in oil prices has an effect on PEMEX revenue that may result in a federal subsidy in order to keep the firm running. PEMEX has historically transferred a massive amount of revenues into the federal government budget, but since 2014 has not done so while borrowing heavily.

Old and new debt instruments are different and the extensive use of CETES has changed completely the manner in which to approach sovereign borrowing. As CETES are issued under Mexican law in pesos but investors can be foreign, the aggregate foreign exchange risk is not completely wiped out for the Mexican Treasury.

12

Portugal's Austerity Bailout

Lessons of a Dangerous Experiment

JOSÉ CASTRO CALDAS

ABSTRACT

In May 2011, a liquidity crisis affecting both the banks and the Treasury triggered the intervention of the Troika in Portugal. Three years later, in May 2014, the Portuguese authorities performed what was then called a clean exit from the 'adjustment' programme. Meanwhile, the Portuguese sovereign debt, which amounted to 98 per cent of GDP in 2011, escalated to 132 per cent in 2014. Immediately after the supposedly clean exit of the program a new banking crisis surfaced. For the public, the fact that an adjustment programme that was justified by a large public debt and financial fragility has produced an even larger debt and a new banking crisis stands out as paradoxical. The public's perplexity is justified. The Portuguese people have learned from experience that fiscal consolidation and internal devaluation in the context of a general economic downturn are unable to deliver a sustainable trajectory of the public debt or a recovery of the banking sector. It has further learned that the short-term recessive effects of fiscal consolidation and internal devaluation may be lasting and may hinder recovery. The active and overall population decreased, long-term unemployment and low investment depleted human capabilities and the capital stock. With the bailout experiment Portugal became a poorer country that must serve a much larger debt. In spite of a positive reorientation of government policies away from austerity, in the present framework of the euro, and absent debt restructuring, the prospects for recovery are bleak.

1. INTRODUCTION

In April 2011, from the 3rd to the 6th, the Portuguese TV Channel TVI broadcasted interviews with the CEOs of the four largest private banks – *Banco Comercial Português* (BCP), *Banco Espírito Santo* (BES), *Banco Português de Investimento* (BPI) and *Santander Totta*. Those CEOs who previously had argued against a bailout of Portugal, similar to those of Greece and Ireland, now claimed that the government should stop resisting the IMF and the EU and request some kind of international loan.

On 6 April, the caretaker Minister of Finance announced, without informing the prime minister, that Portugal would 'apply to the financing mechanisms available in the European frame'.[1] Two hours later the prime minister formally announced the request for 'external assistance'.

What really happened during those days?

The troika's intervention in Portugal is usually described as the bailout of a sovereign cut off from the markets. Although it is true that the sovereign was facing a serious liquidity problem, this interpretation conceals the fact that – given the amounts of state guarantees provided to banks and the precedent set by sovereign bailouts of banks, namely in Ireland – this same sovereign was in turn highly exposed to banks that where facing an even more serious liquidity crisis.

The Portuguese banking system, whose debt towards their foreign counterparts was negligible until the middle of 1990s, had reached a peak of over €140 billion (78 per cent of GDP) in February 2008, when their source of financing dried up. Since then the rollover of their debt was made possible only with the funding of the ECB (see Figure 12.1).

However, the funding of the ECB to the banks was contingent on the availability of eligible collateral. With the downgrading of the Portuguese sovereign debt by all rating agencies, the Portuguese banks were suffering increasing haircuts on the collateral provided, and the prospect for them was one of rejection of Portuguese bonds by the ECB once the rating agencies decided to further downgrade these bonds to junk status.

For the bank CEOs, Portugal should request a bailout, not because there was an eminent risk of sovereign default, but because this was the only possible way for the banks to secure access to ECB funding. In their TV interviews they meant to clearly signal to the government that they were no longer ready to fund the Treasury, and that the government should either trigger the bailout request or face the unthinkable, that is default.

[1] 'É necessário recorrer à ajuda externa da Europa', *Jornal Público* (Lisbon), April 6, 2011, www.publico.pt/economia/noticia/teixeira-dos-santos-e-necessario-recorrer-a-ajuda-externa-da-europa-1488593.

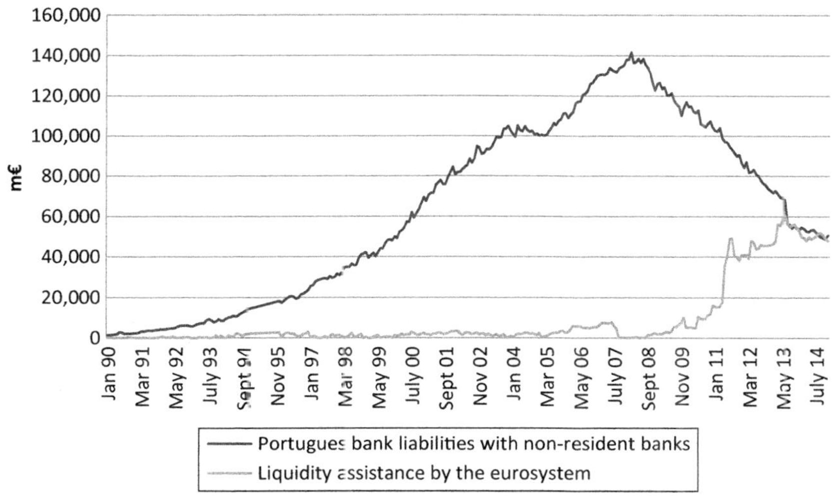

FIGURE 12.1 1990–2014, Portuguese bank liabilities with non-resident banks, and liquidity assistance to Portuguese banks by the Eurosystem.
Source: Bank of Portugal.

In August 2014, three months after Portugal's 'clean exit' from the troika's 'adjustment programme', the announcement was made by the Bank of Portugal that the largest Portuguese private bank – BES – was to be resolved. In December 2015, a smaller bank – BANIF – was also resolved and soon after, the urgent capitalization of the largest Portuguese bank, the state-owned CGD, was called for. The bailout thus concluded with another banking crisis, this time, not one of liquidity but one of solvency, which is still unfolding.

From one banking crisis to the next, Portugal experienced a bailout that has shattered the foundations of its society and aggravated its economic and financial predicaments. In this chapter we briefly survey the process that led to the crisis, the interpretations given of the crisis in the media that shaped the design and implementation of the 'adjustment programme', the assumptions of the bailout and its consequences, and the lessons that may be drawn from the Portuguese financial and social 'experiment'. The chapter concludes with a discussion of the prospects for Portugal within the present EU framework.

II. INDEBTEDNESS WITHIN THE EURO

The indebtedness of the Portuguese banks, since the middle of the 1990s, may be interpreted as part of a process of semi-peripheral financialization initiated in the 1980 and speeded up in the course of construction of the European Monetary Union (EMU).[2]

The first step in this process occurred in 1989 when a revision of the Constitution allowed for the reversal of the nationalization of banks that had been carried out after the democratic revolution of 1974 and led to the privatization of all banks with the exception of Caixa Geral de Depósitos (CGD). With privatization, credit limits and administrative interest rates were removed, and compulsory reserves at the Bank of Portugal drastically reduced. Credit consequently started to expand.

In 1989 the European Banking Directive harmonizing the practices of the European banking sector was transposed to national law, all national controls over the international circulation of capital started to be removed, and the escudo became fully convertible with its exchage rate pegged to a German mark dominated basket of european currencies. From 1990 onward, loans of the Bank of Portugal to the Treasury were reduced and public debt was securitized, open to national banks and foreign investors, and traded on secondary markets.

In the beginning of the 1990, joining the EMU had become for the Portuguese elites a major objective. According to their optimistic conjectures, financial integration in the frame of the EMU would atract capital and lower real interest rates allowing firms to boost investment and production.

What actually happened was substantially different. Portugal entered the euro with an overvalued exchage rate. Portuguese firms in the tradable sectors, mostly price-takers, saw their margins compressed between increasing internal prices and stagnated international prices. Investement thus fled to sectors less exposed to international competion from construction to retail. Foreign credit, at historically low interest rates, channelled by the banking sector to firms and families fuelled the non-tradable sector, notably real estate, construction and housing.

Compared to Greece, Spain and Ireland, countries which have experienced similar processes under the EMU, Portugal's economy stagnated after 2000 until 2008. A number of factors converge to explain this stagnation, namely, the high level of indebtedness of the private sector, the stock exchange crash in 2000, the accession of China to the WTO and of Eastern European countries to the EU – which affected the competiveness of the Portuguese tradable sector and deflected foreign direct

[2] For a description and analysis of this process, which are summarized in the following paragraphs, *see* J. Rodrigues, A.C. Santos and N. Teles, 'Semi-peripheral financialisation: The case of Portugal', *Review of International Political Economy* (2016), 480–510.

investment –, the rise of the exchange rate of the euro in respect to the dollar and the upsurge of oil prices.[3]

Meanwhile, the current account deficit rose from 3.3 of GDP in 1995, to a peak of 12.6 per cent in 2008, and the net international investment position deteriorated from -12.5 per cent of GDP in 1996 to -95,1 per cent in 2008.[4]

While bank external debt increased from 20.4 per cent of GDP in 1995, to 78.6 per cent in 2007, public debt increased from 58.3 per cent, to 68.4 per cent during the same period. However, due to recession, by the end of 2010 public debt had reached 96.2 per cent of GDP and in April 2011 the yields of 10-year bonds in secondary markets reached 9.19 per cent.[5]

The conditions for financing public debt had deteriorated not mainly as a consequence of public indebtedness itself but of the exposure of the treasury to a banking sector experiencing an acute liquidity crisis. However, what emerged in the public space in Portugal was not a combined banking-sovereign liquidity crises, but a sovereign debt crisis due to overspending. The banking system, so the portuguese were told, was sound and safe.

III. NARRATIVES OF THE CRISIS

The ground for the Portuguese bailout was prepared by narratives in the media, that, in attributing the crisis mainly to public overspending and labour costs, were instrumental in devising and implementing the 'adjustment programme'.[6] Those narratives were important for establishing in comon sense terms 'what went wrong' and 'what should be done' to solve the crisis, and in trying to explain and accommodate unexpected adverse events during the implementation of the programme.[7]

In the begining of 2010, what had previously been interpreted as an episode of financial turbulence triggered by events in the American banking sector,

[3] *See* R.P. Mamede, *O que fazer com este país: do pessimismo da razão ao otimismo da vontade* (Lisbon: Marcador, 2015).

[4] Source: Eurostat. [5] Sources: Bank of Portugal and Eurostat.

[6] Economic opinion in the media was, and still is, dominated by a neo-liberal stance. We surveyd and report in this section the writings of leading economic journalists during the 'adjustment' period. *See* J.C Caldas and J.R. Almeida, 'Narrativas da crise no jornalismo económico', *Cadernos do Observatório* 7, (2016) www.ces.uc.pt/observatorios/crisalt/documentos/cadernos/CadernoObserv_VII_mar2016.pdf.

[7] On the importance of narratives, *see* M. Blyth, 'Powering, Puzzling, or Persuading? The Mechanisms of Building Institutional Orders', *International Studies Quarterly* 51 (2007): 761–77, and B. Jessop, 'Narratives of Crisis and Crisis Response: Perspectives from North and South', in *The Global Crisis and Transformative Change*, eds. P. Utting and R.V. Buchholz (Basingstoke: Palgrave Macmillan, 2012), 23–42.

and later as a financial crisis with an economic impact, was construed in the EU as a sovereign debt crisis. Expansionary fiscal measures and bank bailouts, aimed at containing the economic recession caused by the financial crisis, should now, according to the EU institutions, be replaced by fiscal consolidation, aimed at recovering the confidence of financial markets, and internal devaluation, aimed at fostering competitiveness.

In Portugal the government of the Socialist Party, which had engaged in fiscal expansion in 2008 and 2009, closely followed the EU shift. Since March 2010 till September 2010, three programmes enacting fiscal consolidation, privatization, and labour market re-regulation were adopted. A fourth programme, presented in March 2011, would be rejected in the parliament leading the prime minister to resign.

The shift towards austerity required a new narrative. The causes of the crisis were no longer the malpractices and the deregulation of the financial sector, but rather overspending, public and private, and immoderate wages. Already in January 2010 the tone was set up in the media. 'We', had spent beyond our means. 'The public debt, after the immoderation of families, of firms and of banks is the new threat to financial stability'.[8] The nasty consequence necessarily followed: 'When we spend above what we produce, the moment comes when someone must pay the bill';[9] There is no alternative. The markets demand and 'we' must deliver – 'Those in charge are the markets'.[10] 'We' should therefore prepare for sacrifice: 'This fiscal vertigo is odious. But let it come. It will regenerate the economy and prepare the new life after the carnage'.[11]

The troika's 'adjustment programme' was welcomed at the outset by most of the economic journalists as an opportunity for redemption that could not be missed: 'This is a unique opportunity to change era into a regime of nominal stability, with room for merit, in which welfare (and salaries) depend on competitiveness. . . . This means creating, at last, a modern state';[12] 'We have an opportunity to rewrite our history, which is not unique nor the last, but which is a golden one. . . . I already decided how to vote in June 5: I will vote

8 H. Garrido, 'Editorial – O opaco mundo dos subsídios', *Jornal de Negócios* (Lisboa), January 5, 2010. http://www.jornaldenegocios.pt/opiniao/detalhe/o_opaco_mundo_dos_subsiacutedios

9 C. Lourenço, 'A cor do dinheiro – Hallelujah Mr. President!', *Jornal de Negócios* (Lisboa), January 4, 2010. http://www.jornaldenegocios.pt/opiniao/detalhe/hallelujah-mr-president

10 P. Santos Guerreiro, 'Editorial – O sexo fraco da crise', *Jornal de Negócios* (Lisboa), January 21, 2010. http://www.jornaldenegocios.pt/opiniao/detalhe/o_sexo_fraco_da_crise

11 P. Santos Guerreiro, 'Editorial – Acabou a crise, começou a austeridade', *Jornal de Negócios* (Lisboa), May 13, 2010. http://www.jornaldenegocios.pt/opiniao/detalhe/acabou-a-crise-comeccedilou-a-austeridade

12 P. Santos Guerreiro, 'Editorial – Budapeste', *Jornal de Negócios*, p. 3 (Lisboa), April 8, 2011. http://www.jornaldenegocios.pt/opiniao/editorial/detalhe/budapeste?ref=pedro-santos-guerreiro_BlocoArtigos

for the troika and for the reform plan that will allow us to have a very different state, another state, a better state'.[13]

With a new government that claimed ownership of the troika programme in office, the journalists encouraged the prime minister to faithfully implement it: 'Passos Coelho [the new prime minister] must insure an impeccable execution of the troika plan . . . I repeat, either this or chaos'.[14]

However, with time, enthusiasm started to fade. The first surprising event for journalists was the announcement of a 'colossal' fiscal gap by the finance minister which was to be filled with extraordinary taxes. This was met by the journalists with criticism: 'Once again the priority is given to tax hikes with no concrete results in respect to cutting expenditure'.[15] Instead the journalists believed: 'We have to aim at the salaries of public servants, at pensions, we should aim at public firms, at health care and education'.[16]

As recession settled in, with unemployment rising to surprising highs, making it harder to balance the budget, the critical tone raised: 'The consequences of austerity are there. . . . A programme of organized impoverishment, euphemistically called 'adjustment plan' would be unavoidably recessive'. Nonetheless, such a programme made perfect sense . . . 'because the standard of living of the Portuguese must be adjusted to their level of wealth creation. And . . . the country must be prepared to a new reality, for a new Welfare State that will not protect everything and everybody but only those in need, most fragile. And to a new, more competitive, economic state able to promote growth'.[17]

As the economic and social situation further deteriorated, and as in society the mood described by the IMF as 'austerity fatigue' settled in, journalists experienced and expressed an increasing difficulty in framing the negative surprises in a coherent discourse of support to the 'adjustment programme'.

In September 2012, following the announcement of a cut on the firm's contribution to social security to be compensanted by an increase in worker's contributions which was met by the public with huge protest demonstrations,

[13] A. Costa, 'Já decidi em quem vou votar', *Diário Económico* (Lisbon), May 6, 2011 p. 60.

[14] P. Santos Guerreiro, 'Editorial – Trabalhar para aquecer', *Jornal de Negócios* (Lisbon), July 1, 2011. http://www.jornaldenegocios.pt/opiniao/editorial/detalhe/trabalhar_para_aquecer?ref=pedro-santos-guerreiro_BlocoArtigos

[15] J. Vieira Pereira, 'Bloco de notas – Coelho prevenido vale por dois', *Expresso* (Lisbon), July 2, 2011. http://expresso.sapo.pt/opiniao/opiniao_joao_vieira_pereira/coelho-prevenido-vale-por-dois=f659120

[16] P. Santos Guerreiro, 'Editorial – A armadilha dos impostos', *Jornal de Negócios*, (Lisbon), September 6, 2011. http://www.jornaldenegocios.pt/opiniao/colunistas/pedro-santos-guerreiro/detalhe/a_armadilha_dos_impostos?ref=pedro-santos-guerreiro_BlocoArtigos

[17] A. Costa, 'Um novo acordo que já o era antes de o ser', *Diário Económico* (Lisboa), February 29, 2012 p. 72.

the emotional tone in some writings reached paroxysm: 'This isn't working . . . The troika should look the Portuguese in the eyes and reply to three questions: do you really believe that with more and generalized austerity the economy will start growing in the second quarter of next year? Do you really believe that, after having failed this year, Portugal will achieve the brutal deficit compression targeted for each of the two next years? Do you really believe Portugal will be able to pay its public debt. . .?'.[18] The generalized perception was that a recessive spiral had been triggered – 'The concern now is that more cuts in expenditure will have an even worse effect on recession, feeding what is called a recessive spiral and aggravating the social pressure'.[19]

The general outcome was disappointing. The main purpose of the programme – reforming the state – was yet to be accomplished: 'I believed that with a whip on our backs, we would have no choice but reform the state and the country. It is time to say that after having seen what I saw in the last few months (culminating in the government's paralysis) I was completely wrong . . . Portugal is an irreformable country'.[20]

However, by the end of October 2013 with the troika signalling a pick-up in activity and lower unemployment, decompression set in: 'We have to catch this wave of confidence. After all this may turn out better than we expected.'[21]

With the programme about to be concluded it was now time to take stock and discuss the day after. In spite of hopeful signs of recovery, the truth was that overall the opportunity had been missed: '[For the troika] leaving Portugal is a confirmation of success. This is what they came for: to leave one day. Wether the country is left in better or worse condition, that is up to those who stay to decide. They did their job. The government didn't. The structural reforms were neither reforms nor structural. . . The opportunity was lost'.[22]

The implication of having missed the opportunity was that the 'adjustment' should proceed in the future: 'We left the surgery block, but we are still in

[18] P. Santos Guerreiro, 'Editorial – As verdades que agora nos dirão', *Jornal de Negócios* (Lisboa), September 25, 2012. http://www.jornaldenegocios.pt/opiniao/editorial/detalhe/as-verdades-que-agora-nos-diratildeo

[19] P. Santos Guerreiro, 'Mundos e Fundos – A visita da velha senhora', *Revista Sábado* (Lisboa), March 14, 2013 p. 65.

[20] C. Lourenço, 'A cor do dinheiro – Somos um país irreformável', *Jornal de Negócios* (Lisboa), July 2, 2013. http://www.jornaldenegocios.pt/opiniao/colunistas/camilo-lourenco/detalhe/somos-um-pais-irreformavel

[21] H. Garrido, 'Editorial – Afinal a confiança está a regressar', *Jornal de Negócios* (Lisboa), December 5, 2013. http://www.jornaldenegocios.pt/opiniao/colunistas/helena-garrido/detalhe/afinal_a_confianca_esta_a_regressar

[22] P. Santos Guerreiro, 'Leiam os lábios dele', *Expresso* (Lisboa), May 5, 2014 p. 4.

intensive care… Public expenditure is still above the recommended levels. We have to cut deeper. There is no alternative'.[23]

Economic journalism played a crucial role in the 'adjustment programme'. It provided a narrative that explored moral sentiments and common sense views to produce consent for the type of 'adjustment' devised by the EU and the IMF. The sentence 'We spent above our means' – repeated to exhaustion on the press and on TV – signified that 'we' should sacrifice, that is cut spending, public and private, like every indebted family does if it really wishes to honor its commitments.

When the programme started to produce adverse effects, the narrative had to shift to accommodate public discontent while preserving the legitimacy of the core goals of the 'adjustment'. There were problems due to wrong implementation or even bad design of some aspects of the programme. But the 'adjustment' as such – cuts in spending aimed at reducing public provision in health, education and pensions and 'structural reforms' against the 'rigidity' of the labour market – was unavoidable. After all if the 'adjustment' failed to produce the expected results, this was due to the fact that it did not go far enough in reforming the state and the labour market. As a consequence further 'adjustment' would be needed in the future.

IV. THE PORTUGUESE BAILOUT: FROM ASSUMPTIONS TO OUTCOMES

For the IMF, the agency that provided the troika with the knowledge and experience aquired in previous bailouts all over the world, intervention in euro area countries presented a new challenge. However, the Fund was not totally unprepared. A paper written in 2006, precisely about Portugal, by Olivier Blanchard, who in 2011 was the Economic Counselor and Director of the IMF's Research Department, clearly signals that a rational for such interventions was being developed in the Fund even before the outbreak of the Great Recession.[24]

In that paper Blanchard noted that the 'Portuguese economy is in serious trouble: Productivity growth is anemic. Growth is very low. The budget deficit is large. The current account deficit is very large'.[25] He further noted that the situation was the product of an 'investment boom' triggered in the second half

[23] J. Vieira Pereira, 'Bloco de notas – O perigo do crescimento económico', *Expresso* (Lisboa), April 18, 2014 p. 6.

[24] O. Blanchard, 'Adjustment within the Euro. The Difficult Case of Portugal', *Portuguese Economic Journal* 16, no: 1–21.

[25] Ibid., 1.

of the nineties 'by the commitment by Portugal to join the euro' and the resulting 'drop in interest rates and expectations of faster growth',[26] which, in the absence of productivity growth, came to an end in the beginning of the new decade, leading to a slump.

Blanchard then explored the policy options available for Portugal and possibly other euro area countries. The Portuguese problem, whose symptom was the large current-account deficit, was one of competitiveness, defined by Blanchard as determined by 'the inverse of unit labor costs relative to those of the euro area'.[27]

The options available in his view were only two. The first (and most attractive) was 'to achieve a sustained increase in productivity growth'. The second (less attractive) was 'a large decrease in the nominal wage'.[28] However, since productivity was unlikely to 'increase overnight', the fast track left was to 'achieve a decrease in nominal wages – without relying on unemployment to do the job over time'.[29]

Blanchard noted that 'the traditional way to achieve a reduction in real wages is a [currency] devaluation' but that such an option was blocked by Portugal's membership in the euro. He believed, however, that 'the same result can be achieved (…) at least on paper, through a decrease in the nominal wage and the price of non-tradables, while the price of tradables remains the same.' This would require 'coordinated decreases in nominal wages'.[30] Blanchard was not very specific on which policy tools should be mobilized to reduce nominal wages. Implicit however was a thorough reform of the institutions regulating employment protection. The 'Portuguese labor market' – wrote Blanchard – 'is dysfunctional', and 'the main cause appears to be the high degree of employment protection'.[31]

Echoing to some extent Blanchard's analysis[32] the troika's 'adjustment programme', as stated in the Memorandum of Understanding (MoU), was meant to restore growth and competitiveness, reduce public debt and deficit and stabilize the financial system.[33]

Restoring competitiveness and promoting growth, given Portugal's membership of the euro, should rely on a internal devaluation strategy supported by (1) a 'fiscally neutral cut in social security contributions' aimed at increasing profitability in the tradable sector and (2) a deep labour market reform aimed

[26] Ibid., 2. [27] Ibid., 4. [28] Ibid., 2. [29] Ibid., 8. [30] Ibid., 15. [31] Ibid., 14.

[32] *See* A. N. Costa (Ed.), 'Economics and the "real-world": the case of the Portuguese Memorandum', (2015), Mimeo Report, Centre for Social Studies, Coimbra University.

[33] International Monetary Fund, 'Request for a Three-Year Arrangement Under the Extended Fund Facility', 2011, IMF Country Report No. 11/127, p. 25, www.imf.org/external/pubs/ft/scr/2011/cr11127.pdf.

at flexibility. Both policies were targeted to the reduction of labour costs of domestic production.[34]

Other measures to boost competitiveness and growth involved the removal of barriers to entry and the opening up of the non-tradable sector to competition. Most importantly a detailed reform of the judiciary was advanced with the stated aim of improving its efficiency.[35]

The programme included a large and 'front-loaded' fiscal adjustment, two-thirds of which on the expenditure side.[36] The measures focused on expenditure reduction included: (1) the reduction of public wages and of pensions, (2) the reduction of the number of public employees, (3) spending cuts on the health and education sectors, (4) the reduction and better targeting of social transfers, and (5) the suspension of new large infrastructure projects. Large savings were expected from reforms in the health sector through higher user fees, cuts in pharmaceutical spending, and reduction in operational costs of hospitals.[37] On the revenue side, the programme envisioned increasing the share of consumption taxes and reducing tax exemptions.[38]

A 'structural fiscal reform' was advanced, meant to reduce the scope and involvement of the state in the economy through the restructuring of state owned enterprises, the revision of public private partnerships contracts, and privatizations mainly in transport, energy, communications and insurance.[39]

The financial stability measures advanced in the MoU aimed at recapitalizing and ensuring liquidity to the banking sector. Taking access to the exceptional liquidity support from the euro system for granted, the programme raised the government guarantees for uncovered bank bonds and stressed the need for strengthening capital adequacy targets through market-based solutions. A Bank Solvency Support Facility of €12 billion was set up as a 'backstop mechanism' to guarantee that banks were able to reach higher capital requirements on time. Banking regulation and supervision were reinforced, and early intervention and resolution frameworks were enhanced. Measures to tackle private sector indebtedness were advanced to promote an effective 'corporate and household debt restructuring' by, for instance, 'amending the insolvency law and strengthening out of court restructuring incentives'.[40]

The logic of the Portuguese 'adjustment programme' was dependent on the presupposition that the programme's objectives – improving external competitiveness and growth, reducing public debt and deficit, and stabilizing the financial system – could be made mutually consistent and achieved by means of internal devaluation, fiscal consolidation and bank recapitalization.

34 Ibid., 17–18. 35 Ibid., 18–19. 36 Ibid., 11. 37 Ibid., 13. 38 Ibid., 7
39 Ibid., 20. 40 Ibid., 14–15.

Actually, events have shown that those objectives are conflictive. Wage restraint attached to the objective of boosting competitiveness compressed internal demand, generated deflation and affected growth. The compression of internal demand reduced imports. But the contribution of the external sector did not compensate for the compression of internal demand. Fiscal consolidation, given its negative impact on internal demand, also had negative effects on growth and backfired on lower fiscal revenues and higher public expenditure.

Furthermore, the recessive effects of both policies of internal devaluation and of fiscal consolidation brought about more non-performing loans in detriment of the stability of the financial system. Besides, the requirement of banking sector capitalization in the absence of equity coming from the private sector became a burden to the public budget.

All this took place to an extent that far exceeded IMF projections (see Table 12.1). During the bailout period (2010–14), GDP contracted 6 per cent (against a projection of −0.2 per cent by the IMF). Employment decreased 7.4 per cent (against an IMF projection of −1.1 per cent). Particularly serious, due to its implication for the future, was the decline in investment (−29.6 per cent, against an IMF projection −11.3 per cent). Exports expanded, although less than expected by the IMF, and imports contracted, exceeding IMF expectations, and the current account rebalanced.

The negative effects of fiscal consolidation and of wage restraint on growth did backfire, jeopardizing the objective of fiscal adjustment. The fiscal consolidation achieved was of 4 percentage points, against an IMF target of 6.8 percentage points. Between 2007 and 2015 the measures of assistance to the financial sector had an accumulated impact on the public debt of €21 billion (11.5 per cent of 2015 GDP).[41]

Mostly due to the recession, non-performing loans of non-financial firms increased from 5 per cent of the value of all loans to the same firms in 2011, to 15 per cent in 2014 (3 per cent and 5 per cent for non-performing loans of individuals) (see Figure 12.2).

In sum, the 'adjustment programme' achieved only one of its main macroeconomic objectives – the rebalancing of the current account. Due to the unanticipated extent of the recession and the bank bailouts, the fiscal consolidation fell short of the ambitious goals of the MoU and public debt escalated from 96.2 per cent of GDP in 2010 to 130.2 per cent in 2014. In spite

[41] Bank of Portugal, 'Nota de Informação Estatística 56|2016: Dívida pública', April 2016, www.bportugal.pt/pt-PT/Estatisticas/PublicacoesEstatisticas/NIE/Lists/FolderDeListaComLinks/Attachments/211/Divida_Publica-201604.pdf.

TABLE 12.1 *Macroeconomic and social indicators, 2010 and 2014, actual and IMF projection in the MoU*

	2010	2014	Variation 2010–2014 (actual)	Variation 2010–2014 (IMF projection)
Macroeconomic indicators				
GDP (b€, 2010 prices)	179.9	169.1	−6.0%	−0.4%
Gross fixed investment (b€, 2010 prices)	37.9	26.7	−29.6%	−11.3%
Exports (b€, 2010 prices)	53.751	66.158	23.1%	27.4%
Imports (b€, 2010 prices)	67.351	66.666	−1.0%	−2.8%
Employment (million people)	4.914	4.551	−7.4%	−1.1%
Unemployment rate (%)	12.0	14.1	2.1 pp	1.0 pp
General government balance (% GDP)	11.2	7.2	4.0 pp	6.8 pp
General government debt (% GDP)	96.2	130.2	34.0 pp	22.0 pp
Current account balance (% GDP)	−10.3	0.0	10.3 pp	6.5 pp
Net international investment position (% GDP)	−104.3	−114.4	−10.1 pp	−13.9 pp
Population				
Population (million people)	10.573	10.401	−1.6%	
Active Population (15–64) (million people)	5.166	4.976	−3.7%	
Emigration (thousand people during year)	23.760	49.572	108.6%	
Inequality and poverty				
People at risk of poverty or social exclusion	25.3	27.5	2.2 pp	
People under 16 at risk of poverty or social exclusion	27.1	30.8	3.7 pp	
Income quintile share ratio (S80/S20)	5.6	6.2	0.6	

Source: Eurostat, IMF.

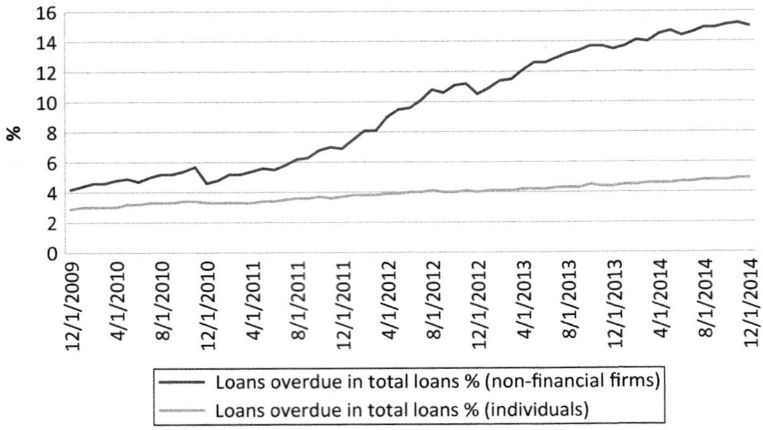

FIGURE 12.2 2009–2014, loans overdue in total loans, non-financial firms and individuals. *Source*: Bank of Portugal.

of the rebalancing of the current account, the external debt (net international investement position) increased, from −104.3 per cent to −114.4 per cent.

The overall social impact of the 'adjustment' was devastating. Mainly due to emigration, the active population and overall population decreased. Poverty, especially child poverty, and inequality in income distribution increased substancialy (see Table 12.1).

In retrospect, the bailout may be interpreted as basically motivated by the concern of safeguarding at all cost the prerogatives of most creditors, namely the large EU banks exposed to 'peripheral' debts. This was done at the cost of social rights of the labouring people, the youth and the pensioners.

As noted by the Committee on Economic, Social and Cultural Rights of the United Nations Economic and Social Council in a 2014 repport that unfortunatly received little or no attention from the Portuguese authorities, the IMF and the EU institutions, 'the financial and economic crisis has had an adverse impact on the enjoyment of economic, social and cultural rights by the population at large, in particular with regard to the rights to work, social security, housing, health and education'. Moreover, various measures in the 'adjustment programme', 'specifically those that target disadvantaged and marginalized individuals and groups, have not been sufficient to adequately protect them against the consequences of the crisis'.[42]

[42] United Nations Economic and Social Council, Committee on Economic, Social and Cultural Rights, 'Concluding observations on the fourth periodic report of Portugal', Geneva, 2014, 1–2.

The 'adjustment' had also political consequences. In the parliament election that took place in October 2015 the coalition PSD-CDS that presided over the 'adjustment' lost 11.8 percentage points compared with its score in June 2011. The Socialist Party improved its score by 4.4 percentage points, and the parties on the left of the socialists increased by 5.4.

This was not a political landslide comparable to those of Greece or Spain. Significant however, is that before the election a new leadership had taken office in the Socialist Party which, after the election, reached an unprecedented agreement with the parties on its left precluding the right wing coalition (PSD+PP) to form a minority government and providing the majority for a socialist government with left-wing support.

V. THE PORTUGUESE BAILOUT: LESSONS LEARNED?

The Portuguese crisis and bailout, as the previous ones in Greece and Ireland, were to some extentent, a real-life experiment. The bailout was conceived as such by the experts who participated in its design, namely the IMF staff, and as such endured, by those who were its subjects.

Although for different reasons, for both, lay people and experts, the experience was distressing. In a interview given after leaving office in the IMF, Blanchard described the crisis as 'a traumatic event during which' economists at the IMF 'had to question many cherished beliefs'.[43]

However, determining whether there were lessons learned from the crisis and the bailout experiments, and which lessons, is a convoluted question. A wide range of people across society probably agree only on not wishing to replicate it. Experts, also tend to disagree. Evidence is always subject to interpertation, and insufficient to establish once and for all the truth or falsity of the pressupositions underpining predictions. Cherished beliefs die hard.

Nonetheless it is possible to identify a number of critical issues exposed by the crisis and the bailout outcomes:

a) The crisis exposed deficiences in the architecture of the euro. In Portugal, the aspiration of joining the euro that prevailed during the 1990s, specially among the elites, gave way to critical and self-critical acessements of that decision. Obviously, misgivings about euro area

[43] 'Interview with Olivier Blanchard. Blanchard: looking forward, looking back', *Survey Magazine*, International Monetary Fund, August 31, 2015, www.imf.org/external/pubs/ft/survey/so/2015/res083115a.htm.

accession do not necessarily translate into crititical opinions on euro area membership, and even less on support to exit.

b) Against the view that prevailed in Portugal, in the EU, and in the IMF, that 'large imbalances in national current accounts were little cause for concern',[44] large imbalaces are indeed a cause for concern, *specially* in a currency union. In a currency union, like the EMU, devaluing the currency is not an option, governments are therefore dragged into internal devaluation as a substitute to external (currency) devaluation. Such an option, as shown in the Portuguese case, may be very effective in lowering imports due to the reduction of internal demand. However, given that internal devaluation is pursued simultaneously by most countries in the currency union, hindering external demand, it may fail to compensate the retrenchement of internal demand or induce the desired reorientation of investment to the tradable sector.

c) The restructuring of public debt was excluded at the outset in Portugal. This followed a similar decision taken in the Greek case, which involved the bending of the rules of the IMF stipulating that access to IMF assistance was conditional on a 'high probability that the member's public debt is sustainable in the medium term'.[45] Arguably, the decision by the IMF to bypass debt restructuring resulted from pressures exercised by the EU, motivated mainly by concerns regarding its impacts on the EU large banks exposed to that debt.

   As it is now openly recognized, '[t]he decision not to seek preemptive debt restructuring … magnified the required fiscal adjustment, and thereby, at least in part, contributed to a large contraction of output …'.[46] Moreover, this decision allowed private creditors to reduce their exposures making any future restructuring much more difficult.

   With the troika's 'adjustment programme' Portuguese public debt increased substantially and is still increasing. Servicing debt is viable only due to the ECB quantitative easying. Once that programme expires the issue of public debt will resurface. And yet, in the EU, debt restructuring, at least in the case of Portugal, remains a taboo subject.

d) The crisis exposed the risks of relying only on financial markets for financing states. A consequence of relying exclusively on financial

[44] Independent Evaluation Office of the IMF, 'The IMF and the Crisis in Greece, Ireland and Portugal: An Evaluation by the Independent Evaluation Office', 2016, vii.

[45] Ibid., 19. [46] Ibid., 15.

markets for financing the Treasury was the increasing interdependence of banks and the sovereign which triggered the bailout in 2011. Another consequence, were the unprecedented speculative movements that drove the yields of the Portuguese bonds to 15 per cent in January 2012.

Conversely, the events have shown that '[c]entral bank purchases of government debt have turned out to be useful to allow for a more gradual fiscal adjustment'.[47] In fact, ECB purchases were what allowed the return of Portugal to market financing of the public debt and the 'clean exit' of Portugal from the bailout.

e) Against the belief once cheriched that positive confidence effects can dominate the adverse effects of cuts in spending or increases in revenues, and lead to 'expansionary fiscal consolidations', the events have shown that fiscal consolidation in a recessive context may even hinder the achievement of fiscal consolidation targets.
f) The crisis and the bailout have challenged the assumption that expenditure-based consolidations are more effective and durable than revenue-based ones. Experience has shown that cuts in expenditure may have stronger recessive consequences and entail higher social costs than income tax hikes. Or in the more moderate language of the IMF '[t]he crisis has not offered conclusive lessons regarding the relative size of revenue and government spending multipliers'.[48]
g) Contrary to the troika's assumptions the experiment is reveiling that the short term recessive effects of the 'adjustment' may be lasting and hinder the potential for recovery. Unemployment fuels emigration and desencourages the long term unemployed, and low investment translates into the obsolescence of the capital stock, both factors decreasing potential output.
h) The crisis and the bailout have highlighted the importance of the media in the framing of perceptions of the public *vis à vis* the crisis and the modalities of crisis response available. With the aim of manufacturing consent for a bailout meant to shift the cost of 'adjustment' from the creditors and the wealthy few to the labouring and unemployed many, the media provided a narrative that presented the bailout and its consequences as a form of punishment for profligacy, which, although

47 International Monetary Fund, 'Reassessing the Role and Modalities of Fiscal Policy in Advanced Economies', 2013, IMF Policy Paper, 13, www.imf.org/external/np/pp/eng/2013/072113.pdf.

48 Ibid., 1.

painful, would bring redemption. The dominance of neo-liberal opinion in the media, the lack of pluralism, has precluded debate and the consideration of alternatives in the public space.

The bailout experiment has challenged the basic theoretical underpinnings of the Portuguese 'adjustment programme'. However the acknowledgement of 'anomalies' by many, including the IMF, does not translate into what philosophers of science would call a paradigm shift. In spite of all evidence the old habits of thought and action tend to prevail. Especially when those habits reflect and reinforce power relations.[49]

VI. LOCKED WITHIN THE DEBT TRAP?

The Portuguese crisis was construed at the outset as a consequence of immoderate government spending, and uncompetitive 'labour costs'. This was supported by an austerity narrative originated in international institutions, like the EU, the IMF and the ECB and actively disseminated internally in the media by economic journalists performing the role of experts.

The austerity narrative, obfuscated the real causes of the crisis – the inflow of capital from the surplus economies of the euro area and its channelling through the Portuguese banking system to the non-tradable sectors of the economy – rooted in the processes of semi-peripheral financialization speeded up by EMU membership. This narrative was instrumental in designing and manufacturing consent for a bailout aimed at safeguarding the prerogatives of most creditors at the cost of social rights of the labouring and the unemployed people, the youth and the pensioners.

The bailout failed in its own terms. It increased sovereign and external debt and produced a solvency crisis in the banking system. Furthermore, it triggered a process of cumulative causation, namely through emigration and under-investment that wore out the capacity for future recovery.

The Portuguese government subsequent to the 2015 parliamentary elections has set out as its mission achieving a turn away from austerity within the rules of the EU Stability and Growth Pact and the Fiscal Compact. This amounts to a very difficult squaring of the circle.

According to the Stability Program 2016–20, presented to the European Commission in April 2016 by the government of Portugal, in order to accomplish the reduction of public debt to 60 per cent of GDP in 2035, even

[49] T.S. Khun, *The Structure of Scientific Revolutions* (Chicago: The University of Chicago Press, 1962).

assuming growth rates above 2.8 per cent until 2020 and moderate public debt interest rates (3.4 per cent), primary budget surpluses increasing from 2.2 per cent of GDP in 2016 to 4.2 per cent in 2020 and the following years are required.[50]

Mainly due to the growing weight of interest on debt which has increased from 2.9 per cent of GDP, in 2007, to 4.6 per cent in 2015, adjustment within the EU rules, would amount to the continuous retrenchment of public expenditure, and therefore of the provision of health and education, pensions, and protection against unemployment and poverty. This would equate to the implementation of a neo-liberal political agenda contrary to the democratic choices of the Portuguese.

The burden of debt is compressing the fiscal space and dragging economic recovery. Stagnation and unemployment are fuelling emigration and demographic decay. An increasing number of people is coming to understand that, in the absence of debt restructuring, and of a reconfiguration of the euro area which would endow it with a robust common budget, the institutions allowing for the emission of debt, and a more democratic legitimacy, the prospects for recovery are bleak. However – given the growing economic and political fragmentation in the EU – developments in this direction are unlikely. Consequently, many, including the author of this chapter, are presently reaching the point of concluding that brighter prospects for the future crucially depend on replacing the presently dysfunctional euro by a more flexible monetary arrangement.

50 The historical record shows that such surpluses are unprecedented in Portugal. To find a surplus (0.1 per cent of GDP) one has to travel back in time to 1997.

13

Don't Waste a Serious Crisis*

Lessons from South Africa's Debt Crisis

DANIEL D. BRADLOW**

ABSTRACT

South Africa has not experienced a sovereign debt crisis since the advent of democracy in 1994. However, it did face a debt crisis in 1985, during the struggle against apartheid. This crisis, in the first instance, was an inter-bank crisis more than a sovereign debt crisis because the apartheid regime, which was largely unable to borrow on international markets due to sanctions, had relied on commercial banks to raise funds on international markets. The crisis was also as much a political as a financial crisis and, in fact, helped contribute to the downfall of apartheid. Despite these unusual features, the 1985 crisis offers a number of lessons about human rights and the management of sovereign debt crises that are still relevant today. This chapter, after a short description of the 1985 South African crisis and its management, explores the lessons that can be learned from this experience and their applicability to sovereign debt crises in emerging markets and developing countries today.

I. INTRODUCTION

To date, South Africa has only experienced one sovereign debt crisis. This occurred in 1985 and it was an episode in the end game of the anti-apartheid struggle. Although, the South African debt crisis was unusual, there are

* Title is based on a quote from President Obama's former chief of staff, Rahn Emanuel, who said 'You never let a serious crisis go to waste. And what I mean by that it's an opportunity to do things you think you could not do before.' *See* www.brainyquote.com/quotes/quotes/r/rahmemanue409199.html.

** The author thanks Nthope Mapefane for her research assistance.

enough similarities between it and other sovereign debt crises that it remains a relevant case study for current sovereign debt crises.

There are three significant lessons that can be learned from the South African crisis. In order to explain these lessons, this chapter is divided into four sections. The first section will provide a brief overview of the South African debt crisis. The second section will highlight changes in the global financial system since the crisis that are relevant to the lessons of the South African crisis. The third section focuses on the lessons from the crisis. The final section is a concluding section.

II. THE SOUTH AFRICAN DEBT CRISIS OF 1985[1]

In the 1980s, South Africa significantly increased its reliance on external debt.[2] Between 1980 and 1984, South Africa's total debt increased from $16.9 billion (equal to 20 per cent of GDP) to $24.3 billion (equal to 46 per cent of GDP).[3] Short-term debt as a portion of total debt increased from 49 per cent in 1980 to over 66 per cent by the end of 1984.[4] By August 1985, when the crisis broke, most of the country's external debt was short-term.[5]

The increase in debt was partly due to a net capital outflow over the first half of the 1980s.[6] This capital flight was attributable to a number of factors, including loss of confidence in the political leadership of the country and in the future of the economy, and to deregulation of the financial markets, which made it possible for South Africans to send their capital abroad.[7] The South African Government (SAG) also allowed domestic interest rates to increase

1 The discussion of the South African debt crisis is based on the description of the crisis in D.D. Bradlow, 'Debt, Development and Human Rights: Lessons from South Africa', *Michigan Journal of International Law* 12 (1991): 647.

2 S. Lewis, *The Economics of Apartheid* (New York: Council on Foreign Relations Press, 1990) 65. In 1956 equity investments represented 75 per cent of total foreign investment, but by the mid-1980s debt, particularly short-term debt, was the major form of external financing.

3 A. Hirsch, 'Sanctions, Loans and the South African Economy', in *Sanctions Against Apartheid*, ed. M. Orkin (Cape Town: David Philip, 1989) 27.

4 Hirsch, 'Sanctions, Loans and South African Economy'; L. Harris, 'South Africa's External Debt Crisis', *Third World Quarterly* 8 (1986): 807; V. Padayachee, 'Private International Banks, the Debt Crisis and the Apartheid State', *African Affairs* 87 (1988): 367; C. Grant, 'The Banks Abandon South Africa', *Euromoney* (1985): 68. *See* generally G. Hufbauer, J. Schott and K. Elliott, *Economic Sanctions Reconsidered: History and Current Policy* (Washington, DC: Institute for International Economics, 1990), 221–35.

5 Hirsch, 'Sanctions, Loans and South African Economy', 272–73; Padayachee, 'Private International Banks', 371–74.

6 Ibid. 7 *See* Lewis, *The Economics of Apartheid*, 154.

sharply so that some South African commercial banks began to borrow externally in the short-term interbank market to fund medium-term credits to South African public and private sector borrowers.[8]

The ease with which South African borrowers were able to obtain funds is surprising.[9] The heaviest borrowing activity occurred when the South African economy was stagnating and per capita income was falling.[10] In addition, South Africa was effectively cut off from IMF financial support and policy advice.[11]

The banks also based their decision to lend to South African borrowers on a flawed assessment of the country's ability to manage its debt. In fact, by early 1985, the banks were concerned about the country's ability to service its 1985–86 debt obligations. In March 1985 Citibank observed: 'South Africa's external finances are in total chaos.'[12] It concluded that 'it is difficult to see how debt refinancing on the scale required … can possibly be achieved.'[13]

In mid-1985 South Africa's political and financial difficulties reached a crisis point. Its economy was experiencing the worst recession since the 1930s, and it was facing the most sustained period of political protest in the country's history.[14] On 20 July, the government imposed a state of emergency and on 31 July Chase Manhattan Bank announced that it would not extend any new credits to South African borrowers nor would it roll over short-term loans that were to fall due in late August. Other banks adopted the same approach.[15] Since there was a 'bunching' of debt payments falling due in

[8] The interest rate differential could be as much as 10–12 per cent. The exchange rate hedges involved the sale of foreign exchange for future delivery on terms that provided the borrower with a fixed exchange rate, thereby placing the risk of currency fluctuations on the SAG. *See* Padayachee, 'Private International Banks', 365.

[9] The borrowers were predominantly private corporations. The sanctions campaign made it difficult, but not impossible, for the public sector to directly raise funds in international markets. Ibid., 366. For a general description of the sanctions campaign's effect on loans to South Africa, *see* J. Hanlon and R. Omond, *The Sanctions Handbook* (Harmondsworth: Penguin, 1987) 333–34.

[10] Padayachee, 'Private International Banks', 365, 370. Hirsch, 'Sanctions, Loans and South African Economy', 271.

[11] J. Morell, 'A Billion Dollars for South Africa', *International Policy Report* (Washington, DC: Centre for International Policy, 1983), 1–3.

[12] Hirsch, 'Sanctions, Loans and South African Economy', 273. [13] Ibid.

[14] *See* sources cited *supra* notes 5–6. The following discussion of the unfolding of the South African debt crisis are based on these sources. For a chronology of the South African debt crisis, *see* Hufbauer, Schott and Elliott, *Economic Sanctions Reconsidered*, 221–35.

[15] Chase Manhattan was not the first bank to take such action but it was the first to do so publicly. Its actions had particular significance because of the influence that Chase Manhattan had, at

the second half of 1985, it was obvious that South African borrowers would be unable to meet their obligations.[16]

The situation was exacerbated by President Botha's 'Rubicon' speech in mid-August. He stated that the country had 'crossed the Rubicon' on the road to reform, but he ruled out political power sharing and blamed 'barbaric communist agitators' for the social unrest in the country.[17]

The reaction to the speech was dramatic and the SAG was forced to close the foreign exchange and stock markets. Before allowing the markets to reopen, the SAG[18] announced that it was declaring a four month moratorium on the repayment of $10 billion of payments falling due on short term debt, primarily interbank debt, owed by private South African banks to private lenders.[19] Foreign government-guaranteed debts, trade credits, Eurobonds, debts of the SAG and IMF funds were excluded from the moratorium. This meant that at the time of the initial debt negotiations the SAG was not legally responsible for the debt and was only seeking to establish an orderly repayment mechanism for private borrowers.[20]

The banks were aware of the political sensitivity of the South African debt negotiations. In the early stages of the crisis they appeared to require the SAG to satisfy certain political demands as a precondition to a successful debt renegotiation.[21] Ultimately, a new one-year debt arrangement was concluded without the SAG satisfying any of these political conditions.[22]

II.A. *The First Interim Arrangement*

The terms of the First Interim Arrangement were that the SAG would make available sufficient foreign exchange to repay 5 per cent ($500 million) of the

that time, with other banks. Hufbauer, Schott and Elliott, *Economic Sanctions Reconsidered*, 223.

[16] For a detailed analysis of South Africa's debt profile at this time, *see* J. Lind and D. Espaldon, South Africa's debt at the time of crisis (San Francisco: CANNICOR Research, 1986).

[17] For more information on South Africa's debt situation at this time, *see* Hufbauer, Schott and Elliott, *Economic Sanctions Reconsidered*, 223; Hirsch 'Sanctions, Loans and South African Economy', 274; Grant, 'The Banks Abandon South Africa', 69.

[18] Proclamation R 157/1985, as issued by the State President of South Africa, *Gov't Gazette* September 1, 1985, at 9926. These measures were eventually extended until March 31, 1986. *See* G.N.R. 2868/1986, in *Gov't Gazette* February 23, 1985 at 10054. The statutes are analysed in E. Du Plessis, 'South Africa's Foreign Debt Moratorium', *Modern Business Law* 8 (1986): 24, 28.

[19] The crisis was a serious one for the banks because a significant amount of the debt was interbank debt. *See* Harris, 'South Africa's External Debt Crisis', 807.

[20] *See* Du Plessis, 'South Africa's Foreign Debt Moratorium', 33.

[21] *See* sources cited *supra* notes 5–6.

[22] *See* Harris, 'South Africa's External Debt Crisis', 803.

principal of the debt over the one year life of the arrangement and the banks would reschedule the remaining $9.5 billion over 12 months.[23]

The interim arrangement provided that each debtor would need to reach a renegotiated agreement, based on the terms of the Interim Agreement, with its own group of creditors. If they did not reach agreement, the original debtor would make payments equal to the local currency equivalent of the original obligation into a Special Restricted Account. These accounts, credited to the original creditor, were held until maturity by the Public Investment Commission (PIC), a public sector entity that invested in public sector stock.[24] The SAG therefore could access these deposits, subject only to the PIC's statutory authority, until the repayment obligation matured.[25] Thus, in financial terms, the agreement was an attractive one for the SAG.

II.B. *The Second Interim Arrangement*

When the first interim arrangement expired, the banks concluded a second interim arrangement with the SAG in March 1987.[26] This three-year arrangement, which terminated on June 30, 1990, continued the basic framework of the first arrangement. It contained no grace period and required repayment of $1.42 billion (13 per cent) of the outstanding affected debt.[27]

[23] Hirsch, 'Sanctions, Loans and South African Economy', 275. *See also* ibid., 804. The banks were free within these parameters to reach their own agreements with their original debtors.

[24] The PIC is a non-banking financial intermediary that receives funds from public sector entities and invests in fixed interest public sector stock. Its scope and responsibilities are set out in Public Investment Commissioners Act, No. 45 of 1984. *See* The Department of Finance, The Public Investment Commissioners, in *The Mechanics of the South African System*, ed. H. Falkena, W.J. Kok and J.H. Meijer (Hampshire: Macmillan Press, 1989), 109–16.

[25] *See* Du Plessis op. cit. (fn 20) at 33. It is important to recognize that this arrangement enabled the SAG to use budgetary resources for other purposes.

[26] Hircsh, 'South Africa's Foreign Debt Moratorium', 275. *See* also Hufbauer, Schott and Elliott, *Economic Sanctions Reconsidered*, 229.

[27] Hufbauer, Schott and Elliott, *Economic Sanctions Reconsidered*, 229. This agreement consists of a letter from the South African Minister of Finance to the banks, dated March 25, 1987, that sets out the terms of the arrangement and stipulates that each letter to each bank is a separate offer which the bank may accept by acknowledging receipt of the letter. Second Interim Arrangement Letter. Appended to the letter was a technical memorandum that discussed how the interim arrangement would operate. Aspects of the Second Interim Arrangements [hereinafter *Technical Memorandum*]. The special restricted accounts are credited to the original creditor who is paid out according to the terms of the Interim Arrangement. As long as the funds were actually held in the accounts, they were

The SAG continued to have access to these funds subject to the statutory mandate of the PIC.[28]

The Second Interim Arrangement also established two mechanisms through which creditors could 'exit' the Interim Arrangement. First, the banks could convert their loans into ten-year exit loans that would not be subject to any future rescheduling.[29] About $5 billion of debt was converted into these exit loans.[30]

The second mechanism was a debt-equity conversion through which the banks could convert their funds into investments in South African enterprises.[31] About $600 million of debt was converted through this mechanism.[32]

II.C. *The Third Interim Arrangement*

In mid-1989 the anti-apartheid movement began to prepare for the negotiation of a Third Interim Arrangement. Its objective was to convince the banks to condition a Third Interim Arrangement on SAG agreement to dismantle apartheid and negotiate with the democratic forces on the establishment of a non-racial democratic constitutional order in South Africa.[33]

available to the SAG that could use the funds to finance public sector securities. *See* Second Interim Arrangements Letter, § 7.ol (c).

28 *See* Public Investment Commissioner's Act 1984, No. 45 of 1984; *see* The Department of Finance, The Public Investment Commissioners, in *The Mechanics of the South African System* eds. H. Falkena et al. (Hampshire: Macmillan Press, 1989) 109–16.

29 *See Ibid.* § I2.

30 *See* Tommey, 'Outlook for Foreign Funding Improving', *The Star*, June 6, 1990; S. Fidler, 'Lenders Take Up S. African Exit Option', *The Financial Times*, May 16, 1989. In May 1989, only $3.5 billion had been converted to exit loans.

31 *Technical Memorandum*, § 6. The financial rand, which trades at a discount to the commercial rand, cannot be transferred out of South Africa. This means that any sale of financial rands represents merely a change in ownership and no net outflow of funds from South Africa. *See* The Bank of Lisbon and South Africa Limited, The Financial Rand Market, in *The Mechanics of the South African Financial System: Financial Institutions, Instruments and Markets, eds.* H. Falkena et al. (Hampshire: Macmillan Press, 1989), 339–40.

32 *See* Tommey, 'Outlook for Foreign Funding Improving'; Fidler, 'Lenders Take Up S. African Exit Option', 4.

33 In April 1989, four South African churchmen, Archbishop Desmond Tutu, Dr Allen Boesak, Dr Beyers Naude and Reverend Frank Chikane, issued an appeal to 14 creditor banks not to reschedule South Africa's debt unless five conditions were met. They were that the SAG must end the state of emergency; release all political prisoners and detainees; unban all political organizations; repeal all racist legislation, including the Group Areas Act, the Land Acts, the Separate Amenities Acts and the Population Registration Act; and establish a process for negotiating a new constitution for a non-racial, democratic, and unitary South Africa. These demands were taken up by the anti-apartheid movement. *See* Commonwealth Committee of Foreign Ministers on South Africa, *South Africa: The Sanctions Report (1989)* [hereinafter

The timing seemed propitious. The democratic forces appeared to be regrouping from the blows they had suffered when the state of emergency was declared, and the South African economy was again in deep crisis.[34] It was well known that South Africa could not repay the $ 8 billion that would fall due when the Second Interim Arrangement terminated.[35] In addition, the country had substantial obligations falling due in 1990–91 on debt outside the scope of the interim arrangement.[36]

These developments appeared to give the banks great leverage over the SAG.[37] The anti-apartheid movement argued that the banks should use this leverage to help end apartheid.[38]

Unfortunately, the anti-apartheid movement's strategy was based on an overly optimistic assessment of the bargaining position of the banks. In 1989 the banks were facing serious problems with their outstanding debts to developing countries, which were accumulating substantial arrears.[39] The strategy also ignored the banks' reluctance to attach political or policy-related conditions to debt renegotiations. Banks had tried this, with a notable lack of success, in Peru in the mid-1970s.[40]

Sanctions Report]; Rescheduling South Africa's Debt: Hearing before the Subcomm. on International Development, Finance, Trade, and Monetary Policy of the Comm. on Banking, Finance, and Urban Affairs, 1O1st Cong., 1st Sess. 101–45 (1989) [hereinafter *Hearings*] Divestment and Non-Equity Links by Transnational Corporations in South Africa, Report of the U.N. Centre on Transnational Corporations, U.N. Doc. EIC. IO/AC.411989/2 (1989) [hereinafter *Divestment Report*].

34 *Ibid, see* Statement of John Lind in Hearings, 76–77; Joffe, 'Economics Not Faith Tell Churchmen Where To Apply Pressure', 15, *The Weekly Mail* (Johannesburg, South Africa), June 23–29, 1989.

35 *See* sources cited in fn 6; *Divestment Report*, 2, 13; K. Ovenden and T. Cole, *Apartheid and International Finance: A Programme for Change* (Australia: Penguin Books 1989), 75–98.

36 The country's total repayment obligations for 1990–91 were estimated to be between $1.5 and 2.0 billion per year. *See Divestment Report*, 2, 13; Statement of John Lind in Hearings, 77.

37 For a detailed discussion of commercial bank exposure to South Africa, *see Divestment Report*.

38 *See* sources cited *supra* note 35.

39 In 1989, total arrears on developing country debt was $79 billion, equal to 6.4 per cent of total debt. About half of this was owed to private creditors. *See* The World Bank, *World debt tables 1990–91: external debt of developing countries – supplement*, World Debt Tables, Washington, DC: The World Bank, 1990–91, 22, http://documents.worldbank.org/curated/en/749481468782376937/World-debt-tables-1990–91-external-debt-of-developing-countries-supplement).

40 *See* R. Plan, *External Debt Restructuring* (Vienna: Manz, 1985) 58–61. The banks had experienced similar problems in their attempts to renegotiate the obligations of the German government in the 1920s and '30s. *See* R. Chernow, *The House of Morgan: An American Banking Dynasty and The Rise of Modern Finance*, (Grove Press, 1990), material at 392–99 is particularly pertinent.

Furthermore, by 1989 the SAG knew it could not expect to receive new money from the banks and so had little incentive to accede to bank demands that it viewed as unreasonable.[41]

The banks were able to use these weaknesses in the anti-apartheid movement's strategy to portray the strategy as financially naive and unworkable.[42] This enabled them to base the South African debt negotiations on their own profit maximizing criteria and to justify the results as being the most 'feasible' under the circumstances. The result was that in October 1989 the SAG and the banks announced that they had concluded a third interim arrangement that followed similar lines to the second agreement.[43] The arrangement significantly alleviated the financial pressure on the SAG.[44]

II.D. *Subsequent Developments*

The dynamics surrounding South Africa's debt changed with the advent of democracy in 1994. While some stakeholders inside the country were urging the new democratic government to rely on doctrines like odious debt[45] to avoid paying back the debts incurred during the apartheid era, the

[41] *See* Recent Developments in South Africa and H.R. 3458: Joint Hearing Before the Subcomm. on International Development, Finance, Trade and Monetary Policy of the House Comm. on Banking, Finance, and Urban Affairs and the Subcomm. on Africa of the House Comm. on Foreign Affairs, 101st Cong., 2d Sess., 101–79 (1990) [hereinafter *Recent Developments*] (Statements of Rodney B Wagner, Vice Chairman, Morgan Guaranty Trust Company, and John I. Simone, Executive Vice-President, Manufacturers Hanover Trust Company). Some South African commentators had begun to argue for a 'unilateral rescheduling.' *See* Ensor, 'SA Should Withdraw from Onerous Debt Arrangements-Academics', 5 *Business Day* (Johannesburg, South Africa), December 29, 1989.

[42] Ibid., *see* Statements of Rodney B. Wagner and John I. Simone in Recent Developments.

[43] The agreement was implemented through a bank acknowledgement of the receipt of a letter dated October 23, 1989, and the accompanying technical memorandum from the South African Minister of Finance.
The third interim agreement, beginning in July 1990, covers US $8 billion in loans and continues the interest rates and provides for the same relending and exit loan options available under the Second Interim Arrangement. According to the arrangement, South Africa would repay about $1.5 billion of the debt over the life of the arrangement. This meant that South Africa would still owe $6.5 billion when the agreement terminated on December 31, 1993. *See* the discussion of the Third Interim Arrangement, *supra* notes 35–43 and accompanying text. On the financial consequences of the Third Interim Arrangement, *see* J. Lind, *The New Interim Agreement Between the Baks and South Africa and Its Implications* (CANNICOR Research, 1989); Tommey, 'Outlook for Foreign Funding Improving.'

[44] *See* 'Swiss Roll-overs', 37 *Financial Mail*, November 16, 1990.

[45] *See*, UNCTAD Discussion Papers *The Concept of Odious Debt in Public International Law*, No. 187, July 2007, UNCTAD/OSG/DP/2007/4, http://www.unctad.org (accessed August 5, 2016) for an overview of the doctrine of odious debt.

government's focus was on establishing its international financial and economic credentials so that it could obtain new financing to begin addressing the huge social and economic backlogs facing the country. The new government, anxious to establish its economic management credentials, concluded that it could gain more from servicing the debt according to its terms than by relying on legal arguments, regardless of how valid they may have been, to avoid paying back the outstanding debts. Thus, post 1994, the government did not seek any further debt renegotiations and continued to service all its outstanding debt according to its terms.

III. CAVEATS: CHANGES IN THE INTERNATIONAL FINANCIAL SYSTEM

The international financial system has changed substantially since the South African debt crisis. A full discussion of all these changes is beyond the scope of this chapter. However, there are two that require some discussion because of their implications for the lessons that are discussed in the next section.

The most significant change is that at the time of its debt crisis, the primary private source of external finance for developing countries was commercial banks. Today, the predominant form in which middle income countries like South Africa access such financing today is through issuing debt securities.[46]

This development has expanded the range of potential creditors for countries like South Africa. The potential bondholders include, in addition to commercial and investment banks, such financial institutions as insurance companies, pension funds, hedge funds, sovereign wealth funds, asset managers and wealthy individuals.

Second, the fact that these securities are liquid means that creditors who lose confidence in a debtor can easily trade out of its bonds. Consequently, on average, the country's bondholders will have a lower tolerance for holding the bonds of risky debtors than was the case with bank creditors.

Also, since the 1980s, the international community has developed a range of international norms and standards that are relevant to sovereign debt renegotiations. These include private industry standards such as the principles on responsible sovereign debt renegotiations developed by the Institute for

[46] *See*, Republic of South Africa, National Treasury, Budget Review, 24 February 2016, 86; *also see*, for example, M. Wolf, *Fixing Global Finance* (Baltimore: John Hopkins University Press: 2008); M. El-Erian, *When Markets Collide: Investment Strategies for the Age of Global Economic Change* (New York: McGraw-Hill Education, 2008).

International Finance (IIF),[47] and standards developed within the UN system on principles of responsible sovereign borrowing and lending;[48] on responsible investing;[49] and on sovereign debt renegotiations and human rights.[50] They also include international regulatory standards such as the Basel Committee on Banking Supervision's guidelines on capital adequacy,[51] and the standards relating to supervision in the financial sector, with one set of principles for supervisors dealing with banks,[52] insurance companies[53] and investment banks and securities firms.[54] More recently, the international community has developed standards for promoting more socially responsible corporate, including financial institution, conduct. These standards include the UN Guiding Principles on Business and Human Rights,[55] the OECD

[47] *See* Institute of International Finance (IIF), *Principles for Stable Capital Flows and Fair Debt Restructuring in Emerging Markets* (March 31, 2005), www.iif.com/topics/principles-stable-capital-flows-and-fair-debt-restructuring.

[48] *See* UNCTAD, Principles on Promoting Responsible Sovereign Lending and Borrowing, UNCTAD/GDS/DDF/2012/Misc.1 (January 10, 2012), http://unctad.org/en/PublicationsLibrary/gdsddf2012misc1_en.pdf.

[49] *See* UNEP Principles on Responsible Investing (PRI), www.unpri.org.

[50] *See* U.N. Human Rights Council: Guiding principles on foreign debt and human rights, annexed to the Report of the Independent Expert on the effects of foreign debt and other related international financial obligations of States on the full enjoyment of all human rights, particularly economic, social and cultural rights, Cephas Lumina, U.N. Doc. A/HRC/20/23 (April 10, 2011); G.A. Res. 68/304 (September 17, 2014); Annex to Resolution 20/10 of the U.N. Human Rights Council, The Effects of Foreign Debt and Other Related International Financial Obligations of States on the Full Enjoyment of All Human Rights, particularly Economic, Social and Cultural Rights, U.N. Doc. A/HRC/RES/20/10 (July 18, 2012) UNGA Basic Principles on Sovereign Debt Restructuring Processes G.A. Res. 69/319 (September 10, 2015), www.un.org/en/ga/search/view_doc.asp?symbol=A/RES/69/319.

[51] *See* Basel Capital Accord: International convergence of capital measurement and capital standards (July 1988), www.bis.org/publ/bcbs04a.htm; Basel II: International Convergence of Capital Measurement and Capital Standards: a Revised Framework, June 2004, www.bis.org/publ/bcbs107.htm; Basel III: A global regulatory framework for more resilient banks and banking systems, December 2010, www.bis.org/publ/bcbs189_dec2010.htm.

[52] The Basel Committee on Banking Supervision: Core principles for effective banking supervision (2012), www.bis.org/publ/bcbs230.htm.

[53] International Association of Insurance Supervisors (IAIS), INSURANCE CORE PRINCIPLES (Updated 2015), www.iaisweb.org/page/supervisory-material/insurance-core-principles//file/58067/insurance-core-principles-updated-november-2015.

[54] International Organization of Securities Commissions (IOSCO): Objectives and Principles of Securities Regulation (June 2010), www.iosco.org/about/?subsection=about_iosco.

[55] United Nations Office of the High Commissioner for Human Rights, UN Guiding Principles on Business and Human Rights, U.N. Doc. HR/PUB/11/04, www.ohchr.org/Documents/Publications/GuidingPrinciplesBusinessHR_EN.pdf.

Guidelines on MNEs,[56] the Global Compact,[57] and industry standards and codes like the Equator Principles[58] and ISO 26000.[59]

IV. THREE LESSONS FROM THE SA DEBT CRISIS

The South African debt crisis, in the context of its time, was particularly complex for two reasons. First, the biggest part of the renegotiated debt was short-term inter-bank debt rather than medium term debt as was the case in most sovereign debt crises of the time. Second, the debt crisis, because of its roots in South Africa's apartheid system was more politicized than in most crises.

Nevertheless, the negotiations between the SAG and its creditors were similar to those in most sovereign debt crises. They were essentially about trying to reach a mutually acceptable agreement on how to adjust the terms of South Africa's debt so that it was able to both comply with its commitments to its creditors and manage its other commitments as a sovereign.[60] As a result, the crisis offers three lessons that are relevant to the management of sovereign debt crises today.

IV.A. *Lesson 1: Finance Is All about Money*

This seemingly obvious point has an important implication. The contractual arrangements for financial transactions are carefully negotiated to provide maximum possible legal protections to the creditors and to ensure that they have the legal means to efficiently enforce their rights.[61] However, whether

56 OECD, Guidelines for Multinational Enterprises (May 25, 2011), www.oecd.org/daf/inv/mne/48004323.pdf. This version of the Guidelines includes, for the first time, a section on human rights.

57 U.N. Global Compact, The Ten Principles of the Global Compact (January 31, 1999), www.unglobalcompact.org/what-is-gc/mission/principles.

58 Equator Principles (EP) III (June 2013), www.equator-principles.com/.

59 ISO 26000 Guidance to Social Responsibility (November 1, 2010), www.iso.org/obp/ui/#iso:std:iso:26000:ed-1:v1:en.

60 *See*, generally, O. Lienau *Rethinking Sovereign Debt: Politics, Reputation and Legitimacy in Modern Finance* (Harvard University Press, 2014); L. Buchheit and R. Lastra (eds.) *Sovereign Debt Management* (Oxford University Press, 2014). The fact that the apartheid government had a particularly racialized and constricted view of its sovereign obligations is relevant to the way in which the negotiations were structured and the range of potential outcomes but not to the underlying dynamic of the negotiations. *See*, section II of this chapter for a description of the negotiations.

61 *See*, for example, P. Wood, *Law and Practice of International Finance* (Sweet & Maxwell, 2008); Buchheit and Lastra, *Sovereign Debt Management.*

the creditors decide to utilize these rights to enforce the debt or to renegotiate terms with the borrower will depend on which option is likely to produce the larger financial return. Conversely, the debtor will be influenced in its approach to its financial obligations more by its calculus of whether it can increase the available financial resources by performing its contractual obligations or by keeping the money owed and defaulting on these obligations than by the strength of its legal position.

The significance of this lesson was demonstrated during the unfolding of the South African debt crisis. In the initial phase of the crisis, the SAG made a distinction between different types of debt. It remained current on its trade financing obligations and on its debts to its official creditors in order to minimize the risk that it would be cut off from these key sources of external finance. Similarly it decided that it would be able to conserve precious foreign exchange if it could compel the commercial bank creditors of South African commercial banks to convert their inter-bank debts into medium term debts. This meant that, ironically, the fact that South Africa was unlikely to gain access to new financing strengthened its bargaining position with the creditors who knew that they could only realistically hope to be repaid if they reached an agreement with South Africa. Moreover, once the banks' funds were trapped in South Africa, the SAG's bargaining position continued to strengthen. This is indicated by the relatively more flexible approach that the banks took in the second and third interim agreements than in the first interim agreement.

The converse situation prevailed after the advent of democracy in South Africa. The new government knew that it was viewed with suspicion by the banks and that if it wanted to borrow in the future it would need to establish its credentials as a reliable participant in international financial markets. Consequently, the government had a strong incentive to perform its contractual obligations, knowing that the reward would be access to the financing needed to deal with the difficult social and economic conditions that the government had inherited. The new government's needs, therefore, had the effect of enhancing the bargaining position of the creditors which were the very institutions that South Africa had to convince of its reliability as a debtor.

From a purely legal perspective the SAG's position is puzzling. Apartheid had been declared a crime against humanity[62] and it seemed possible for the

[62] International Convention on the Suppression and Punishment of the Crime of Apartheid. Adopted by the General Assembly of the United Nations on November 30, 1973, G.A. res. 3068 (XXVIII), U.N. Doc. A/9030 (1974), 1015 U.N.T.S. 243, entered into force July 18, 1976, https://treaties.un.org/doc/publication/unts/volume%201015/volume-1015-i-14861-english.pdf.

government to demonstrate that at least a portion of its debt was used to support apartheid and was therefore odious debt. However, the cost of relying on this legal argument was clear. While the government could have won this argument in a court of law, the response of the financial institutions could have been to congratulate South Africa on its legal victory and to inform it that they were not planning to lend it any new money. Since the banks are under no duty to lend to any particular borrower, the SAG would have had to accept this reduction in their access to international finance. Thus, the victory could have been a pyric one obtained at a high price.

This lesson should not be read to mean that the legal issues in financial transaction are unimportant or that the careful attention paid to structuring and negotiating them is a waste of time. In fact, the parties' calculation of how they can maximize their financial returns is influenced by the terms of the debt contracts and the applicable governing law. Moreover, the discussions between the parties takes place in the shadow[63] of the law applicable to the parties and their transaction. Thus, in effect the ways in which the legal issues are addressed in the debt agreements helps shape the options available to the parties in the debt renegotiations.

IV.B. *Lesson 2: The Unaddressed Suffering Caused by a Debt Crisis Becomes the Legacy Haunting a Country's Future*

In brief, this lesson is that the failure to deal with the social, political and economic issues that are the proximate causes of a debt crisis creates a legacy that haunts the debtor's efforts to shape a sustainable future after the debt crisis.

It would have been unrealistic to expect that the democratic forces in South Africa could have used the 1985 debt crisis to force the apartheid government to the negotiating table and to fully address the legacy of apartheid. However, it was not unrealistic to think that the country could have used the debt crisis to initiate some structural economic and social reforms that began undoing the terrible burden that apartheid had imposed on the country. This did not happen for a number of reasons. At the onset of the crisis, the apartheid government resisted the notion that the debt crisis was caused by its policies. It had the bargaining power to block any creditor efforts to impose political reforms as a condition for debt renegotiation. In addition, the banks were reluctant to insert themselves into the process of social and economic change

63 R. Mnookin and L. Kornhauser Lewis, 'Bargaining in the Shadow of the Law: The Case of Divorce', *The Yale Law Journal* 88 no. 5 (1979): 950–97.

in South Africa. Their reluctance was based on concerns that included a fear that they would be held responsible if their efforts to promote reform failed, either because the SAG failed to implement the reforms or they did not produce the desired outcome.[64]

The parties' failure to exploit the opportunities created by the crisis, left many stakeholders in South Africa angry that they were being forced to pay back apartheid debts despite having been adversely affected by the debts. This legacy has continued to influence South Africa. This can be seen, for example, in the efforts by civil society to advocate for a repudiation of the South African debt,[65] by the inclusion of banks in the apartheid litigation in the US[66] and in the efforts that some civil society groups made to oppose the Barclays purchase of ABSA bank in the early years of this century.[67] It may also contribute to the mixed response of South African financial institutions to demands to change their operating practices significantly and provide more adequate and appropriate financial services for small and medium sized enterprises and poor people.[68]

Although there is no way to know with certainty, it is possible that if South Africa and its creditors had used the debt to help promote social and economic reforms the legacy of the crisis might have been more positive than it has actually turned out to be. It is also possible that if the crisis had been used in this way the South African social and economic situation today may be more transformed, and the SAG's capacity to deal with the challenges of poverty, inequality and unemployment more effective.

IV.C. *Lesson 3: Soft International Norms and Standards Are Beneficial to Sovereign Debt Workouts*

At the time of the South African debt crisis there were no international norms and standards that were clearly applicable to sovereign debt workouts.

64 Ibid.

65 P. Bond, *Against Global Apartheid South Africa Meets the World Bank, IMF and International Finance* (UCT Press, 2003); J. Rubin 'Challenging Apartheid's Foreign Debt.' (1997), http://citeseerx.ist.psu.edu/viewdoc/download?doi=10.1.1.516.2414&rep=rep1&type=pdf.

66 Ntsebeza v. Ford Motor Co. (In re South African Apartheid Litig.), 15 F. Supp. 3d 454 (S.D.N.Y. 2014).

67 Jubilee News, *Jubilee Grabs Barclays & Absa by the Horns!*, www.apartheid-reparations.ch/documents/suedafrika/JubeeNL1-05.pdf.

68 FinScope Report, *Financial Access and SME Size in South Africa*, January 2016, www.finmark.org.za/sites/publication/financial-access-and-sme-size-in-south-africa/; FinScope Consumer Survey South Africa (2014), www.finmark.org.za/sites//wp-content/uploads/pubs/MedRel_FS_SA_20141.pdf.

This meant that there were no international norms to guide the creditors, the South African government or the anti-apartheid movement on how to structure either the sovereign debt renegotiation process or the outcomes on the substantive issues in the renegotiated agreement.

Today the situation would be different. There are a range of non-binding international norms and standards they can be used by interested stakeholders to assess the performance of the parties in sovereign debt renegotiations.[69]

One group of standards relate to financial sector regulation. For example, the Basel Committee on Banking Supervision's standards dealing with capital adequacy for banks, assign different risk weightings to different bank assets and then calculate how much capital each bank should have based on the composition of its asset portfolio and the total value of its risk weighted assets.[70] Given the political situation and the parlous state of the economy in South Africa in 1985, it is likely that these standards would have resulted in the banks having to set aside a relatively large amount of capital to cover their renegotiated South African debt. This in turn could have resulted in the banks taking a harder line with South Africa in the renegotiations, thereby, at least inadvertently, promoting the agenda of the anti-apartheid movement.

Second, since the time of the South African debt crisis, entities such as the IIF, UNCTAD and the UNGA have developed guidelines on sovereign debt renegotiations that are intended to help its members and their sovereign debtors to reach more sustainable agreements.[71] All these instruments stress that the debt renegotiations should be transparent, which could have helped increase pressure on the banks to be tougher on its South African debtor.

Third, the existence of standards like the UNGPs[72] would have had a particular resonance in the case of the South African debt crisis.[73] They would have given anti-apartheid activists a benchmark that they could have used to evaluate the performance of the banks in their negotiations with South Africa. They would also have been able to use this benchmark to push the banks to reach a more socially responsible resolution with South Africa. In particular, they could have pushed the banks to undertake a more rigorous and more socially and human rights focused due diligence of South Africa before agreeing to a debt renegotiation.

69 *See supra* notes 57–61. 70 *See supra* note 53. 71 *See supra* notes 49 and 50.

72 *See* UN Guiding Principles on Business and Human Rights.

73 *See*, D.D. Bradlow, 'Can Parallel Lines Ever Meet? The Strange Case of the International Standards on Sovereign Debt and Business and Human Rights', 2016 41 *Yale Journal of International Law* 205, for a discussion of how the UNGPs can be applied to a sovereign debt renegotiation.

This lesson suggests that the development of international standards, even though they are non-binding, can be a positive development for promoting more responsible sovereign debt renegotiations. At a minimum these standards may enhance the position of those stakeholders who are monitoring a particular debt renegotiation and are advocating for a more socially responsible outcome.

V. CONCLUSION

The South African debt crisis of the 1980s is a useful case study because it demonstrates a number of lessons that are still relevant today, even though international finance has changed significantly since the crisis. Even though apartheid made the South African crisis unique in a number of ways, the underlying economic causes and debt renegotiation process were sufficiently similar to other sovereign debt renegotiations that it offers three lessons that are more generally applicable to sovereign debt renegotiations.

14

Lessons from South Korea

A Developmental Mindset Makes a Difference When Governing the Financial Economy

ELIZABETH THURBON

ABSTRACT

Like countless countries grappling with the challenge of late development, South Korea has – since the 1960s – accumulated large volumes of foreign debt. And like so many others, Korea has subsequently suffered a series of debt crises, some prompting intervention by the International Monetary Fund (IMF). Yet unlike other countries, Korea has tended to recover swiftly from each crisis, most recently the 1997–98 regional turmoil and the 2008 Global Financial Crisis. Moreover, despite recurrent debt crises, Korea has managed to stay a successful course of economic development. So what might policymakers elsewhere learn from Korea's experience of debt-based development, and from its management of recurrent debt dilemmas? In this chapter I examine the critical role played by Korean policymakers in governing the country's debt-based development strategy from the 1960s to the 1990s, and in mitigating the worst effects of its 1997–98 and 2008 financial crises. I conclude by drawing lessons from the Korean experience for policymakers elsewhere.

I. INTRODUCTION

Like countless countries grappling with the challenge of late development, South Korea has since the 1960s accumulated large volumes of foreign debt. And like so many others, Korea has subsequently suffered a series of debt crises, some prompting intervention by the International Monetary Fund. Yet unlike other countries, Korea has tended to recover swiftly from each crisis, most recently the 1997 regional turmoil and the 2008 Global Financial Crisis (GFC). Moreover, despite recurrent crises, Korea has managed to stay a relatively successful course of economic development. This is not to deny the existence of serious economic and social challenges in Korea, not least the growing income inequality of recent years. Nevertheless, Korea's rapid industrial transformation and its advances in human development since the 1960s are rare accomplishments globally – especially in the context of high levels of foreign indebtedness. For this reason, Korea's debt-based development experience has long attracted interest from policymakers elsewhere facing similar debt and development challenges.

So what might others learn from Korea's experience of debt-based development, and from its management of recurrent debt dilemmas? The answer to this question will almost certainly vary depending on who is asked, with economists and political scientists emphasizing very different variables. As I am a political scientist, my answer to the 'lessons from Korea' question focuses primarily on politics, and more specifically on *policymakers*. One of the most important lessons from Korea, and potentially the most empowering for policymakers elsewhere, relates to the critical role played by a key segment of Korea's policymaking elite in strategically governing the nation's financial development. Since the 1960s, these policymakers have sought to proactively manage Korea's integration into global financial markets and to mitigate its most developmentally detrimental effects. I call this group Korea's developmentally minded policymakers.[1]

In the sections that follow, I briefly investigate where these policymakers came from and how they managed Korea's debt-based development strategy relatively effectively from the 1960s to the 1990s. I then examine Korea's experience of the 1997 and 2008 financial crises. I discuss both the causes of these crises in Korea and the role played by the nation's developmental elite in crisis management and recovery. I conclude by drawing out lessons for policymakers and policymaking elsewhere.

II. ORIGINS OF THE DEVELOPMENTAL MINDSET

From the 1960s until today, Korea's developmentally minded policymakers have typically occupied key positions in the governmental apparatus including the Presidential Office, the Finance Ministry, the Bank of Korea and Korea's numerous development banks, such as the Korea Development Bank. As their label implies, they are distinguished by a shared *mindset* or way of thinking

[1] This chapter draws on arguments presented in my book, E. Thurbon, *Developmental Mindset: The Revival of Financial Activism in South Korea* (Ithaca: Cornell University Press, 2016).

about the primary purpose of finance on the one hand, and the appropriate role of financial policymakers on the other.[2]

In the developmental mindset, the primary purpose of finance is to serve the *productive* economy, and in doing so to advance the techno-industrial development of the nation. The developmental mindset thus implies a particular way of thinking about the role of financial policymakers: they should strategically intervene in the market to help connect the financial and productive sectors of the economy, and to ensure that financial resources flow to areas deemed 'strategic' by the state. Korea's developmental policymakers are neither all-powerful nor infallible. Their interventions have at times hindered rather than helped Korea's economic and social circumstances. Nevertheless, without reference to their role, it is impossible to fully explain the success of Korea's debt-based development strategy, or the country's relatively swift recovery from successive debt crises.

The origins of a developmental mindset in Korea can be traced to the shared formative experiences of Korea's first developmental elite under Japanese colonialism (1901–45). From the 1930s, many Koreans were enlisted into the Japanese army and into the 'policy banks' established to fund Korea's development as a Japanese supply base. These Koreans saw how Japan's military planners perceived industrial strength as the key to national power and prestige. They also saw how Japanese bankers mobilized vast sums of money and pumped it into industrial projects designated as strategic by the state. These shared experiences shaped the thinking of Korea's first policy elite as they set about building an independent nation. This elite was led by Park Chung Hee, South Korea's president from 1961 to 1979. With a small group of nationalists in the Korean army, Park seized power in a military coup fifteen years after Japan's World War II defeat and eight years after the Korean War left the peninsula divided in two, with the South heavily dependent on US aid and military protection.

Japanese colonialism and US dependence had bred in Park and his loyalists a fierce nationalism and desire to secure Korea's national independence and to build its international prestige. Economic catch-up with Japan and the West was seen as central to this goal, and to restoring the livelihood and pride of the Korean people. The colonial experience had shown Park how a government could strategically manipulate an economy for nation-building purposes. Upon seizing power, Park set about building the institutional

[2] *See* ibid., Chapters 1, 2 and 4. The following sections draw on these chapters.

architecture that would enable him to translate his developmental ambitions into action via an ambitious debt-based development strategy.

III. MANAGING KOREA'S DEBT-BASED DEVELOPMENT STRATEGY, 1961–1993

Korea's revolutionary leaders saw a debt-based development strategy as the only viable option for numerous reasons. The first was their own experience under Japanese rule; they had seen the transformative potential of this approach. The second was Korea's parlous economic circumstance. Resource poor and with no viable export base, Korea could not self-fund its development at the outset. FDI was not seriously considered thanks to the colonial experience and fierce nationalism it had bred. For Korean policymakers, foreign borrowing was the only option – at least until they could expand Korea's export (and thus income, savings and investment) base.

So how did policymakers ensure that foreign loans met productive ends? The answer lies in the institutional innovations carried out in Park's first years as President. One of Park's first moves was to centralize power in the Presidential Office and to concentrate economic policymaking responsibility in two small, elite bureaucratic bodies directly answerable to the President: the Economic Planning Board (charged with devising national development plans) and the Ministry of Finance (to oversee their financing). The Bank of Korea was subordinated to the MOF so that growth could be pursued without constraint. The banking system was then nationalized and colonial era 'development banks' including the Korea Development Bank (KDB) revived. Key ministerial and banking posts were then filled with officials loyal to Park and his ambitions – and to a developmental view of finance. The developmental mindset was reinforced and perpetuated by the regular circulation of key elites through the Presidential Office and through rigorous bureaucratic recruitment and socialization processes.[3]

By the late 1960s, Korea's entire financial policymaking apparatus was geared to the goal of rapid industrialization and export expansion via a debt-based development strategy.[4] Even as national income and (government-

[3] For a detailed examination these bureaucratic restructuring and socialization processes, *see* the two chapters by B-K Kim: 'The Labyrinth of Solitude: Park and the Exercise of Presidential Power', and 'The Leviathan: Economic Bureaucracy under Park', both in *The Park Chung Hee Era: The Transformation of South Korea*, eds. B-K Kim and E.F. Vogel (Cambridge, MA: Harvard University Press, 2011).

[4] For details of financial sector restructuring and the rise of financial activism under Park, *see* Thurbon, *Developmental Mindset*, chapter 4.

compelled) savings increased exponentially over the 1960s and 1970s, it could not keep pace with Park's aggressive investment and export expansion plans, which demanded continued foreign borrowing. However only banks and firms with government approval could borrow overseas, and development banks played a critical role mediating between local borrowers and foreign lenders, ensuring that foreign loans reached strategic ends.

Foreign loans flowing into projects deemed strategic by the state received a full government guarantee. So while Korea's foreign debt was directed towards private firms, the government was ultimately liable for these debts should things go wrong. To prevent things going wrong, the government closely monitored the performance of firms receiving government-backed loans. Recipient firms were mainly export-oriented firms in strategic industries, and were held to strict performance criteria, including production, technology improvement and export targets.[5] Failure to meet targets saw firms denied future funding. These measures meant that foreign loans typically found productive, income-generating activities, improving repayment chances. To further ensure their creditworthiness the government limited the number of local firms allowed to operate in strategic industries. The aim was to promote competition while minimizing the risks of over-capacity and declining earnings. Korea's large, family owned firms, the chaebols, were the primary targets of government lending. Indeed Korea's debt-driven development strategy was primarily responsible for these firms' massive growth and expansion over the 1970s and 1980s.

Between the 1960s and 1990s, this strategy delivered one of the most remarkable industrial transformations in world history. Industrial transformation went hand in hand with impressive advances in human development, from improving income equality to outstanding advances in education, health and life expectancy. Nevertheless, Korea's development strategy was not free of problems and perversions. Three in particular eventually brought it un-stuck.

The first was a heavy reliance on oil imports. This left Korea's export-oriented economy vulnerable to fluctuations in oil prices, especially when

[5] For the foundational account of the conditional nature of financial assistance in Korea, *see* A. Amsden, *Asia's Next Giant: South Korea and Late Industrialization* (New York: Oxford University Press, 1989). For a theoretical justification of this approach, *see* A. Amsden, *The Rise of 'The Rest': Challenges to the West from Late-Industrializing Economies* (New York: Oxford University Press, 2001) and Mathews 'Latecomer Industrialisation' in *Elgar Handbook of Alternative Theories of Economic Development*, eds. J. Ghosh, R. Kattel and E. Reinert (London: Edward Elgar, 2016). On conditionality as a hallmark of developmentalism *see* E. Thurbon and L. Weiss, 'The Developmental State in the Late 20th Century', in J. Ghosh et al. (ibid).

price hikes coincided with weak global demand. This occurred twice in the 1970s, resulting in debt crises and forcing the government to turn to the IMF. Korean policymakers pursued the most unconventional of responses to these crises: using IMF assistance to restructure debts while simultaneously upgrading and expanding industrial production, hoping to grow Korea out of crisis when external conditions improved.[6] Korea did recover swiftly from the 1973–74 and 1979–80 downturns. However these policy responses did nothing to reduce the instabilities inherent in its debt-based development strategy. The second problem was the rapid growth of the chaebols and an increasingly imbalanced industrial ecosystem, where smaller firms found it hard to thrive. As non-chaebol firms accounted for the overwhelming majority of employment in Korea, their hardships were felt society-wide. The third problem was that Korea's development strategy was carried out by authoritarian regimes masquerading as democratic ones. So, despite improvements in national income and human development, calls for political and economic liberalization grew ever stronger over the 1970s and 1980s. Elections were held in 1980 and 1988, but both saw military men with scant commitment to democratic ideals elected as president. It was not until 1993 that Koreans elected their first real civilian president, Kim Young Sam. Kim swiftly delivered on his promise of wholesale economic liberalization. Four years later, Korea experienced the worst financial crisis in its history.

IV. THE 1997 CRISIS AND KOREA'S DEBT-BASED DEVELOPMENT STRATEGY

The 1997 crisis was different from those Korea had previously experienced, in cause and effect. When the crisis broke, mainstream Western commentary identified as its primary cause Korea's state-directed, debt-based development model.[7] Yet in reality that model – described earlier – had been effectively dismantled by the mid-1990s. Contrary to the conventional wisdom of the day,

[6] Woo's foundational *Race to the Swift* (1991) provides a detailed account of Korea's debt-driven development experience from the 1960s to the 1980s and its management of the financial crises during this period. J-e. Woo, *Race to the Swift: State and Finance in Korean Industrialization* (New York: Columbia University Press, 1991).

[7] For two excellent accounts and critiques of the initial Western interpretation of the 1997–98 crisis, *see* R. Wade and F. Veneroso, 'The Asian Crisis: The High Debt Model Versus the Wall Street-Treasury-IMF Complex', *New Left Review* 228 (1998): 3; and Chang, Ha-Joon, Park Hong-Jae and Chul Gyue-Yoo, 'Interpreting the Korean Economic Crisis: Financial Liberalization, Industrial Policy and Corporate Governance', *Cambridge Journal of Economics* 22, no. 6 (1998): 735–46.

the primary cause of Korea's 1997 crisis was the government's aggressive pursuit of financial liberalization under President Kim Young Sam, starting in 1994.[8] This pursuit was domestically designed rather than externally imposed. While Korea had come under relentless US pressure to liberalize its financial markets since the early 1980s, previous Korean presidents had largely resisted those calls. Kim YS took a very different position to his predecessors. So enthusiastic were Kim and his chief advisors about financial liberalization that during negotiations for OECD entry, the Korean team offered liberalizing concessions that went far beyond what the OECD required or expected.

How might we explain this dramatic policy shift? The answer lies with the changing balance of power within the Korean state between developmental and liberally minded policymakers. From the 1970s, liberal ideas came to resonate strongly within some segments of the bureaucracy, especially the EPB. As Korea's debt-based strategy succumbed to oil shocks and lurched into financial crisis during the 1970s, liberally minded policymakers became convinced that Korea's state-guided model was the fundamental problem, and financial liberalization the only answer. The appeal of liberal ideas was by no means universal. Bureaucrats in the Ministry of Finance, the Bank of Korea and key industry ministries remained wedded to a developmental view of finance and a strategic role for the state. So too did President Park Chung Hee and his two successors, Chun Doo Hwan and Roh Tae Woo (who were less developmentally diligent than Park, but not hostile to financial activism). However, presidential support for financial activism changed dramatically with the election of President Kim Young Sam, Korea's first real civilian president and its first liberally minded leader. Given the institutional power of the president in Korea, Kim's strong support for financial liberalization made a dramatic policy shift possible.

Between 1994 and 1996, the Kim administration pursued a rapid, reckless and ill-designed approach to financial liberalization. Restrictions on short-term capital flows were abolished while prohibitions on the establishment of

[8] For detailed accounts of the limitations of Korea's approach to financial liberalization in the early 1990s under President Kim Young Sam, and contrasts of this account with more 'developmental' approaches to liberalization elsewhere in East Asia, *see* E. Thurbon, 'Two Paths to Financial Liberalization: South Korea and Taiwan', *Pacific Review* 2 (2001): 241; and E. Thurbon, 'Ideational Inconsistency and Institutional Incapacity: Why Financial Liberalization in South Korea Went Horribly Wrong', *New Political Economy* 3 (2003): 341; E. Thurbon, 'The Developmental Logic of Financial Liberalization in Taiwan' in *Institutions and Market Economies: The Political Economy of Growth and Development*, ed. W. Garside (London: Palgrave Macmillan), 87–106. The reminder of this section draws on these accounts.

merchant banks were simultaneously lifted. Inexperienced banks led Korea's headlong charge into short-term foreign borrowing. Between 1993 and 1996, Korea's external debt increased from US$ 43 to 104 billion, of which close to 60 per cent was short-term. Liberalization was accompanied by the abandonment of strategic industrial governance. Investment restrictions designed to prevent overcapacity in key export sectors were removed. Before long, short-term loans were being plied by banks into long-term investments by medium-sized chaebols looking to aggressively expand into once forbidden strategic sectors. The result was predictable – the build-up of massive debt-to-equity ratios by the chaebols, combined with over-capacity and falling earnings in key export industries. The party came to an abrupt halt in 1997 when instabilities in South East Asia spooked foreign lenders and sparked unprecedented capital flight. With the exchange rate plummeting, Korean firms and banks found themselves unable to roll over short-term loans, and stuck with huge dollar-denominated liabilities. Within months, Korea was forced into the arms of the IMF.

V. KOREA'S RESPONSE TO AND RECOVERY FROM THE 1997–1998 CRISIS

The causes of the 1997 turmoil were different from Korea's earlier episodes. However newly elected President Kim Dae Jung (1998–2002) responded in ways reminiscent of Korea's traditional developmental regimes.[9] Like his predecessor, President Kim DJ was a life-long campaigner for democracy and a vocal advocate of chaebol reform. But unlike Kim Young Sam, Kim DJ was not hostile to the idea of strategic industrial governance or financial activism. Indeed, Kim DJ soon proved himself a strong advocate of strategic financial and industrial governance – so long as it was aimed at disciplining and streamlining the chaebols and promoting the development of non-chaebol firms, which he saw as critical to Korea's future techno-industrial competitiveness. Kim's proclivity for strategic activism was reflected in some of his first moves as President. He began by closing Korea's most troubled financial institutions and merging and nationalizing others. He then set about disciplining and streamlining the chaebols with a view to restoring profitability and their capacity to repay loans. This involved several rounds of aggressive, state-led restructuring in which overextended firms were ordered to swap or sell assets to achieve the rationalization of production lines, or face bankruptcy.

9 On these similarities, *see* J. Cherry, 'Big Deal or Big Disappointment? The Continuing Evolution of the South Korean Developmental State', *Pacific Review* 3 (2006): 327.

While some weaker firms didn't survive the shake-up, Korea's key conglomerates emerged streamlined and stronger than ever. Korea's development banks then helped to recapitalize these firms, allowing them to swiftly resume production and export activities.

The swift recovery of the chaebols' export earnings drove the recovery of the Korean economy as a whole, allowing the government to repay its IMF debt ahead of schedule. Yet this was not before the IMF's initial response to the crisis brought the country to its knees. The story of the IMF exacerbating the 1997 crisis has been well told.[10] Suffice to note the key points. Although Korea's debt problems lay principally with the private sector, and although the government maintained sound fundamentals right up until the crisis broke, the IMF responded as if government profligacy and excessive market interference were the key causes of Korea's woes. The IMF thus ordered the government to raise interest rates, slash government spending and implement a comprehensive programme of financial liberalization and deregulation along with sweeping corporate and labour market reforms. By (incorrectly) signalling to foreign investors that Korea's economic system was fundamentally flawed, the IMF triggered a second wave of capital flight. As foreign funding evaporated and the prospect of national default loomed, President Kim took the unprecedented step of asking ordinary Koreans to donate their own personal gold to the government – even their jewellery – to help it keep the nation afloat. The public's response was overwhelming, with an estimated $2 billion collected under the gold donation scheme. Some Koreans even donated their wedding rings to the national cause.

Yet despite this shaky start, the government's subsequent management of the crisis proved effective. The Kim regime took a two-step approach to recapitalizing Korean banks and re-igniting productive investment: encouraging FDI and expanding financial activism.

V.A. *Recapitalization via FDI*

The IMF's rescue package came with numerous conditions, including the removal of almost all restrictions on FDI, even in the banking sector, and the introduction of a fully floating exchange rate system.[11] FDI liberalization

[10] *See* Wade and Veneroso, 'The Asian Crisis.'

[11] For a detailed examination of the role of foreign investment in banking sector reform under Kim Dae Jung, *see* T. Kalinowski and C. Hyekyung, 'Bank Nationalization, Restructuring and Reprivatisation: The Case of Korea since the Asian Financial Crisis', *Korea Observer* 1 (2010): 1.

was deeply controversial in Korea, given its colonial history and pervasive nationalist sentiment, which had been actively fostered by the Park regime. Nevertheless, President Kim and his advisors were not opposed to the idea of FDI in the banking sector. They hoped that the injection of foreign capital, technology and expertise would not just stabilize the local system but also have positive upgrading effects. And local opposition to FDI was temporarily neutralized by the fact that Korea had no domestic options for recapitalization, given the crisis situation. Between 1998 and 2006, foreign ownership in the Korean banking system increased from 18 to 65 per cent. To further promote financial stability, strict debt-to-equity limits were imposed on the chaebols. The stock market was also further opened to foreign investment – a move the government hoped would help further reduce the chaebols' debt-reliance. Foreign ownership of shares in Korea's flagship chaebols thus increased significantly. However foreign ownership did not translate into managerial control, which remained in Korean hands.

These measures helped to recapitalize Korean banks and reduce the chaebols' debt-reliance. Yet it was not long before FDI inflows bumped up against political limits. Over 1997–98, the Korean won plummeted against most major currencies thanks to capital flight and exchange rate liberalization. Devaluation made Korean financial and corporate assets relatively cheap for foreign investors, especially from the US and Europe. Between 1998 and 2000, foreign investors were able to snap up intrinsically valuable Korean assets at fire-sale prices. This riled the Korean public, many who had donated their own gold at the height of the crisis to help save these very assets.

Resistance to growing foreign bank ownership also emanated from within the state, the backlash led by developmentally minded policymakers in the Bank of Korea and the Ministry of Finance. Their opposition soon put the Kim government's further privatization plans on hold. Policymakers' concerns related to the impact of foreign bank entry on productive investment levels. For as the early 2000s progressed, it became clear that foreign-owned banks and branches were disinclined to lend to Korean firms for productive purposes. Their preference was to pursue short-term profits through real estate and consumer lending, and by facilitating derivatives trades. The unwillingness of private banks to lend to Korean firms was exacerbated by a newfound risk-aversion on the part of the chaebols. Badly burnt by the IMF crisis, the chaebols proved increasingly reluctant to expand their investments at home, preferring to retain rather than reinvest their profits. Following China's 2001 WTO entry, when the chaebols did decide to reinvest, it was often in China not Korea. These problems provide the context for second step of the government's crisis response.

V.B. *Expansion of Financial Activism*

The government's concern with boosting productive investment and securing Korea's future techno-industrial competitiveness informed the second step of its crisis recovery strategy: the revival of financial activism. This principally involved expanding the financing activities of Korea's development banks. In the post-crisis period, a key focus of these banks was Korea's non-chaebol firms in industries deemed strategic, especially information and communications technology (ICT) industries. President Kim saw ICT as critical to Korea's future as a high-wage, high value-added economy. He also understood that raising the technology and export competitiveness levels of Korean SMEs was crucial to this goal. To this end, given the reluctance of private banks to lend to smaller firms, the government re-purposed Korea's development banks as venture capital firms. Over 1998–2000, Korea's development banks flooded the market with venture funds. This resulting start-up boom helped absorb many of the highly skilled professionals made redundant through post-crisis chaebol restructuring. The dot-com bust of 2001 proved fatal for many start-ups. But this did not deter the continued expansion of financial activism as the 2000s progressed. Increased development bank lending was accompanied by government efforts to foster the local bond market as an additional financing mechanism for Korean firms.[12]

These measures saw Korea recover swiftly from the crisis. Nevertheless, as the 2000s progressed, a new series of instabilities emerged that would expose Korea to the 2008 global financial crisis.

VI. BETWEEN THE CRISES: THE EMERGENCE OF NEW INSTABILITIES

From the early 2000s, a two-tier financial system emerged in Korea. The first tier was made up of private commercial banks reluctant to lend to non-chaebol firms and a preference for consumer, real estate and derivatives-focused financing. This preference was particularly strong among foreign banks branches, which under IMF reforms had been left greater scope than local banks to engage in the trading of forex derivatives. The second tier consisted of state-owned development banks charged with the task of filling the growing void in 'real economy' financing. They focused mainly on lending to and investing in non-chaebol firms engaged in manufacturing activities. However

[12] *See* L. Rethel 'The New Financial Development Paradigm and Asian Bond Markets', *New Political Economy* 15 (2010): 4.

the government's financial activism could not insulate Korea from the major headwinds that buffeted the economy as 2008 crisis loomed. These headwinds – with origins in reforms imposed by the IMF in 1997 – eventually culminated in Korea's exposure to the 2008 disaster.

In 1997, the IMF required Korea to remove almost all restrictions on foreign investment in the stock and bond markets, and to implement a fully floating exchange rate system. These developments produced a new host of challenges for Korean policymakers anxious to maintain financial stability and productive investment. As Korea began to recover from the crisis, it experienced huge volumes of foreign capital inflows, attracted by a depressed Korean Won and bargain basement asset prices. Before long, those inflows exerted upward pressure on Korean asset prices and the Won. From 2005, Won appreciation became a major problem for Korean exporters, undermining their competitiveness. Where the government may traditionally have intervened to devalue the Won, the free-floating exchange rate system prevented a direct response. And indirect responses, such as lowering the domestic interest rate, were ruled out by the real estate bubble, the other by-product of capital inflows. Lower interest rates would only fuel that fire.

Given the Won's relentless rise, Korean exporters began looking for ways to hedge against future increases. They did not have to look far, with foreign bank branches aggressively pushing one solution: the purchase of forward forex contracts, financed through short-term borrowing (the cheapest option). As noted earlier, under IMF reforms, foreign bank branches were exempt from forex trading regulations. Unlike Korean banks, they were free to promote forex futures as the obvious option for Korean firms. Foreign bank branches thus became the primary transmission lines of the GFC to Korea – accounting for the lion's share of short-term foreign debt and derivatives exposure on the eve of the crisis.[13]

However, foreign bank branches and Korean exporters were not solely responsible for the explosion in forex derivatives trading and the accumulation of short-term debt. Korean policymakers also inadvertently exacerbated these trends through their efforts to lower the exchange rate via indirect means: encouraging capital outflows. In 2005 the government removed restrictions on outbound investments in foreign real estate and stock markets. The result was a spectacular increase in capital outflows. Unfortunately however, the anticipated depreciation of the Won did not eventuate. For Korean investors also sought to hedge their investments through the purchase of forward forex

[13] On the role of foreign bank branches in precipitating the crisis, *see* H. Cho, *South Korea's Experience with Banking Sector Liberalization* (Amsterdam: SOMO, 2010).

contracts, again largely financed by short-term loans. Upward pressure on the Won thus continued unabated.

Thus by 2008, Korea found itself again laden with short-term foreign debt, leaving it vulnerable to any shock that might trigger capital flight. That shock eventually came with the implosion of the US housing market and the Lehman Brothers bankruptcy in September 2008. The panic was immediate. In the month of October alone, capital flight from Korea reached a massive $25.5 billion – approximately 3 per cent of GDP. This was around four times greater than the worst month of the 1997. Between September and December, the Won lost 30 per cent of its value against the dollar and foreign reserves plummeted by 20 per cent. Export earnings plunged by more than 30 per cent and stock values by approximately 20 per cent. This led the IMF to downgrade Korea's 2009 growth forecast from 2.5 per cent in November 2008 to minus 4 per cent in January 2009.[14] Yet, as we shall see, the government's response saw Korea recover swiftly, eventually posting positive growth in 2009, despite the growing global calamity.

VII. THE GFC: RESPONSE AND RECOVERY

Korea's swift recovery from the GFC can be largely attributed to the response of its financial policymakers under Korea's newly elected President Lee Myung Bak (2008–13). Lee had swept to power in 2008 on a wave of 'developmental nostalgia'. Years of financial instability and jobless growth had fuelled in Korea pervasive scepticism about the benefits of 'free markets' and their ability to deliver stability, employment and growth. Developmental nostalgia manifested in the stated desire of many Koreans for a strong leader willing to pursue bold development initiatives aimed at a national economic revival. Lee MB capitalized on this sentiment, offering himself as a twenty-first-century Park Chung Hee. Lee promised to pursue as president ambitious, government-led projects aimed at kick-starting a new growth era. Yet no sooner had he assumed the presidency that the GFC hit, making crisis management Lee's primary challenge.

Lee's first reactions revealed his developmental inclinations and ensured that his crisis response would be shaped by developmental ways of thinking about finance. Over 2008 and 2009, Lee surrounded himself with advisors who envisaged a far stronger role for the state in regulating financial markets than existed at the time. Among the most influential were former MOF

[14] D. Cho, 'The Republic of Korea's Economy in the Swirl of Global Crisis,' (2009) ADBI Working Paper 147, 4. Tokyo: Asian Development Bank Institute.

bureaucrats Kang Man-Soo and Park Jae-wan, and internationally admired Oxford-trained economist Shin Hyun-song. Between 2008 and 2010, these men served as Lee's Minister of Finance and Strategy, First Economic Secretary and Chief advisor on international finance respectively. Lee's crisis team was united by their rejection of free-market fundamentalism and their belief in the necessity and desirability of capital controls. Shin played a particularly important role in designing the re-regulatory measures introduced by Korea in 2010. But before they could consider regulatory redesign, policy-makers had to deal with the immediate task of crisis management.

The Lee government's crisis response was the opposite of that adopted in 1997 under the auspices of the IMF.[15] In 2008, the Bank of Korea slashed interest rates in half while the Finance Ministry ramped up government expenditure, introducing two emergency budget packages totalling nearly 4 per cent of GDP, providing an effective counter-cyclical stimulus. Then, to prevent a full-blown banking crisis, the government announced the temporary guarantee of banks' short-term foreign debts. This was seen as credible by foreign lenders in 2008 because, unlike in 1997, Korea's foreign reserves were *greater* than its short-term foreign debts. In 2008 the government allowed the Won to plummet in value directing reserves towards bank stabilization instead of squandering them on defending the Won. Bank stabilization was also easier in 2008 because post-1997 reforms had required Korean banks to adhere to new BIS-stipulated reserve ratios. So despite capital flight, Korea did not succumb to a banking crisis in 2008. No major bank bailouts were needed, nor did loan growth stall significantly.

Moreover, despite plummeting profits, Korea's export sector remained largely immune to crisis. Thanks again to post-crisis reforms, the chaebols had much lower debt-to-equity ratios in 2008 than in 1997. Moreover, following China's 2001 WTO entry, chaebol exports were now directed largely towards China, which remained relatively immune from the crisis. Chaebol exports thus picked up swiftly from early 2009 when the immediate shock of the crisis settled. Their export earnings revival was also helped by Korea's plummeting exchange rate. By Q2 of 2009, chaebol exports had thus recovered well, again helping to drive national recovery.

Yet the fortunes of non-chaebol firms were not as rosy. As the crisis intensified, the reluctance of banks to extend liquidity to smaller

[15] Some excellent studies compare Korea's policy responses to the 1997 and 2008 financial crises and draw policy lessons for Korea. For example: Cho, 'The Republic of Korea's Economy' and L. Keun, G. Kim, H-K Kim, and H-S Song, 'A New Macro-Financial System for a Stable and Crisis-Resilient Growth in Korea', *Seoul Journal of Economics* 2 (2010): 145.

firms – despite government pleas – riled state officials. As 2009 progressed, officials from the President down began to criticize private banks for continuing to pay dividends to shareholders instead of extending loans to cash-strapped local firms. From mid-2009, a narrative emerged from the government that Korea needed to rethink the purpose of the financial sector, and take urgent efforts to re-link its financial and productive sectors. With the economy stabilized, policymakers turned their attention from crisis management to recovery. Their approach was twofold: the re-regulation of short-term capital controls to ensure stability, and the expansion of financial activism to boost productive investment and kick-start a new growth era.

VII.A. *Capital Control Re-Regulation*

The GFC provided the political space for Korean policymakers to think creatively about regulatory measures that might help prevent future crises. By 2010, the scale of the GFC and its impact on emerging economies especially had softened international attitudes toward capital controls – at least in times of crisis. As 2010 progressed, the IMF, World Bank and Asian Development Bank all released statements supportive of some form of capital controls in times of crisis. Shin Hyun-song, Lee's top advisor on International Finance and globally respected scholar of capital controls, was an important contributor to this international debate. It was Shin who led Korea's team of financial reformers as they mapped out a series of reform proposals for the nation. In 2010, four key reforms were devised and implemented. They included: a tax on the non-deposit liabilities of banks to discourage banks from holding excessive dollar-denominated debt; a tax on foreign purchases of government bonds to promote bond market stabilization; endorsing government intervention in the foreign exchange market in times of disorder; and lowering the foreign exchange derivatives ceilings for local and foreign banks. These measures were designed to limit currency trading and the build-up of short-term debt and to prevent capital flight.

Korean policymakers trod very carefully in introducing these measures so as not to spark international or domestic opposition – or capital flight. In 2010 Korea was also Chair of the G20 and wanted to avoid any perception that it was turning its back on the liberal international economic order. Policymakers thus strategically adopted 'market-friendly' language in justifying these measures, labelling them 'macro-prudential regulations' rather than 'capital controls.'[16] They also waited until after the November G20

[16] For an illuminating analysis of Korean policymakers' management of the politics of capital control re-regulation, *see* K.P. Gallagher, 'Countervailing Monetary Power: Re-regulating

summit – where they secured G20 endorsement for 'defensive capital controls' for emerging economies – to implement them. Following their implementation, in early 2011 the measures received the explicit endorsement of the IMF, which released a report highlighting the positive impact of capital controls in Korea.

Yet it is important to re-emphasise that not all aspects of financial activism have been supported or successful in Korea; developmentally minded policy-makers are neither all powerful nor infallible. For example, Finance Minister Kang's exchange rate interventions over 2008–09 aimed at artificially lowering the Won were especially controversial. This measure benefitted Korean exporters (namely, the chaebols), but was deeply unpopular with the wider public who felt the full brunt of its inflationary effects. The public backlash saw President Lee reluctantly stand down Kang as Minister in 2009. However, Lee soon appointed Kang as Chairman of the KDB, where he oversaw the second part of the government's crisis recovery strategy: the expansion of financing by Korea's development banks aimed at kick-starting productive investment and igniting a new growth phase.

VII.B. *Expansion of Financial Activism*

I have elsewhere told the story of the revival of financial activism in post-2008 Korea.[17] Suffice to note here the key points. When President Lee came to power Korea had experienced a decade of jobless growth and was facing growing competition from China. Like his predecessors, Lee believed that to break out of the middle income trap and join the ranks of advanced economies, Korea would have to rapidly improve the competitiveness of its non-chaebol firms, which accounted for over 98 per cent of Korean employment. It would also need to find new, high-tech industries in which it could lead from the outset rather than simply follow advanced-country firms. Yet realizing this vision required sufficient financing for non-chaebol firms. And as we have seen, private banks were reluctant to provide this.

The government's response to this challenge was to aggressively expand financing by Korea's development banks. Under Lee, funds were overwhelmingly channelled to firms in 'green growth' industries – such as electric vehicles, smart grids and new and renewable energies, which the government identified as the most promising new growth industries. By attempting to seize

Capital Flows in Brazil and South Korea', *Review of International Political Economy* 1 (2015): 77.

[17] Thurbon, *Developmental Mindset*.

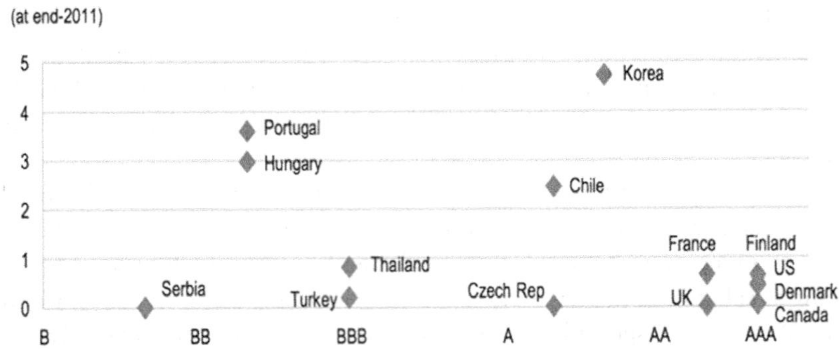

FIGURE 14.1 Government SME financing as a percentage of GDP. Reproduced with permission from Fitch, *Korea's Policy Financial Institutions*, 2013 Special Report. Seoul: Fitch Ratings. *Note*: Horizontal axis = ratings by Fitch.

the global lead in these industries, policymakers hoped not only to secure Korea's future competitiveness, but also to address energy insecurity and climate change concerns, boosting Korea's international profile.[18] Korea now stands out among OECD countries in terms of the role of development banks in its banking system. In 2015, state-owned policy banks accounted for approximately 30 per cent of all bank lending in Korea. The Korean government is also exceptional in its financing of SMEs (see Figure 14.1).

The GFC's impacts on the Korean population were thus comparatively mild. Employment growth fell by only 1 per cent during the crisis, and Korea's unemployment rate remains low by international standards. This is not to downplay the persistence of major social and economic challenges. But in the absence of financial activism, the experience of ordinary Koreans since the GFC is likely to have been worse.

VIII. CONCLUSION

It is arguably unhelpful to draw specific policy lessons from Korea for other countries. Korean policies often worked because they were designed to address the particular challenges facing the nation at different moments in history. And as Korea's experience with the IMF in 1997 revealed, making 'one size fits all' policy recommendations divorced from national context can be deeply

[18] On the developmental underpinnings of Korea's Green Growth strategy, *see* S-Y Kim and E. Thurbon, 'Developmental Environmentalism: Explaining the Embrace of Green Growth in Korea', *Politics and Society* 2 (2015): 213.

damaging. Rather, the most important lessons from Korea relate to the critical role played by *developmentally minded policymakers* who since the 1960s have been motivated by a primary goal: to keep connected the financial and productive sectors of the economy, and to ensure that the financial market serves rather than destabilizes the 'real' (read: export and job creating) economy. Financial activism has not always been successful. But it has tended to help rather than hinder Korea's development efforts for at least two reasons. First, Korean policymakers' have often shared a well-developed sense of public service and commitment to the pursuit of national over personal or political goals. Goal orientation has meant that where financial activism has been deployed, it has often been on a conditional basis, contingent upon longer-term goals being met. Second, financial activism in Korea has been shaped by commitment to a clear *goal* rather than a set of rigid, ideologically informed policy prescriptions. Policymakers have thus been willing to experiment with a range of policies, combining liberalization with strategic interventionism to discover what works, adapting their approaches to changing circumstances. But while Korea's financial policies have adapted and evolved, their overarching goal – to have finance serve the productive economy – has remained relatively constant. This makes Korea a worthy case study for policymakers elsewhere grappling with their own unique debt and development challenges.

15

The Spanish Crisis

The Trouble of Managing Debt Overhang in an Imperfect Monetary Union

JOSÉ ANTONIO ALONSO

ABSTRACT

Spain has been one of the European countries more affected by the financial and economic crisis. Prior to 2007, Spain could be presented as a good example of responsible management of fiscal policy, with surplus in the public budget and a very limited ratio of public indebtedness. The main economic problems were located in the enormous deficit in the current account and the external private debt accumulated. Part of this debt was employed in adding fuel to the real estate bubble. The crisis seriously affected those parts of the financial system (Cajas de Ahorro) more linked with the real estate sector, obliging public authorities to a massive public bailout programme. As a consequence, private debt was transformed into public debt, the public budget fell into significant deficits and GDP growth turned negative. The Spanish government adopted an extreme adjustment programme as a condition for receiving external financial support and recovering economic equilibrium. Nowadays, the Spanish GDP is still 10 per cent lower than that of 2007 and social costs of the adjustments have been tremendous, while the ratio of external public debt has climbed to its highest historical levels and the economic recovery is fragile. The chapter analyses this process and argues that the economic policy adopted by the EU and applied in Spain, far from having attenuated the crisis and offered a solution to the countries affected by debt overhang tended to make the situation more difficult. The chapter defends that the relief for the problem of sovereign debt will require both a policy change in the EU, with creditor countries adopting an expansive fiscal policy, and a reform of EU institutions in order to complete and rebalance the Monetary Union.

1. INTRODUCTION

Economic historians remind us that the Spanish state has frequently used debt as a source of public financing. In fact, history says that Spain is one of the countries in the world with the longest list of debt defaults.[1] That is not surprising if we bear in mind the crucial role that public debt had both in the fragile financial sustainability of the Spanish empire as well as in financing the numerous wars in which the Spanish monarchy was involved between 1500 and 1800. Later, in the nineteenth century and the first half of the twentieth some civil wars (including that of colonial independence in Latin America) were responsible for many other periods of debt overhang that required subsequent renegotiation processes with creditors.[2]

The Franco dictatorship was – also in this field – an abnormal period, which distanced Spain from international financial markets. The State abused the inflationist tax and the financial repression in order to finance fiscal imbalances. The new democratic regime, after the late seventies, tried to sort out this area and to progressively move Spanish policy and institutions in terms of debt towards those in operation in other European countries. The fiscal capacity of the State was strengthened, with a tax reform, a regulated debt market was developed, through programmed auctions, incentives were established to attract investors and the range of bonds was diversified.[3]

As a result of this process, Spain was one of the latest European countries in attaining international standards in responsible debt management.[4] The task was not an easy one because there were important economic crises in the period, when Spain had to make intensive use of debt. The most serious period was in the early nineties when public debt reached more than 60 per cent of GDP. The recovery of economic growth, after 1996, and the processes of privatization of public companies implemented by the first government of José María Aznar put the ratio of public debt to GDP in a path of progressive reduction.

Between 1996 and 2007, Spain underwent a period of remarkable economic boom. Spain grew at a faster rate than its peers, it reduced unemployment, improved its fiscal balance, the inflation differential was

[1] *See*, for example, C.M. Reinhart and K.S. Rogoff, *This Time Is Different. Eight Centuries of Financial Folly* (New Jersey: Princeton University Press, 2009).

[2] *See* F. Comín, *Las crisis de deuda soberana en España (1500–2015)* (Madrid: Catarata Ediciones, 2016).

[3] I. Ezquiaga, *El mercado español de deuda del Estado. Estructura y formación de precio* (Barcelona: Editorial Ariel, 1991).

[4] Reinhart and Rogoff, *This Time Is Different*.

contained and the ratio of public debt to GDP was maintained at a much lower level than that agreed at Maastricht. As a result, Spain became one of the most disciplined pupils in the convergence process defined by the Monetary Union. Encouraged by those results, there was a generalized feeling of success in Spanish society, which was stimulated by complacent comments by politicians.

In 2009, as a result of the crisis, all those parameters had changed: with the Spanish economy plunged into a sharp recession, unemployment grew, the fiscal balance showed an enormous deficit and debt began to grow fast. The intensity of the change stunned Spanish society. What had happened? In barely two years, it had gone from being a model country, which met its international commitments, to a bankrupt economy and one of the main risk factors for the sustainability of the European Monetary Union (EMU).

The reaction of the authorities was late and hesitant until in 2010 the government felt obliged to accept the conditions imposed on it by the European authorities, including a constitutional change prompted from abroad. The medicine fuelled internal devaluation, through a severe adjustment in public spending, dried up credit, aggravated the recession and increased unemployment. During the presidency of Jean-Claude Trichet, the European Central Bank (ECB) limited its activity to monitor inflation, avoiding to assume the role of a lender of last resort in support of the indebted countries. With financial markets in tension after the Greek crisis, the Spanish government had to face speculators attacking sovereign debt without monetary policy and with severe fiscal restrictions.

The disciplined submission of the national authorities to the dictates of the European Union (EU), the progressive relegation of EU authorities to the leadership of Germany (and partly France) and the evidence of the mistaken management adopted in response to the crisis fed the distancing of citizens from the political class and the institutions, both nationally and at a European level. The economic crisis was therefore followed by a political crisis, which can most clearly be seen in the transformation of the parliament, with the emergence of two new political forces, one of which is the heir to movements expressing citizens' indignation.

In the last two years, 2015 and 2016, the economic situation improved noticeably. The change in direction adopted by the European Central Bank (ECB) played a crucial role in that improvement. From 2013, the ECB got involved in providing liquidity to European economies and from 2015 in buying debt from countries with problems. The consequent lowering of interest rates and risk spreads notably reduced the cost of debt. At the same time, the lowering in oil prices, the improvement in the ranking of Spain as a tourist destination (due to the increased insecurity in competitor markets) and the improvement in the competitiveness of exports laid the foundations for some degree of economic recovery. However, the ratio of debt to GDP still increased up to 2015, as a consequence of both the needs of new loans for refinancing floating debts and the persistence of public deficit. Official foresights expect that the debt ratio will begin to decrease in 2017. Given the part that international factors have played in improving economic conditions, there is a risk that if those conditions change, so will the state of the Spanish economy, with a subsequent risk to its debt sustainability.

The present chapter aims to recount and interpret what has taken place in the Spanish economy during the last two decades. However, it also aims to make the case for a number of lessons that can be drawn from the Spanish case. Firstly, it argues that economics, as a discipline, is not able to predict the onset of financial crises. It is pointless, therefore, to reproach economists for not having warned of the crisis earlier, but they can be reproached for not having highlighted the imbalances of the economy and the risks of those imbalances. Secondly, it argues that the economic policy adopted by the EU and applied in Spain, far from having attenuated the crisis and offered a solution to the countries affected by debt overhang tended to make the situation more difficult, seriously compromising the future of the Euro. In choosing those options, the particular interests of countries able to impose their criteria – particularly Germany – weighed heavily. Lastly, it argues that the relief for the problem of sovereign debt in some European countries in these last two years, including in Spain, has a fragile basis and is highly dependent on international conditions being maintained. If we want to provide a true and fair solution to debt, we need a policy change in the EU and a reform of its institutions.

II. COULD THE CRISIS HAVE BEEN PREDICTED?

Financial markets are inherently volatile since the prices of assets are influenced by the processes of expectation formed by agents in relation to the future.[5] This behaviour of financial markets is related to the asymmetric information between the moneylender and the borrower and to the unavoidable uncertainty that characterizes financial transactions. We can seek to partially correct such characteristics through more precise and transparent

[5] Ch. Wyplosz, 'International Financial Stability', in I. Kaul et al., *Global Public Goods: International Cooperation in the 21 Century* (New York: United Nations Development Programme, Oxford University Press, 1999).

information but nothing guarantees that the problem will be totally resolved. Historical experience is riddled with the failed behaviour of agents attributed with powerful and sophisticated information about the markets.

The latest grounds for such a result have to do with the inter-temporal nature of the transactions carried out in the capital markets; in the end, the exchange is between the present capacity to spend (creditor) and the promise of a future payment (debtor). But the future is impossible to predict, especially if it seems conditioned on a dynamic of self-fulfilling expectations. In terms of consistent modelling, this implies the existence of more than one equilibrium, which means that the same economic foundations can produce diverse results and, therefore, clearly, they are unpredictable.

Economists have tried to minimize the consequences of these characteristics and have tried to convey to society the idea that they are capable of anticipating them and predicting financial crises.[6] The technical apparel that accompanies their econometric exercises converts their predictions into little more than esoteric, giving citizens the idea that their opinions are based on irrefutable scientific foundations. Understandably, when the crisis arrived in 2008, some of the public turned against economists: where were you and why did not you see this coming, they seemed to say. The baseless expectations that were fed about the forecasting ability of Economics turned into justified criticisms of the standing of the profession.

II.A. *Three Large Imbalances*

If economists are not able to predict the onset of a crisis, they must, however, draw our attention to those imbalances that imply risks to the stability and growth of the economy. In the case of the Spanish economy, the boom that came before the crisis brought with it three worrying trends that very few people wanted to see back then: a large external imbalance, increased private sector debt and the progressive creation of a property bubble.

II.A.1. External Imbalance

It is common for the Spanish economy to run a deficit in the current account. This result is due to the high dependence of the economy on imports, particularly in energy and intermediate goods, and on its traditional net

6 Criticism of those aspects has been developed, among others, by H. Minsky, *Can It Happen Again? Essays on Instability and Finance* (Armonk, ME: Sharpe, 1982); and P. Davidson: *Financial Markets, Money and the Real World* (Cheltenham: Elgar, 2002).

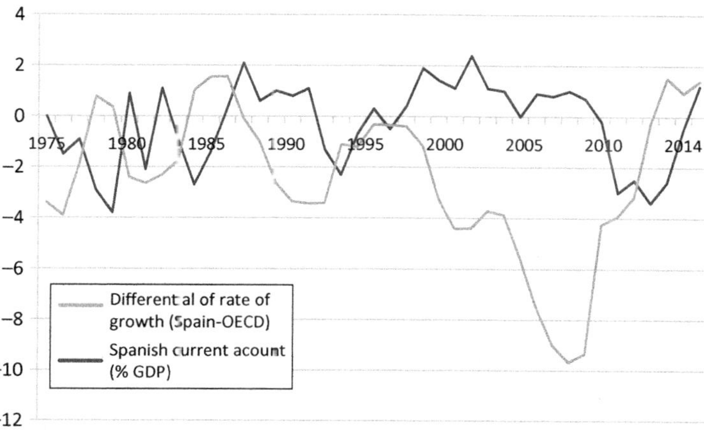

FIGURE 15.1 Comparative growth and the Spanish current account.
Source: Eurostat and World Bank.

demand for capital in international markets. However, traditionally, when the deficit came close to 4 per cent of the GDP, it was deemed necessary for the Spanish economy to carry out an economic adjustment that basically consisted of devaluating the currency and a programme of restrictive fiscal and monetary measures. The current account served, therefore, as a major constraint on the growth of the Spanish economy (Figure 15.1).

The last operation of this type was produced as a result of the realignment of exchange rates that took place due to the European Monetary System crisis, in 1992. The Peseta devalued as many as four times, allowing the Spanish economy to recover its lost competitiveness and to rebalance its current account. In fact, the current account became virtually balanced between 1994 and 1996 and, driven by foreign demand, and with some internal reforms, one of the longest periods of economic boom began in the Spanish economy.

Between 1997 and 2007, Spain had virtually a decade of growth at a rate 30 per cent higher than the OECD average. The consequence of this process was the progressive worsening of the current account balance, which became particularly pronounced after the joining of the Euro. The deficit exceeded the threshold of 4 per cent of GDP in 2000, and reached the incredible rate of 10 per cent in 2007 and 2008. Spain became the OECD country with the greatest current account deficit in relation to GDP and the second in terms of the volume of its deficit (after the United States). Was that situation sustainable?

II.A.2. Increase in Debt

Spain began its early democratic years with a limited public debt. At the end of the eighties, a big programme of public investment in infrastructure was promoted in order to prepare some international events to be hosted in Spain in 1992 (among them, the Olympic Games). A serious crisis in the early nineties climbed the ratios of unemployment and public deficit. As a consequence, public debt began to grow until it reached more than 65 per cent of GDP in 1997 (Figure 15.2). The Aznar government implemented a process of liquidating the debt, in order to move the Spanish economy closer to the Maastricht agreements. The process was based on two main sources: (1) a significant increase of tax collection, derived from the effect of more active economic growth; and (2) the one-off income obtained from one of the most intense wave of privatization of public companies.

Between 1999 and 2007, while Germany and France increased their debt by 5 per cent points in relation to their GDP, Spain reduced its by almost 30 per cent points (going from 64 per cent to 36 per cent of GDP). In fact, before the crisis, Spain was one of the countries in the European Union with the lowest ratio of public debt: its ratio to GDP was half Germany's and France's (36 per cent compared to 65 per cent and 64 per cent respectively) and was almost a third of Italy's (103 per cent).

However, while public debt was reduced, debt taken on privately accelerated quickly. Families were the first agent to take on debt; then, after the entrance into the EMU, companies increased also their debt. In any case,

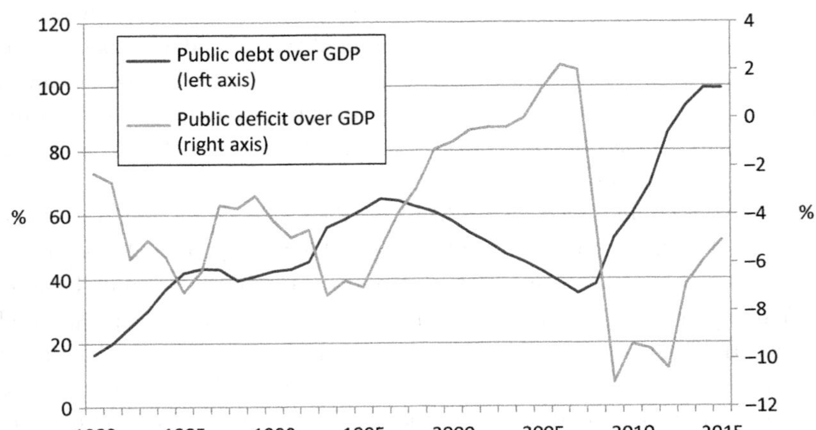

FIGURE 15.2 Spanish public debt and public deficit.
Source: Banco de España.

the debt that grew at the sharpest rate was that of financial institutions: while family and company debt doubled between 1998 and 2007 that of financial institutions multiplied by nine.

As a result of all that the aggregated Spanish debt was equivalent to 430 per cent of GDP prior to the crisis, with private debt amounting to 384.5 per cent. Did not that amount to a clear risk?

II.A.3. Property Bubble

The third risk factor took the form of a boom in the property sector (an excessive increase in the supply of new housing) along with a property boom (an increase in the prices based on expectations they would later be worth more). The data seemed to support that phenomenon. In terms of the boom, between 2000 and 2007 close to 700,000 new properties were built a year. As the authorities recognized, albeit with a tone of pride rather than worry, more homes were being built in Spain than in Germany, France, Italy and the United Kingdom together.

In terms of prices, their index in real terms (outstripping the evolution of consumer prices) doubled in a similar period compared with Italy or the United States, countries that also underwent a property boom. That increase in prices can only be partially attributed to structural factors, such as the improvement in family incomes or the increase in demand due to a wave of immigration. In fact, empirical studies suggest that about two-thirds of the spiralling prices were due to pure speculation.[7]

This growth in the construction sector helped to reduce unemployment, to increase the wealth of families and to expand the taxes the administrations could collect. The problem lay in the fact that the foundations for growth were clearly unsustainable.

II.B. *The Imbalances No One Wanted to See*

Given the magnitude of the imbalances, we need to ask why their seriousness was not highlighted and why the dominant economic opinion was so complacent and trusting while the crisis was being incubated. Confusion, ideological prejudices and economic interests were factors that have contributed to explain that behaviour of analysts and politicians. There was confusion over the novelty that the EMU brought with it and how the new economic

[7] M. Sebastián, *La falsa bonanza* (Barcelona: Península, 2016).

environment could condition economic policy responses; there also were ideological prejudices because of the widespread conviction (with neoliberal roots) that the market was a correct evaluator of risks, meaning present profitability trends for assets were considered the best predictors of future profitability; and, finally, there were political and economic interests because many social segments and economic groups benefited from the boom.

For many analysts the incorporation of Spain into the European Monetary Union made the current account deficit virtually irrelevant. The constraint imposed by the obligatory correction when the Spanish economy reached a current account deficit of 4 per cent of GDP seemed definitively eradicated. After all, had not Spain hit a deficit of 10 per cent without any problems of international financing? The argument used to justify that verdict was that the EMU made Spain the equivalent of a region in a federal country. Was the current account deficit of Extremadura, California or Bavaria important? The European Commission itself contributed to this poor interpretation. In its report '*One market, one money*' it argued that current account imbalances were the expression of the movement of capital searching for profitability differentials between the EMU member countries. If that was the case, why worry?

However, those interpretations did not take into account that: (1) the EMU lacked the characteristics of an optimum monetary union with high differences in productivity among members, and large freedom of capital movement but not for labour; (2) there was no fiscal union guaranteeing transfers from regions with surpluses to those with deficits; and (3) the ECB's mandate was limited and its neutrality towards countries was disputable.[8]

The same argument was used to judge the surging private debt. If the debt were public, it would be judged as problematic, but since it was that of private agents, which supposedly process the market's signals of profitability and risk, why worry? There was no shortage of analysts who even considered the process of increasing indebtedness to be positive since it showed the capacity of Spain to make the most of the new possibilities for international financing that seemed to be ushered in by the EMU.

Lastly, the hardest imbalance to diagnose and treat was the property bubble, basically because some factors (such as the migration inflow) could also contribute to the rise in prices. In any case, there were a lot of signals that the property prices had climbed beyond these structural causes. The resistance to recognizing the problem was linked to the effect that bursting the property

[8] *See*, for example, L. Svensson, 'The foreign exchange risk premium in a target zone with devaluation risk', *Journal of International Economics* 33 (1992).

bubble could have on growth, employment, the health of financial institutions and the wealth of families. In addition to those reasons, how could a property bubble be tackled if control over the best instrument for fighting it – interest rates – had been lost?

III. OWN CAUSES AND OUTSIDE CAUSES

The imbalances mentioned were driven by very diverse factors, some of which were linked to the international sphere; others were entirely within the control of national authorities.

The first decade of the new millennium was characterized by the excess of international liquidity as a factor, which was the result of the non-functioning savings capacity of countries, which had surplus trade balances (exporters of revalorized commodities or, like China, of manufacturers). Within Europe there was similar imbalance, with Germany amassing trade surpluses that were channelled to the Southern European countries. Experience shows that excess liquidity, in a context of unregulated and highly competitive financial markets, tends to produce imbalances that emerge either as speculative bubbles, as imprudent processes of indebtedness or as both. That is what happened at the end of the seventies, causing a debt crisis in the developing world; and the same thing happened at the origin of the current crisis.

This context affected the EU, which had implemented an imperfect monetary union. It was imperfect in its origins because the region did not meet the requirements of an optimum monetary area but also because its institutional design was inadequate. In the case of an asymmetric shock, the vulnerability of the system was high because it lacked political and fiscal unity and because the central bank had a deliberately limited mandate (only related to combat inflation). In order to overcome the heterogeneity among members, the EMU defined a group of poorly founded criteria of convergence. One sign of the poor design of these criteria is that Spain met them all but did not avoid the crisis. Reality showed that these criteria were: (1) partial because they failed to include areas (such as the inflation of assets or levels of private debt) that are a source of risks in a context of fixed exchange rates and (2) imperfect because they have a pro-cyclical tone that does not help to preserve medium-term stability.

The problems were exacerbated by inadequate management by the EMU authorities. The first one lay in the maintenance of an interest rate that was too low for those countries with greater potential growth. There was a conceptual difficulty – that of an imperfect monetary area where the desirable conditions for some countries (Germany, for example) may not be adequate for others

(Spain or Portugal). Looking for a balance between those needs was not simple, but the data suggest that the ECB was very far from a position that could be considered impartial. The application of the Taylor rule to the EMU economies shows the ECB's reference interest rate was much closer to the conditions of Germany than those of Spain.[9]

The persistence of interest rates below the appropriate level for Spain fed the expansion of credit, facilitated the use of international financing and blew up the property boom. Additionally, in a highly competitive context, it stimulated financial institutions to fight for assets, seeking to increase their market quota as a way of improving profitability. This process particularly affected the Savings Banks (Cajas de Ahorro), a form of semi-public financial organizations that had traditionally focused its business locally and which underwent an intensive process of expansion, associated with the financial boom.

The data is indisputable: the relation between credits and deposits grew 70 per cent between 1996 and 2008. And that figure is partial since part of the loan activity of the banks was beyond assets, through securitization, grouping credits together and placing them on the market. That process was accompanied by a change in the way of how banks financed credit, which went from depending on client deposits to use of foreign debt, both through the interbank market as well as through the capital market.

Therefore, the conditions of the context and, in particular, the tone of the monetary policy adopted by the EMU stimulated the imbalances that led to the crisis although there were also national decisions that laid the foundations of the process. Although we could mention some others, there are four elements that are particularly relevant:

- Firstly, the failures in banking supervision. It is difficult to understand the crisis without discussing the central role the financial institutions played in it, above all if we take into account the important weight that banks have in the Spanish economy. The banking supervisor, the Banco de España, was not capable of identifying the risks associated with the rapid expansion of some banks – particularly the Cajas de Ahorro – nor was it able to check the high dependency of many of them on property credit. The accumulation of risks was high in a context in which governments told society Spain had some of the most solid banks in the world. Although that verdict could be applied to some – very few – of the large banks, it was certainly not the case with the situation in many of them.

9 *See* F. Nechio, 'Monetary Policy When One Size Does Not Fit All', Federal Reserve Bank of San Francisco (FRBSF Economic Lette Vol. 18), 2011.

- Secondly, the anti-cyclical provisions of the Banco de España, designed in a very innovative way when Spain joined the European Monetary System, were relaxed. These provisions corrected the predominantly pro-cyclical tone that characterized the Basel rules and established a barrier to the cyclical component of the capital markets. Unfortunately, that regulation was progressively relaxed from 2000, eliminating one of the factors that would have moderated the process of foreign debt.
- Thirdly, land was liberalized and carte blanche was given to local administrations to draw up planning rules and to reclassify land. In a context of limited public resources, the sale of land and property promotions became one of the most profitable sources of raising funds for those administrations. That process nurtured some episodes of corruption by elected authorities and political parties in the last few decades that are now under trial.
- Lastly, the house purchase market (rather than the rental market) was stimulated through diverse means. Among them: tax breaks were established for buying property, the loan could cover a very high proportion of the mortgaged asset value (high loan-to-value ratio) and, finally, a mortgage law that overprotected lenders against borrowers was maintained in force (in which, for example, the return of the house for settling the debt was not admitted).

IV. FROM PRIVATE DEBT TO PUBLIC DEBT

As has been highlighted, Spain entered the crisis having obtained a comfortable fiscal surplus the previous year of close to 2 per cent, and with a ratio of public debt to GDP that was among the lowest in Europe. In a very short space of time, those two characteristics were sharply changed: the surplus became a deficit of 11.1 per cent in barely two years; and the ratio of public debt to GDP reached 60 per cent in 2010, maintaining an upward trend up to 2016. At the same time, the unemployment rate climbed from 8 per cent in 2007 to 26 per cent in 2012 (Figure 15.3). In barely three years, Spain went from being a model economy to having the kind of parameters of a wartime economy.

The most important factors explaining those changes are easily identifiable. On the one hand, the effect that the recession generates on the fiscal balance through the weight of automatic stabilizers: the fall in tax revenue and the increase in costs associated with unemployment benefits. Debt also became notably more expensive as the result of the contagion effect from the debt crises particularly in Greece, which significantly raised the cost of the debt.

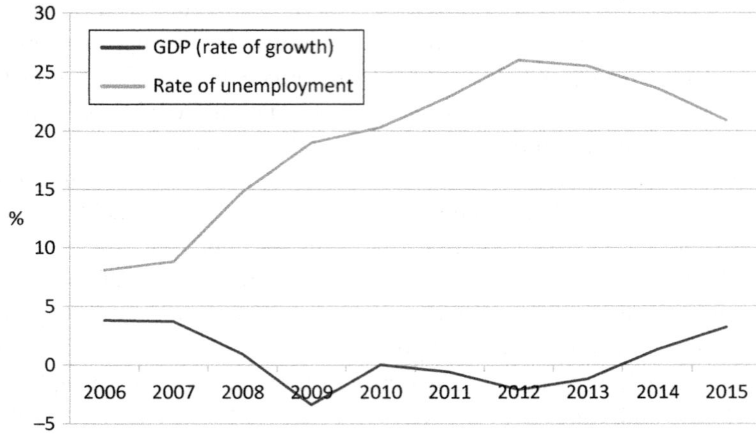

FIGURE 15.3 Growth and unemployment.
Source: Eurostat.

Finally, the third large factor was due to the impact of the rescue of those banks most affected by the devaluation of their assets on public resources. That financial rescue, through the Orderly Bank Restructuring Fund (FROB), increased debt by €19 billion between 2009 and 2012.

That process was initially accompanied by three relevant changes in the debt configuration: (1) the increase in floating debt as a result of the recurrent needs of the financing of the public sector; (2) the change of those holding the debt, with the share of non-residents reducing (from more than 50 per cent to 38 per cent in 2012); and (3) the change in the nature of part of the capital, as the State took the debt issued by other organizations. As a consequence, the share of public debt as a total of capital considerably increased.

The authorities took some time to recognize the seriousness of the situation. In 2010, however, the evidence became irrefutable and the socialist government of José Luís Rodriguez Zapatero had to carry out a programme of severe cuts to public spending, including reducing payments to civil servants and freezing pensions. Under pressure from EU authorities (particularly from the then ECB governor), a reform of article 135 of the Constitution was implemented urgently with the aim of giving guarantees to the priority payment of public debt and ensuring budget stability in the medium term. That shameful episode was added to the long history of international creditors meddling in the sovereignty of debtors. The novelty of the case was that this time the interference was between developed countries that are part of the same "club".

Neither the cuts nor the constitutional reform succeeded in calming investors. In 2011, Spain went through its most critical moment. The markets doubted that the public deficit could be reduced at the planned rate and that with an internal devaluation policy Spain could grow enough to exit the debt trap in which it was immersed. That year the attacks by speculators accentuated, confident of a sure profit since Spain lacked the instruments to fight those attacks and since the ECB was opposed to buying the debt of countries with problems. Speculators had never found themselves in a panorama that was so secure and profitable.

In 2012, Spain had a new significant increase of the debt. However, on this occasion this increase was mainly caused by one-off events that rose debt (with a single effect at the time). Those included: (1) the creation in 2012 of the Fund for the Financing of Payments to Suppliers, in order to avoid budgetary restrictions and late payments affecting private business (which increased debt by 2.7 per cent of GDP), (2) the contributions to the European Financial Stability Fund (EFSF), that was substituted in 2012 by the European Stability Mechanism (ESM), which increased the debt by 1.7 per cent and 0.4 per cent of GDP, respectively; and (3) the creation in 2011 of the Fund for the Amortization of the Electricity Deficit (FADE), aimed at managing the deficit tariff of the energy sector.

The situation changed in the summer of 2012 when the ECB governor announced his intention to do 'whatever it takes' to save the euro, which was a form of recognizing that the attacks on the European periphery were a way of attacking the euro. That process was begun with the injection of liquidity into banks through the Long-Term Financing Programme. That policy was not only a way of overcoming the drying up of credit produced by a collapse in the inter-banking market but also a way of recovering the profitability of financial institutions. Banks could access credit at interest rates close to zero and with those resources they could acquire Spanish public debt at a profitability of over 5 per cent, which could also be used as a guarantee in access to new ECB credits.

From 2015, the ECB added to that policy another more active policy of buying public debt from Eurozone countries as a heterodox instrument for monetary expansion (through the Outright Monetary Transactions Programme). As a result of those moves, the markets calmed down and both the risk spread and interest rates fell. This change in monetary policy was also accompanied by a fiscal proposal, which was equally expansive, the 'Junker plan', which still has to be developed.

With hindsight, the attitude of the EU authorities, particularly in the first period of the crisis, was clearly mistaken. During the period of the most virulent attacks by speculators against countries in the European periphery, countries were abandoned to their luck, knowing they lacked the means to counter those attacks. All the EU pressure was aimed at demands for abrupt fiscal consolidation, which not only deepened the recession in the affected countries, but also damaged society and made governability difficult. In that context, it was arduous for countries to emerge from the debt trap, putting at risk the general framework for the euro.

Despite the rhetoric that accompanies European integration, EU authorities behaved in a very similar way to the lenders in the case of the debt of the developing world in the eighties. As back then, the costs of correction were distributed in an unbalanced way, to the detriment of the debtor. The conditions of support designed by the 'troika' (the EC, the ECB and the IMF) were taken to an extreme, with limited respect to national sovereignty and democratic demands of the indebted country, implying high social and human rights cost; big institutional investors (such as banks), were protected and rescued with public resources, while savers and small investors were left to their own fate; and the demanded public spending cuts exceeded what the governments could manage, while scrapping any possibility of restructuring debt. When debt restructuring did happen, as in the Greek case, the deal seemed more designed to save the creditors (given the exposure of French and German banks) than to improve the conditions of debtors. It was those same creditor interests that ended up relegating the management of the crisis to the EU bodies; and it was those same interests that initially prevented the ECB from buying public debt from countries being attacked by speculation.

The tip of the iceberg of the poor policy was that until 2012 the ECB did almost exactly the opposite of what it should have done: in the run-up to the crisis it had interest rates that were excessively low, which encouraged debt and the creation of speculative bubbles in the European periphery countries; and after the crisis, when the Federal Reserve began cutting interest rates, to 2 per cent in 2007, the ECB decided to increase them in 2008 to 4.25 per cent to tackle inflationary expectations that no one saw. Only the reaction of the ECB after 2013 and, more actively, in 2015, have managed to compensate for this series of blunders, even if the formal mandate of the BCE is still inappropriately defined.

V. BUT IS THE DEBT SUSTAINABLE?

In 2016 accumulated public debt is around 100 per cent of GDP. This is the highest rate since 1910. The Government expects that the ratio will begin to be reduced after 2017. The relevant question, therefore, is what we should expect in the future.

The data from the last two years are fuelling optimism. Thanks to a fall in labour costs, the Spanish economy improved its competitiveness, with exports growing at very notable rates, not just in goods but also in services. At the same time, the sum of imports has fallen as a result of the cheapening in raw materials, particularly oil prices. As a result, the trade deficit has fallen (to 2.4 per cent of GDP in 2015) and has turned the current account deficit into a surplus. External demand, therefore, has helped to activate the economy and in the last two years GDP has undergone visible growth. Additionally, after the change in the ECB policy, there has been a relaxation in the debt market, facilitating the renewal of bonds and reducing costs. The average cost for issuing Spanish debt was below 1 per cent in mid-2015 and marginal rates for auctions of six-month papers were negative.

These are all positive factors. However, they are very dependent on conditions in the broader context. Shadows emerge if we look at the domestic economy. On the one hand, Spain has to manage its debt in a context of a still very sizeable public deficit, which refuses to disappear. It is also difficult for the pace of GDP to be maintained if cuts punish investment in fields such as education and technology, fields that should support productivity growth and if international conditions become less favourable.

The renewal of the last Stability Program (2016–19) illustrates that vulnerability. Given the lowering of forecasts for the world economy, Spain had to reduce its GDP growth estimates by 0.5 per cent points for 2018 (2.5 compared to 3 per cent), the estimated public deficit was increased by close to two points (from −0.3 to −2.2 per cent) and public debt by more than four points (from 93.7 to 97.9 per cent).

If international context become more adverse, therefore, the conditions for debt sustainability could be put at risk. That hypothesis cannot be ruled out if we take into account the process announced by the US Federal Reserve to increase interest rates and the end of the policy of massive debt purchases by the ECB. The lower growth of emerging countries, including China, introduces another factor of uncertainty that needs to be considered.

That is why in order to reduce the risks the EU needs to implement what it did not want to do at the start: (1) accompany expansive monetary policy, which has its limits, with growing doses of expansive fiscal policy, that have not been seen so far; (2) revise the conditions of debt sustainability of affected countries in order to offer a solution (including restructuring) to those with serious solvency problems; and (3) adapt the processes of fiscal consolidation to the conditions required for economic growth and for guaranteeing basic public services to citizens and the democratic conditions of governability of the countries affected.

VI. A FEW LESSONS

Throughout the present chapter, we have tried to interpret the process that led to the debt crisis in Spain. We have highlighted the imbalances that caused it; we have also considered the evolution of the Spanish economy in the last few years, analysing the behaviour of national and EU authorities; and, finally, we have discussed the conditions that could affect the debt problem in the immediate future.

We can present four main lessons:

- Firstly, Economics cannot predict crises and should be honest with society about that limitation. While crises cannot be predicted, the risks of certain imbalances can be highlighted. To do that, it is important for economists to remain sceptical about the possibilities of markets to self-regulate and to expect them to adequately evaluate risks.
- Secondly, in a context of fixed exchange rates (and even more so in a monetary union) capital inflows can be a source of instability, generating processes of excessive indebtedness or speculative bubbles. In those cases, without monetary policy tools, countries need to make a more intensive use of fiscal policy and regulatory mechanisms. The application of fiscal rules can be useful, but only as long as they have a counter-cyclical nature, which is not the case with the EMU convergence criteria. It is also necessary to take a broader view on risks and, in addition to inflation, deficit and public debt, macroeconomic policy should consider the evolution of asset prices, credit expansion and the current account balance.
- Three, the policy of entrusting the solving of crises affecting the European periphery to internal devaluation of indebted countries has been shown over time to not just be unfair but also inefficient. It is unfair because it leads to imbalanced sharing of costs between creditor and debtor countries; and the greatest sacrifice falls on the sectors of the population with lowest incomes in the debtor countries (families and the unemployed). It is inefficient, because it has a recessive bias, which makes it more difficult for indebted countries to reduce the ratio of debt to GDP.
- Lastly, if we want to protect the monetary union from the risks of asymmetric shocks, we need to advance in the political, fiscal and

banking union, formally increasing the ECB mandate. It is also necessary to add an accompanying expansive fiscal policy to the expansive monetary policy; making progress on partial debt mutualization of member countries; and to study the debt restructuring of those countries with serious solvency problems, which implies to build an institutional procedure for treating sovereign insolvency.

16

Conclusions

What Has Been Learned?

JUAN PABLO BOHOSLAVSKY AND KUNIBERT RAFFER*

Drawing conclusions from the cases analysed in this volume, as well as from the history of sovereign debt crises, it seems that – except by some people in academia – very little has been learned. The same policy mistakes have been made for decades. This is particularly worrying in democratic contexts as scientific knowledge should be a pillar in policy decisions.

As explained in the introduction, some stakeholders benefiting from the current situation see no reason for change, others not benefiting may be more ready to consider revising practices that have failed in the past. Yet, the former may consider some regulatory or policy changes to better protect their rights against strategic defaults. The latter may appreciate knowing more about, and understanding available policy and legal options better, as well as their social, economic and political effects. They might wish information on how to prevent and deal with financial and debt crises better and in a way that is human rights sensitive. This group is likely to include not only creditors and debtors that are genuinely open to improvements and to protecting public goods in the financial sector but also people in creditor and debtor countries that want to lobby their representatives.[1]

Which lessons can be drawn from this book's country studies? While readers will find in the chapters a number of specific lessons to be learned, we recap here some essential lessons drawn from considering all these cases in a systematic and holistic way.

* The authors wish to extend their gratitude for the comments to the drafts of this chapter received from José Antonio Alonso Rodríguez, Alfredo Fernando Calcagno, José Castro Caldas, Matthias Goldmann and Martín Guzman.

1 *See* on this relation principal – agent O. Lienau, *Rethinking Sovereign Debt: Politics, Reputation, and Legitimacy in Modern Finance* (Cambridge, MA: Harvard University Press, 2014), esp. 100ff, 193ff.

In practically all cases of debt crises financial liberalization and capital account liberalization occurred before the crisis and were apparently either the cause of this crisis or at least fostered the crisis considerably. This ranges from the so-called Euromarket starting in the 1960s and producing the 1980 crises in Latin America to present day debt crises. This Euromarket has nothing to do with the present currency. It was a xeno-market, mainly of dollars in Europe, thus escaping regulatory oversight both in the currency's home country and in the host country. It was a neo-liberal free market hailed as a huge success and proof that state regulation is unnecessary at best if not pernicious. This *de facto* deregulation – technically it was no deregulation as the Euromarket had never been regulated anyway, although domestic markets from which the money fled were regulated – allowed countries from the South access to easy money. Not infrequently, credits were even thrusted upon them. Following W. Wriston's dictum that sovereigns would always exist and thus repay, and encouraged and applauded by OECD governments and multilateral institutions, commercial banks lent aggressively, disregarding the most elementary rules of prudent banking. Bankers thrusting credits on countries cashed their bonus payments and changed to another employer. Historically unique, syndicated lending not bonds, characterized Euromarket loans. The 1982 debt crisis changed this euphoria about the Euromarket, but not the trend towards further reducing regulatory supervision.

In contrast to the eurozone debt crisis, the Fed warned about the potential risk of the growing involvement of US banks in Latin American and other Southern countries. 'In 1977, during a speech at the Columbia University Graduate School of Business, then-Fed Chairman Arthur Burns criticized commercial banks for assuming excessive risk in their Third World lending'.[2] By 1982 the nine largest US money-centre banks held Latin American debt amounting to 176 per cent of their capital; their total Southern debt was nearly 290 per cent of capital. Did banks already then calculate that they would be bailed out in spite of warnings – even in spite of the law, as later against the eurozone's non-bailout clause?

It seems they did. In the early 1970s the Indonesian national oil company Pertamina had amassed uncontrollable debts. According to a report by the US Senate Committee on Foreign Relations[3] apparently no one, including

[2] J. Sims and J. Romero, 'Latin American Debt Crisis of the 1980s' Federal Reserve History, November 22, 2013, www.federalreservehistory.org/Events/DetailView/46.

[3] US Senate Committee on Foreign Relations, Bretton Woods Agreements Amendments Act of 1977, US Senate, 95th Congress, 1st Session, Report No. 95-603 (Washington DC: Government Printing Office, 1977).

commercial banks themselves, knew how much precisely. A one year stand-by agreement was concluded with the IMF, putting a ceiling on Indonesia's external borrowing and a specific sub-ceiling on Pertamina's. Foreign banks rushed in to go on lending, using technical tricks (such as rolling over short term loans) to escape those ceilings and disregarding outspoken warnings by the US government. When the crisis broke the US government immediately helped. Sovereign lending was riskless for banks, the Senate Committee concluded.

Economically, bank behaviour was perfectly rational – a clear case of moral hazard, produced by OECD-governments. Demanding high spreads they charged what they could get and lent as much as they could, obviously confident that their governments would help them when – rather than if – in trouble.

A scapegoat was easily found: after applauding the so-called successful recycling of Petrodollars – an untruth because funds from balance of payments surplus OPEC countries, though substantial, were not – relatively speaking – that big, OPEC and 'recycling' have been used as a convenient scapegoat for the debt crisis in spite of quantitative evidence.[4]

A much overlooked contributing factor was that banking regulations have been dismantled, regulatory norms have become deferential to and accommodated the wishes of the financial sector. Basel II (internal risk assessment, i.e. Lehman judging their own risk exposure) is a case in point. Already the first neo-liberal crisis – Chile 1982, which was obliterated by the 'big' Mexican crisis in the same year – clearly showed what to expect. Chile 1982 was already a 'modern' or 'second generation' crisis, a repressed testimony of the unwillingness of neo-liberal politicians in the North to learn and to fend off damages from their constituencies and the poor.

The paramount importance of capital controls as a way to prevent and face debt and financial crises emerges from our chapters. The rapid granting of banking licenses – new banks were founded as money flowed into the country – overtook the increase in capability to effectively supervise a rapidly expanding sector in Indonesia. This is not totally unlike the global situation. Indonesia's experience was the rehearsal for many of the events and policy choices in the eurozone crisis, as the author notes, and an action replay of Chile's hushed up 1982 crisis. In Korea, the primary cause of the 1997 crisis

[4] K. Raffer and H.W. Singer, *The Foreign Aid Business: Economic Assistance and Development Co-operation* (Cheltenham: Elgar, 1996) 123–33; or K. Raffer and H.W. Singer, *The Economic North-South Divide, Six Decades of Unequal Development* (Cheltenham: Elgar, 2001), 133–37.

was the government's aggressive pursuit of financial liberalization; in liberalized Korea foreign bank branches, exempt from forex trading regulations, became the primary transmission lines of the global financial crisis of 2008. Free capital movements were one important cause of the crisis in euroland, a region of totally free capital transfers. These were fuelled by huge balance of trade imbalances within the eurozone, another construction error of the euro.

As a member of the Organization of Eastern Caribbean States and the East Caribbean dollar zone Grenada shows similarities to the eurozone. Iceland liberalized as demanded by neo-liberal theory, allowing three banks to accumulate unpayable debts. In Argentina the military dictatorship replaced the developmental state by ultra-liberal policies including trade and capital-account liberalization, income concentration and financial deregulation. Debts exploded and the 'foundation' for a continuing crisis was laid, exacerbated later by further neo-liberal policy errors such as the currency board peso-dollar. Historically, exchange rate rigidness, even if not as pronounced as with a currency board, has usually contributed to capital inflows and thus eventually to crises. Daring introduce capital control, though only on a limited scale, Malaysia successfully escaped catastrophe during the Asian crisis. Mexico's 'Tequila Crisis' (1994–95) could not have occurred as it did without liberalizing regulatory changes Her tesobonos happened to be rated BBB, beyond the reach of 'small guy investors' and pension funds before these regulatory changes. The Asian crisis had striking similarities to the Mexican crash. Strongly propagated, especially by the IMF, undue capital account liberalization has been a reliable recipe for crisis. The IBRD even drew parallels between the Southern Cone and the Mexican crises and the Asian crisis.[5] Why did the Bretton Woods institutions (both not normally known for their restraint in giving advice) not warn those countries to proceed more slowly with cautious sequencing as they knew to be the appropriate policy before this crisis and as they do today – pointing at already available evidence, instead of applauding too quick liberalization and those inflows of volatile capital? An insoluble enigma.

Meanwhile even the IMF, set to get capital account liberalization into its statutes (which explicitly allow, occasionally even demand capital controls) right during and after the Asian Crisis has eventually admitted that capital controls could be necessary, though only under special circumstances as defined by the IMF.

[5] IBRD, '1998 Annual Review of Development Effectiveness', OED, Task Manager: Robert Buckley, Washington DC, 1999, 2.

In the light of historical evidence the present US administration's intention to 'review' the Frank-Dodd Act,[6] which means deregulating substantially again, bodes ill for stability in the future. Though Frank-Dodd is certainly not beyond critique, it improved the situation. Repealing it largely or totally may well pave the way to the next debt crises.

Debt crises have changed radically from government over-indebtedness (as in Latin America except in Chile in the 1980s) to private debt burdens socialized by the government (so-called second generation debt crises). But the crises after the 1970s could not have happened without liberalized and uncontrolled capital flows. Both generations of crises are caused by undue liberalization and deregulation. In Korea, foreign bank branches accounted for the lion's share of short-term foreign debt and derivatives exposure on the eve of the crisis. This same build-up seems to be happening again. This is disquieting because in virtually all cases excess liquidity – easily available credits – acted as a fire accelerant, and markets are highly liquid right now. A similarly deregulated but illiquid market could not have lent that liberally. In the words of UNCTAD:

> According to the Bank for International Settlements, the debt of non-financial corporations in these economies increased from around $9 trillion at the end of 2008 to just over $25 trillion by the end of 2015, and doubled as a percentage of gross domestic product (GDP) – from 57 per cent to 104 per cent – over the same period. Past experience shows that if much of the non-performing private sector debt is large and denominated in foreign currency, as in Latin America, for example, it tends to end up on public balance sheets, thus risking a sovereign external debt crisis.[7]

This conclusion evidenced by country experiences in this book holds as long as governments are prepared – willingly, enticed by orthodox economists or forced by other governments and/or IFIs – to cut down prudent precautions against insufficiently controlled capital mobility, and to do anything to save speculators and other 'investors', even at the cost of violating human rights, once the crisis has broken. As long as this does not change we have to expect yet another debt crisis.

6 J. Cox, 'What Is Dodd-Frank? And Is Trump About to Cause Another Financial Crisis? The US President Is Expected to Order a Review of the Dodd-Frank Act', *Independent*, February 3, 2017, www.independent.co.uk/news/business/news/what-is-dodd-frank-and-are-we-heading-for-another-financial-crisis-regulation-crash-banks-donald-a7560641.html.

7 UNCTAD, 'Trade Development Report 2016', Geneva, 2016, IV; 'these economies' refers to emerging economies.

Most debt crises preferred saving foreign creditors' income and bonus payments over the population's social and economic rights. This is particularly and more clearly, but not only, apparent in the case of the second generation of debt crises. It runs counter to the solution found for over-indebtment in all civilized legal systems that protect a minimum of human and social rights of defaulted debtors. Argentina immediately after debt restructuring, but much more prominently Iceland, show that it is indeed possible to implement solutions that require creditors fairly sharing a significant part of the losses (as usual in all insolvency laws) while trying to shelter the most vulnerable groups hit by crises.

Defects in the international financial architecture have allowed so-called vulture funds to become a business model that hampers solutions between sovereign debtors and creditors willing to accept reality. The vulture funds litigation saga against Argentina in US courts dramatically tells us how disruptive these creditors (and judicial rulings supporting their views) can be for debt restructurings and debtors' economies. When US judge Griesa prohibited Argentina to continue serving her bonds in the US and elsewhere to restructured *bona fide* creditors until it paid those plaintiffs 100 per cent of their bonds[8] (disregarding the obvious extraterritorial effects of this decision)[9] many people realized things had gone too far.[10]

The fundamentally wrong decision to opt for US jurisdiction is one easily fixable problem. A British court (in *Kensington International Ltd v. The Republic of the Congo*) rightfully refused to take other *bona fide* creditors hostages in order to help vultures[11] – unlike judge Griesa. In 2015 Belgium passed legislation limiting vulture fund litigation (which is, by the way, currently challenged by a Cayman Islands based hedge fund, NML Capital Ltd., before the Constitutional Court of Belgium). Emulating this legislation, in 2016 France passed a new law preventing vulture funds and other creditors

8 *See* in detail M. Guzmán, 'An Analysis of Argentina's 2011 Default Resolution', CIGI Papers, N° 110, October 2016.

9 In 2014 Argentina filed a lawsuit against the United States before the International Court of Justice (ICJ) on the basis that the judgement had violated its sovereignty. Yet, the ICJ did not have a chance to discuss on the merits of the complaint due to lack of jurisdiction, ICJ, Press Release No. 2014/25, August 7, 2014.

10 *See* the UN Human Rights Council resolution (A/HRC/27/L.26) condemning the activities of vulture funds for their impacts on the capacity of governments to fulfil their human rights obligations, September 23, 2014.

11 Kensington Int'l Ltd. v. Republic of the Congo (Kensington I), 2003 WL 1935493 ¶¶ 2–3 (C.A. May 13, 2003); cf. also E. Kingdon, 'Leveraging Litigation: Enforcing Sovereign Debt Obligations in Nml Capital, Ltd. v. Republic of Argentina', *Boston College International and Comparative Law Review* 37 (2014): 36.

from seeking large profits providing the debtor state is recipient of official development assistance, it was in default or near to when the debt was purchased by the creditor, and the default was less than four years ago or the restructuring terms were accepted by at least 66 per cent of debt holders.

The case of Zambia is prominent. A vulture fund based in the British Virgin Islands, called Donegal International, sued Zambia for US$ 55 million (nominal value) after purchasing bonds for US$ 3.28 million. The High Court of England and Wales decided that the Zambian state had to pay the plaintiff US$ 15.4 million,[12] which amounted to 65 per cent of what Zambia had saved in debt relief in 2006 through the Multilateral Debt Relief Initiative (MDRI).

This case, which caused strong emotions within the NGO community has some peculiarities. The original debt claim was $15 million granted by Romania in 1979 so that Zambia could buy Romanian exports. In 1999, both Donegal, a vulture fund based in the British Virgin Islands, and Zambia offered to buy this debt at a discount. Although Zambia's offer was slightly higher, Romania chose to sell the claim to Donegal.[13] Apparently, continuing relations with a debtor in arrears with whom Romania had repeatedly negotiated from 1984 onwards without reaching a satisfying agreement was seen less appealing than Donegal's offer. Aware that Zambia was very likely to participate in the Heavily Indebted Poor Countries (HIPC) Initiative, the fund offered slightly more than Romania could expect to recover if Romania participated in HIPC. Romania thus chose to avoid HIPC relief. Zambia claimed in court that the debt was invalid as there was evidence that Donegal's local agent had bribed civil servants to pass the debt to Donegal rather than allowing Zambia to pay it off at a heavily discounted rate to Romania.[14] One should note, though, that the British court – in contrast to Griesa – only recognized part of Donegal's claim, not the full amount.

The Paris Club admonished official creditors against assigning away their responsibility to deal with low-income sovereign debt within internationally accepted frameworks. Furthermore, this case seems to have influenced national laws against vulture litigation.

In 2010, the UK passed a law preventing claims against heavily indebted poor countries that exceed the amount which a holdout creditor would have

[12] Donegal International Ltd. v. Zambia, High Court of Justice (England and Wales), [2007] EWHC 197 (Comm.).

[13] Cf. T. Laryea, 'Donegal v. Zambia and the Persistent Debt Problems of Low-Income Countries', *Law and Contemporary Problems* 73 (2010): 193–200.

[14] A. Beattie, 'Vulture Fund' in Zambia Debt Case Gain', *Financial Times*, February 16, 2007, www.ft.com/cms/s/0/23104b92-bd5e-11db-b5bd-0000779e2340.html?ft_site=falcon&desktop=true.

received had he accepted the debt agreement. In 2013, the UK Act was replicated in the Crown dependencies of Jersey, Guernsey and the Isle of Man. Still, although an improvement, rule of law minded national courts and laws are no substitute for a global sovereign insolvency procedure.

Criticizing only professional holdouts, unpleasant as some may be, is nevertheless barking up the wrong tree. This allows critics to feel moral outrage and the satisfaction of fighting evil, but the fact is largely ignored that holdouts only use (and are allowed to abuse) the legal framework governments provide. This fundamental difference between private creditors that are subject to laws and official creditors that are making them and are obliged to defend decent legal standards must not be obfuscated.

Legal and ethical norms valid in all municipal laws, such as debtor protection, have been denied to the peoples of sovereign debtors, making big strides back into archaic forms of debt laws. With creditors being judges, bailiffs and experts in their own cause, present conditions are worse than antique laws, where after all only judges, not one party, could decide over the debtor. Especially Northern countries have established a state of lawlessness, and contempt for the most basic norms of the rule of law in sovereign debt relations.

This is why the United Nations 'Basic Principles for Sovereign Debt Restructuring' approved by the General Assembly in 2015 are an important global tool to guide debt crises resolutions according to robust legal and economic principles aimed at protecting public goods and human rights.[15] But, as explained in this book's introduction, Argentina, the sponsor of this initiative, capitulated to vulture funds in 2016 in order to regain access to international financial markets. Argentina is not a developed country – not one of those Northern countries that voted against or abstained this United Nations resolution – which blatantly ignored these principles, but one of those debtor countries that would supposedly most benefit from a legal framework on debt restructurings

This reflects how complex collective actions problems of debt restructurings and international relations regarding debts are. Everybody benefits from a good system but nobody wants to shoulder the cost of creating it. The lesson should be that some form of fair and enforcing mechanism becomes necessary as well as more international consensus building around these principles. Reputational costs from not following the UN principles are near to zero, and this should change.

[15] *See* J.P. Bohoslavsky and M. Goldmann 'An Incremental Approach to Sovereign Debt Restructuring: Sovereign Debt Sustainability as a Principle of Public International Law', *Yale Journal of International Law* 41, no. 2 (2016): 13ff.

There is also another complexity: how to reconcile applicable principles whose implementation may lead to contradictory outcomes. Here too the Argentinean case is a useful example. If it were true (it is not in our view) – as the Argentine government argued in 2015 – that repaying vulture funds would be the entry point for regaining access to international financial markets and rebuilding the fiscal space needed to promote social and economic rights in the country, thus violating the principle of granting equal treatment to creditors (not paying restructured creditors the same as holdout creditors) would collide with the principle of sovereign policy space (i.e. countries' right to decide and implement their own economic policies, including – we insist, though it is wrong in our view – capitulating to vulture funds). This possible legal tension is actually acknowledged and solved by the United Nations 'Basic Principles for Sovereign Debt Restructuring', which says 'A Sovereign State has the right, in the exercise of its discretion, to design its macroeconomic policy, including restructuring its sovereign debt, which *should not be frustrated or impeded by any abusive measures*' (principle 1, stress added by us). In turn, they also establish that 'Equitable treatment imposes on States the duty to refrain from arbitrarily discriminating among creditors, unless a different treatment is justified under the law, is reasonable, and is correlated to the characteristics of the credit, guaranteeing inter-creditor equality, discussed among all creditors (. . .)' (principle 5). Finally, they state that 'Majority restructuring implies that sovereign debt restructuring agreements that are approved by a qualified majority of the creditors of a State are not to be affected, jeopardized or otherwise impeded by other States or a non-representative minority of creditors, who must respect the decisions adopted by the majority of the creditors' (principle 9).

Most domestic laws do not explicitly deal with or solve these legal tensions, refusing to apply what they found to be the best and fairest solution to a national debt overhang to international (sovereign) debtors. Vulture funds take advantage of it. Some countries, such as the UK, Belgium or France, moved into this direction and have deliberately solved this problem – at least for the poorest countries (see preceding) – but most national laws are often interpreted to still uphold that professional holdouts have a valid legal title to full repayment, even at the cost of human rights. Such legal interpretations are likely to violate human rights and contradict human rights obligations of not only debtor states but also of developed states in which courts hold out creditors find their way. Progress exists but is still very slow.

The underlying linchpin solving this kind of legal conflicts is that creditors and debtors cannot just sideline human rights obligations when implementing the principles on debt restructurings. People taking decisions (be they negotiators or judges) should be aware that the scope of the *pacta sunt servanda* principle is limited by human rights.[16] The economic translation of this legal principle is that ensuring debt sustainability while safeguarding human rights and debtor protection should be the main goal of debt restructurings.

Dealing with the legal conflict proposed here, it must be said that while it cannot be theoretically excluded that fully reimbursing vulture funds could under closely specified circumstances also help realize human rights within debtor countries, this is usually not the case. Therefore, benefits to human rights have to be duly proven by carrying out a sophisticated and rigorous human rights impact assessment.[17] It is hard to think how letting vulture funds get their own way can be, from a human rights perspective, a better solution than reaching a universal, reasonable and sustainable debt restructuring agreement.

This implies to say that human rights law enters the scene even before defining legal limits to austerity policies. It has to be assessed whether there are any viable human rights compliant policy alternatives to austerity or fiscal consolidation available, including tax reforms and criteria to distribute financial losses between debtor and creditors and among creditors themselves in order to create the necessary economic environment and debt conditions that facilitate the full realization of economic and social rights.

A case in point is South Africa. Having every possible legal argument in its favour, it did not invoke the illegality or odiousness of the debt incurred by the Apartheid regime, apparently afraid not to regain access to financial markets if it had not acted so. Were the effects of this decision in terms of justice, truth, memory, compensation and non-repetition carefully considered? Was this decision really necessary for regaining capital market access? And what about the incentives for other indebted countries going through post authoritarian periods?

The South African case is even more complex, as the author explains in his chapter. Failing seriously to deal with social, political and economic problems

[16] On how and why human rights are an essential part of the concept of sovereignty, *see* broadly Lineau, *Rethinking Sovereign Debt*. Elaborating on the interrelation of financial and human rights obligations in the field of debt restructurings, *see* J.P. Bohoslavsky, report to the UN General Assembly, 'Report on sovereign debt restructurings', A/70/275, August 4, 2015.

[17] 'Human Rights Impact Must Be Addressed in Vulture Fund Litigation – UN Experts', United Nations, Geneva, November 27, 2014, www.ohchr.org/EN/NewsEvents/Pages/DisplayNews.aspx?NewsID=15354; and 'Hold-Out Deal in Argentina Makes Solving Debt Crises More Difficult, UN Rights Experts Say', United Nations, Geneva, March 8, 2016, www.ohchr.org/Documents/Issues/IEDebt/IEArgentina8Mar2016_en.pdf.

that are at the roots of debt crisis creates a legacy that impairs debtor's efforts to shape a sustainable future.

As analysed by Dani Rodrik,[18] debt crises caused by neo-liberal liberalisation were successfully used to enforce even more neo-liberal 'reforms', a very illogical strategy if governments and IFIs really wanted to fight crises, but extremely logical if the real aim is diverting public money to private pockets. IMF staff have usually seen the onset of a crisis as 'an opportunity to assist the reformist economic team in carrying out financial sector reform and deregulation,'[19] which had been identified as a priority in IMF evaluation reports. The EU Commission and the ECB see the euro-crises in precisely the same way, combining the shifting of costs from speculators and banks onto the poor with further neo-liberal 'reforms'. In a private conversation Amartya Sen called the Greek case 'fascinating because it is one of those curious situations in which creditors extend new loans under conditions that guarantee they will not get their money back.'[20] Rodrik explains it. As official creditors do not really lose *their own* money but the money of taxpayers they themselves suffer no losses.

Only Iceland has successfully chosen a totally different way to fight its debt crisis. Apparently, debt crises usually serve a hidden pro elite agenda.[21] It must also be said that higher spreads for countries were justified by purportedly higher risks. But when risk strikes, taxpayers bail out those charging risk premia.

On the other hand too low spreads, as brought about by negligent politics in the eurozone, are a wrong signal to the markets and would-be creditors. They naturally egg creditors on to lend too much. So did political assertions that euro-countries cannot and will not go bankrupt.

In particular the experiences of European countries described in this book are very clear – abundantly so in Greece, arguably less so elsewhere – in terms of the ineffectiveness of austerity and fiscal consolidation policies in the context of weak internal and external demand to overcome macro-economic

[18] D. Rodrik, 'Understanding Policy Reform', *Journal of Economic Literature* XXIV (1996): 1ff.

[19] IMF-IEO (Independent Evaluation Office of the International Monetary Fund), 'The IMF and Recent Capital Account Crises: Indonesia, Korea, Brazil', IMF, Washington, DC, 2003, 13.

[20] Y. Varoufakis, 'Greek Debt Denial: A Modest Debt Restructuring Proposal and Why It Was Ignored', in *Too Little, Too Late, The Quest to Resolve Sovereign Debt Crises*, eds. M. Guzman, J.A. Ocampo, J.E. Stiglitz (New York: Columbia University Press, 2016), 100.

[21] *See* this strategy in the field of sovereign debt and labor rights in the context of economic adjustment and austerity, J.P. Bohoslavsky, report to the UN Human Rights Council, 'Labour rights in the context of economic adjustment', A/HRC/34/57, December 2016.

and financial problems in a socially sustainable way. This fact makes a strong case in favour of consistent fiscal and monetary policies, as well as of an institutional framework for allowing and properly shaping sovereign debt restructurings – including the possibility (necessity) of granting debt relief. Such a framework would fit together wonderfully with the 'no-bailout clause'. Unlike bailouts it would fit the declared intentions of the founders of the euro like a glove.

Most cases presented in this book tell us that frameworks for debt sustainability analysis should be based on a more comprehensive understanding of debt sustainability, incorporating human rights and social and environmental dimensions. Debts that might be repayable from a financial point of view might not be so from a social and human rights perspective, thus financially unsustainable if everything that has to be taken into account is properly taken into account.

Is foreign debt the only way for developing economies to take off? Brazil's case tells us there is an option that needs to be considered: generating national resources through strengthening the domestic productive structure in order to stimulate growth and produce domestic savings. Of course, this alternative economic and financial strategy might not work for all countries, but it is rarely considered in the public debate before simply deciding to borrow externally.

In countries adopting fixed exchange rates, particularly in the context of monetary unions, capital flows (including private and public indebtedness) can be a source of instability. Given the legal impossibility of using monetary tools to overcome financial and debt crises, counter-cyclical fiscal policies need to be seriously considered. Of course, if such fiscal policies are not allowed, withdrawing from these orthodox and fixed currency arrangements should be considered as an option (*see* on this Chapters 9 and 12, on Ireland and Portugal respectively). On the other hand one must also stress that there exists a bailout prohibition for euro-countries that – if not violated – would have precluded the detrimental effects of these crises on human rights and development, naturally at a cost – costs to speculators and other creditors shielded by Brussels.

Again, except from Iceland, countries do not discuss how to reform and mobilize tax policies to tackle debt and financial crises which includes expanding the fiscal space to protect core human rights, reducing economic inequality[22] and implement countercyclical strategies.

[22] *See* J.P. Bohoslavsky, 'Economic Inequality, Debt Crises and Human Rights', *Yale Journal of International Law* 41, no. 2 (2016): 177–99.

The Ecuadorian case shows how important it is not to mix arguments that support the principle indicating that some debts must not be repaid because they are illegitimate (cases of financing of criminal regimes or corruption, for instance) with the fundamental insolvency principle that establishes that if a debt cannot be repaid because of insufficient debtor's assets, debt must be reduced. The Ecuadorian case did not shed light on the differences between these two principles, nor provide a viable definition of illegitimacy. Legally speaking, its arguments were often not correct. It was nevertheless a powerful weapon against creditors afraid of what the debtor government might come up with soon. The promiscuous use of both principles might even be counter-productive for an agenda that promotes global and robust principles for debt restructurings and for the development of a legal framework to prevent lending/borrowing practices that facilitate human rights violations.

An expression that has become quite popular recently is 'bailing in'. It is supposed to be the opposite of bailing out the private sector. Bailing out official lenders, such as the ECB, should of course continue according to those eagerly using the wrong expression bailing in. Logically, the opposite of bailing out is not bailing out. The very expression 'bailing in' private or other creditors is absurd, recalling E.A. Blair's famous book 1984. It purports that people having nothing whatsoever to do with the crisis are somehow, quite possibly unfairly, drawn into it. Private creditors were already 'in' by lending without any need of being bailed in, admittedly egged on by public sector failures in most if not all cases. Then public authorities bailed them out, breaking the law in the case of the eurozone, in order to protect lenders from the results of their own lending decisions and the market: corporate welfare for speculators and banks financed by cutting down social expenditures, pensions, and investments into science and research. This is a clear and deliberate choice. Logically, official creditors were absolutely indignant at the end of 2016 when the Greek government decided to grant a special payment to the poorest pensioners after and because Greece's primary surplus substantially exceeded the target set with creditors.[23] What seems to have angered official creditors that presumably would have eagerly accepted similar sums being used to entertain high ranking EU-officials or guarantee speculators' profits, is that this money was used to secure human rights and without Greece's democratically elected officials first devoutly asking permission from official

[23] 'Ohne Gläubiger zu fragen: Griechenland zahlt Rentnern Weihnachtsgeld', *Der Spiegel*, December 9, 2016, www.spiegel.de/wirtschaft/soziales/griechenland-zahlt-rentnern-ein-extra-weihnachtsgeld-glaeubiger-wurden-nicht-gefragt-a-1125178.html.

and unelected EU creditors. The latter would most likely have denied this abuse of money to fight hunger and misery.

When Draghi finally proposed imposing losses on holders of senior bonds issued by the most severely damaged Spanish savings banks in order to save taxpayers' money in July 2012 – a sharp turnaround of ECB policy – finance ministers immediately rejected this, protecting 'the market' from the market mechanism. In Greece, meanwhile, the private sector had a second haircut, not because of the need to ensure human rights, but to protect EU officials and their wrong decisions luring private creditors into lending to Greece.

In other countries the pull factor of wrong regulatory decisions is less pronounced, although it did play a non-negligible role. But anyway the word 'bailing in' is wrong, and one must suspect deliberately chosen to give a wrong impression.

It is important to keep the financial and productive sectors of the economy connected, as financial intermediaries have the function to channel savings (Asian countries such as Korea have traditionally a very high savings rate) to the real economy – productive investments. Several countries such as South Korea, having a developmental mindset, acted accordingly.

Apart from debt service, finance nowadays does not take other more important aspects into account – such as human rights – not because this is written in stone, but because strong interests control the public economic discourse in a way that social and human rights considerations are regarded as, if not completely irrelevant for finance, highly distortive for financial relations and institutions. As we have seen in the chapter studying this case in detail as well as in this concluding chapter, the Icelandic experience clearly shows that this assumption is deeply flawed.

Finally, one lesson that comes up from every single case is debt sustainability analyses are still overwhelmingly based on undue optimism and a narrow understanding of sustainability, focusing primarily on the ability of a country to pay back its debt without having to resort to exceptional financing. This explains why debt relief is often *too little*.

A debt can be regarded as 'sustainable' as long as the State is able to service its debt, even when at the same time significant parts of its population are starving – in that case most States would violate international law on human and social rights. It is dramatically clear that frameworks for debt sustainability analysis need to be reviewed to be based on a more comprehensive understanding of debt sustainability, incorporating human rights and the social and environmental dimensions of sustainability. Keeping in mind that financial decisions and economic policies are based on debt sustainability analyses, projections of repayment capacities of borrowing states need to ensure that the obligations of States to guarantee core economic, social and cultural rights to their population can be fulfilled.[24]

Reckless lending and borrowing, euphoria, and then crashes, are often accompanied by economic crimes. Providing the right legal incentives to those taking financial decisions might constrain their options. While impunity guarantees new reckless behaviour, accountability plays, to some extent, a preventive role. The efforts made by Iceland to hold bankers accountable are remarkable in the light of modern financial history. In contrast, in Iceland there appear to have been hardly cases dealing with criminal or non-criminal aspects of (at least) negligent behaviour of officials in charge of supervising the banking industry and, in any case, with no meaningful outcome in terms of holding them responsible. Yet, accountability should also reach governmental officials. Another necessary innovation is holding politicians financially and – where applicable – criminally responsible for their actions. Economically formulated: making textbook microeconomics work better in the real world.

[24] J.P. Bohoslavsky, report to the UN General Assembly, 'Integrating Human Rights into Debt Policies to Counter New Debt Vulnerabilities', August 5, 2016, A/71/305; and M. Guzman and D. Lombardi, 'Assessing the Appropriate Size of Relief in Sovereign Debt Restructuring', 2016 (mimeo), providing specific criteria for assessing the appropriate size of debt relief.

Index